Answering Questions With Statistics

Robert Szafran

Stephen F. Austin State University

Los Angeles | London | New Delhi
Singapore | Washington DC

SAGE

Los Angeles | London | New Delhi
Singapore | Washington DC

FOR INFORMATION:

SAGE Publications, Inc.
2455 Teller Road
Thousand Oaks, California 91320
E-mail: order@sagepub.com

SAGE Publications Ltd.
1 Oliver's Yard
55 City Road
London EC1Y 1SP
United Kingdom

SAGE Publications India Pvt. Ltd.
B 1/I 1 Mohan Cooperative Industrial Area
Mathura Road, New Delhi 110 044
India

SAGE Publications Asia-Pacific Pte. Ltd.
33 Pekin Street #02-01
Far East Square
Singapore 048763

Associate Editor: Vicki Knight
Assistant Editor: Lauren Habib
Editorial Assistant: Kalie Koscielak
Production Editor: Brittany Bauhaus
Copy Editor: Gillian Dickens
Typesetter: C&M Digitals (P) Ltd.
Proofreader: Jennifer Gritt
Indexer: Rick Hurd
Cover Designer: Bryan Fishman
Marketing Manager: Helen Salmon
Permissions Editor: Adele Hutchinson

Icons that mark the "Math Tips," "Research Tips," and "SPSS Tips" © iStockphoto.com/scottdunlap

Printed in the United States of America

Library of Congress Cataloging-in-Publication Data

Szafran, Robert F.

Answering questions with statistics/Robert Frank Szafran.

p. cm.
Includes bibliographical references and index.

ISBN 978-1-4129-9132-2 (pbk.)

1. SPSS (Computer file) 2. Social sciences—Statistical methods. I. Title.

HA29.S954 2012
005.5'5—dc23   2011020538

This book is printed on acid-free paper.

11 12 13 14 15 10 9 8 7 6 5 4 3 2 1

Brief Contents

Detailed Contents

PART II: DESCRIPTIVE STATISTICS: ANSWERING QUESTIONS ABOUT YOUR DATA

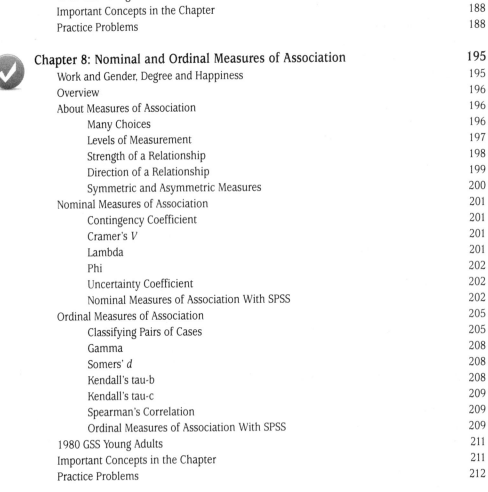

About the Author

Robert Szafran is the Regents Professor of Sociology in the Department of Social and Cultural Analysis at Stephen F. Austin State University in Texas. A passionate believer in the ability of all college students to master and enjoy basic statistical analysis, he teaches courses in research methods and data analysis and also demography and labor force analysis. He has received both College and University Excellence in Teaching Awards. Past director of his university's First-Year Seminar Program and its Inter-disciplinary Linked Courses Program, he has also served as department chair. He received his Ph.D. in Sociology at the University of Wisconsin at Madison.

Preface

To the Instructor

This book arose out of dissatisfaction. I wanted a data analysis text that was sufficiently broad, within the reach of today's average student, and interesting:

- a text that covered most of the statistical techniques routinely appearing in the professional literature of social service professionals;
- a text that did not discourage students with numerous mathematical formulas;
- a text that saw statistics as a means to an end rather than as an end in itself;
- a text that would work with students in a variety of social science majors; and
- a text that conveyed the satisfaction and, yes, even fun of finding answers to substantive questions.

None of the available texts fully accomplished what I wanted. So this book was written. After several years of classroom testing and fine-tuning, I believe the current text achieves what I and, hopefully, you are looking for.

A Unifying Substantive Question: How Have Young Adults Changed in 30 Years?

For most of us, statistics are a means to an end; they are tools for answering questions. Where most social science data analysis texts go wrong is that they focus on the tool and ignore the question. Not so here! When statistics are presented as means for answering a question rather than ends-in-themselves, they become aids rather than obstacles.

How are today's young adults different from the young adults of 30 years ago, and how have the young adults of 30 years ago changed as they have become today's middle-age adults? The examples and practice problems in every chapter address these questions—questions that will engage college students of all ages who wonder how America is changing and how they themselves may change as they grow older.

The Book's Organization

The book is divided into three parts: Part One has chapters that introduce data analysis and SPSS, Part Two contains eight chapters on descriptive statistics that begin with frequency tables and go through multiple regression, and Part Three includes six chapters on inferential statistics.

Part One:

Getting Started begins by answering some questions most students have right at the start—questions like why study data analysis, and how much math and computer knowledge is required? Essential concepts from research methods relevant for data analysis are also explained. In Part One, students are guided through a very simple data analysis session and are shown how to create a data set of their own.

Part Two:

Descriptive Statistics: Answering Questions About Your Data demonstrates procedures to use when the analyst is concerned only with describing the cases for which he or she actually has data. Statistics summarizing single variables (univariate statistics) are presented first and then statistics summarizing relationships between variables (multivariate statistics). Frequency tables, measures of central tendency, measures of dispersion, crosstabs, measures of association, subgroup means, and regression are all covered as are bar charts, pie charts, histograms, and clustered bar charts. This section also includes a chapter on data management and data transformation techniques.

Part Three:

Inferential Statistics: Answering Questions About Populations explains procedures that allow the analyst to draw conclusions about the population from which his or her sample of cases was randomly selected. It begins with a simple chapter on the statistical theory behind inferential statistics. A four-step approach to hypothesis testing is introduced in the next chapter and demonstrated with one-sample *t* test hypotheses. The remaining chapters present different types of hypothesis tests, including paired samples, independent samples, one- and two-way analysis of variance (ANOVA), and chi-square. A concluding chapter reexamines measures of association and regression but this time using them for inferential purposes.

Distinctive Things About the Book's Organization

Start-of-Chapter Diagrams

Each chapter begins with an opening diagram that shows where the chapter's material fits into the big picture. It indicates if the chapter is primarily about data management, descriptive statistics, or inferential statistics and if the chapter addresses univariate or multivariate statistics. It lists the statistics and SPSS procedures introduced in the chapter and what kinds of questions these statistics and procedures are good at answering.

Broad Coverage of Statistics With Minimal Statistical Theory

To introduce the wide range of statistical techniques found in the social science literature, this text keeps to a minimum formulas and statistical theory. The time and space saved in this way permit a broader coverage of univariate and multivariate, descriptive and inferential statistics. The only formulas presented in the text are reproduced on the pages that start Parts Two and Three of the book, which makes those pages handy for review purposes.

A Review of (or Brief Introduction to) Research Methods

This text is not a combined research methods and data analysis text. It does, however, include in the first chapter a brief explanation of concepts from research methods that are essential for data analysis. If students have already had research methods, this chapter provides a review. If they have not had research methods, this chapter provides just enough background to make it possible to succeed at data analysis.

Regression Covered in Both the Descriptive and Inferential Parts of the Book

Regression is one of the few procedures discussed in both the descriptive and the inferential parts of the book. This allows for more extensive coverage, and experience shows that most students more quickly grasp the fundamentals of the procedure if it is first presented as a descriptive technique with its inferential aspects then added later.

A Simple Four-Step Procedure for Hypothesis Testing

Students often become frustratingly confused by the details of statistical hypothesis testing. In this text, a simple four-step approach is taught that involves (1) statement of hypotheses, (2) examination of sample data, (3) determination of significance level, and (4) conclusion. Each type of hypothesis test presented in the book makes use of these same four steps. Hypothesis testing becomes an easy technique for getting an answer to a substantive question rather than a quagmire in which the substantive question is lost sight of or judged not worth the pain of answering.

Practice Problems Are a Big Part of This Text

They appear at the end of all chapters. Those that can be answered without using statistical software appear first, followed by those requiring software.

While the examples in the chapters answer questions about young adults in 1980, only the answers to the problems at the end of the chapters reveal what young and middle-age adults are like today and how they differ from their counterparts of 30 years ago. This makes the practice problems doubly useful: Students learn data analysis techniques but also get answers to questions they actually care about.

Many of the practice problems conclude with instructions to "summarize in a few well-written sentences what you found." For univariate problems, students are asked to summarize in 50 words or less; for multivariate problems, 100 words or less. Why ask for verbal descriptions when the student has already reported the numbers? Because verbal descriptions force students to grapple with what the numbers mean, and they teach students how to communicate their findings to others. The 50- and 100-word limits will force students to be clear, concise, and judicious about what gets described and what doesn't. The end-of-chapter summaries of what was revealed in the chapter about young adults in 1980 can serve as models for the practice problem summaries.

Glossary Terms

Important terms are printed boldface the first time they appear in the text. In addition to being described in the text, they and their definitions also appear in the end-of-book glossary.

Concept Checks

Concept check boxes appear two or three times in each chapter. Each includes just a few questions about important ideas that have already been presented in the chapter. Students should try to answer each of these questions, and if they can't, they should go back and find the answers.

Important Concepts Listed at the End of Each Chapter

Mostly these are glossary terms used in the chapter. They may be terms first introduced in this chapter, but they may also be terms introduced earlier but feature prominently in the present chapter. The lists of concepts will also include important ideas, techniques, and procedures from the chapter. These lists can be used by students as a check of their conceptual mastery of the chapter.

SPSS

SPSS is thoroughly integrated into this text. The dialog boxes and output were produced using *IBM®SPSS® Statistics 20,* which will be referred to in the text simply as SPSS. Students will need to own or have access to a recent version of SPSS. They should have no difficulty following the examples and completing practice problems if they are using slightly older or, in all likelihood, newer versions of SPSS. Even the simplest SPSS package, the student version, with its limit of 1,500 cases and 50 variables, is adequate for reproducing the examples in the chapters and completing all the practice problems. Upon completion of the text, students will have sufficient proficiency to justifiably list SPSS as a skill on their resumes.

Step-by-Step Explanations of SPSS Procedures

Every SPSS procedure is described clearly with step-by-step instructions. What's more, the examples in the book make use of data that can be downloaded from the book's website (www. sagepub.com/szafran), which means students can even begin to learn the techniques by duplicating the examples in the chapters themselves.

Numerous Examples in Every Chapter

Every statistic and data analysis technique is demonstrated in the text by one or more examples. The examples are clear and easy to follow. Sometimes a particular statistic makes sense when students read about it, sometimes when they see an example. Either way, the text has it covered.

General Social Survey Data

The text comes with an SPSS data file named *fourGroups.sav,* which includes responses from the 1980 and 2010 General Social Surveys but only from respondents who were in their 20s or in their 50s at the time of the survey. Thus, the cases in the data set form four identifiable groups: 1980 young adults, 1980 middle-age adults, 2010 young adults, and 2010 middle-age adults. There are a total of 1,258 cases and 48 variables in the data file.

By including data from all four groups in a single file, students won't have to switch from one data set to another when answering questions about different groups, and they will be able to conduct analyses that include more than one group. Students will, however, need to learn how to tell SPSS which group(s) to include in an analysis. That can easily be done using the *Select Cases* procedure in SPSS.

The variables in the data set represent respondent answers to questions about subjective beliefs (e.g., freedom of speech, abortion, religiosity, overall happiness) as well as objective characteristics (e.g., type of hometown, years of schooling, marital status, income). Persons familiar with General Social Survey data sets will recognize almost all of the variables used here. The names, variable labels, value labels, and coding for only a handful of variables have been changed from their original General Social Survey format to make them easier for students to comprehend and use.

I welcome your comments about and suggestions for the text. You can reach me at rszafran@sfasu.edu.

Robert Szafran

To the Student

How are today's young adults different from those of 30 years ago, and how have the young adults of 30 years ago changed as they have become middle-aged? You will know when you finish this book.

What? You thought this was a statistics text. Well, it is. But, you see, few social scientists and even fewer students find statistics themselves inherently interesting. For most of us, statistics are just tools for answering questions. Where most data analysis texts go wrong is they focus on the tool and ignore the question. Not so here! When statistics are presented as means for answering a question rather than ends-in-themselves, they become aids rather than obstacles.

In this text, the questions you will answer will be about today's young and middle-age adults: How are they similar? How are they different? How do they compare to young and middle-age adults of 30 years ago? These are questions that should interest college students of all ages who wonder how America is changing and how they themselves may change as they grow older.

Real Data About Real People

Every 2 years, the National Opinion Research Center conducts interviews with a large random sample of adult Americans. Funded by the National Science Foundation and known as the General Social Survey, these interviews include questions about subjective beliefs such as freedom of speech, abortion, religiosity, and overall happiness as well as objective characteristics such as type of hometown, years of schooling, marital status, and income. The data file you can download from this textbook's website (www.sagepub.com/szafran) includes the answers given by persons who were in their 20s or in their 50s when they participated in the 1980 or 2010 General Social Surveys. This is the data set you will use to answer questions about young and middle-age adults now and 30 years ago.

The Book's Organization

The book consists of three Parts: Part One contains two introductory chapters, Part Two has eight chapters on descriptive statistics, and Part Three includes six chapters on inferential statistics.

Part One:

Getting Started begins by answering some questions you may have right at the start—questions like why study data analysis, and what preparation do you need? Essential concepts from research methods relevant for data analysis are also explained. In Part One, you will be guided through a very simple data analysis session and be shown how to create a data set of your own.

Part Two:

Descriptive Statistics: Answering Questions About Your Data shows you procedures to use when you just want to describe the cases for which you have data. Frequency tables, measures of central tendency, measures of dispersion, crosstabs, measures of association, subgroup means, and regression are all covered as are bar charts, pie charts, histograms, and clustered bar charts. This section also includes a chapter on data management and data transformation techniques.

Part Three:

Inferential Statistics: Answering Questions About Populations explains procedures that allow you to draw conclusions about the population from which your sample of cases was randomly selected. The section begins with a simple chapter on the statistical theory behind inferential statistics. A four-step approach to hypothesis testing is introduced in the next chapter and demonstrated with one-sample *t* test hypotheses. The remaining chapters present different types of hypothesis tests, including paired samples, independent samples, one- and two-way analysis of variance (ANOVA), and chi-square. A concluding chapter reexamines measures of association and regression but this time using them for inferential purposes.

Learning Aids to Take Advantage Of

Start-of-Chapter Diagrams

Before beginning each chapter, take a few moments to study its opening diagram. It shows where the chapter's material fits into the big picture. You will see if the chapter is primarily about data management, descriptive statistics, or inferential statistics and if the chapter shows how to describe single variables or the relationships between variables. You will also see what statistics and computer procedures are introduced in the chapter and what kinds of questions these statistics and procedures are good at answering.

Practice Problems Are a Big Part of This Text

They appear at the end of all chapters. Those that can be answered without using statistical software appear first, followed by those requiring software.

If you really want to find out about young and middle-age adults today, you have to do the practice problems. While the examples in the chapters answer questions about young adults in 1980, the practice problems ask questions about the 2010 young and middle-age adults. By answering those questions, you will be not only learning data analysis techniques but also finding out how the current generation of young people differs from the last generation and how one generation of young people changed as they got older.

Many of the practice problems conclude with instructions to "summarize in a few well-written sentences what you found." For simple problems, you'll be asked to summarize in 50 words or less; for more complex problems, 100 words or less. Why are you asked to compose verbal descriptions of your findings when earlier in these same problems, you already reported the values of relevant statistics? Because verbal descriptions force you to grapple with what the numbers mean and teach you how to communicate your findings to others. The 50- and 100-word limits will force you to be clear, concise, and judicious about what gets described and what doesn't. Here is a hint for composing those verbal summaries: Near the end of most chapters are summaries of what the chapter found out about young adults in 1980. These summaries run about 50 to 100 words long and can serve as models for the summaries you will have to write.

Glossary Terms

Data analysis inevitably comes with terms that need to be understood. Important terms are printed boldface in the text the first time they appear. In addition to being described in the text, they and their definitions also appear in the end-of-book glossary.

Concept Checks

Concept check boxes appear two or three times in each chapter. Each includes just a few questions about important ideas that have already been presented in the chapter. Try to answer each of these questions. If you honestly can't, it means your mind was on auto-pilot as you read the last few pages. Go back and find the answers.

Important Concepts Listed at the End of Each Chapter

Mostly these are essential terms used in the chapter. They may be terms first introduced in this chapter or terms introduced earlier but feature prominently in the present chapter. The lists of concepts will also include important ideas, techniques, and procedures from the chapter. Reviewing these lists provides a check of your conceptual mastery of the chapter.

SPSS

Learning how to use a statistical software package is an essential part of this book. Fortunately, statistical software these days is easy to master. The dialog boxes and output in this book were produced using *IBM®SPSS® Statistics 20,* which will be referred to in the text simply as SPSS. The "20" refers to Version 20 of this software, but you should have no difficulty following the examples and completing practice problems if you are using a slightly older or newer version. When you finish this book, you should list SPSS proficiency on your resumes. It is a valuable skill that many employers will recognize.

The complete SPSS package includes many statistical procedures—far more than are discussed in this book. Fortunately, users can purchase less than the complete package. Even the simplest SPSS package, the student version, with its limit of 1,500 cases and 50 variables, is adequate for reproducing the examples in the chapters and completing all the practice problems.

Step-by-Step Explanations of SPSS Procedures

Every SPSS procedure is described clearly with step-by-step instructions. The examples in the book use the same data file you will be using to answer the practice problems at the end of the chapters. That means you could begin to learn the techniques by duplicating the examples in the chapters themselves. The dialog boxes and output you see on your computer will match what appears in the text.

Work Hard and Enjoy the Power

While everything in this text has been designed to help you easily learn data analysis, in the end it comes down to whether you are willing to make the effort. No one learns data analysis by being passive; it is necessarily an active endeavor. Sections of text need to be read slowly and thoughtfully and, sometimes, read a second time. You need to read the data analysis examples in the text as if you were doing them yourself. And you need to do the practice problems at the end of the chapters. For some, learning data analysis will be easy; for others, it will be more difficult—but all of you are capable of learning this material.

It has often been said that knowledge is power. The knowledge you are about to acquire about doing data analysis and correctly interpreting its results will set you apart not only from most of the general public but also from most college graduates. Others will defer to your conclusions. Data analysis is a tool that can be used again and again to unlock more and more knowledge. By learning data analysis well, you will be acquiring the power to affect not only your own life but the well-being of your community, your profession, and your society.

I welcome your comments about and suggestions for the text. You can reach me at rszafran@sfasu.edu.

Robert Szafran

Acknowledgments

As with any text, credit for the finished product needs to be shared. My colleague Ray Darville has over the years taught with early versions of this text and has offered many useful suggestions and corrections. I thank him sincerely. Thanks also go to my colleagues Jerry Williams and Ryan Button for valuable feedback and recommendations. Reviewing textbook manuscripts when done well is a difficult and time-consuming task. The reviewers of this manuscript did their jobs well and I thank them. It is a much better text for their labors.

The students who used earlier versions of this text provided a valuable service for me and for future students. At times, they directly pointed out difficulties in the text, more often their homework and tests indirectly highlighted shortcomings in the material. As so often happens, I learned from my students.

Finally, I wish to express appreciation to the editors and staff associated with SAGE who have made the preparation of this text so much easier and the final product so much better. Vicki Knight, senior acquisitions editor, has been wonderful to work with, as have Kalie Koscielak, Lauren Habib, Brittany Bauhaus, and Gillian Dickens.

I am most appreciative of the constructive comments and suggestions that were provided by reviewers of the manuscript at various stages:

Barry J. Babin, *Louisiana Tech University*

Gary Bamossy, *George Washington University*

Hyejeung Cho, *University Of Texas at San Antonio*

Tom Collinger, *Northwestern University*

Georgiana Craciun, *Slippery Rock University*

Gopela Ganesh, *University Of North Texas*

Ronal Goldsmith, *Florida State University*

Jared M. Hansen, *University of North Carolina at Charlotte*

Min-Young Lee, *University Of Kentucky*

Charlotte H. Mason, *University Of Georgia*

Camelia Micu, *Fairfield University*

Jason Siegal, *Claremont Graduate University*

M. Joseph Sirgy, *Virginia Tech*

PART I

GETTING STARTED

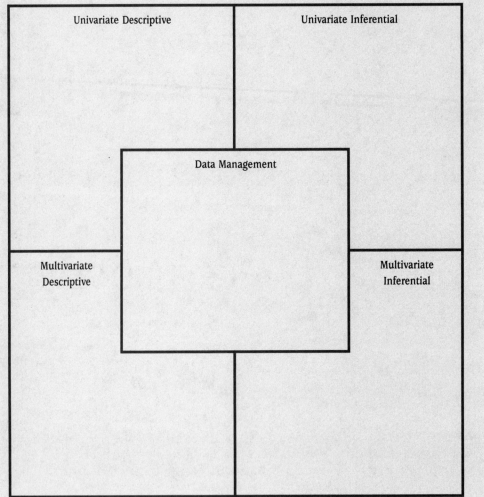

Questions and Tools for Answering Them
(Chapter 1)

Univariate Descriptive	Univariate Inferential

Data Management

Multivariate Descriptive	Multivariate Inferential

Introduction 1

In this chapter, you can learn

- what you can find out about data analysis from this book,
- why data analysis is important,
- how much math and computer knowledge you will need to use this book,
- some concepts from research methods that are essential for data analysis, including

  - cases and units of analysis;
  - variables, attributes, and levels of measurement;
  - reliability and validity;
  - independent, dependent, and control variables;
  - requirements for demonstrating causality; and
  - probability and nonprobability sampling.

Welcome to *Answering Questions With Statistics*. This book has been written to help you learn data analysis: how to do it yourself and how to understand what others have done. Since this is probably your first comprehensive introduction to data analysis, the material is presented in a simple, straightforward way. While there is much to learn, most is easy to understand. To be successful at mastering data analysis, you don't need to be a math whiz, but you do need to be disciplined. You need to read the chapters carefully, follow the examples in the chapters, and do the practice problems. By doing that, when you complete this book, you will understand and be able to do the statistical procedures most commonly used by social scientists. So, let's begin.

About Learning Statistics

Statistics Are Tools for Answering Questions

Statistics are just tools. They help us answer questions and make decisions. While you can admire the beauty of statistics and the elegance of the math behind them, most people who use statistics just want to find something out. Statistics are a means to an end, not an end in themselves. That is the approach this book will take.

RESEARCH TIP

What's the Difference Between Statistics and Data Analysis?

Statistics focuses on the properties of the statistic itself. It explains why the statistic works. The statistic is an end in itself. Data analysis takes a more applied approach. It emphasizes how to correctly use a statistic to answer a question. The statistic is a means to an end. This textbook is all about data analysis.

Almost every example in this book and almost every practice problem flow directly from one central question: Have young adults changed in 30 years? This question can be taken two ways: "How do the young adults of today compare to the young adults of 30 years ago?" and "How have the attitudes and behaviors of those young adults of 30 years ago changed now that they are middle-aged?" These questions are relevant to anyone of any age who wonders how America is changing and how they themselves have changed or will change as they grow older.

The companion data file to this book, which can be downloaded from the book's website, has information on 1,258 persons who were respondents to the General Social Survey (GSS). The GSS is a national sample survey of adult Americans funded by the National Science Foundation and currently carried out every other year by the National Opinion Research Center. Our 1,258 persons represent four distinct groups: *1980 young adults, 1980 middle-age adults, 2010 young adults, and 2010 middle-age adults.* As the names indicate, the first two groups come from the 1980 GSS, the last two from the 2010 GSS. The two young adult groups were in their 20s when they took part in the GSS; the two middle-age adult groups were in their 50s. The four groups come from three different generations: The 1980 middle-age adults are from America's World War I generation, the 1980 young adults and the 2010 middle-age adults are from the same baby boom generation at two different points in time, and the 2010 young adults are from Generation Y. Table 1.1 shows the actual years of birth for the groups and some alternate names that will sometimes be used for the groups.

With data on these four groups, we can ask and answer some interesting questions: What was each of the four groups like? How do 2010 young adults compare to 1980 young adults? How does the generation gap between young and middle-age adults today compare to the generation gap of 30 years ago? And how have the 2010 middle-age adults changed from the 1980 young adults they were? (The fiftysomethings who answered the GSS in 2010 and the twentysomethings who

RESEARCH TIP

More About the General Social Survey

For more information about the General Social Survey, visit http://www.norc.org/projects/General+Social+Survey.htm.

The complete citation to the data file from which our 1980 and 2010 data came is as follows: Tom W. Smith, Peter V. Marsden, Michael Hout, and Jibum Kim: *General Social Surveys, 1972–2010* [machine-readable data file]. Principal Investigator, Tom W. Smith; Co-Principal Investigators, Peter V. Marsden and Michael Hout, NORC ed. Chicago: National Opinion Research Center, producer, 2005; Storrs, CT: The Roper Center for Public Opinion Research, University of Connecticut, distributor. 1 data file (55,087 logical records) and 1 codebook (3,610 pp).

Table 1.1   The 1,258 Persons We Will Study Are Divided Into Four Groups

Group	Year of Birth	GSS Year	Age at the Time of the GSS	Number of Persons in Data Set
1980 young adults (1980 twentysomethings)	1951 to 1960	1980	20 to 29	327
1980 middle-age adults (1980 fiftysomethings)	1921 to 1930	1980	50 to 59	212
2010 young adults (2010 twentysomethings)	1981 to 1990	2010	20 to 29	341
2010 middle-age adults (2010 fiftysomethings)	1951 to 1960	2010	50 to 59	378

answered the GSS in 1980 are not the same individuals since the GSS takes a new random sample of the population each time it is conducted, but they come from the same baby boom generation at two points in time: young adulthood and middle age.)

The data analysis examples in the chapters will show you what the 1980 young adults were like. To find out what the 2010 young and middle-age adults were like and how much change has occurred in 30 years, you will have to do the practice problems at the end of each chapter. Practice problems are an essential part of learning data analysis. Inevitably, you learn by doing.

What Can You Expect to Learn About Data Analysis?

As you find out about young adults and how they have changed, you will be learning

- how to understand statistical information when it is presented to you and
- how to produce meaningful statistical information.

This book's first purpose is to make you an informed consumer of statistics. Almost everywhere you look, you see statistical information. It is in newspapers and on the evening news. It is certainly in textbooks and in professional journals. You will find information being communicated in statistical form in reports done by you or for you in your job. We have all heard how easy it is to lie with statistics, but that depends on how much the person receiving the information knows about statistics. A person who knows nothing about statistics can be easily fooled, but to fool a person who knows her way around data analysis is not so easy.

This book's second purpose is to make you a competent producer of statistical information. To do this, you will be introduced to and use one of today's most commonly used statistical software packages—*IBM®SPSS® Statistics*. It is used in colleges and graduate schools, in government offices, in welfare agencies and police departments, and in private businesses. ("SPSS" is the shorthand way that we will refer to *IBM®SPSS® Statistics*.) Knowing how to use SPSS is a concrete skill that employers value. Once you have mastered the SPSS techniques described in this text, you should indicate on your resume that you have knowledge of SPSS. It is that valuable!

Why Is Data Analysis Important?

You are probably taking a course in data analysis because your major department requires it. That should tell you data analysis is pretty important. Many licensing exams in social service professions test for the material taught in data analysis, and many graduate and professional programs build on the skills taught in data analysis.

But why do your major departments want you to take data analysis? Why do licensing exams test for data analysis knowledge, and why do graduate and professional programs want you to learn even more about data analysis? Some of the reasons are that understanding data analysis makes you

- a better citizen,
- a better professional,
- a better administrator, and
- a better policy maker.

As a citizen, you have a responsibility to understand the issues of the day, to comprehend the extent of social problems and the effectiveness of current programs, and to choose between the proposals of competing political candidates. A democracy depends on an informed electorate. You cannot consider yourself informed in the 21st century without a working grasp of statistics.

As a professional, you have an ethical responsibility to provide the best available service to your clients—whether those clients are recipients of welfare programs, students in a classroom, or citizens seeking safety under police protection. Hopefully you are a concerned, caring individual, but that is not what will make you a professional. Knowing the effectiveness of alternative treatment programs and administering the best available treatment is what makes you professional. You cannot do that without knowledge of statistics.

As a supervisor of other professionals—and many of you will rise to managerial positions—you will be called upon to make decisions about your agency's staffing, your office's programs, and your department's effectiveness. Without basic data analysis skills, you will lack the tools necessary to make the best decisions.

Important policy decisions in our businesses, communities, and governments are not made solely on statistical evidence. But without a grasp of statistical techniques, your chances of getting a seat at the table where important decisions are made are slim, and your chances of holding that seat, should you happen to get it, even slimmer.

How Much Math or Computer Knowledge Do You Need?

As far as this text is concerned, you knew enough math when you graduated from high school and probably from grade school. This is not a math text. While you will see the formulas for some of the simpler statistics and occasionally use those formulas to calculate statistical values, you will usually depend on the computer to calculate those values.

But what if you have forgotten most of the math you knew when you graduated high school? Take heart—much of it comes back very quickly. Having said that, if you are seriously concerned about your math skills, here are some suggestions:

- If you have not yet taken and passed a college-level math course, any college-level math course, do that before taking data analysis. Any math course will remind you of those math principles you knew when you graduated from high school.
- Find a math review book for students preparing for college entrance exams such as ACT, SAT, or even a college entrance basic skills test. Ignore the geometry, ignore the trigonometry and any calculus, and ignore any advanced algebra. Just review the arithmetic and the simplest algebra.

Don't worry! You almost certainly know enough math.

But do you need to have taken a course in probability and statistics before taking data analysis? The more you know about probability theory and formal statistics, the better you will understand how the statistics described in this book work and why you can have confidence in them. But do you need a probability and statistics course to understand and master the data analysis techniques described here? No.

So, if you have taken a probability and statistics course, will you learn anything new here? Yes. Because this book does not go into the theory behind particular statistics, it has time to introduce more statistics than are usually covered in probability and statistics courses. More important, you will see the statistics being used in context—specifically in a social science context. You will see in what situations social scientists choose which statistical tools and how social scientists move from statistical results to decisions.

Since SPSS is a computer software program, do you need to know a lot about computers or programming? Absolutely not! SPSS is not a programming language like Java, C++, or Pascal. Those are computer languages in which users write commands observing the language's specific rules of syntax. SPSS is a statistical application. It consists largely of pulling down menus, making selections, pointing and clicking. Although most versions of SPSS do provide users with the option of writing syntax commands, which can dramatically save time when doing certain complex or often repeated procedures, we will stick with just pulling down menus, making selections, and pointing and clicking.

The mechanics of using SPSS are few in number and simple to learn. After just a few chapters, getting SPSS to do what you want will be no problem. The bigger tasks will be deciding what you want SPSS to do and drawing conclusions from the output SPSS provides you.

CONCEPT CHECK

Without looking back, can you answer the following questions:

- Who are the four groups we will be comparing in the chapter examples and practice problems?
- In what roles will you be better because you understand data analysis?

If not, go back and review before reading on.

Looking Ahead

The rest of this chapter reviews some important research methods concepts. Chapter 2 then walks you through a simple SPSS session using an already existing data set, and it shows you how to create an SPSS data set on your own. Once you understand these things, you are ready to begin answering questions with statistics. Starting with Chapter 3, chapters start off with questions about 1980 young adults. Each chapter presents the data analysis techniques needed to answer those questions. The practice problems at the end of each chapter then give you a chance to use those techniques to see how young adults have changed in 30 years.

Essential Concepts From Research Methods

Before you can use data analysis to answer questions, you need to understand some things about how data are collected. Data collection techniques are often referred to as research methods. Data analysis and research methods go hand in hand. Which statistical techniques you can use depend on how the data were gathered. In turn, decisions about how to gather data depend on which statistical techniques you want to use. It is the classic chicken-and-egg question about what to study first: research methods or data analysis. That is why some schools have students learn methods first and others data analysis first.

The remainder of this chapter describes some concepts from research methods that are particularly important for doing data analysis. Whether this is a review for you of material you covered before or a preview of what you may be studying in more depth in the future, read carefully. The terms and ideas described in this chapter are used frequently in the chapters ahead.

Cases

Science proceeds by means of comparison. Social scientists rarely study just one person or one family or one community. They study many individuals (or families or communities), looking for ways in which they are similar and ways in which they differ and then seeing if some of those differences are related. And, if they are related, they try to understand why.

In survey research, each individual who completes a questionnaire represents a separate **case.** In a study of U.S. states, each of the 50 states would represent a case, and the researcher's data set could be described as consisting of 50 cases.

Depending on the researcher and the type of study being done, cases may also be referred to as subjects, participants, or observations.

Statistical analysis can reveal patterns in the characteristics of cases—patterns that the unaided researcher might miss. The greater the number of cases being studied, the harder it is to detect subtle or complex patterns in the data, and social scientists often analyze data sets containing hundreds or thousands of cases, making statistical analysis essential.

The data analyst needs to know what the cases in a data set represent. In the majority of social science data sets, the cases represent individual persons. But in some data sets, the cases represent something else. The cases might represent families, occupations, unions, nations, or many other possibilities. The **unit of analysis** is simply a way of referring to what the cases in a study are. Knowing what the cases in a data set represent is important because the analyst is justified in drawing conclusions only about the units of analysis for which she has data. For example, if we have data on counties, we can legitimately talk about the characteristics of counties and how certain county characteristics are related to other county characteristics. If we were to talk about the characteristics of individuals and how those individual characteristics are related when all we have are data describing counties, we would be exceeding the limits of our data and committing what is termed an **ecological fallacy,** which is the assumption that what is true about groups must inevitably also be true of the members of those groups.

Data sets generally do not mix together different units of analysis. A data set of 1,500 cases might consist of data on 1,500 individual persons or 1,500 different families, but it would not consist of data on mostly individuals but with a few families thrown in. Whenever you are using a data set for the first time, be sure to find out how many cases there are and what the cases represent.

Variables

Scientists are interested in the differences between cases. For example, families differ in income and in type of residence. Universities differ in the selectivity of their admission standards and whether they are public or private. Any dimension on which the cases in a study differ is known as a **variable.**

As you can imagine, cases can differ in many ways. Individuals, for example, differ physically; they also differ in attitudes and values, the frequency with which they do certain things, in their religious and political affiliations, and so on. No study records all the variables on which cases differ.

A researcher decides which variables to study based on a theoretical perspective, a review of the literature, logical thinking, a hunch, or preliminary unstructured observation.

Deciding which variables to include in a study and which to exclude is tough. Every variable included will require more time, energy, and money devoted to data collection. Every variable excluded will be a possible answer to a question that will go unexplored.

Data sets differ in the number of variables they contain. A data set could consist of just a single variable but usually contains more than that. Data sets based on answers to large surveys often include hundreds of variables.

Theoretical Definition

Variables are usually referred to by a brief name such as *gender, social class,* or *occupation,* but that name is really just an abbreviation. A researcher needs to know, and anyone reading the researcher's results needs to know, what the researcher means by that name. When the researcher says *gender,* what does he mean by that term? Or when she says *social class?* Or *occupation?* Each variable, besides having a name, needs to have a **theoretical definition**. Sometimes called a nominal definition, a theoretical definition is like the definition you would find in a dictionary. It explains in abstract terms what the researcher means by a certain variable name.

Two researchers might theoretically define the same variable name in different ways. There is absolutely nothing wrong with that, although it will complicate communication between the researchers. The important thing is that each researcher and her audience know what is being meant when that researcher uses that variable name.

Operational Definition

A theoretical definition clarifies for both the researcher and his audience what is meant by a particular variable name. But using that variable in an empirical study requires more. A researcher must know and be able to explain to others precisely how that variable is going to be measured. The description of the procedure by which a variable is going to be measured is known as the **operational definition.**

A good operational definition should indicate how the measurement will be done. Will it be based on observing the case or by asking a question of the case or, perhaps, by examining something produced by the case such as a journal entry? If you are going to measure a variable by asking a question, what specifically will that question be and, very importantly, how will the person indicate his answer? Will he give an unstructured answer or choose from designated categories and, if the latter, what are those categories? Will the variable be measured by asking just one question or will multiple questions be needed, and if multiple questions are required, how will the several answers be combined into an overall score?

Even if two researchers agree on the theoretical definition of a variable, they might operationally define it differently. That is their right, although it will again complicate communication between the researchers and make a straightforward comparison of their results difficult. The important thing is that each researcher and his audience know what is being measured when that researcher uses that variable name.

Within a single data set, researchers should not change the operational definition they are using for a variable. You cannot measure readiness for college by administering the ACT exam to half your subjects and the SAT exam to the other and treating the scores as if they all came from the same operational definition.

Attributes

Part of the operational definition is a clear specification of the categories or attributes that make up the variable. These are the possible scores or values cases may receive on the variable. For example, the variable gender would probably have the categories male and female. Social class might be operationally defined as consisting of the categories lower class, middle class, and upper class. The variable number of children might be operationally defined as consisting of the categories 0, 1, 2, 3, 4, 5, and on up to the highest integer needed. Normally, the attributes of a variable are constructed so that every case will find one and only one category that fits. (Having cases fit into one and only one category is sometimes accomplished by instructions on survey questions or directions to observers that state to use one and only one answer category.)

Once you know the attributes that make up a variable, all the other information in the operational definition about whether to ask questions or observe, what question or questions to ask, and how to combine answers to several questions can be thought of as the procedure to follow to figure out which is the correct attribute for each case. It is very important that the same procedure be followed for each case. Although the result of applying the procedure to different cases may be different— that is, some cases end up in one category while other cases end up in other categories—the procedure to determine the appropriate category needs to be applied consistently. If the procedure is done one way for some cases but another way for other cases, then the procedure itself rather than the actual differences in the cases may be determining into which category the case is placed.

As noted earlier, researchers may operationally define the same variable differently. That extends to differing on the number of attributes that make up the variable. For example, take the variable age. One researcher may operationally define the variable age as the number of full days a person has lived since birth. That would result in a great many attributes since a centenarian has lived approximately 36,525 days! Another researcher might operationalize the same variable as age at last birthday. That would result in far fewer attributes. The researcher who uses age at last birthday but defines the attributes in terms of categories (0 to 9, 10 to 19, 20 to 29, 30 to 39, 40 to 49, and so on as needed) would have still fewer attributes. Still another researcher might operationalize age as young, middle aged, and old. One way of operationalizing age is not necessarily better than another. However, how a variable is operationalized will affect which statistics can be used in its analysis.

Variables differ in the number of attributes that make them up. In the simplest situation, a variable has just two attributes, for example, female and male, yes and no, agree and disagree. A variable with just two attributes is known as a dichotomy. Dichotomies sometimes receive special treatment in data analysis. Of course, a variable could not have just one attribute. Variables are dimensions on which cases differ. If there is but one attribute, then there is no possibility for cases to differ. A dimension on which cases do not differ either because there is no alternative category or because all the cases fall into just one category is referred to as a constant.

At the other extreme, variables may have a very large, even an infinite, number of attributes. If the variable is population size and the cases are nations and the attributes are the set of positive integers (1, 2, 3, 4, 5, and on up as high as needed), we would have more than 1,300,000,000 attributes since China has a population in excess of 1.3 billion persons. Now, you might say, that's true, but many of those attributes won't be used. Since there are only about 200 nations in the world, no more than 200 attributes, and possibly less if any countries have identical populations, will have any cases in them. However, the list of attributes that make up a variable does not depend on which attributes are actually used in a data set. An unused attribute is still an attribute for that variable.

Researchers distinguish between discrete and continuous variables. A **discrete variable** has a finite and usually small number of attributes, whereas a **continuous variable** has a large, theoretically infinite, number of attributes. The distinction is an important one because discrete and continuous variables sometimes require different statistical techniques. Continuous variables are always based on a numeric scale of measurement, but not all numeric scales are continuous variables. Continuous variables have a potentially infinite number of possible values between any two attributes. For example, the percentage of a population that is female could have a value (or attribute) of 55%. It could also have a value of 56%. Between those two values, however, there are an infinite number of possible values. The percentage female could be 55.5%, 55.25%, 55.125%, and so on. By comparison, consider the variable number of children. Both 3 and 4 are legitimate values. But there are no values between 3 and 4 that are possible. No one has 3.5 children. Thus, number of children is a discrete variable. Had a researcher been comparing nations, however, and the variable been average number of children, fractional values become possibilities, and the variable would be considered continuous. Variables whose attributes are not numeric quantities such as political party affiliation (Democrat, Republican, other, none) or degree of agreement with a particular statement (strongly disagree, moderately disagree . . . moderately agree, strongly agree) are always considered discrete variables. Another term sometimes used for discrete variables is *categorical variables*.

Levels of Measurement

A fundamental concept for data analysis is **level of measurement.** Based on the properties possessed by a variable's attributes, the variable can be described as having a nominal, ordinal, interval, or ratio level of measurement. You set a variable's level of measurement, whether you realize it or not, when you operationally define the variable. Decisions made early in the research process such as the answer choices you are going to provide for a question in a survey, the recordkeeping procedures to be used by observers, or the classification systems to be used in analyzing artifacts determine a variable's level of measurement. Although the critical decisions are made early in the research process, the consequences of those decisions about level of measurement only show up when you are ready to do data analysis. You must know the level of measurement of every variable you use in your analysis because which statistical procedures are legitimate to use and which are not depend on the level of measurement of the variables involved.

In most research methods classes, four distinct levels of measurement are introduced: nominal, ordinal, interval, and ratio. For an introductory course in data analysis such as this one, however, the distinction between interval and ratio does not matter. None of the statistics introduced in this book require a ratio level of measurement. So, you will not need to distinguish between interval and ratio levels. Those last two levels are combined so that there are just three levels of measurement:

nominal, ordinal, and **interval/ratio.** (As you will soon see, SPSS gives the name *scale* to this combined interval/ratio level of measurement.)

Nominal is considered the lowest level of measurement, next comes ordinal, and interval/ratio is considered the highest. Nominal attributes have the least information in them, ordinal attributes have more information packed in them, and interval/ratio attributes have the most usable information. Correspondingly, nominal variables support the fewest legitimate statistical procedures, ordinal variables support more, and interval/ratio support the most.

In deciding a variable's level of measurement, you need to know the attributes that make up the variable. In deciding about level of measurement, the number of cases that fall into particular attributes makes no difference. Level of measurement can be determined before any of the data are actually collected.

Nominal

You can determine a variable's level of measurement by asking just three yes/no questions about the attributes that make up the variable. Figure 1.1 shows you the questions and what to do with the answers.

The first question is "Do the attributes cover all the possibilities without overlapping?" You want to create a set of attributes so that every case finds one and only one attribute that fits it. Sometimes this is accomplished with instructions like "choose one and only one of the following answers," "choose the one best answer," or "check the one category that comes closest to what you observed." In fact, unless told otherwise, you can assume respondents, observers, and examiners were told to choose one and only one attribute.

Figure 1.2 repeats the flowchart of questions in the previous figure but at each stopping point shows an example of a variable that would have traveled that path.

One stopping point is if the answer to the first question is no. The variable "personal income last year," as operationalized in Figure 1.2, does not even have a nominal level of measurement. The categories overlap. Someone with exactly $10,000 income could go into either of two categories; the same is true for someone with $30,000 or $50,000 income. Overlapping categories is a surprisingly common mistake in designing operational definitions, and it needs to be corrected before the data start to be collected. There is usually no good way to fix the problem after the fact. So be sure to carefully examine and pretest your research instruments before using them!

Now consider a variable that records the state in which a person was born. Its attributes appear in Figure 1.2. These attributes cover all the possibilities without overlapping. For this variable, the answer to the first question is yes.

If the answer to this first question is yes, then the variable's level of measurement is at least nominal. Mathematically, if you are comparing two cases on a nominal variable, you can state whether the two cases are equal (=) or not equal (≠). That may not seem like much, but it is a start and will allow you to generate frequency distributions.

Ordinal

The second question is "Can the attributes be put in a natural order from low to high?" Can the categories that make up the variable be arranged so they represent increasing amounts of what the variable measures? In practical terms, if you put each attribute on a card, mixed them up, and tossed them on

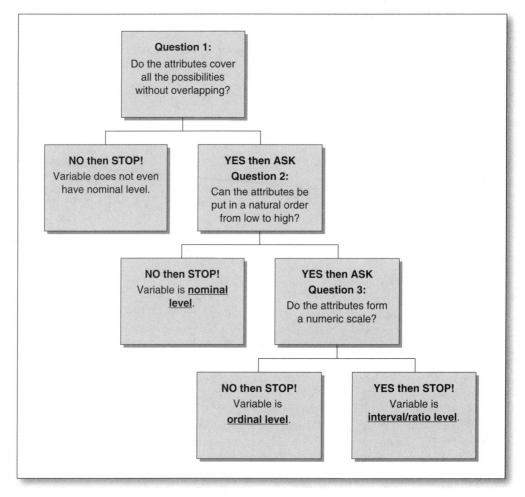

Figure 1.1   Determining a Variable's Level of Measurement

the floor, would a reasonable person be able to put them in order from low to high? If so, then the attributes have rank order. Remember that the order must be based on what the variable is trying to measure. Alphabetical order does not count nor does an order based on how many cases chose each attribute.

The attributes for state of birth do not possess a natural order. No matter how much you personally favor one state over another, the attributes are just different from one another. They lack a natural rank order. So the variable state of birth is a nominal-level variable.

Now consider a variable that records the extent of a person's agreement or disagreement with the statement "I am looking forward to learning more about data analysis." The attributes appear in Figure 1.2. Assume respondents were told to select the single answer that most accurately describes their attitude. For this variable, the set of attributes not only represents all the possibilities without overlapping but also can be put in order from least agreement (strongly disagree) to most agreement (strongly agree).

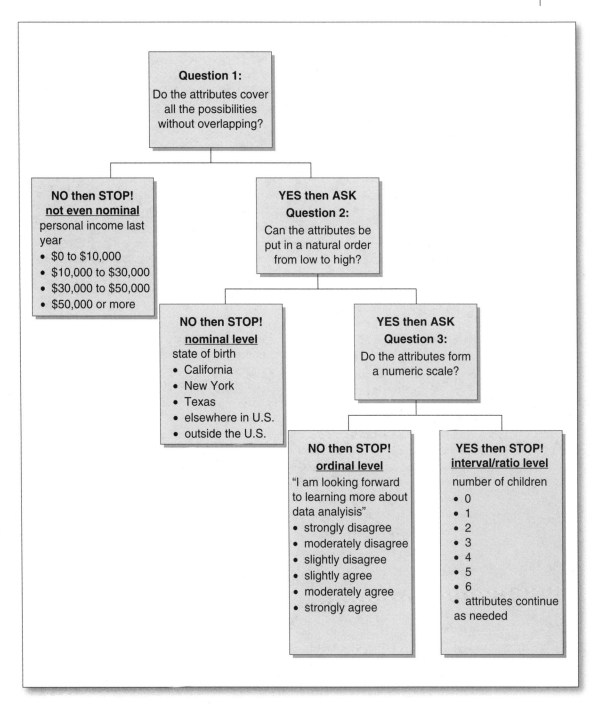

Figure 1.2 Determining a Variable's Level of Measurement With Examples

If the answer to the question about all possibilities without overlapping is yes and the answer to the question about a natural order is yes, then the variable is at least ordinal. When comparing two cases on an ordinal variable, not only can you state whether the two cases are equal or not equal, but if they are unequal, you can also describe the first case as less than (<) or greater than (>) the second case. As you gain mathematical operations, you gain statistical tools.

Interval/Ratio

The third and final question is "Do the attributes form a numeric scale?" The issue here is, after the attributes are put in rank order, whether the amount of difference between any two adjacent attributes is the same as the amount of difference between any other two adjacent attributes. This property is sometimes referred to as a fixed unit of measurement. And the only way we can precisely say how different one attribute is from its neighboring attributes is if the attributes form a numeric scale.

The attributes of the variable measuring agreement or disagreement with the statement about data analysis certainly have a natural order, but they do not represent a numeric scale. It is not clear precisely how large the difference is between adjacent categories. While moderately disagreeing represents more agreement than strongly disagreeing, how much more agreement does it represent? Nor is it clear that the distance between any neighboring attributes is always the same. For example, is the difference between strongly and moderately disagreeing the same amount of difference as between slightly disagreeing and slightly agreeing? You can't say because the attributes do not represent a numeric scale. Therefore, this variable has just an ordinal level of measurement.

Now consider a variable that records the number of children a person has. The attributes start at 0 and increase by 1, going as high as necessary for the case with the greatest number of children. This variable's attributes cover all possibilities without overlapping, can be put in a natural order from low to high, and form a numeric scale. You know precisely how much of a difference there is between any two adjacent attributes: exactly one child.

If the answer to the third question is yes, then you have an interval/ratio variable. Number of children is interval/ratio. With a numeric scale, you gain the mathematical operations of addition (+) and subtraction (–). When two cases are not equal, not only can you state whether the first case is less than or greater than the second case, but you can also subtract the value of the lower case from the value of the higher case to determine how many units apart they are on the numeric scale. Correspondingly, you could add a certain number of units to the value of the lower case to make it equal the value of the higher case. Not surprisingly, the advantages of a numeric scale are substantial for statistical analysis.

SPSS TIP

Caution: When Numbers Don't Represent Numeric Attributes

You will soon see that many nominal and ordinal variables are represented by numeric codes when entered into SPSS. Just because a variable's attributes are represented by numeric codes does not make the variable interval/ratio. The attributes themselves, and not just their codes, must correspond to numeric quantities.

Difficult to Determine

With practice, determining the level of measurement of most variables becomes relatively simple. However, a few variables can still be difficult to classify. Even professional researchers disagree about how to treat certain sets of attributes.

A few difficult situations occur with sufficient frequency that guidelines for classifying them are presented here. These may or may not be the same guidelines as your instructor uses. Check with your instructor and follow her or his guidelines.

One commonly occurring difficult situation is when the attributes represent groups of numeric values. Assume you are gathering data about the students in a college data analysis class. Here are two variables each with two different sets of attributes.

- Number of colleges ever attended (1, 2, 3 or 4, 5 to 7, 8 or more)
- Number of colleges ever attended (1 or 2, 3 or 4, 5 or 6, 7 or more)
- Test grade (less than 50, 50 to 59, 60 to 69, 70 to 79, 80 to 89, 90 to 100)
- Test grade (less than 51, 51 to 60, 61 to 70, 71 to 80, 81 to 90, and 91 to 100)

All of these sets of attributes include an **open-ended attribute** or category. For the first two, the open-ended category is at the end; for the last two, it is at the beginning. One of the guidelines used in this text for determining level of measurement is to ignore open-ended categories. Make your decision about level of measurement based on the other categories. Ignoring open-ended categories is usually safe because experienced researchers typically use open-ended categories only where they expect few if any cases.

Even after we have agreed to ignore the open-ended category, however, these four sets of attributes represent still another difficulty. Notice that in the first and third sets of categories, the attributes are not equally wide. For the first set of attributes for number of colleges, the categories include 1 value, 1 value, 2 values, and then 3 values. For the first set of attributes for test grade, all but the last category include 10 values; the last category includes 11 values. In contrast, the categories for the second set of attributes for number of colleges each include exactly 2 values, and the categories for the second set of attributes for test grade each include exactly 10 values. This makes a difference for determining level of measurement. When some or all of the attributes represent groups of numeric values, you need to check the width of the attributes. If they are all equally wide, the variable is classified as interval/ratio, but if the attributes differ in width, the variable is classified as ordinal. (If the categories differ in width, then the distance from the middle of one category to the middle of the next category is not always the same, which means there isn't really a fixed unit of measurement even though the attributes form a numeric scale.) For the four sets of attributes listed above, the first and third represent an ordinal level of measurement, while the second and fourth represent interval/ratio.

This means that even if a variable's attributes represent all the possibilities without overlapping each other, have an inherent order, and represent a numeric scale, the variable might not be interval/ratio. If the attributes are of unequal width, this text classifies the variable as ordinal. A common example of this occurs in regard to measures of income. Surveys will ask respondents to choose from categories such as $0 to $9,999, $10,000 to $29,999, $30,000 to $59,999, $60,000 to $99,999, and $100,000 or more. Because these categories are of unequal width, the attributes represent just an ordinal level of measurement. To specifically avoid level of measurement problems, many researchers prefer not to ask respondents to choose from groups of values. Respondents, on the other hand, often prefer choosing from groups of values—particularly on items that may be sensitive or difficult to recall precisely.

Dichotomies represent still another challenging situation. When it comes to levels of measurement, dichotomies are quite flexible. While normally thought of as nominal variables whose attributes are simply different from one another (e.g., male or female, left-handed or right-handed), they are sometimes seen as also having rank order (e.g., disagree or agree) and are even treated as interval/ratio by some statistical procedures when the dichotomous attributes represent the presence or absence of a particular characteristic. Because dichotomous variables are used in such diverse ways, be sure to ask your instructor how she or he wants you to handle them. This text usually treats dichotomies as nominal-level variables.

CONCEPT CHECK

Without looking back, can you answer the following questions:

- What are some common units of analysis in social science research studies?
- What are variables and attributes?
- What are the three levels of measurement used in this text?
- What are the three questions to ask about a variable's attributes to determine that variable's level of measurement?

If not, go back and review before reading on.

Reliability and Validity

Operational definitions should be both reliable and valid. **Reliability** is often defined as consistency of measurement. An operational definition is consistent or reliable if you get the same scores for cases the second time you measure them as you did the first time you measured them. That assumes, of course, that not enough time has passed between the first and second measurements for the underlying characteristic to have changed. An operational definition would not be very reliable if, when you remeasured subjects, persons whom you first classified as very liberal were now being classified as slightly conservative and if those who were moderately conservative on first measurement were moderately liberal on second measurement. You expect your measurement procedure to put cases in the same attributes or at least nearly the same attribute the second time as it did the first time.

To assess an operational definition's reliability, a researcher may literally retest, re-observe, or re-measure some of the cases and statistically assess how well the scores the cases received the first time match the scores they received the second time. Alternatively, if an operational definition uses not just one question to measure a variable but several questions all aimed at the same underlying concept, reliability can be assessed by examining how well the answers to the different questions match one another. SPSS has several statistics you can use to assess the reliability of an operational definition.

Validity can be briefly defined as measuring what you intend to measure. Validity refers to the goodness of fit between your theoretical definition and your operational definition. Are you measuring what you intend to measure?

Compared to reliability, where you are assessing the match between two sets of scores, validity is more difficult to measure because you are talking about the match between your theoretical definition of the concept and a set of scores produced by your operational definition. Assessing the fit between something abstract (theoretical definition) and something concrete (the scores produced by your operational definition) can only be done indirectly. Sometimes the fit is judged on logical grounds and sometimes on statistical grounds. SPSS can help with the statistical assessment of validity.

Both reliability and validity as described here are characteristics of individual variables. Some (hopefully all) of the variables in a study may have good reliability and good validity, some may have good reliability but poor validity, and still others may have poor reliability and poor validity.

Both the producers and the consumers of research should be concerned about the reliability and validity of the variables used. When variables lack reliability and validity, you can have no confidence in the conclusions of the research. Checking the reliability and validity of operational definitions can be tedious work. It is best done and sometimes can only be done by the researcher who originally gathers the data. When you can't rigorously assess the reliability or validity of a variable's operational definition, at least ask yourself if a researcher's questions, observation techniques, or classifying procedures would likely yield consistent measures if they were repeated (that is reliability) and ask yourself if they are really getting at what the variable is calling itself (that is validity). If either answer is no, the results of the analysis, no matter how good looking, are questionable.

Relationships Between Variables

Sometimes social scientists are interested in just a single variable. For example, how many persons voted for each candidate in an election? More often, however, they look at the relationship between variables. For example, is there a relationship between a person's gender and his or her choice in an election? Much of this text will be about statistically assessing the relationships between variables.

Independent and Dependent Variables

When considering the relationship between two variables, social scientists often think of one variable as influencing the other. For example, there is probably a relationship between the amount of time students spend studying for a course during the first few weeks of the semester and the grade they receive on the first exam. Most people believe that amount of study time influences how well a person does on the exam.

When you are thinking of one variable as influencing the other, the variable that is doing the influencing is called the independent variable, and the variable that is being influenced is the dependent variable. In the previous example, amount of study time would be the independent variable and exam grade would be the dependent variable.

A variable is independent or dependent only in the context of a relationship. One variable by itself is neither independent nor dependent. Furthermore, the same variable in one relationship may be dependent, but in a different relationship, it may be the independent variable. In the previous example, first exam grade was the dependent variable. However, in the relationship between the variables first exam grade and time spent studying in the weeks following the first exam, first exam grade is the independent variable.

For many of the statistical procedures covered in this book, you will need to distinguish between the independent and dependent variables. It is sometimes difficult to make that determination. Here are some things that can help. First, if one of your variables occurred earlier than the other variable, the variable that occurred first is the independent variable. So, one of the things you can ask yourself is which variable happened first. Which occurs first in a person's life, his or her gender or current marital status? Gender, of course, so gender is the independent variable.

Second, when the time sequence of the variables is not clear, consider if one of your variables represents a broad orientation while the other reflects a more specific opinion or behavior. Usually, broader orientations develop earlier and change less frequently than specific opinions or particular behaviors. For example, which reflects a broader orientation: political party affiliation or preferred candidate in the upcoming election? Since political party affiliation is a broader orientation, it is the more likely independent variable.

For many pairs of variables, you can imagine influence moving in both directions. For example, consider the two variables mother's educational level and daughter's educational level. While daughters could certainly be influenced by their mothers, it is also possible that a mother might be so impressed by a daughter's educational accomplishments that the mother returns to school. The third suggestion for identifying the independent and dependent variables is to consider both directions in which influence might flow and pick the more common or more likely direction. Although some mothers may be influenced by their daughter's educational achievements, the influence of a mother's level of education on a daughter's educational level is the more common path of influence, so mother's education would be the independent variable. Just because it is possible that for some cases, the influence flows in the opposite direction, this should not stop you from identifying the independent and dependent variables. Base your decisions on what is the more likely flow of influence. Only when influence is almost equally likely to flow in either direction should you not identify independent and dependent variables.

Control Variables

In the real world, few dependent variables are influenced by just one independent variable. For example, a grade on a first exam can be influenced not only by amount of time spent studying but also by other factors such as class attendance, year in school, and initial interest in the subject, to name just a few.

Identifying the separate effect of each independent variable on the dependent variable can be tricky because independent variables are sometimes related to one another. For example, you are interested in the effect of study time on test grade. But it is probably true that persons who study more also typically attend class more often. So, when you see that persons who study more tend to get better grades, is it really the effect of study time or is it just the hidden effect of class attendance?

This is where the notion of **control variables** comes in. A researcher will want to control the effect of the other independent variables to better perceive the effect of the one independent variable in which she is primarily interested. Controlling a variable can be done in one of two ways. First, you can control a variable by turning it into a constant. For example, you might limit your study of the relationship between study time and exam grades to only those students who had perfect clas attendance. If you did that and still found that students who studied more got better grades, it could not be because of better class attendance because all the cases in the study had the same level of attendance. The problem with controlling a variable in this way is that you may end up with only a few cases to study, and you would probably want to repeat your study to see if study time affects grades similarly for students with near-perfect attendance, fair attendance, and awful attendance. The second technique to control a variable is to statistically control its effect. Many SPSS procedures can statistically control the effect of other independent variables. Those techniques identify the **net effect** of individual variables on the dependent variable, net effect meaning the effect when the other independent variables have been controlled.

Causality

It takes some pretty strong evidence to support the claim that one variable *causes* another to change. To prove causality, you must demonstrate three things. First, you must show that the two variables are statistically related (sometimes referred to as **covariation**). Second, you must show that changes in the independent variable preceded changes in the dependent variable (sometimes referred to as **temporal sequence**). Third, you must show that the relationship between the two variables is true, that it is still present when you have controlled for all other variables that might be creating the covariation (sometimes known as **nonspuriousness**).

The first requirement of covariation is easy to test. Many of the procedures covered in this book will reveal whether two variables are statistically related. While it is encouraging when the statistical relationship is a strong one, moderate or even weak statistical relationships are sufficient evidence for covariation. All that must be shown is that there is some statistical relationship.

The second requirement of temporal sequence does not depend on any statistical test. Can you be sure, or at least reasonably confident, that what you are claiming is the cause (i.e., the independent variable) happened before what you are claiming is the effect (i.e., the dependent variable)? Sometimes the research design employed by the researcher involves repeated measurements of the same variables over time. Such a design allows a researcher to note when certain changes occur. Sometimes researchers control when subjects are exposed to certain things. That also facilitates determination of temporal sequence. However, in cross-sectional studies, which are conducted at just a single point in time, researchers may have to depend on logic to determine the probable sequence of events. This constitutes the weakest evidence of temporal sequence.

The toughest requirement to meet is nonspuriousness. If something is spurious, it is false. It is not what it appears to be. To prove that the relationship is nonspurious, the researcher must show that the statistical relationship remains when all possible other independent variables have been controlled. The problem is that there are an infinite number of other possible causes for the dependent variable. The statistical techniques mentioned above, which allow you to statistically control the effects of other variables, are helpful but cannot eliminate all other possibilities. If you have controlled for what seem to be the most likely alternative causes and the statistical relationship between the independent and dependent variables remains, you can be reasonably confident that the relationship is nonspurious. Ultimately, though, only the true experimental designs that involve random assignment of subjects to groups and manipulation of the independent variable permit researchers to exclude all other possible explanations and definitively demonstrate nonspuriousness. Regrettably, practical and ethical considerations prohibit the use of true experimental designs to study many important social research questions. That is why researchers turn to quasi-experimental and nonexperimental research designs. While these designs only suggest rather than prove causality, they provide at least some understanding into topics that are ill-suited for experimental research.

All of this talk of causality is to remind you to be humble in describing the results of your data analysis. Claims about one variable being the cause of another should be made only when there is evidence for all the requirements of causality. Be glad when you can speak of moderate and strong relationships in which the temporal sequence is relatively clear and you have controlled for the most likely alternative explanations.

Sampling

Sampling is a complex topic. Just a few of the ways in which it affects data analysis are mentioned here. The topic of sampling is more fully discussed later in the book when statistics are introduced that draw conclusions about populations from sample data.

A researcher typically has some group of entities (perhaps persons, families, organizations, or nations) about which she would ultimately like to make statements. This group is known as a **population.** For some studies, the population of interest might be students currently enrolled at a university; for others, it might be all the households in a particular city or all the states that make up the United States. For example, a population of frequent interest in this book is "1980 young adults," that is, all those persons in 1980 who were residing in the United States and who were in their 20s.

The members of a population are referred to as the **elements** of the population. When a researcher gathers information about each and every element of the population, that researcher has done a **census.** It is important to understand that when you see reference to a census in this book, it does not necessarily mean the Decennial Census of Population and Housing done in the United States every 10 years. Any data set with information on every element in the researcher's population of interest can be referred to as a census.

Obviously, some populations are very large, and conducting a census of such a population would be time, energy, and resource expensive. Fortunately, relatively precise statements about populations can be made with a high level of confidence from certain types of samples.

There are two broad categories of sampling techniques: **probability** and **nonprobability.** In probability sampling, every element in the population must have some chance of being selected into the sample, and it must be possible to actually calculate each element's chance of being selected. Sampling procedures that do not meet these requirements are called nonprobability procedures. Nonprobability sampling techniques include quota sampling, purposive (or judgmental) sampling, snowball sampling, and convenience (or reliance on available subjects) sampling. Nonprobability sampling is often quicker and less expensive than probability sampling, and it is sometimes the only approach possible when going after difficult to identify populations. However, it is not possible to estimate the amount of sampling error in the results of nonprobability samples. That restricts the types of statistical analyses that can be done with the data.

Probability sampling techniques include simple random sampling, systematic random sampling, stratified random sampling, and multistage (or cluster) random sampling. Although often more time-consuming and expensive, probability samples produce data for which it is possible to estimate the extent of sampling error. That opens up additional data analysis possibilities.

As a data analyst, you need to know whether the data set you are using was the result of a census, a probability sample, or a nonprobability sample. Knowing how the cases were selected enables you to correctly choose statistical procedures and allows you to avoid making inappropriate generalizations about the population from which the cases in the data set came.

CONCEPT CHECK

Without looking back, can you answer the following questions:

- What is the difference between reliability and validity?
- What are the differences between independent, dependent, and control variables?
- To show that a causal relationship exists, what three things are required?
- What is the difference between a census and a sample?
- What are some types of nonprobability sampling and some types of probability sampling?

If not, go back and review before reading on.

Important Concepts in the Chapter

attribute

cases

census

constant

continuous variable

control variable

covariation

dependent variable

dichotomy

discrete variable

ecological fallacy

element

independent variable

interval/ratio

level of measurement

net effect

nominal

nonprobability sampling techniques

nonspuriousness

open-ended attribute

operational definition

ordinal

population

probability sampling techniques

reliability

sampling

temporal sequence

theoretical definition

unit of analysis

validity

variable

Practice Problems

1. Indicate how many cases there are in the study and what the unit of analysis is for each of the following:
   a. In a study of individual behavior in public places, a researcher reports that over a period of several weeks, she gathered data on 253 young persons "hanging out" at a mall.
   b. The General Social Survey randomly selects 1,500 adult Americans to interview. Each respondent is asked a number of questions about his values, opinions, and behaviors.
   c. Surveys were sent to 50 rural churches inquiring about their organization, services, and membership.

2. For each of the following, provide a brief theoretical definition and a brief operational definition:
   a. a variable named "self-confidence"
   b. a variable named "social class"

3. You are doing a study of currently enrolled college students. Provide a complete set of attributes for each of the following variables. (Remember that a single attribute can represent a group of different values.)
   a. academic major
   b. percent of classes attended
   c. number of pets owned
   d. satisfaction with college

4. For each of the following variables, indicate if it would be continuous or discrete:
   a. number of Olympic medals an athlete has won
   b. an individual's fastest time in the 100-meter sprint
   c. number of persons living in a household
   d. average household size in a county

5. Regarding level of measurement,
   a. What are the three questions to ask about a variable's attributes to determine that variable's level of measurement?
   b. What sequence of answers to those questions identifies a nominal variable?
   c. What sequence of answers to those questions identifies an ordinal variable?
   d. What sequence of answers to those questions identifies an interval/ratio variable?

6. You are examining a variable's attributes. They represent all the possibilities without overlapping one another, and they have an inherent order. However, they do not form a numeric scale. What level of measurement does the variable have?

7. For each of the following variables, indicate its level of measurement:
   a. a city's average annual rainfall measured in tenths of inches (attributes: 0.0, 0.1, 0.2, . . .)
   b. whether a person voted in the last presidential election (attributes: yes, no)
   c. income last year (attributes: $0, $1 to $9,999, $10,000 to $24,999, $25,000 to $74,999, $75,000 to $149,999, $150,000 or more)
   d. frequency of feeling in the presence of the supernatural (attributes: never, occasionally, frequently, always)
   e. number of days missing from work (attributes: 0, 1, 2, 3–5, 6–10, 11 or more)
   f. age at last birthday (attributes: 0 to 9, 10 to 19, 20 to 29, 30 to 39, 40 to 49, 50 to 59, 60 to 69, 70 to 79, 80 and older)

8. "I never get the same waist measurement twice. The directions always say to relax but they don't say whether to inhale or exhale. Sometimes I inhale and then measure; sometimes I exhale and then measure." Does this statement describe a reliability problem or a validity problem? Explain.

9. If you are concerned that a variable isn't really measuring what the variable's name implies, are you concerned about reliability or validity?

10. For each of the following expressions, identify the independent variable and the dependent variable:
   a. "Absence makes the heart grow fonder." (variables: degree of fondness and distance)
   b. "Too many cooks spoil the broth." (variables: number of cooks and quality of the broth)

11. I am interested in the effect of using a fertilizer on plant growth. Since I know that amount of light will also affect plant growth, I will make sure that the plants receiving the fertilizer get the same amount of light as the plants not getting the fertilizer. In this example,
   a. What is the independent variable?
   b. What is the dependent variable?
   c. What is the control variable?

12. What three things must be shown to prove causality?

13. A researcher has data for a large number of subjects on the social class of the family in which each person was raised and each person's level of self-confidence at age 20. There is a strong positive correlation between the two variables. What else must the researcher show to prove that being raised in a higher social class causes higher self-confidence?

14. Explain the difference between a census and a sample.

15. Identify for each of the following whether it is a probability sampling technique or a nonprobability sampling technique:
   a. systematic random sampling
   b. quota sampling
   c. snowball sampling
   d. simple random sample
   e. convenience sampling

16. An instructor wants to know how much time the students in his class spent studying for an exam. For each of the following, does the resulting data set represent a census, a probability sample, or a nonprobability sample?
   a. The instructor asks the first five students coming to class the next day.
   b. The instructor randomly selects five students to ask.
   c. The instructor asks each and every student in the class.

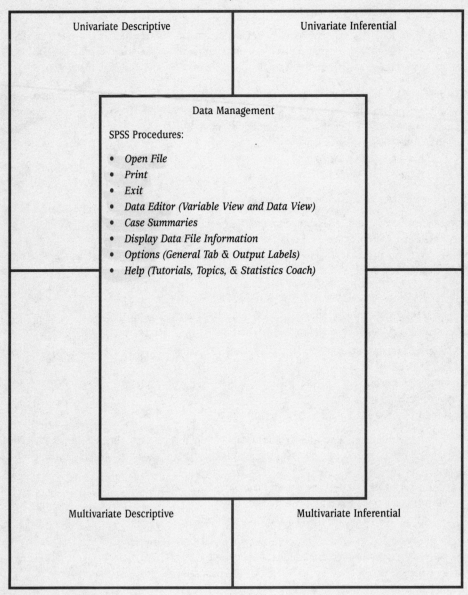

Questions and Tools for Answering Them
(Chapter 2)

Univariate Descriptive	Univariate Inferential

Data Management

SPSS Procedures:

- *Open File*
- *Print*
- *Exit*
- *Data Editor (Variable View and Data View)*
- *Case Summaries*
- *Display Data File Information*
- *Options (General Tab & Output Labels)*
- *Help (Tutorials, Topics, & Statistics Coach)*

Multivariate Descriptive	Multivariate Inferential

Data Sets 2

In this chapter, you can learn

- how to use an SPSS data set that someone else created,
- how to create your own SPSS data set,
- how to quickly familiarize yourself with the variables in a data set,
- how to set SPSS variable lists and output labels to your preferences, and
- how to use the *Help* capabilities built into SPSS.

Overview

To do data analysis, you need data. The actual collecting of which is often a long and difficult job. But once that chore is finally done, the fun begins. Data analysis is like the last chapter in a mystery novel where things that were hidden are now revealed. You see the complete distribution of scores on your variables and discover how those variables relate to one another. Hypotheses get tested and found to be supported or not supported.

If you are using a statistical application such as SPSS to help with the data analysis (and these days even small data sets are routinely analyzed with the aid of statistical software), the data have to be in a form that the statistical application can recognize and work with. This chapter will start you working with SPSS and show you how to use SPSS data sets that have been put together by others and how to put together your own SPSS data set.

About SPSS

The complete SPSS software package includes a large variety of data management and statistical tools, and it regularly comes out with updated versions that add additional tools, increase user-friendliness, and improve the appearance of certain types of output. In fact, the complete title of the software used for this book is *IBM®SPSS® Statistics 20*. The 20 indicates that this is Version 20 of SPSS. For the data analysis techniques covered in this book, differences in recent versions are relatively minor. Using older versions of SPSS should pose no difficulties for you, but it is a good idea to confirm that with your instructor if you are using an older version.

SPSS TIP

Moving Files Between Different Versions of SPSS

If you are using a different version of SPSS than your instructor or fellow students or campus computer lab, you should know that output saved as a file by one version of SPSS often cannot be opened by other versions of SPSS, and while newer versions of SPSS can usually read data sets created by older versions, older versions may not be able to read data sets created by newer versions.

You may be doing your SPSS work on your own computer, a friend's computer, or possibly in a school computer lab. If you are purchasing your copy of SPSS or deciding where you will do your SPSS work, be sure to check the hardware requirements for the version of SPSS. There is usually no problem, but older personal computers sometimes lack the memory, speed, storage capacity, or video resolution required by newer versions of SPSS.

SPSS is normally sold in modules. The complete package is very powerful and quite expensive, but SPSS is also sold in smaller student packages at reduced cost. Even the most basic student package is still an impressive piece of statistical software. It is not quite as powerful as the regular base module (e.g., it cannot handle more than 50 variables or more than 1,500 cases), but these limitations are not a problem for most analyses, and they certainly are not a problem for this text. The more complete the SPSS package you are using, the more options you may see on various pull-down menus; the less complete the package, the fewer options. But all of the procedures used in this text are available on all SPSS packages, even the simplest student package.

Although using SPSS is quite simple, almost everyone feels better if they try it the first time with someone else. Sometimes, we overlook the simplest things, and a friend can spot our mistake. Remember, everyone learns by making mistakes. The more you explore within SPSS, trying new things, the more you will learn.

Using an Already Existing SPSS Data Set

The easiest way to learn how to use an already existing SPSS data set is to walk through a simple SPSS session. This will give you a hands-on experience using the software. Most SPSS sessions consist of five parts: starting SPSS, opening a data set, doing some statistical analysis, printing some or all of the results of your analysis, and exiting SPSS.

SPSS TIP

Downloading the **fourGroups.sav** *SPSS Data File*

The data file you will need to follow along with the examples in this book and to do the practice problems is available at www.sagepub.com/szafran. Download the file to your hard drive or flash drive. It is an SPSS data file, so it can only be opened and read using SPSS.

Starting SPSS

There are a variety of ways of starting SPSS. Double-click on the SPSS icon if it appears on your computer desktop, click on SPSS in your start menu (the list of applications that appears when you click on the Windows start button in the lower left corner of the desktop), or use Windows Explorer to find and double-click on the "spss.exe" file in the SPSS folder in the Program Files folder on your hard drive. (Double-clicking on the name of an SPSS data file in Windows Explorer will both start SPSS and open the data file.)

When SPSS opens, you will see what appears to be an empty spreadsheet. If a dialog like the one in Figure 2.1 appears in front of the spreadsheet, simply click the cancel button in the dialog to make it disappear. Some people like to use that opening dialog to get started, but others don't; in any case, you need to know how to work without it since that opening dialog may be permanently suppressed on some machines that you use.

Opening a Data Set

There are times when you will need to create your own SPSS data set. Most of the time, however, you will be using an SPSS data set created by someone else. There are several ways to tell SPSS which data set you want to use. While you may quickly figure out some simpler ways to open files, a procedure that works in almost all situations is to pull down the *File* menu, move your cursor to *Open,* move your cursor to *Data,* and click.

File | *Open* | *Data*

An open file dialog similar to Figure 2.2 appears. It lists the contents of the folder from which you last opened an SPSS data file. If the data file you now want is in that data set, simply open it the way you open files for other Windows applications. If the data file is in some other folder, move to the appropriate folder and open the file.

When a data set is opened, what looks like a spreadsheet with information appears. The spreadsheet may consist of just numbers, just words, or a combination of the two. For now, do not worry about how the data set appears on the screen. The different formats will be discussed later in the chapter.

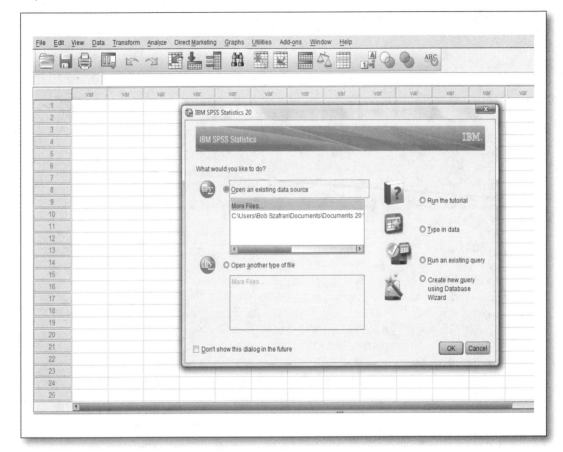

Figure 2.1   Opening Dialog (Can Be Permanently Suppressed)

Doing Some Analysis

One of the simplest types of analysis is a frequency table. Frequency tables are discussed in detail in the next chapter. For now, we will merely have SPSS generate one for us.

Pull down the *Analyze* menu, move your cursor to *Descriptive Statistics,* move your cursor to *Frequencies,* and click.

Analyze | Descriptive Statistics | Frequencies

A dialog similar to Figure 2.3 opens up.

On the left of the dialog is a list of the variables in the data set. In Figure 2.3, this list consists of variable labels. They are in the order in which the variables appear in the data file. (Later in this chapter, you will see how you can control the appearance of this list.) If you move your cursor over the part of the variable label that is visible, the complete label appears along with the variable name.

If there are many variables, a scroll bar is provided. Choose a variable in the list that you suspect will have just a few attributes and double-click on it. That moves the variable into the previously empty variable list near the center. Now click the OK button.

Instead of the spreadsheet screen, you now see the output screen. It is divided into two panes. In the right pane, you will see the tables, charts, and text produced by the SPSS procedures you ran.

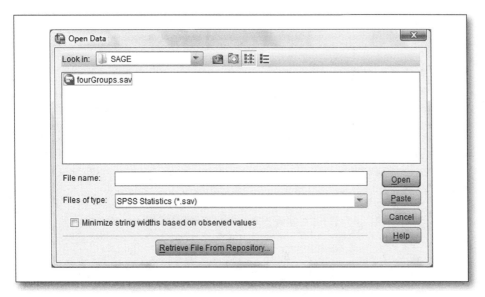

Figure 2.2   Dialog to Open a Data File

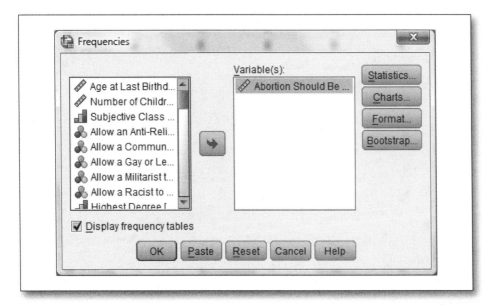

Figure 2.3   Dialog to Create a Frequency Table

In the left pane is an outline of the SPSS output. It is like a table of contents. Clicking on something in the outline pane moves the output in the right pane to what you have selected.

If you picked a variable with a small number of attributes, your output will be relatively short. On the other hand, variables with many attributes can generate very large frequency tables.

Although much of it is self-explanatory, for now, don't worry about making sense of the frequency table output.

Printing Some Output

You will often want to print some or all of your output. You may need it for homework or to show someone or simply for your own future use.

With the output screen in front of you, simply pull down the *File* menu and click *Print*.

File | Print

A dialog similar to Figure 2.4 appears. If the computer you are using is connected to more than one printer, choose the printer you want.

If you wanted just a certain part of your output to be printed, you could have selected just that part by clicking on that part in the outline pane before going to the *Print* procedure.

When you click OK, the output is sent to the printer.

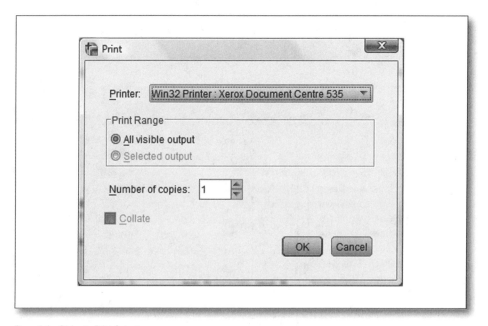

Figure 2.4   Dialog to Print Output

SPSS TIP

Printing Landscape Often Saves Paper

The output produced by SPSS often fits poorly on letter-size paper. Tables get broken up and spread across pages, making them difficult to read. Interpreting output is much easier when viewed on the screen. When you do print, landscape orientation often saves paper and keeps more of a table together.

To print landscape, pull down the *File* menu, click on *Page Setup*, and choose landscape. This should be done while viewing output on the screen and before going to the *Print* dialog.

Exiting SPSS

When you are done with your analysis and you have printed what you want, you are ready to exit SPSS. One way to do that is to pull down the *File* menu and click *Exit*.

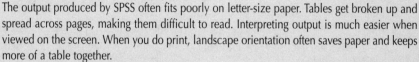

File | Exit

When you do that, SPSS may ask you some questions before it closes. If you created a data set during this SPSS session or if you made any modifications in a preexisting data set, you will be asked if you want to save the data set. If you have created a new data set and have not saved it yet, you almost certainly want to save the data file. If you were working with a preexisting data set and made some changes or additions to it, you may or may not want to save the now modified data file. Be careful here! You have been working with a copy of the data set. The original version is still on the hard drive or wherever you got it from. If you save the now modified file with the same name as the original, the original version is lost to you. Only the modified version will be available for future SPSS sessions. That may be what you want. If you want to keep both the original and the modified versions, however, then be sure to give the modified file a different name.

SPSS will also ask if you want to save your output. Not only can you save SPSS data files, but you can also save output files. If you say yes, a dialog will open asking where you want the file saved and what you want to name the file. In a future SPSS session, you could open up the output file you saved from this previous session. One reason for doing this might be because the computer you were working on was not connected to a working printer. You could take your output file to some other computer that has SPSS and is connected to a working printer and print some or all of your output. However, SPSS output files can only be opened and read by SPSS. You cannot open that output file in Microsoft Word or any other program besides SPSS. Also, one version of SPSS may not be able to open output files created by a different version of SPSS.

Creating an SPSS Data Set

Using an existing SPSS data set is easy, but someone had to create that data set, and sometimes that someone will be you. You may need to create an SPSS data set to do the analysis for a research project, or you may want to statistically examine some data for work.

As an example, we will create a small data set based on answers given by the first 10 persons to return a questionnaire. The questionnaire uses some of the same questions used in the General Social Survey (GSS). The data appear in Table 2.1.

Table 2.1   Data From 10 Questionnaire Respondents

Survey ID	Age at Last Birthday	Sex	Number of Children	Self-Described Social Class	Self-Described Political Orientation
A01	41	Male	3	Middle class	Moderate
A02	44	Female	2	Upper class	Liberal
B01	19	Female	0	Middle class	"Don't know"
B02	82	Male	4	Middle class	"Don't know"
B03	86	Male	0	Upper class	No answer
B04	33	Female	1	Lower class	Conservative
C01	50	Male	1	Working class	Moderate
D01	No answer	Male	"Don't know"	Middle class	Liberal
D02	41	Female	8	Middle class	Conservative
D03	22	Male	0	Upper class	Liberal

Creating a data set in SPSS requires you to enter information using two screens. One is labeled "Variable View" and the other is "Data View." Getting to these screens is easy. If you are just starting your SPSS session, the program opens with the variable view and data view screens. If you have already been working with some other data set in SPSS and now want to create a new data set, you can simply pull down the *File* menu, move your cursor to *New*, move your cursor to *Data*, and click.

File | *New* | *Data*

You tell SPSS the characteristics of each of your variables using the variable view screen, and you enter your data using the data view screen.

Data View

You can tell which screen you are looking at by the tabs in the lower left. If data view is not the top tab, just click on the data view tab to bring it to the top. The data view screen you see should be similar to Figure 2.5.

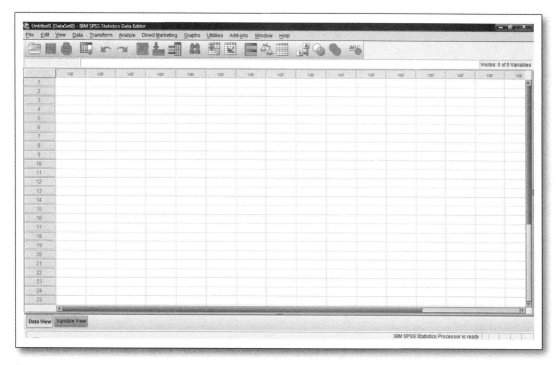

Figure 2.5   Data View

This is the screen you will use to enter data. The rows represent the cases in your data set. Information for each case in your data set will be entered on a separate row. For example, if you have 250 cases in your data set, you will create a data matrix involving 250 rows.

The columns represent the variables in your data set. Information for each variable will be entered in a different column. If your data set includes 13 variables, your data matrix will have 13 columns.

The data matrix obviously resembles a spreadsheet with the rows representing cases and the columns representing variables. Also like a spreadsheet, where any row and column cross is referred to as a cell. In a cell, you indicate which attribute of a variable describes that particular case. The information entered into each cell is often referred to as a value. Obviously, some values may appear frequently in a column if that attribute of the variable describes many of the cases. Other values may appear infrequently if they describe only a few cases. For example, in a data set where the cases represent persons and one of the variables is "number of children," you would probably see many 0s, 1s, and 2s in the column for that variable but relatively few, if any, 16s, 17s, or 18s.

Before entering data into the data view screen, it is best to tell SPSS about the variables that make up the data set. For that we switch to variable view.

Variable View

Switch to variable view by clicking on the variable view tab in the lower left. The variable view screen you see should be similar to Figure 2.6.

Figure 2.6   Variable View

Notice that in variable view, the rows represent variables and not cases. You can specify up to 11 properties about each variable, although you will often use the default settings supplied by SPSS for these properties. The following pages describe each of these properties. The completed variable view screen after all the variables' properties have been set appears later in the chapter as Figure 2.10.

Name

Each variable must have an SPSS name. Without a name, you would have no way to indicate which variable you are talking about. There are certain rules for selecting names:

- Two variables in the same data set may not have the same name.
- The name can be up to 64 characters long, but shorter names make output and variable lists easier to read.
- The name must begin with a letter or @. (Under certain circumstances, names may also begin with # or $.)
- The name may include letters, numbers, and some symbols (e.g., #, $, _, @). SPSS will tell you if you use an illegitimate character. Unfortunately, % is an illegitimate character.
- Letters can be upper- or lowercase in variable names.
- Spaces are not permitted within variable names.

You want your variable names to be as informative as possible but also as short as practical. Fortunately, variable labels (described later in this chapter) provide a way to attach some additional information to variable names.

Since every variable must have a name, SPSS will create a name if you enter data for a variable that you have not named yourself. But SPSS uses very unimaginative names, such as var00001 and var00002. Clearly, it is better to create your own names if you want each name to jog your memory about what the variable represents.

For our survey data set, the variable names will be ID, AGE, SEX, CHILDREN, CLASS, and POLVIEWS. Variable names do not need to be capitalized. They are capitalized in this text only so that you can more quickly recognize them as variable names.

Prefered: Numeric or (text strings) – where were you born.

Type

SPSS can work with many different types of variables. Depending on their type, SPSS stores, displays, and analyzes them differently. This book uses just two types of variables: **numeric variables** and **string variables.** Do not confuse these with level of measurement or discrete versus continuous. By type, SPSS is referring to the types of characters that can be used when entering data in the data view screen.

For numeric variable values, you may only enter numbers, decimal points, negative signs, and positive signs. If you type any other character, including a space, as a data value, SPSS will not accept the value. (Actually, leading spaces and trailing spaces are OK; it is a space within an entry that SPSS will not accept.)

While SPSS has very strict rules about numeric variables, almost anything goes for string variables. Numbers, symbols, spaces, uppercase letters, lowercase letters, and punctuation are all permissible.

Since there are almost no rules for entering string variables, you might wonder why not make all variables string? In fact, however, string variables are used very infrequently because substantially fewer statistical procedures can be done with string variables.

You may notice in variable view that as soon as you enter a name for a variable, SPSS inserts many other properties for that variable. These are defaults. They are the typical properties of variables. In many cases, the defaults will be just what you want, but not in all cases. Notice that the default for type is numeric.

It may seem obvious that interval/ratio variables will be numeric, but what about nominal and ordinal variables? They are usually numeric as well. They are made numeric by assigning a numeric code to represent each attribute. For example, the variable CLASS has four attributes: lower class, working class, middle class, and upper class. Rather than actually typing in those words when entering the data (which would make this a string variable), the codes 1, 2, 3, and 4 will be used to represent the four attributes. When entering the data, only 1s, 2s, 3s, and 4s are typed. Using numeric codes saves time and, more important, makes available the statistical procedures that require numeric variables. It is important to understand, however, that assigning numeric codes to a variable's attributes to qualify it as a numeric variable does not change the variable's level of measurement. CLASS is ordinal, and assigning numeric codes to represent the attributes does not change that fact.

You might be thinking that it is well and good to save time by entering numbers instead of words, but how long will it be before you forget what the numeric codes represent? As you will see when value labels are discussed in a few pages, SPSS gives you a way to attach a verbal reminder to these numeric codes of what each represents.

So, when would you want to use a string variable? The most common reason is to put some identifying information for each case into the data set—identifying information that requires the use of more than just numbers. For example, in a data set where the cases represent nations, you might want to include the name of the country as a string variable. Although you would not actually use the string variable in any statistical analysis, having that information in the data set can be very helpful for identification purposes. Say you are doing some analysis and notice the largest population for any country is 1.3 billion persons. You might want to know which country had that population. You could go to the data set, find the case that had a value of 1.3 billion for its population, and glance over at the column for the string variable name to see which country's characteristics you are looking at. Or what if in analyzing the data for population size, you find that the minimum value is −340000? Since population size cannot be negative, you know that the data must have been entered incorrectly. You go to the data set to find which country has this obviously incorrect value, then go to the source for the information to find what the correct value should be, and correct the data set.

RESEARCH TIP

String Identifiers and Promises of Confidentiality

When the cases in your data set represent persons, organizations, or any entities to whom you have promised confidentiality, it is not good to include a string variable that broadcasts the identity of the case. Better to use an identifying code that requires access to a key that is only available to the principal researcher.

When the data have been gathered anonymously, there is obviously no way to tie the data back to a particular person or organization, but you still might use an identifying code so that data can be traced back to a particular questionnaire to check possible data entry errors.

How do you change a variable's type? Simply click on that cell where the type column and the variable that you are working on cross. A gray area appears toward the right of the cell. Click on that and a dialog similar to Figure 2.7 opens. (If you originally clicked toward the right part of the cell, the dialog immediately opens.)

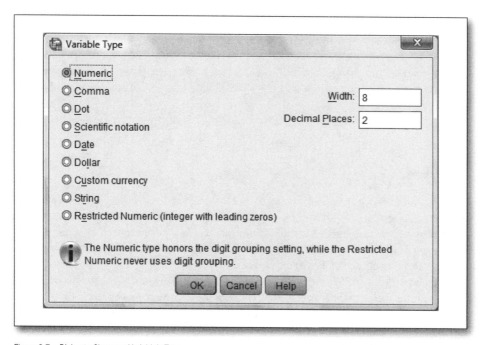

Figure 2.7   Dialog to Change a Variable's Type

You can see the many types of variables SPSS recognizes. If numeric is selected as the type, the dialog has a place to designate width and decimals. If string is selected, the dialog has a place to designate characters (which means the same as width). You can specify those things here or by using the next two columns in variable view.

In our survey data set, only ID will be a string variable. Its maximum number of characters will be set to 6 since that seems slightly larger than the longest identifying code we could possibly need. The other variables will be numeric.

Width

Width controls how large a value you can enter for that variable for any case in the data set. For example, the value −13.5 is five characters wide and the value *orange* is six characters wide. The effect of the width setting on numeric variables is relatively modest, however, since SPSS will often let you exceed what you have set as the maximum width. Often but not always! For example, you can exceed the specified width when entering data for a numeric variable in data view, but you cannot exceed the specified width when identifying values that will be assigned particular value labels (discussed in a later section). Since you cannot always exceed the specified width of numeric variables, the best advice is to set the width a bit larger than you think you will need for the largest value.

Width (or characters) matters very much, however, for string variables. If you try to enter more characters than the specified width for a string variable, only the specified number of characters will be entered in the data set. Any additional characters are not recorded. The key, therefore, is to specify a width for each string variable that will accommodate your widest value. To estimate what that is, try to quickly locate or imagine your longest value, count the characters (being sure to include spaces, punctuation, and any other symbols), and add a few extra to be on the safe side. You can change the specified width later if you come across any even wider value as you are entering your data, but it is you who will have to do it. SPSS will not automatically accept the wider value.

In our survey data set, the width for ID was set at 6. All the other variables use the default width of 8.

Decimals

Values for numeric variables may include a decimal point and one or more numbers after that decimal point. For example, grade point average is routinely recorded to two decimal places. SPSS assumes by default that numeric variable values will have two numbers after the decimal place. Even if you do not enter a decimal point followed by any numbers, the value in the data set will appear with a decimal point followed by two zeroes.

If you want more than two decimal places to show for the values for a numeric variable, simply increase the number of decimal places. When you click the cell, two arrows appear toward the right of the cell. You can use them to increase or decrease the number of decimal places. You can also highlight the number of decimal places currently appearing in the cell and type in your preferred number. If you want to make the same change for many variables in your data set, you can use the *Copy* and *Paste* options in the Edit menu to copy a cell with the desired number and paste that value in the desired other cells.

Setting the number of decimal places only affects the number of decimal places that appear in data view and in any SPSS output where data values are presented. In fact, SPSS records all numeric values for calculation purposes to at least 16 decimal places. If decimal is set to a certain number and you enter more numbers after the decimal point, that additional information is recorded by SPSS and will appear if you decide to increase the number of decimal places appearing.

For string variables, the number of decimal places appears as zero and is pale. That number cannot be changed because the concept of decimal places makes no sense for string variables. The values for string variables are whatever, and only whatever, gets entered as their values. SPSS never recognizes string variable values as numbers; they are just strings of characters.

In our survey data set, the number of decimal places for all of the numeric variables has been set to 0 since none of the values for these variables require decimal places.

No space
No numbers
No simbuls

copy & paste in the Box
Question

Chapter 2 :: Data Sets | 41

Label

Variable names are limited to 64 characters, and spaces are prohibited. However, SPSS gives you the option of assigning a variable label to a variable name. Depending on how you set your output label options (described later in the chapter), these variable labels may appear in your SPSS output and can provide a fuller description of what the variable actually represents. SPSS itself does not care whether you provide variable labels. They are strictly for the convenience of human users. They play no part in any statistical calculations. However, since it's possible to quickly forget what a variable name represents, you should enter a variable label whenever the variable name "does not say it all." For our survey data set, variable labels were added for every variable.

Variable labels can include anything: numbers, symbols, spaces, uppercase letters, lowercase letters, and punctuation. Variable labels can be as long as 256 characters in length; however, variable labels that long can badly clutter up the output and, in some output, may be truncated. Less is better if you have said everything that is needed.

To enter a variable label, just click in the appropriate cell and type your label. To modify an existing variable label, double-click on the label and then click where you want to make your insertion and enter your changes. To replace an entire label, click just once in the cell and type your new label.

Values

Higher # — For
Lower # — aghinst   1—10

Just as you can attach labels to variable names, you can attach labels to the codes representing the attributes of a variable. Remember how the attributes lower class, working class, middle class, and upper class were represented by the codes 1, 2, 3, and 4, thereby making it a numeric variable? With value labels, you can remind yourself what each numeric code represents.

These value labels function similarly to variable labels except that variable labels attach to the variable name, whereas value labels attach to the individual attributes of a variable. Once again, depending on how you set your output label options, the value labels may appear in your SPSS output next to the numeric codes you used to enter the data. It does not matter to SPSS whether you provide value labels. Like variable labels, they are strictly for the convenience of human users and play no part in any statistical calculations.

Value labels can include anything: numbers, symbols, spaces, uppercase letters, lowercase letters, and punctuation. Value labels can be as long as 120 characters in length; however, long value labels, just like long variable labels, can clutter up the output and may be truncated because of space limitations in some output. Once again, brevity is best.

Not all variables benefit from value labels. Because the meaning of numeric values for interval/ratio variables is usually obvious, value labels are rarely needed. For example, the meaning of the attribute 54 for the variable "age at last birthday" is pretty obvious and does not need a label attached to it saying "fifty-four years." The nominal and ordinal variables are usually the ones where you want to create value labels to help you remember what the numeric codes represent.

You can attach value labels to all the possible values for a variable, none of the possible values, or just some of the possible values. For example, even for the variable age at last birthday, if the highest value you chose to use was 89 and that described persons who were 89 or older at their last birthday, you might attach the value label "89 or older" to the value 89 to remind yourself what an 89 represents. That might be the only value label you create for this variable.

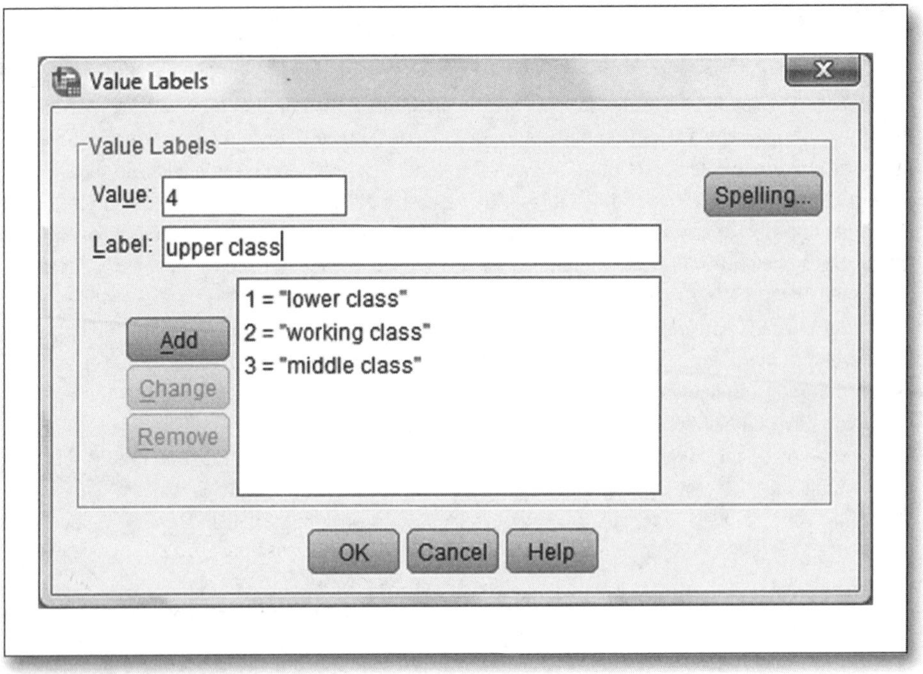

Figure 2.8   Dialog for Setting Value Labels

To create value labels, click toward the right side of the cell where the column headed "Values" and the row for your variable cross. A dialog similar to Figure 2.8 opens up.

In the value field, enter one of the codes used for the attributes. In the label field, enter the label you want attached to that code. Now click the add button. The code with its label appears in the list of value labels for this variable. Repeat this process until you have created all the labels you want for this variable. Clicking the OK button closes the dialog. You can reopen this dialog to add, change, or delete labels whenever you wish. If several variables in your data set use the same numeric codes and labels, you can copy and paste this "Values" cell to save time.

For our survey data set, value labels were created for all the variables except ID. For SEX, value labels were added to identify males and females. For CLASS and POLVIEWS, labels were used to indicate what class and what political orientation the numeric codes represent. For AGE, a label was added to the value 89 to indicate this category includes persons 89 and older just as a label was attached to the value 8 for CHILDREN to point out that this category includes persons with 8 or more children. For AGE, CHILDREN, CLASS, and POLVIEWS, labels were added to certain values to show why cases might have missing data. More will be said about this in the next section. (We are creating some value labels and, in the next section, creating some user-missing codes that are not actually needed for our small data set of 10 cases. These value labels and user-missing codes do appear in the larger data set that you will be using throughout this book, however, and creating them now will give you familiarity with how the larger GSS data set is designed.)

Missing

Almost inevitably data for some cases on some variables end up missing. Survey respondents may not know the answers to some questions, they may refuse to answer other questions, and they may legitimately skip specific questions because those questions are not relevant to their situation.

If a cell is left empty in a data matrix, SPSS will always recognize that as missing data. SPSS uses a **system-missing** code to represent an empty data cell. That is just a fancy way of noting that it is built into the SPSS system to recognize empty cells as missing data for that case on that variable.

Cases with missing data on a particular variable are excluded whenever a statistic involving that variable is calculated. That only makes sense since we do not have the data needed to include the case.

Researchers often do not care why a value is missing for a particular case for a particular variable. All that is noteworthy is that it is missing. In such cases, they simply leave the data cell blank and let SPSS treat it as a system-missing code regardless of whether it was missing because the answer was unknown, the respondent refused to disclose the answer, or the question was not relevant.

Sometimes, however, researchers want to keep track of the reasons why the data are missing. To do so, they reserve special codes, called **user-missing** codes, for the possible reasons why data might be missing. There are two things to bear in mind if you want to record the reason for a missing value. First, do not choose values that could also be legitimate values for a variable. Consider the confusion that would occur if a researcher decided for the variable "age at last birthday" to use the code 21 to indicate the respondent refused to answer the question. Some cases would be getting a code of 21 because that is how old they were at their last birthday, while other cases would be getting a code of 21 because they refused to disclose their age, but once the data were entered into the data matrix, there would be no way to separate one group of 21s from the other. Better to use as a missing value code some value that could not naturally occur such as −1. No one is −1 years of age. Or you could use 98 as a missing value code for "no answer" *if* you established an open-ended category like 89 for all persons 89 or older.

That brings us to the second consideration. You need some way to tell SPSS that the value, for example, −1, you are using for a certain type of missing data represents a missing value. If you fail to tell SPSS, the program will treat −1 as a perfectly valid value and include it in the calculation of any statistics involving this variable. Telling SPSS which values represent missing data is the purpose of this column in variable view. These are called "user-missing" values because they are not built into the SPSS system but rather are defined by you, the user. Simply click toward the right side of the cell. A dialog similar to Figure 2.9 opens up.

The default setting is "no missing values." (That means no user-missing values. Blank data cells are always recognized as system-missing values.) You have two options for specifying user-missing values. The first option lets you specify one, two, or three discrete values as user missing. The second option lets you specify a range of values as user missing and also, if you wish, one discrete value outside that range.

For our survey data set, user-missing values were set for AGE, CHILDREN, CLASS, and POLVIEWS.

Cases with user-missing values are excluded from statistical analyses just as are cases with system-missing values.

Figure 2.9   Dialog to Set User-Missing Values

For any user-missing values you create, you may want to go back to the values column and cre-ate labels if you have not done so already. The labels will remind you what each user-missing value represents.

Columns

The columns specification controls how many characters for a data entry will actually appear in data view. Be careful not to confuse the width and columns specifications. Width affects what is stored in computer memory; columns affects what is visible in data view. Even if more characters are stored in the memory, only the number of characters stated in the columns specification will appear.

If a string variable value is larger than the column width, SPSS starts at the beginning of the value and shows as many characters as will fit in the column. If a numeric variable value is larger than the column width, SPSS will first try to shorten the appearance of the value by rounding off decimal places. (Of course, the full value without any rounding remains in the computer's memory, and the full value would be used for any calculations.) If eliminating decimal places does not sufficiently shorten the appearance of the value, SPSS will convert the value to scientific notation if space permits. Scientific notation can shorten the length of extremely large or extremely small values. It may, however, involve some loss of precision in the appearance of the number due to rounding. If there is insufficient space to represent the number using scientific notation, SPSS will simply replace the number with a string of asterisks to indicate the columns specification is too small to show the number.

(handwritten top margin: File Data Analize — Mostly Used)

MATH TIP

Understanding Scientific Notation

It does not happen often, but occasionally SPSS will save space by showing numbers in scientific notation. Here are some examples:

$$3.14E+05 \qquad 6.60E-05 \qquad -7.15E12 \qquad -1.25E-04$$

Scientific notation in SPSS takes a very large or very small number and expresses it as a single integer plus two decimal places times a power of 10. To convert the scientific notation back into regular numbers, you simply have to move the decimal point a certain number of places to the right (if the number after the E is positive) or a certain number of places to the left (if the number after the E is negative). Remember that the positive or negative sign after the E is only telling you whether to move the decimal point to the left or to the right. It does not tell you anything about whether the original number is positive or negative. To determine that, just look to see if there is a negative sign or not in front of the entire number.

Sometimes the positive sign after the E is omitted. If there is neither a positive nor a negative sign after the E, move the decimal point to the right.

The four numbers above when converted from scientific to regular notation become

$$314,000 \qquad 0.000066 \qquad -7,150,000,000,000 \qquad -0.000125$$

(handwritten right margin: Data View Variable)

(handwritten right margin: output)

(handwritten right margin: NO SAVE change in)

Clicking the columns cell toward the right reveals two arrows that you can use to raise or lower the number of characters to be shown. You can also highlight the current columns specification and type in your preferred specification. For now, column width for all variables in our sample data set will be left at the default setting of 8.

(handwritten right margin: SPSS)

Align

The align specification also only affects the appearance of the data in data view. You have a pull-down menu to indicate if you want the values for a particular variable left-justified, center-justified, or right-justified. Alignment settings have no effect on the statistical calculations. For our survey data set, none of the defaults were changed. By default, numeric variables are right-justified and string variables are left-justified.

Measure

(handwritten: (Scale)(ordinal)(Nominal) Rank/order — Most Important!!)

This next column in variable view is to record each variable's level of measurement. Using a pull-down menu, you can specify nominal, ordinal, or scale. **Scale** is the same as interval/ratio. If you specified a variable's type as string, SPSS assumes the variable is nominal. You can change the level

(handwritten bottom: 3 choices)

(handwritten bottom: Variable View To Enter Data)

(handwritten bottom: inport =)

to ordinal, but you cannot change it to scale. If you specified a variable's type as numeric, SPSS shows the level of measurement as unknown. You can then change the level to nominal, ordinal, or scale.

Many beginning SPSS users assume this column does more than it really does. It is a good place to record each variable's level of measurement. What the specification in this column usually *does not do* is warn you when you are about to ask for a statistical procedure that is beyond a variable's level of measurement.

SPSS excludes string variables from the list of available variables for certain statistical procedures but that is because of the variable's type, not its level of measurement. SPSS tries to be helpful by inserting symbols (three balls for nominal, three bars for ordinal, a ruler for scale) in front of the variable's name in variable lists to remind you of the variable's level of measurement, but in most cases, it does not stop you from using variables in inappropriate statistical procedures. The responsibility is always on you to consider each variable's level of measurement and to only ask for appropriate statistical procedures.

In our sample data set, ID and SEX are nominal, CLASS and POLVIEWS are ordinal, and AGE and CHILDREN are scale (interval/ratio).

Role

SPSS lets you specify what role a variable will play in statistical analyses, for example, if a variable will always be used as an independent variable (what SPSS calls an input role) or a dependent variable (what SPSS calls a target role). Specifying roles for variables is useful when data sets have been collected for very specific analytical purposes and only for those purposes. The GSS is not a single-purpose data set. Variables play many different roles depending on the research question. For our sample data set, the roles have all been set to none. This was done by using the pull-down menu hidden at the right of the cell. Later in this chapter, you will also see how this role function can be turned off, thereby ignoring any preset roles.

Figure 2.10 shows variable view with all of the information entered for our survey data set.

File Edit View Data Transform Analyze Direct Marketing Graphs Utilities Add-ons Window Help

	Name	Type	Width	Decimals	Label	Values	Missing	Columns	Align	Measure	Role
1	ID	String	6	0	Identifying Code Placed on Survey upon Return	None	None	8	Left	Nominal	None
2	AGE	Numeric	8	0	Age at Last Birthday	{89, 89 or ol...	97, 98, 99	8	Right	Scale	None
3	SEX	Numeric	8	0	Respondent's Sex	{0, male}...	None	8	Right	Nominal	None
4	CHILDREN	Numeric	8	0	Number of Children	{8, eight or ...	9	8	Right	Scale	None
5	CLASS	Numeric	8	0	Subjective Class Identification	{1, lower cla...	7 - 9, 5	8	Right	Ordinal	None
6	POLVIEWS	Numeric	8	0	Think of Self As Politically Liberal, Moderate, ...	{1, liberal}...	8, 9	8	Right	Ordinal	None
7											
8											
9											
10											
11											
12											

Figure 2.10   Variable View With the Settings for Our Sample Data Set

Returning to Data View

Returning to data view, you will notice the names of the variables now appear above the columns. If you changed the size of the columns while in variable view (we did not), those changes would also be evident.

Before entering your data, take a look at the tool bar, which is the bar with the buttons below the menu bar. Find a button with an icon that looks like a fork in the road with one road leading to the number 1 and the other leading to the letter A. When you move your cursor over it, the phrase "Value Labels" appears. Click it a few times. It is actually an on/off switch. When the cursor is not on the button, notice how the button appears either pushed in or not. Click it so that it is not pushed in. What this button does will be explained after the data are entered.

Data entry is very simple, but, depending on the length of the data set, it can be very tedious. It must always be done carefully!

Begin with the cell in the upper left corner. This is where you enter the value of the first variable for the first case. If the variable is a numeric variable, you will only be keying in numbers, possibly a decimal point, and possibly a negative sign. If it is a string variable, you could be keying in anything. When you are finished entering in that value, you can move to the right (to enter the value for the second variable for the first case) by hitting the right arrow key or you can move down (to enter the value for the first variable for the second case) by hitting the enter key. Depending on how the data you are going to enter are organized, it may be easier to enter the values for all the variables for the first case and then do the same for the next case and the next and so on, or it may be easier to enter the values for the first variable for all the cases and then do the same for the second variable, then the third variable, and so on. It makes no difference how you do it.

As soon as you enter the first value for a case, two things happen. First the case number in the left margin of the data matrix darkens. This is because SPSS now knows that case exists. These case numbers in the left margin are not a variable. If the cases in your data set get sorted into a different order, these numbers in the left margin do not move. So, if you want each case to have an ID number that stays with the case no matter how the data set gets resorted, you need to create it as a variable in your data set.

The second thing that happens is that as soon as one value for a case is entered, a small dot appears in each of the other cells for that case. That dot is the system-missing value indicator for SPSS. Since you have entered one value for that case but not yet entered any other values, those other values are missing, at least for the moment. As you move to those cells and enter the appropriate values, they cease to be missing.

The importance of care when entering data cannot be overstressed. While some data entry errors may become obvious later, many will not. No matter how small the data set and no matter how carefully you entered the data, go back over your data matrix and check the entries. Even better, since most people, at least occasionally, tend to see what they thought they entered rather than what they really entered, find a friend who might owe you a favor and have him or her check your work.

Before going on to other things, return to the button on the tool bar that looks like a fork in the road. This button controls whether the data matrix shows the actual values you entered or, for those variables with value labels, the value labels attached to the values. Click on this "value label" button so it appears pushed in. For those variables with value labels, the cells in the data matrix are now showing the value labels rather than the actual numeric values you entered. If the label is cut off because the column is too narrow, you can click and drag the right edge of the column next to the variable name further to the right. Click the value labels button again and the numeric values reappear. Some people prefer to see the value labels in the data matrix; others prefer the numeric values that were entered. You can choose whichever you prefer.

Figures 2.11 and 2.12 show our sample data set. Figure 2.11 shows the actual data that were entered. Figure 2.12 shows the value labels replacing the numeric codes that had labels.

	ID	AGE	SEX	CHILDREN	CLASS	POLVIEWS	var	var	var	var
1	A01	41	0	3	3	2				
2	A02	44	1	2	4	1				
3	B01	19	1	0	3	8				
4	B02	82	0	4	3	8				
5	B03	86	0	0	4	9				
6	B04	33	1	1	1	3				
7	C01	50	0	1	2	2				
8	D01	99	0	9	3	1				
9	D02	41	1	8	3	3				
10	D03	22	0	0	4	1				
11										
12										

Figure 2.11   Data View With Data as Entered

File	Edit	View	Data	Transform	Analyze	Direct Marketing	Graphs	Utilities	Add-ons	Window	Help

1 : ID | A01

	ID	AGE	SEX	CHILDREN	CLASS	POLVIEWS	var	var	var
1	A01	41	male	3	middle class	moderate			
2	A02	44	female	2	upper class	liberal			
3	B01	19	female	0	middle class	don't know			
4	B02	82	male	4	middle class	don't know			
5	B03	86	male	0	upper class	no answer			
6	B04	33	female	1	lower class	conservative			
7	C01	50	male	1	working class	moderate			
8	D01	no answer	male	don't know / no answer	middle class	liberal			
9	D02	41	female	eight or more	middle class	conservative			
10	D03	22	male	0	upper class	liberal			
11									
12									

Figure 2.12   Data View With Value Labels Substituting for the Actual Data

Saving Your Data Set

Having spent all this time defining your variables and entering your data, you want to save your work. Even if the data set is small and you think you have done all the analysis you could ever want, save your data set! It is easy to do and may save having to re-create the data set later. Simply pull down the *File* menu and click on *Save*.

File | *Save*

A dialog similar to Figure 2.13 opens.

Like other Windows applications, the first time you save a file, you must indicate where you want to save it (c: drive, d: drive, or wherever) and the file name. Whatever you name the file, SPSS will add the extension .sav to indicate that this is an SPSS data file.

RESEARCH TIP

Save Your Data Often

Many researchers do not wait until they have finished entering the data to save the file they are creating. After every sizable chunk of work, they save it. For very large and/or very important data files, careful researchers have them saved in more than one location (and not just two locations on the same computer).

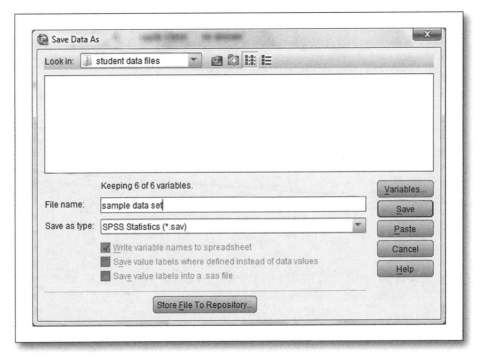

Figure 2.13   Dialog to Save a Data Set

Printing Data

You may want to print a copy of the data that you entered. A printed copy can be useful for checking to make sure you entered the data correctly. The simplest way to print your data is to simply pull down the *File* menu and click *Print* when you are in data view. If a section of the data matrix is highlighted, only that section will get printed. To eliminate any highlighting, simply press the < Esc > key.

File | Print

Another way to print your data is to pull down the *Analyze* menu, move your cursor to *Reports,* and click *Case Summaries*.

Analyze | Reports | Case Summaries

The *Case Summaries* procedure can do a lot more than simply list your data, but that is the only thing we need right now. When you click on *Case Summaries,* a dialog opens up similar to Figure 2.14.

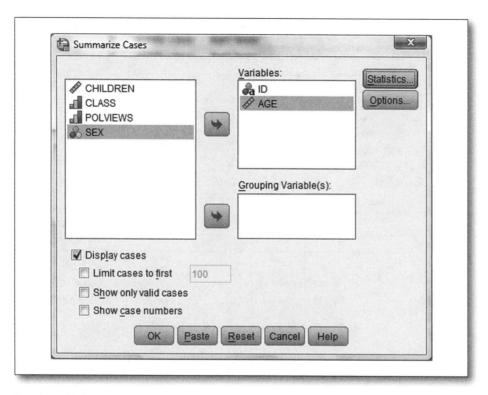

Figure 2.14   The *Summarize Cases* Dialog

Move the variables whose values you want printed from the list on the left to the "Variables" list in the upper middle part of the dialog. Do this by clicking once on a variable name and then clicking on the arrow that points to the "Variables" list. You can move one, some, or all of the variables from the list on the left to the variables list on the right. Do not put anything in the list labeled "Grouping Variables." Next, look at the lower left area of the dialog. Make sure "Display cases" is checked. You can limit the number of cases for which you will see the data, but if you wish to see all the cases, make sure "Limit cases to first ___" is not checked. "Show only valid cases" and "Show case numbers" should also not be checked. Finally, click OK.

Figure 2.15 shows the output for our sample data set from the *Case Summaries* procedure.

The "Case Processing Summary" box tells you how many cases had valid data ("included") and how many had missing data ("excluded") on each of the variables. The "Case Summaries" box lists the values of the variables for each of the cases. In the columns, the values for each case are shown along with the value label if there is one. At the bottom of the column, you are told the "Total N." The uppercase letter N is frequently used to represent the number of valid cases. Valid cases are nonmissing cases.

Case Processing Summary

	Cases					
	Included		Excluded		Total	
	N	Percent	N	Percent	N	Percent
ID	10	100.0%	0	.0%	10	100.0%
AGE	9	90.0%	1	10.0%	10	100.0%
SEX	10	100.0%	0	.0%	10	100.0%
CHILDREN	9	90.0%	1	10.0%	10	100.0%
CLASS	10	100.0%	0	.0%	10	100.0%
POLVIEWS	7	70.0%	3	30.0%	10	100.0%

Case Summaries

	ID	AGE	SEX	CHILDREN	CLASS	POLVIEWS
1	A01	41	0 male	3	3 middle class	2 moderate
2	A02	44	1 female	2	4 upper class	1 liberal
3	B01	19	1 female	0	3 middle class	8 don't know
4	B02	82	0 male	4	3 middle class	8 don't know
5	B03	86	0 male	0	4 upper class	9 no answer
6	B04	33	1 female	1	1 lower class	3 conservative
7	C01	50	0 male	1	2 working class	2 moderate
8	D01	99 no answer	0 male	9 don't know / no answer	3 middle class	1 liberal
9	D02	41	1 female	8 eight or more	3 middle class	3 conservative
10	D03	22	0 male	0	4 upper class	1 liberal
Total N	10	9	10	9	10	7

Figure 2.15   Output From the *Case Summaries* Procedure

You could print just this "Case Summaries" box by going to the outline pane (on the left of the screen), clicking "Case Summaries" to select just this part of your output, and then printing.

Printing Variable Information

You may want a printed copy of the variable information you entered in variable view. The simplest way to do that is, when you are in variable view, to press the < Esc > key to make sure no section is highlighted and then pull down the *File* menu and click *Print*.

File | Print

Unfortunately, doing this will not show all the value labels you created, and the full variable labels may be truncated.

An alternative method of printing variable information is to pull down the *File* menu, move your cursor over *Display Data File Information,* and click *Working File:*

File | Display Data File Information | Working File

This generates output that can be printed. Figure 2.16 is an example of the output produced by the *Display Data File Information* procedure.

The "Variable Information" box shows all the information in variable view except the value labels. Print format and write format did not appear in variable view, but they are based on variable type (A for string and F for numeric), width, and decimals. The value labels you created appear in a separate box called "Variable Values."

SPSS TIP

Adjusting Output Table Column Width

The original "Variable Information" box in the *Display Data File Information* output was not as neat as it appears in Figure 2.16. The columns were all of identical width, which meant some were too narrow for their content to be read easily and some too wide.

To change the appearance of output tables, move your cursor onto the table you want to adjust and double-click. By doing that, a window opens in which you can customize the appearance of the output. You can click and drag the edges of columns to adjust their width. When you are satisfied, simply click outside the window. The changes you made are now reflected in your output

---

Running the *Display Data File Information* procedure is also a good way to become initially familiar with a data set created by someone else. You will see the properties of each variable, including its value labels. In this way, you will know which variables are and are not in the data set and, for those that are, important information about how they were measured. This will give you a good idea about what types of research questions the data set could be used to answer and which statistical procedures would be both appropriate and useful with each variable.

Importing Data From Excel

If your data already reside on a Microsoft Excel spreadsheet, you can easily import them into SPSS without having to retype them. A simple method is to copy the cells from your Excel spreadsheet

Variable Information

Variable	Position	Label	Measurement Level	Role	Column Width	Alignment	Print Format	Write Format	Missing Values
ID	1	Identifying Code Placed on Survey upon Return	Nominal	None	8	Left	A8	A8	
AGE	2	Age at Last Birthday	Scale	None	8	Right	F8	F8	97, 98, 99
SEX	3	Respondent's Sex	Nominal	None	8	Right	F8	F8	
CHILDREN	4	Number of Children	Scale	None	16	Right	F8	F8	9
CLASS	5	Subjective Class Identification	Ordinal	None	10	Right	F8	F8	7 through 9, and 5
POLVIEWS	6	Think of Self as Politically Liberal, Moderate, or Conservative	Ordinal	None	8	Right	F8	F8	7, 8, 9

Variables in the working file

Variable Values

Value		Label
AGE	89	89 or older
	97[a]	question not asked
	98[a]	don't know
	99[a]	no answer
SEX	0	male
	1	female
CHILDREN	8	eight or more
	9[a]	don't know / no answer
CLASS	1	lower class
	2	working class
	3	middle class
	4	upper class
POLVIEWS	1	liberal
	2	moderate
	3	conservative
	7[a]	question not asked
	8[a]	don't know
	9[a]	no answer

a. Missing value

Figure 2.16 Output From the *Display Data File Information* Procedure

and paste them into the SPSS data matrix. However, a more efficient method that can also import the names of the variables from Excel to SPSS is to pull down the *File* menu, move the cursor to *Open,* and click on *Data:*

File | Open | Data

When the open file dialog appears, indicate that you want to see Excel-type files. Then select the desired file and click "Open." Before the file opens, another dialog will appear asking if SPSS should read the variable names from the first row of the Excel spreadsheet. If it should, leave the box checked; if it should not, uncheck the box. If you are importing an Excel file with multiple worksheets in it, SPSS will give you an opportunity to specify which worksheet you want imported.

When the Excel file is opened in SPSS, SPSS will look at the data and try to make reasonable decisions about the type, width, decimals, alignment, and level of the variables. Be sure to go to variable view and make any corrections. While in variable view, add any needed variable labels, value labels, and user-missing values.

SPSS can also import data from spreadsheets and applications other than Excel.

Setting SPSS Options

Like many other software applications, SPSS lets you customize certain things about how it appears on the screen. Ask your instructor how he or she wants you to set your SPSS options. The option changes described here will make your SPSS dialogs and outputs look like those in the rest of this book.

The next time you start SPSS, pull down the *Edit* menu and click on *Options.*

Edit | Options

You will see a dialog similar to Figure 2.17 open up with many tabs near the top.

Click on the "General" tab if that tab is not already in the front. Under "Variable Lists," click "Display names" and click "Alphabetical." By making these choices, the list of variables that appears for almost every SPSS procedure will be much easier to use. Instead of the list consisting of variable labels (take a look at Figure 2.3), which are often too long for the variable list box, the list will consist of variable names (now look at Figure 2.14), and the variable names will be in alphabetical order, which makes it much easier to locate the variable you are looking for.

Still on the general tab, click "Use custom assignments" under "Roles." This turns off the predetermined roles that appear in variable view.

Now click on the "Output Labels" tab. The dialog should now look similar to Figure 2.18.

There are four options that can be set. The first two control labeling in the outline pane; the second two control labeling in the right pane where tables, charts, and text appear. For the output shown in this book, the first pull-down menu was always set to "Names," and the second pull-down menu was always set to "Labels." The third pull-down menu was usually set to "Names," and the fourth pull-down menu was usually set to "Values and Labels."

SPSS TIP

Customizing Your Output

Set these "pivot table labeling" options to make your output look its best. If you think your output has too much labeling or not enough labeling, reset these options and repeat your analysis. Your new output will reflect your new option settings.

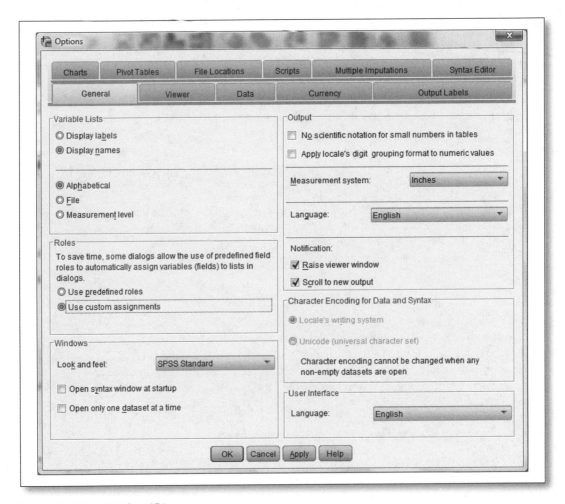

Figure 2.17   Options Dialog, General Tab

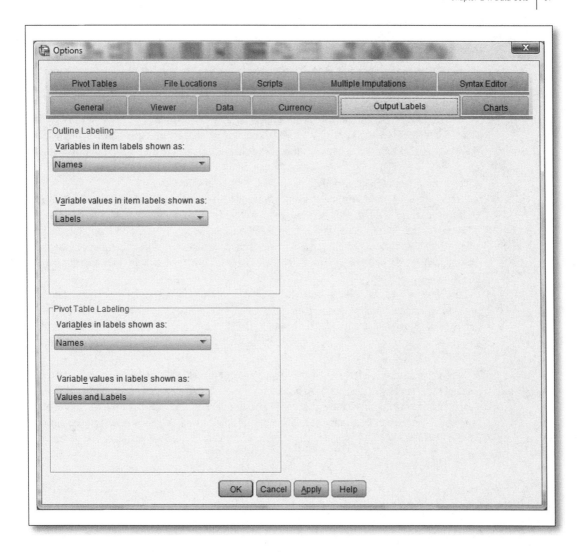

Figure 2.18   Options Dialog, Output Labels Tab

Once you have set these options, click OK. These options remain in effect for the copy of SPSS running on this computer until someone changes those options. That is good news if you are running SPSS on your own computer since you will have to change the options only once. If you use SPSS in a computer lab or on someone else's machine, you should check to see if the options are set the way you want them to be each time before beginning your work.

SPSS Help Capabilities

Like many software programs, SPSS has some very useful help mechanisms built right into the program. With them you may be able to answer questions and solve problems for yourself when neither your instructor nor your fellow students are handy.

The *Help* menu lists several options. *Tutorial* will give you a self-paced guided tour through data analysis with SPSS. Like most machine-based tutorials, it is "one size fits all" and will not let you ask questions or skip things you already know. Nevertheless, you can learn an awful lot from it. The tutorials are designed for persons just becoming familiar with SPSS data analysis. The more you already know about SPSS, the more tedious these tutorials would be.

Topics, another option on the help menu, is where you would turn when you have a more specific question. You can seek your answer by identifying the "contents" of your question, or you can use the "index" to search for help based on specific keywords or do a general "search" of the SPSS help files based on particular words in your question. Topics is probably the most used help function in SPSS. Even regular SPSS users find they need help with specific details, and here is where they go.

The *Statistics Coach* option on the help menu can give you advice about which statistical procedures you could use depending on the nature of the question you want answered. It is like having a statistical consultant available 24/7. This help function is particularly good for professionals who know something about statistics but only infrequently are called upon to actually do some data analysis.

SPSS can also give you location-specific help. Many of the dialogs have help buttons that explain some of the choices you have to make or can make when doing a particular procedure. Also, positioning the cursor over an element in a dialog or output and clicking the right mouse button often can get you very specific assistance. Help is not available for every element in every dialog or output, in which case nothing happens when you right-click. But often help is there.

CONCEPT CHECK

Without looking back, can you answer the following questions:

- Why should you run *Display Data File Information* the first time you use a data set created by someone else?
- How do you get dialogs to list variable names rather than variable labels?
- What are two ways to get location-specific help from SPSS?

If not, go back and review before reading on.

Important Concepts in the Chapter

Case Summaries procedure

cell

Data View

Display Data File *Information* procedure

exiting SPSS

importing data

level of measurement

numeric variable

opening a data set

printing output

saving a data set

scale

scientific notation

setting SPSS options

SPSS Help capabilities

starting SPSS

string variable

system-missing

user-missing values

value label

variable label

variable name

Variable View

Practice Problems

1. In data view,
   a. Do the cases correspond to rows or to columns?
   b. Do the variables correspond to rows or to columns?

2. Would you go to variable view or to data view for each of the following?
   a. to see the set of value labels for a variable
   b. to see a variable's level of measurement
   c. to see the user-missing value codes
   d. to see what value a particular case had on a particular variable
   e. to see which case(s) had a particularly unusual value on a variable

3. Which of the following MUST a variable have: a variable name, a variable label, value labels, or user-missing values?

4. For each of the following, indicate if it is a legitimate variable name or not:
   a. %female
   b. female%
   c. 2friends
   d. friends2

5. Explain the difference between what SPSS calls numeric and string variables.

6. Convert each of the following numbers from scientific notation to normal notation:
   a. 4.32E+05
   b. 4.32E–02
   c. –9.87E08
   d. –9.87E–03

7. What name does SPSS use for what we are calling the interval/ratio level of measurement?

8. SPSS puts symbols in front of the variables in a variable list to indicate each variable's level of measurement. What level of measurement is indicated by each of the following?
   a. three balls
   b. three bars
   c. a ruler

9. You are creating a data set that includes a numeric variable called testScore. Possible scores on the test go from 0 to 100. You want to create a user-missing code to indicate that a student has no test score because he or she was absent the day of the test. For each of the following, indicate if it would be a smart choice for a user-missing code or not, and why:
   a. –1
   b. 0
   c. none
   d. (simply leave the cell blank)

10. Which of the following SPSS procedures would be best for each of the following tasks?
    - Case Summaries
    - Data View
    - Display Data File Information
    - Help | Topics | Index
    - Help | Tutorials
    - Options (General tab)
    - Options (Output Labels tab)
    - Variable View

    a. change a value label
    b. familiarize yourself with the variables in a new data set
    c. have SPSS use variable names instead of variable labels in variable lists
    d. have only variable names and not variable labels appear in output
    e. find out what the term *roles* refers to in SPSS

Problems Requiring SPSS

11. Open the SPSS data file that accompanies this text. Its name is *fourGroups.sav*. Be sure you have set your SPSS options as described in this chapter. Run a *Frequencies* procedure for the variable GROUP. Print your output.

12. What follows is output from the *Display Data File Information* procedure. Use SPSS to create the data set it describes. After using Variable View to define the variables, use Data View to enter the data that follow the *Display Data File Information* output. Enter your name and your (made-up) stats as the sixth case. Run the *Display Data File Information* procedure to show how you defined your variables and print your output. Also print a copy of the Data View screen after you have entered your data.

Variable Information

Variable	Position	Label	Measurement Level	Role	Column Width	Alignment	Print Format	Write Format
PLAYER	1	Lastname, Firstname	Nominal	None	20	Left	A20	A20
YEAR	2	Year in College	Scale	None	8	Right	F8	F8
HEIGHT	3	In Inches	Scale	None	8	Right	F8	F8
POSITION	4	<none>	Nominal	None	8	Right	F8	F8
FIELD	5	Field Goal Percent	Scale	None	8	Right	F8	F8
FREE	6	Free Throw Percent	Scale	None	8	Right	F8	F8
POINTS	7	Average Per Game	Scale	None	8	Right	F8.1	F8.1

Variables in the working file

Variable Values

Value		Label
POSITION	1	guard
	2	forward
	3	post

	PLAYER	YEAR	HEIGHT	POSITION	FIELD	FREE	POINTS
1	Baker, Jordan	2	68	1	40	62	13.3
2	Buchanan, Daisy	2	65	2	42	69	7.8
3	Buchanan, Tom	4	74	3	38	74	12.5
4	Carraway, Nick	1	72	1	45	55	8.8
5	Gatsby, Jay	3	70	2	37	75	5.4
6							
7							

13. Use SPSS to create a data set for the following data. You will have to name the variables and decide on their properties. After defining the variables, enter the data. Run the *Display Data File Information* procedure to show how you defined your variables and print your output. Also print a copy of the Data View screen after you have entered your data.

President	Year Inaugurated	Total Years in Office	Political Party	Prior Elected Office	Popular Vote When First Elected
Dwight D. Eisenhower	1953	8	Republican	None	55.4
John F. Kennedy	1961	2	Democrat	Senator	50.1
Lyndon B. Johnson	1963	6	Democrat	Vice-President	61.3
Richard M. Nixon	1969	5	Republican	Vice-President	43.6
Gerald R. Ford	1974	3	Republican	Vice-President	Not elected
James E. Carter	1977	4	Democrat	Governor	51.0
Ronald W. Reagan	1981	8	Republican	Governor	51.6
George H. Bush	1989	4	Republican	Vice-President	53.9
William J. Clinton	1993	8	Democrat	Governor	43.3
George W. Bush	2001	8	Republican	Governor	49.7
Barack H. Obama	2009	Still in office	Democrat	Senator	52.9

14. Create a data set of your own. It should have at least five variables and at least five cases. At least one variable should be a string variable. At least three variables should have variable labels. At least one variable should have value labels. At least one variable should have a user-missing value. After defining the variables and entering the data, run the *Display Data File Information* procedure to show how you defined your variables and print your output. Also print a copy of the Data View screen after you have entered your data.

PART II

DESCRIPTIVE STATISTICS

Answering Questions About Your Data

Formulas Appearing in Part Two (Chapters 3–10):

$$\text{percent} = \frac{\text{row frequency}}{\text{grand total}} \times 100$$

$$\text{row percent} = \frac{\text{cell count}}{\text{row total}} \times 100$$

$$\text{valid percent} = \frac{\text{row frequency}}{\text{valid total}} \times 100$$

$$\text{column percent} = \frac{\text{cell count}}{\text{column total}} \times 100$$

$$\text{range} = \text{maximum} - \text{minimum}$$

$$\text{total percent} = \frac{\text{cell count}}{\text{table total}} \times 100$$

$$\text{mean} = \frac{\sum X_i}{N}$$

$$Y = a + b(X)$$

$$\text{variance} = \frac{\sum (X_i - \bar{X})^2}{N - 1}$$

$$Y = a + b_1(X_1) + \ldots + b_n(X_n)$$

$$\text{standard deviation} = \sqrt{\text{variance}}$$

$$\text{regression residual} = Y - \hat{Y}$$

$$\text{coefficient of determination} = R^2$$

$$\text{variance} = \text{standard deviation}^2$$

$$\text{coefficient of alienation} = 1 - R^2$$

$$z\text{-score}_i = \frac{(X_i - \bar{X})}{\text{stdev}}$$

$$\text{raw score}_i = (z\text{-score}_i \times \text{stdev}) + \bar{X}$$

Questions and Tools for Answering Them
(Chapter 3)

Univariate Descriptive	Univariate Inferential
Questions:	

Questions:

- How many persons are in this category? In that category?
- What percent of cases got this score? Got that score?
- What percent of persons got that score or less? That score or more?
- What does the distribution of scores look like?

Statistics:

- Frequency
- Percent
- Cumulative percent
- Pie chart
- Bar chart
- Histogram

SPSS Procedures:

- *Frequencies*
- *Chart Editor*

Data Management

Multivariate Descriptive

Multivariate Inferential

Frequency Tables and Univariate Charts

In this chapter, you can learn

- how to find the number of cases and the percent of cases in each category of a variable,
- how to use and when to use cumulative percents,
- how to find the number of missing cases on a variable, and
- how to visually display the distribution of cases on a variable using a pie chart, bar chart, or histogram.

Religion, Family, and Highest Degree

Now we start answering questions with statistics. The examples in the chapters will ask and answer questions about *1980 young adults*. When you do the practice problems at the end of the chapters, you will find out about *2010 young adults, 2010 middle-age adults,* and, occasionally, *1980 middle-age adults.*

It is important to understand that in Part Two of this book (Chapters 3–10), the answers we get to our questions are not about all young adults in 1980 and 2010 or all middle-age adults in 1980 or 2010. Our answers will only tell us about those twentysomethings and fiftysomethings who took part in the 1980 General Social Survey and those twentysomethings and fiftysomethings who took part in the 2010 General Social Survey. Eventually, you will learn how to answer questions about all twentysomethings and all fiftysomethings in 1980 and all twentysomethings and all fiftysomethings in 2010, but that comes later. First, we just look at the persons who actually answered the questions that gave us the data in our data set. To remind you when our conclusions are only about those persons who participated in the General Social Survey, the letters GSS will be included in the name of the group: *1980 GSS young adults, 1980 GSS middle-age adults, 2010 GSS young adults,* and *2010 GSS middle-age adults.* When the conclusions are about all twentysomethings or all fiftysomethings in 1980 or in 2010, GSS will not be included in the name of the group.

In this chapter, frequency tables and univariate charts will be used to answer the following questions:

- What percent of 1980 GSS young adults had no religious affiliation?
- How strong were the attachments to organized religion of 1980 GSS young adults?
- What percent of 1980 GSS young adults grew up in two-parent households? In one-parent households? In no-parent households?
- What was the most common number of siblings reported by 1980 GSS young adults? How many had no siblings, in other words, they were only-children?
- What kinds of educational degrees did 1980 GSS young adults have?

Once the basic techniques of the chapter have been explained, the following questions about the 1980 GSS young adults will also be quickly answered:

- How do they break down in terms of sex? In terms of race?
- What percent grew up in rural areas? In small towns? In big cities?
- What percent were working full-time?
- Were most already married? Were some of them already divorced?

As you read through the chapter, you will discover the answers to these questions. Then, in the practice problems, you will see how the 2010 GSS young adults and the 2010 GSS middle-age adults compare to these 1980 GSS young adults.

RESEARCH TIP

Stop and Think About What You Expect to Find

After you see statistical results, it's easy to say, "How boring! I already knew that." Or, "Common sense would have told you it was that." But did you? Would it?

Before you look at the results of any analysis, stop and ask yourself what you expect to find. A moment's reflection on what you believe to be true can make data analysis a lot more interesting. Only if you first thought about what you expected can you congratulate yourself for being right or improve your knowledge by realizing you were wrong.

Organization of the Book

Have you noticed the diagrams at the start of each chapter? They show the underlying organization of this book. Almost all of Part Two (Chapters 3–10) explains **descriptive statistics.** Descriptive

what you see

statistics summarize the cases in your data set and only those cases. Descriptive statistics are not designed to draw conclusions about any larger groups for whom you don't have complete data. That is what **inferential statistics** do, and in Part Three (Chapters 11–16), we will cover those.

In both the descriptive and the inferential parts of this book, univariate statistics are covered first (Chapters 3, 4, 11, and 12) followed by multivariate statistics (Chapters 6–10 and Chapters 13–16). **Univariate statistics** tell you about single variables. They might tell you a variable's average or its range, but they will never tell you how one variable is related to another variable. Relationships between variables are reported by **multivariate statistics.** A correlation coefficient is an example of a multivariate statistic because it describes the relationship between two variables. (The simplest multivariate statistics are **bivariate statistics.** They tell how just two variables are related to each other. Bivariate statistics are sometimes treated separately from more complex multivariate statistics, but we will simply include them under the multivariate statistics heading.)

Chapters 2 and 5 of this book are primarily concerned with data management. These chapters explain things like how to create data sets, how to select just certain cases to analyze, how to modify the coding scheme of a variable, and how to create new variables from existing variables.

Each chapter's opening diagram reveals where the chapter fits into the larger picture. The diagram will show you the statistics and SPSS procedures covered in the chapter and what types of questions those statistics and procedures can answer for you.

There are very few statistical formulas included in the book. The few that are included in the chapters are reprinted on the pages that introduce Part Two and Part Three of the book. That makes those pages handy summary sheets at least for the formulas.

Limiting the Analysis to Just One Group

The SPSS data file that you will need for the practice problems in this book and, if you choose, for duplicating the examples in the chapters is available at www.sagepub.com/szafran. The file name is *fourGroups.sav.* That one file includes data from all four groups: 1980 GSS young adults, 1980 GSS middle-age adults, 2010 GSS young adults, and 2010 GSS middle-age adults. However, to duplicate the examples in the chapters and to do the SPSS practice problems at the end of the chapters, you will typically need to select just one of these groups for analysis.

Selecting just a single group is quite simple. One of the variables in the data set is named GROUP. The twentysomethings who took part in the 1980 GSS have a value of 1 on GROUP, the fiftysomethings who took part in the 1980 GSS have a value of 2, the twentysomethings who took part in the 2010 GSS have a value of 3, and the fiftysomethings who took part in the 2010 GSS have a value of 4.

You simply have to tell SPSS to include in the analysis only those cases with the proper value on the variable GROUP. How you do this is described in more detail at the beginning of Chapter 5, but here is a short version.

Pull down the *Data* menu and click on *Select Cases*.

Data | Select Cases

In the dialog that opens, select the option "If condition is satisfied" and then click the "If" button just below it. Another dialog will open. Find and double-click the variable GROUP in the variable list. That puts the variable GROUP in the box at the top right. Now type or use the keypad in the dialog to enter an equal sign and the number of the group you want (1, 2, 3, or 4) after GROUP (for example, GROUP = 1). Finally, click "Continue" to close this second dialog, and then click OK to close the first dialog.

The select cases criterion you set remains in effect until you change it, open a new data set, or end your SPSS session.

SPSS TIP

To Duplicate the Examples in This Chapter

To duplicate the examples in this chapter, use the *fourGroups.sav* data set. Before doing any of the statistical procedures, set the select cases condition to GROUP = 1.

CONCEPT CHECK

Without looking back, can you answer the following questions:

- What is the difference between descriptive and inferential statistics?
- What is the difference between univariate and multivariate statistics?
- How do you limit your SPSS analysis to just one group of cases?

If not, go back and review before reading on.

Generating Frequency Tables

To generate a frequency table, pull down the *Analyze* menu, move your cursor over *Descriptive Statistics,* and click on *Frequencies.*

Analyze | Descriptive Statistics | Frequencies

A dialog similar to Figure 3.1 appears.

On the left is an alphabetical list of the variable names in the data file. (If your list is not in alphabetical order or is showing variable labels rather than names, you have your *Options* for variable lists set differently. Refer back to "Setting SPSS Options" in Chapter 2.) Move one or more

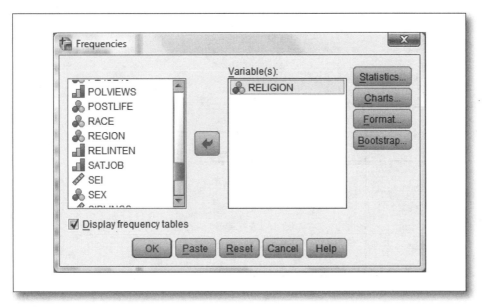

Figure 3.1   Dialog to Create a Frequency Table

variables from the list on the left to the "Variable" list in the center. (Moving more than one variable into the variable field does not make this multivariate. Frequency tables remain a univariate procedure because separate frequency tables will be created for each variable you specify.)

Frequency tables can be created no matter what level of measurement you have. However, continuous variables are usually poor choices for frequency tables because they have so many attributes, and each attribute typically describes no more than a few cases. Discrete variables with a relatively small number of attributes typically make the most useful frequency tables.

The *Frequencies* procedure can do many more things, but for now we just want a frequency table. Make sure that the dialog condition "Display frequency tables" is checked. Then click OK. Figure 3.2 shows the *Frequencies* procedure output for religious affiliation (RELIGION), and Figure 3.3 shows the output for strength of religious affiliation (RELINTEN).

The Parts of a Frequency Table

Output from the *Frequencies* procedure begins with a box titled "Statistics." Since we did not ask for any statistics, all we get are the default statistics: the number of cases in the data set with valid (not missing) values on this variable and the number of cases in the data set with missing values. This latter number includes both cases with system-missing values and cases with user-missing values. There were no missing data on religious affiliation, but seven cases had missing data on strength of

Statistics

RELIGION

N	Valid	327
	Missing	0

RELIGION

		Frequency	Percent	Valid Percent	Cumulative Percent
Valid	1 Protestant	186	56.9	56.9	56.9
	2 Catholic	95	29.1	29.1	85.9
	3 Jewish	6	1.8	1.8	87.8
	4 Other	5	1.5	1.5	89.3
	5 none	35	10.7	10.7	100.0
	Total	327	100.0	100.0	

Figure 3.2   *Frequencies* Output for RELIGION for 1980 GSS Young Adults

Statistics

RELINTEN

N	Valid	320
	Missing	7

RELINTEN

		Frequency	Percent	Valid Percent	Cumulative Percent
Valid	0 no religion	35	10.7	10.9	10.9
	1 not very strong	183	56.0	57.2	68.1
	2 strong	102	31.2	31.9	100.0
	Total	320	97.9	100.0	
Missing	8 don't know	2	.6		
	9 no answer	5	1.5		
	Total	7	2.1		
Total		327	100.0		

Figure 3.3   *Frequencies* Output for RELINTEN for 1980 GSS Young Adults

religious affiliation. The name of the variable appears just above the statistics box. (Remember that you can control whether your output uses variable names, variable labels, or both by setting the SPSS options to your preferences. Refer back to "Setting SPSS Options" in Chapter 2.)

Next comes the frequency table itself. At the far left of a frequency table, you will usually see the words *Valid, Missing,* and *Total.* Look, for example, at the frequency table for RELINTEN in Figure 3.3. The first part of the frequency table reports on cases with valid (not missing) answers. This is usually the largest part of the frequency table. The second part reports on cases with missing answers, and the third part reports on all of the cases combined. This third part is always just a single line. If a variable has no missing data, like RELIGION in Figure 3.2, "Missing" and "Total" are omitted from the far left side of the table.

The *Frequencies* procedure only lists attributes that were used by at least one case. If there were other attributes but no cases used them, those other attributes are omitted from the frequency table.

For each attribute that does appear in the table, you see the numeric code used for the attribute and the value label, if there is one, attached to that code. (You can also control whether your output shows just values, just value labels, or both. Refer back to Chapter 2.) If there is more than one valid attribute used, the total number of valid cases is also reported in the table. Similarly, if there is more than one missing code used, the total number of missing cases is also reported in the table.

The Frequency Column

The frequency column simply tells you the number of cases that had the attribute named at the beginning of the row. For example, 186 of these *1980 GSS young adults* reported they were Protestant and 95 reported they were Catholic.

MATH TIP

Calculating Frequency Values

If you understand the structure of a frequency table, someone could remove a number from the table and you should be able to calculate it on your own. In Figure 3.2, if someone spilled ink on the number 186 for the frequency of Protestants, could you figure it out yourself? You know there are a total of 327 valid cases. Add up the number of cases in the other valid categories (95 + 6 + 5 + 35) and subtract the sum (141) from 327 to get 186!

In Figure 3.3, if the printer failed to print the total number of respondents who have missing data on this variable, you could simply add together the number of persons in each missing data category (2 + 5) to find out there are a total of 7 missing cases.

There is often more than one way to figure out a missing number in a table.

The Percent Column

The percent column tells you the percent of all the cases in the data set that have a particular value on this variable. The phrase "all the cases in the data set" includes both cases with valid values and cases with missing values. For example, in Figure 3.2, we see that 10.7% of 1980 GSS young adults did not belong to an organized religion. In Figure 3.3, we see that 1.5% of 1980 GSS young adults gave no answer, not even a "don't know," when asked about the strength of their religious affiliation.

SPSS TIP

What Does "All the Cases in the Data Set" Mean If You Are Using Select Cases?

When you use *Select Cases,* you temporarily reduce the size of your data set to just those cases that meet your selection criterion. If you have selected just some cases to include in the analysis, as we have when we set *Select Cases* to GROUP = 1, then the phrase "all the cases in the data set" should be interpreted as "all the cases in the data set that meet the selection criteria."

MATH TIP

The Value of Percentages

By expressing the frequency of an attribute as a percent, it is easier to tell if the attribute occurs relatively often or relatively rarely. For example, you are told that 35 of the 1980 GSS young adults reported no religious affiliation. Is that a lot or a little? To know that, you have to know how many cases there were all together. When you are told there were a total of 327 cases, you then mentally estimate what percent 35 is of 327 cases. Instead of having to do the mental math, the percent column tells you that 10.7% of these persons were unaffiliated.

Why are percents such a popular way of presenting information? Because the number of cases in an analysis varies from data set to data set but percents are always based on 100. Expressing information as a percent is a way of standardizing the information, which makes it easier to comprehend and compare to other information.

Any percent in the percent column was calculated by taking the frequency for that row, dividing by the total number of cases in the data set, and multiplying the result by 100 to express it as a percent.

$$percent = \frac{row\ frequency}{grand\ total} \times 100$$

In Figure 3.3, for example, the percent of all 1980 GSS young adults who reported a strong religious affiliation is 102 (the frequency for that row) divided by 327 (the total number of cases in the data set) multiplied by 100. If you did the calculation, you would get a number that, when rounded to one decimal place, is 31.2—just like SPSS. Numeric results are often rounded in SPSS output. Numbers are rounded not only to fit them into limited spaces but also because we usually do not need or want numbers expressed with many decimal places. Just so you know, however, SPSS stores the results of these calculations in its own memory to many more decimal places, and it is possible for users to access those more precise numbers (although we will not do so in this text).

SPSS TIP

Rounding Numbers Down to Fewer Decimal Places

Analysts often round the numbers from SPSS output down to fewer decimal places than appeared in the output when they report their results. In this text, numbers will not be rounded down. The reason for not rounding down is to make it as clear as possible where the numbers are coming from in the output. Ask your instructor if you should round down numbers or report them exactly as they appear in your output.

The Valid Percent Column (ALL)

The valid percent column tells you the percent of all the valid cases that have a particular valid value. For example, of those valid (in other words, not missing) cases on strength of religious affiliation, 31.9% reported they were strong members of their religion. The difference between the percent column and the valid percent column is that the former is describing an attribute _as a percent of all the cases in the data set,_ while the latter is describing an attribute _as a percent of the valid cases in the data set._ The valid percent column does not consider the missing cases. There is no percent calculated for them, and they are not included in the base upon which the percents are calculated.

If there are any missing cases for a variable in the data set, the valid percents will differ from the percents in the percent column. When there are only a few missing cases in a data set, as with strength of religious affiliation (Figure 3.3), the two sets of percents will differ only slightly. In fact, when only a few cases in a large data set have missing data, the percents and the valid percents will appear not to differ at all, but this is only because the differences are hidden when SPSS rounds the percentages. Of course, when there are no missing cases on a variable, as with religious affiliation (Figure 3.2), the percents and the valid percents actually are identical.

To calculate a valid percent, you simply take the frequency for the row, divide by the total number of valid cases, and multiply by 100.

$$\text{valid percent} = \frac{\text{row frequency}}{\text{valid total}} \times 100$$

Let's look again at those reporting a strong religious affiliation. The valid percent for strong religious affiliation is once again 102 (the row frequency) but this time divided by 320 (the total number of valid cases) multiplied by 100. The answer rounded to one decimal place is 31.9. The valid percent for strong religious affiliation differs slightly from the simple percent because the seven missing cases were included in the denominator for the simple percent but not in the denominator for the valid percent.

The Cumulative Percent Column

The last column is the cumulative percent column. It gives you a running total of the valid percents. It tells you the percent of the valid cases that are in that row of the frequency table or in the rows above that row. The cumulative percent column, like the valid percent column, is only concerned with valid cases.

Consider Figure 3.2. For 1980 GSS young adults, 56.9% of the valid respondents are Protestant; 85.9% are Protestant or Catholic; 87.8% are Protestant, Catholic, or Jewish; 89.3% are Protestant, Catholic, Jewish, or some other religion; and 100.0% are Protestant, Catholic, Jewish, some other religion, or no religious affiliation.

Since the cumulative percent gives you a running total of the valid percents, the first cumulative percent will always perfectly match the first percent in the valid percent column, and the last cumulative percent will always be 100. There are several ways to calculate the cumulative percents between the first and last one. The simplest way is to take the *valid* percent for the row you are on and add it to the *cumulative* percent from the row just above where you are. For example, if you want to calculate for yourself the cumulative percent of 1980 GSS young adults who were Protestant, Catholic, Jewish, or some other religion, you simply add the valid percent for other (1.5) to the cumulative percent for the row above (87.8). You get 89.3, which is exactly what SPSS shows.

SPSS TIP

"I Got a Different Result Than SPSS!"

Now try calculating the cumulative percent for Catholic in Figure 3.2. You add 29.1 to 56.9 and get 86.0, but SPSS is showing 85.9! What went wrong? The answer is nothing. Sometimes the cumulative percent you calculate by adding the valid percent to the previous cumulative percent will differ slightly from the result SPSS reports. SPSS is doing its calculations with the very precise numbers stored in the computer's memory, not with the rounded numbers you are seeing and using. Even though SPSS then rounds its result before displaying it, a calculation done with more precise numbers will sometimes produce a result, even a rounded result, slightly different from a calculation done with less precise numbers. Don't worry about it.

Using Frequency Tables

Valid Percents

So, what good are frequency tables? Their most common use is to show the share of respondents falling into each of the variable's attributes. How many 1980 GSS young adults were Protestant? Catholic? Jewish? Other religionists? No religionists? Since percents are easier to interpret than frequencies, most times people want to know the percent of cases in each category.

Usually, persons are interested only in the valid cases. That is an important point to understand and bears repeating: Persons asking questions about the data are usually only interested in the cases with valid data. Because of this, the column that is used the most in frequency tables is the valid percent column.

When asked what percent of respondents gave a particular answer or fell into a particular category, report the valid percent. You can assume that the questioner is not concerned with the missing cases—otherwise, he would be explicit about that in the question. So, if someone asked what percent of 1980 GSS young adults described their religious affiliation as "not very strong," the answer to give would be 57.2%—not 56.0% and certainly not 183.

Percents

Well, if valid percents are so good, what purpose does the percent column serve? Its most common use is to judge whether there is a problem with missing cases. When you see a substantial percent of cases with missing values (perhaps 10% or more), you should be curious. There may or may not be a problem.

Sometimes a large proportion of respondents are appropriately told to skip a question that would not be relevant. For example, only persons who report that they have one or more children might be asked their age when their first child was born. All those with no children would be classified as missing cases on the variable about age at the birth of the first child, and that would not be a problem.

Sometimes surveys include a very large number of questions—more questions than most respondents would sit still to answer. A common strategy is to identify certain core questions that are asked of all respondents. The remaining questions are divided into groups. Any single respondent is asked only certain groups of questions. Which groups of questions he or she is asked might be based on the flip of a coin. This results in many questions having substantial nonresponse, but again, this would not be a problem.

What is a problem is when the percent of cases refusing to answer or saying they "do not know" is large. This may reflect a methodological flaw in the data-gathering procedure. The danger is that there is **response bias,** that is, the persons who did respond are systematically different from the persons who did not. In such a situation, the assumption that the valid responses are representative of the entire group of cases that make up the data set may be a false assumption.

To know whether you should be concerned about a large percent of missing cases, you need to know the cause of the missing cases. User-missing values can enable a researcher to distinguish among the reasons why data are missing. When 10% or more of the cases that should have had valid answers are missing, you need to limit your confidence in the data for that variable. You should also point out this problem of missing data to any persons to whom you present your results.

Frequencies

Among other things, the frequency column tells you the actual number of valid cases you have for the variable. Most researchers and research audiences are more interested in results based on a substantial number of valid cases than on a few. One problem with just reporting percents is that the audience has no idea on how many cases the percents are based. As you will see in Part Three, inferential statistics formally consider sample size in the process of making population inferences. But even for descriptive statistics, the number of valid cases is relevant information.

The frequency column can also point out if you made certain types of data entry errors and how many of these errors you made. On a variable with valid codes of 0, 1, and 2 and with user-missing codes of 7, 8, and 9, there should be no cases with values other than those. If a frequency table reveals two cases with values of 3, you have made a mistake in entering the data, and you can search the data set to find the two cases with 3s and correct them. Unfortunately, frequency tables cannot reveal all data entry errors. If a particular case should have a 0 on this variable but instead has a 1, the problem will not be revealed in the frequency table because both 0 and 1 are legitimate codes.

Cumulative Percents

The cumulative percent column is probably the least used column because it answers a question (what percent of the cases have this value or one of the prior values) that researchers only sometimes ask. When a researcher asks that question, though, the cumulative percent column is just what she or he wants.

Cumulative percents are used more often with ordinal and interval/ratio variables because the attributes that make up those variables have an inherent order to them. When attributes have a natural order or rank, it makes more sense to ask, "What percent of the cases had *at least* a particular level on a variable?" or "What percent had a particular score *or more*?" Occasionally, cumulative percents can even be useful with nominal variables if the order of the attributes, although arbitrary, is nevertheless meaningful such as the order of the attributes for religious affiliation in Figure 3.2. The first two rows (Protestant and Catholic) are the two *big* religions in the United States, the first three rows represent the *traditional* religions in the United States, and the first four rows together represent *all* religions.

How useful cumulative percents are may depend on the order in which the attributes appear in the frequency table. For ordinal and interval/ratio variables, you might want the attributes listed in increasing order of magnitude (low, medium, high) or decreasing order of magnitude (high, medium, low). For any level-of-measurement variables, you might want to know "What percent of cases fell into the three most popular categories?" in which case you'd like the attributes in order of decreasing frequency, or you might ask, "What percent of cases chose a category other than one of the four most popular?" in which case you would want the attributes in order of increasing frequency.

You can ask for a different order for the attributes when you create your frequency table. If you click on "Format" in the dialog that first opens up when you start the *Frequencies* procedure (see Figure 3.1), a dialog similar to Figure 3.4 opens.

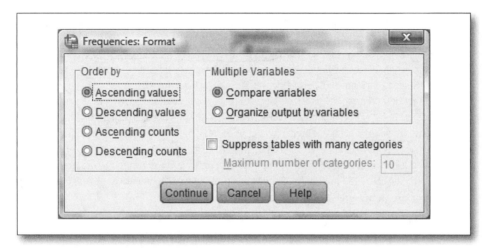

Figure 3.4   Dialog to Set the Order of Attributes

Toward the left, you have options for the order in which the valid attributes will be listed. The default is ascending value order (the category coded 1, then the category coded 2, and so on). "Descending values" reverses that order. You can also ask for the attributes to be listed in ascending or descending order based on how many cases are in each attribute. Once you have made your choice, click "Continue" to return to the original dialog.

CONCEPT CHECK

Without looking back, can you answer the following questions:

- What kinds of questions are answered with valid percents?
- What kinds of questions are answered with frequencies (the actual number of cases in each category of the variable)?
- What kinds of questions are answered with cumulative percents?

If not, go back and review before reading on.

Univariate Charts

pie
bar
histogram

A picture is worth a thousand words, and sometimes worth a thousand numbers, too! For most people, visual images have a dramatic impact that numbers lack. It is usually easier to recall a conclusion if it was supported by a well-constructed chart than if it was supported only by numbers.

There are a variety of ways in SPSS that you can request charts. The *Frequencies* procedure is one of the simplest. From *Frequencies,* you can request a pie chart, a bar chart, or a histogram. All three are **univariate charts**—that is, they display the results for just a single variable.

To request one of these charts when doing *Frequencies,* click the "Charts" button on the *Frequencies* dialog (see Figure 3.1). A dialog similar to Figure 3.5 appears.

You can request a bar chart, pie chart, or histogram. You can choose only one. If you request a bar chart or pie chart, you can choose to have frequencies or percentages displayed with the chart. The percents are valid percents. Whether you choose frequencies or percents, the relative sizes of the slices in the pie or the bars in the bar chart will be the same.

Once you have made your selection, simply click "Continue" to return to the original dialog. If you want only the chart and not the frequency table itself, you can uncheck the "Display frequency tables" checkbox on the original dialog (see Figure 3.1).

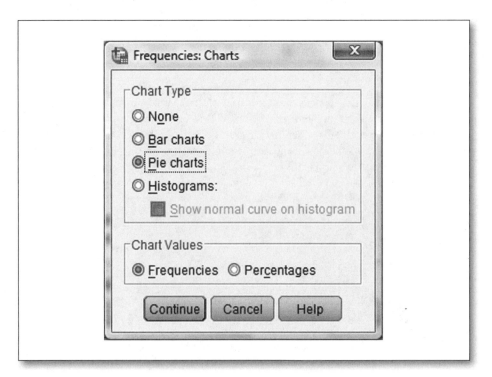

Figure 3.5   Dialog to Request a Chart From the *Frequencies* Procedure

Pie Charts

[handwritten note: Nominal, can be used with nominal, ordinal, or interval]

Pie charts are nominal charts, meaning they can be used to illustrate the distribution of cases on nominal, ordinal, or interval/ratio variables. All that they require is that the attributes be different from one another. Like frequency tables, pie charts become less useful as the number of attributes becomes large. A pie with 4 or 5 distinct slices is easy to comprehend; a pie with 14 or 15 slices becomes too confusing to quickly grasp.

Figure 3.6 uses a pie chart to show the living arrangements for the 1980 GSS young adults when they were age 16.

Almost three fourths were living with both parents. Next most common was living with just a single parent. Living with a parent and a stepparent was less common than living with just one parent. Of course, you could obtain the same information from a frequency table. The advantage of a pie chart or any graphic is that it gives the information more impact and makes it more memorable by adding a visual dimension.

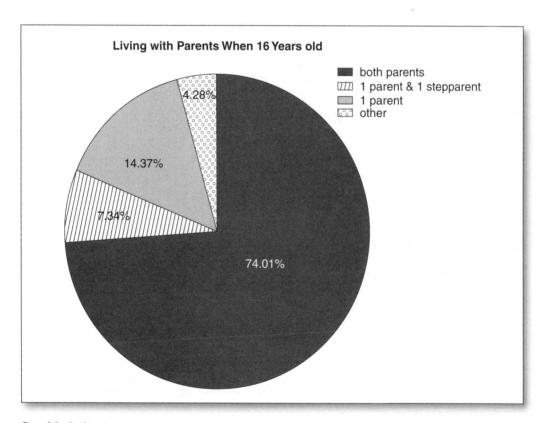

Figure 3.6   Pie Chart for Living Arrangements at Age 16 of 1980 GSS Young Adults

The pie chart in Figure 3.6 is not exactly the pie chart originally produced by SPSS. That original pie chart had no labels showing what percent of the pie was represented by each slice. SPSS provides a *Chart Editor* that lets you modify the appearance of your chart. *Chart Editor* is available for every chart SPSS creates. *Chart Editor* has many options, and the best way to get to know it thoroughly is to experiment with it. What follows are instructions to create the pie chart in Figure 3.6:

1. Move your cursor over the pie chart in your output and double-click. This opens up the chart editor screen similar to Figure 3.7. You will notice that it has a different menu bar and task bar.

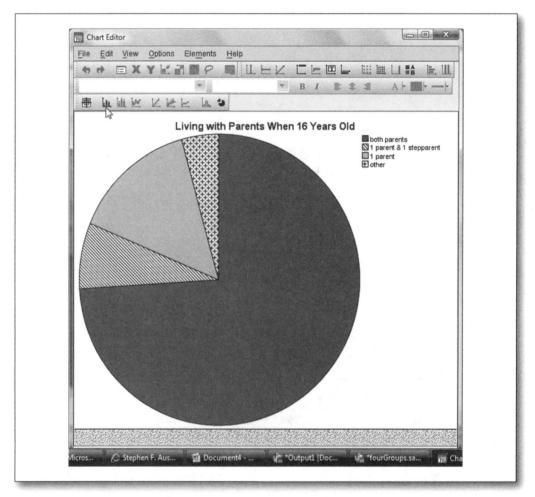

Figure 3.7   *Chart Editor* for Customizing a Chart's Appearance

2. To get the percents to appear for each pie slice, click the "show data labels" button in the tool bar. (In Figure 3.7, the cursor is pointing to it. When you move your cursor over the button, a "show data labels" message appears.) When you click on this button, data labels will appear for each pie slice. A "Properties" dialog may also open up. If it does, simply close it or drag it out of the way so you have a clear view of the chart editor.

3. To increase the size of the data labels that are now in each pie slice, change the font size specification on the tool bar from "auto" to the desired size.

4. To exit *Chart Editor* and return to your SPSS output screen, pull down the *File* menu and click *Close*. The changes you made in *Chart Editor* now appear on the pie chart in your output.

Bar Charts   *nominal* *ordinal*

Bar charts are another nominal charting technique. They are most frequently used to visually show the distribution of cases on nominal or ordinal variables. Pie charts use the size of a slice to show the valid percent of cases described by a particular attribute; bar charts communicate the same information using the height of bars. Because the bars appear along a horizontal line, bar charts can communicate the order of attributes much better than the slices of a circular pie can.

Figure 3.8 shows a bar chart with percentages for the variable DEGREE. This is the highest educational degree the GSS respondent had earned by the time of the survey. It becomes immediately clear from the histogram that a high school degree was by far the most common highest educational degree for these 1980 GSS twentysomethings. More than two thirds report that as their highest degree at the time of the survey, while only about one seventh have a bachelor's or graduate degree. (Keep in mind that these are the highest degrees this sample of twentysomethings had earned by the time of the survey. Many were still in school, and some would undoubtedly go on to earn higher degrees.)

The horizontal axis of a bar chart does not represent a numeric scale. Therefore, the distance between bars does not reflect how much difference there is between the attributes represented by the bars. Consistent with this, gaps are not left on the horizontal axis for unused attributes. For example, if no 1980 GSS young adults had an associate's degree as their highest degree, the bar chart in Figure 3.8 would not have left a space for that attribute. The bachelor and graduate degree bars simply would have shifted left.

The bar chart as originally produced by SPSS did not have the percents for each bar appearing. To get those, it was necessary, as with the pie chart, to go into *Chart Editor* and request data labels. *Chart Editor* was also used to add the "%" signs to the data labels. This was done through the "Number Format" tab on the "Properties" dialog in *Chart Editor.*

Histograms   *must be interval*

Histograms are the third type of univariate chart available through the *Frequencies* procedure. Variables represented by histograms must be interval/ratio because, unlike the bar chart, the base of a histogram does represent a numeric scale. Figure 3.9 shows a histogram for the number of siblings reported by 1980 GSS young adults.

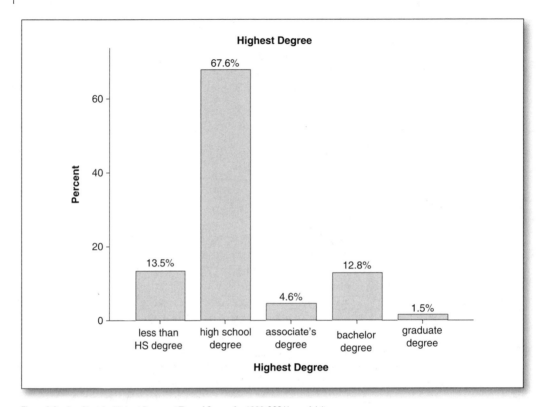

Figure 3.8 Bar Chart for Highest Degree at Time of Survey for 1980 GSS Young Adults

Histograms give you a visual sense of the distribution of cases on a variable. You can quickly see that the most common numbers of siblings reported were between one and five. (If you are thinking in terms of number of children in the family, be sure to add one for the respondent. Also, remember that when the GSS asks about siblings, the respondent is told to include stepsiblings, adopted siblings, and deceased siblings.)

Histograms look like they are made up of bars, but they are more properly referred to as bins. Each bin covers a part of the number line, and every case falling on that part of the number line is counted in that bin. So, even though number of siblings is a discrete variable with only whole-number values possible, the first bin in Figure 3.9 counts all the cases with −0.5 up to but not including 0.5 siblings, the second bin counts all the cases with 0.5 up to but not including 1.5 siblings, and so on through the histogram. The right-most bin in a histogram includes both the lower bound and the upper bound of its range on the number line. In Figure 3.9, the right-most bin counts all the cases with 19.5 up to and including 20.5 siblings. These ranges for the bins may sound silly when dealing with a discrete variable such as siblings, but they make a lot of sense when working with a continuous variable.

To the right of the histogram, SPSS reports the variable's mean, standard deviation, and number of valid cases. Means and standard deviations are univariate statistics we will discuss in the next chapter.

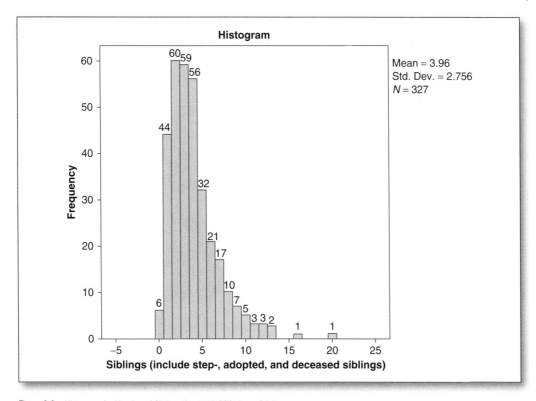

Figure 3.9   Histogram for Number of Siblings for 1980 GSS Young Adults

While a bar chart's horizontal axis is just a place on which to rest the bars, a histogram's horizontal axis represents a number line. That is why gaps are left in a histogram for ranges of values that have no cases. There were no 1980 GSS young adults in our sample with 13.5 up to but not including 15.5 siblings, so the histogram in Figure 3.9 leaves a gap at that point. In other words, the bins have no cases.

The histogram as originally produced by SPSS did not have the frequencies appearing for each bin. To get those, it was necessary, as with the pie chart and the bar chart, to get into *Chart Editor* and request data labels. Unlike pie charts and bar charts, SPSS does not give you the option with histograms to choose percents instead of frequencies.

Other Univariate Charts

Other univariate charts are available through other procedures in SPSS. Pie charts, bar charts, and histograms are probably the simplest and most often used. They have the added advantage of being easily requested through the *Frequencies* procedure. To see the full range of charts available with SPSS, pull down the "Graphs" menu and select "Chart Builder." *Chart Builder* requires a little more time to learn, but it has great versatility. Anyone who will make frequent use of charts to represent data is encouraged to take the time to learn to use *Chart Builder.*

CONCEPT CHECK

Without looking back, can you answer the following questions:

- Histograms require what level of measurement?
- What is the difference between a bar chart and a histogram?
- How do you get into *Chart Editor* in order to customize the appearance of a chart?

If not, go back and review before reading on.

More Frequency Tables

Now that you understand the parts of a frequency table and the functions they serve, here are some additional frequency tables that you can use to answer the questions at the start of this chapter. Figure 3.10 shows the classification of 1980 GSS young adults by gender.

SEX		Frequency	Percent	Valid Percent	Cumulative Percent
Valid	0 male	133	40.7	40.7	40.7
	1 female	194	59.3	59.3	100.0
	Total	327	100.0	100.0	

Figure 3.10 *Frequencies* Output for Sex for 1980 GSS Young Adults

Figure 3.11 shows the racial classification of 1980 GSS young adults. Over the years, the GSS has changed how it measures race. You should read the research tip about race to better understand the changes.

RESEARCH TIP

The GSS and the Variable RACE

The manner in which race was measured changed between the 1980 and 2010 General Social Surveys. In 1980, race was imputed by the interviewer and only explicitly asked if questionable. An instruction to interviewers stated that Hispanics appearing to be white should be classified as white and not as other.

In 2010, however, the GSS was using a measurement procedure for race similar to that adopted in the 2000 U.S. census. This new procedure allowed persons to self-identify their racial ancestry rather than to have it observed and classified by an interviewer. Thus, the race variable in 2010 is based on self-perception rather than physical appearance. There were several consequences of that change, one being that many Hispanics chose to identify their race as Hispanic rather than white.

As you will see in the practice problems, the racial composition of the 2010 GSS respondents, including the 2010 GSS middle-age adults, is noticeably different from the 1980 GSS young adults. In part that reflects changes in the U.S. population due to immigration and fertility, but it also reflects changes in methodology.

		Frequency	Percent	Valid Percent	Cumulative Percent
RACE					
Valid	1 white	291	89.0	89.0	89.0
	2 black	33	10.1	10.1	99.1
	3 other	3	.9	.9	100.0
	Total	327	100.0	100.0	

Figure 3.11 *Frequencies* Output for Race for 1980 GSS Young Adults

Respondents to the GSS are asked what kind of place they were living in when they were 16 years old. On the basis of their answer, they can be placed in one of five categories: farm/countryside, small city, medium city, suburb of large city, and large city. Small cities are those with a population less than 50,000. Medium cities have populations from 50,000 to 250,000. Large cities have populations in excess of 250,000. Figure 3.12 shows the places where 1980 GSS young adults were living at age 16.

The GSS asks respondents what their primary work activity was in the week before the survey. Figure 3.13 shows the answers given by 1980 GSS young adults. To interpret these results correctly, it is important to understand that the GSS tells respondents to select only one category, and the category they select should be the first category that applies. So, for example, the 7.0% who are classified as "in school" are persons in school and not doing any of the things listed earlier in the frequency table. If a respondent were attending college and working part-time, that person would be counted only in the "working part-time" category. The total percent of 1980 GSS young adults in school at the time of the survey was almost certainly higher than 7.0%, just as the total percent who were taking care of a household was almost certainly higher than 17.7%, but we cannot tell from these results how much higher. Another note: One answer category for this question does not

PLACE16

		Frequency	Percent	Valid Percent	Cumulative Percent
Valid	1 country, farm	74	22.6	22.6	22.6
	2 small city	100	30.6	30.6	53.2
	3 medium city	51	15.6	15.6	68.8
	4 suburb of large city	44	13.5	13.5	82.3
	5 large city	58	17.7	17.7	100.0
	Total	327	100.0	100.0	

Figure 3.12 *Frequencies* Output for Place Where Raised for 1980 GSS Young Adults

WORKSTAT

		Frequency	Percent	Valid Percent	Cumulative Percent
Valid	1 working full-time	187	57.2	57.2	57.2
	2 working part-time	32	9.8	9.8	67.0
	3 employed but not currently working	9	2.8	2.8	69.7
	4 unemployed but looking for work	16	4.9	4.9	74.6
	6 in school	23	7.0	7.0	81.7
	7 keeping house	58	17.7	17.7	99.4
	8 other	2	.6	.6	100.0
	Total	327	100.0	100.0	

Figure 3.13 *Frequencies* Output for Work Status for 1980 GSS Young Adults

appear in Figure 3.13 because none of the 1980 GSS young adults chose it. That category was "retired," which was coded 5.

Figure 3.14 shows the marital status of 1980 GSS young adults at the time of the survey. While couples who are separated might be considered legally married, the GSS has always treated it as a separate category. No 1980 GSS young adults were "widowed" (which would have been represented by a code of 2) at the time of the survey, so that category does not appear in the frequency table.

MARITAL

		Frequency	Percent	Valid Percent	Cumulative Percent
Valid	1 married	172	52.6	52.6	52.6
	3 divorced	18	5.5	5.5	58.1
	4 separated	12	3.7	3.7	61.8
	5 never married	125	38.2	38.2	100.0
	Total	327	100.0	100.0	

Figure 3.14 *Frequencies* Output for Marital Status for 1980 GSS Young Adults

1980 GSS Young Adults

The chapter began with some questions about 1980 GSS young adults. On the basis of our analyses, what do we now know?

- 1980 GSS young adults had certainly not turned their back on organized religion—89.3% belonged to some religion. Only 10.7% reported no religious affiliation. Also, their religious affiliations were quite traditional. Protestantism and Catholicism were by far the most common religions. Only 1.5% of these 1980 twentysomethings belonged to a religion outside the Judeo-Christian tradition.
- More than half of the 1980 GSS young adults said their affiliation to a religion was not very strong: 31.9% said their affiliation was strong, 57.2% said not very strong, and 10.2% had no religious affiliation.
- Most 1980 GSS young adults grew up in two-parent families. Almost three fourths reported at age 16 living with both parents, 14.4% reported living with just one parent, and only 7.3% reported living with a parent and a stepparent.
- The most often reported number of siblings was two, closely followed by three, closely followed by four. Only 6 of the 327 twentysomethings in the 1980 GSS reported having no siblings.
- Two thirds of the 1980 GSS young adults had only a high school degree at the time of the survey. Only about one in seven had a bachelor or graduate degree. Of course, some of these 1980 GSS young adults were still in school when they participated in the GSS, so we might want to call this "highest degree so far."
- Women substantially outnumber men in our 1980 GSS young adults data set (59.3% compared to 40.7%). Since the number of twentysomething males and females in the U.S. population is relatively even, the difference may reflect the greater difficulty survey researchers often have in reaching and getting the cooperation of males. Males were also more likely than females to be in the military or in prison, which would put them outside the GSS sampling population.
- The 1980 GSS young adults were very white, 89.0% white. Blacks made up 10.1% of the data set, and persons neither white nor black made up just 0.9%. (Be sure to read the methodological note in the chapter about how race was measured.)

- More than half of the 1980 GSS young adults were raised in rural or small town settings: 22.6% grew up on a farm or in the countryside, and 30.6% grew up in a small city. Only 17.7% grew up in a large city, while 13.5% grew up in a suburb of a large city.
- More than half of the 1980 GSS young adults were employed full-time the week before the survey. Only 7.0% were going to school while not employed and looking for employment. And 17.7% were keeping house while not employed, not looking for employment, and not going to school.
- Most 1980 GSS young adults (52.6%) were currently married at the time of the survey. Another 9.2% had been married but were now separated or divorced. Only about one third (38.2%) had never married by the time of the survey.

Important Concepts in the Chapter

bar chart	inferential statistic
bars and bins	multivariate statistic
bivariate statistic	percent column
Chart Editor	pie chart
cumulative percent column	response bias
descriptive statistic	univariate chart
Frequencies procedure	univariate statistic
frequency column	valid percent column
histogram	

Practice Problems

1. Explain the difference between descriptive and inferential statistics.

2. Explain the difference between univariate and multivariate statistics.

3. Are the statistics in a frequency table descriptive univariate, descriptive multivariate, inferential univariate, or inferential multivariate?

4. For each of the following situations, would inferential statistics be appropriate?
   a. You just want to talk about the cases for which you have data.
   b. Your data represent a census of the population.
   c. Your data represent a nonprobability sample of the population.
   d. Your data represent a probability sample of the population.

5. For each of the following, state if it can legitimately be done only for interval/ratio variables, only for ordinal and interval/ratio variables, or for any level of measurement variables:
   a. frequency table
   b. pie chart
   c. bar chart
   d. histogram

6. Calculate the numbers in the following table that have been replaced by xxx. Do this yourself. This isn't an SPSS problem.

StudentMajor

		Frequency	Percent	Valid Percent	Cumulative Percent
Valid	Criminal Justice	2	XXX	XXX	XXX
	Social Work	9	XXX	XXX	XXX
	Sociology	8	XXX 32	XXX 40	XXX
	Other	1	XXX	XXX	XXX
	Total	20	80.0	100.0	
Missing	Not Reported	5	XXX 20		
Total		25	100.0		

÷ TOTAL   ÷ w/out missin

7. What column in a frequency table should be used to answer each of the following questions:
   a. What percent of the valid cases have a particular attribute?
   b. What percent of all the cases in the data set have a particular attribute?
   c. What percent of the cases have a particular attribute?
   d. What percent of the cases have this attribute or one of the previously listed attributes?
   e. What is the actual number of cases that have a particular attribute?

8. Which column in a frequency table is used most often to report results?

Problems Requiring SPSS and the *fourGroups.sav* Data Set

9. (*1980 GSS middle-age adults*) This problem looks at the religious affiliations of the fiftysomethings who took part in the 1980 GSS. For this problem, consider "traditional American religions" to mean Protestant, Catholic, and Jewish. (Variables: RELIGION; Select Cases: GROUP = 2)
   a. What percent of 1980 GSS middle-age adults
      i. belonged to a traditional American religion?
      ii. belonged to a religion but not a traditional American religion?
      iii. did not belong to a religion?
   b. Summarize in a few well-written sentences totaling 50 words or less what you found out about the religious affiliation of 1980 GSS middle-age adults.

10. (*2010 GSS young adults*) This problem looks at the religious affiliations of the 2010 GSS young adults. For this problem, consider "traditional American religions" to mean Protestant, Catholic, and Jewish. (Variables: RELIGION; Select Cases: GROUP = 3)
   a. What percent of 2010 GSS young adults
      i. belonged to a traditional American religion?
      ii. belonged to a religion but not a traditional American religion?
      iii. did not belong to a religion?

b. [Figure 3.2 shows for the 1980 GSS young adults that 87.8% belonged to a traditional American religion, 1.5% belonged to a nontraditional religion, and 10.7% belonged to no religion.] Summarize in a few well-written sentences totaling 50 words or less the similarities and/or differences in the religious affiliations of the 1980 and 2010 GSS young adults.

11. (*2010 GSS young adults*) This problem looks at how strongly the twentysomethings who took part in the 2010 GSS identified with a religion. (Variables: RELINTEN; Select Cases: GROUP = 3)
    a. What percent of 2010 GSS young adults
        i. identified strongly with their religion?
        ii. identified but not strongly with their religion?
        iii. had no religious affiliation?
    b. Summarize in a few well-written sentences totaling 50 words or less what you found out about how strongly the 2010 GSS young adults identified with a religion.

12. (*2010 GSS middle-age adults*) This problem looks at how strongly the fiftysomethings who took part in the 2010 GSS identified with a religion. (Variables: RELINTEN; Select Cases: GROUP = 4)
    a. What percent of 2010 GSS middle-age adults
        i. identified strongly with their religion?
        ii. identified but not strongly with their religion?
        iii. had no religious affiliation?
    b. [Figure 3.3 shows for the 1980 GSS young adults that 31.9% identified strongly with their religion, 57.2% identified but not strongly, and 10.9% had no religious affiliation.] Summarize in a few well-written sentences totaling 50 words or less the similarities and/or differences in the strength of religious identification of these two groups of baby boomers—the 1980 young adults and the 2010 GSS middle-age adults.

13. (*1980 GSS middle-age adults*) This problem looks at the types of families in which our oldest generation of GSS participants were raised. These fiftysomethings in 1980 were in their teens during the 1930s and 1940s. (Variables: FAMILY16; Select Cases: GROUP = 2)
    a. Create a pie chart showing the types of families 1980 GSS middle-age adults reported living in when they were 16 years old. Have the chart show the valid percent associated with each pie slice. What percent of 1980 GSS middle-age adults reported living
        i. with both parents?
        ii. with just one parent?
        iii. with one parent and a stepparent?
    b. Summarize in a few well-written sentences totaling 50 words or less what you found out about the types of families in which 1980 GSS middle-age adults were raised.

14. (*2010 GSS young adults*) This problem looks at the types of families in which the twentysomethings from the 2010 GSS were raised. These twentysomethings were in their teens during the 1990s and 2000s. (Variables: FAMILY16; Select Cases: GROUP = 3)
    a. Create a pie chart showing the types of families 2010 GSS young adults reported living in when they were 16 years old. Have the chart show the valid percent associated with each pie slice. What percent of 2010 GSS young adults reported living
        i. with both parents?
        ii. with just one parent?
        iii. with one parent and a stepparent?

b. [Figure 3.6 shows for the 1980 GSS young adults that 74.0% lived with both parents, 14.4% lived with just one parent, and 7.3% lived with a parent and a stepparent.] Summarize in a few well-written sentences totaling 50 words or less the similarities and/or differences in the types of families in which the 1980 and 2010 GSS young adults were raised.

15. (*2010 GSS young adults*) This problem looks at the educational degrees the twentysomethings who took part in the 2010 GSS had at the time of the survey. (Variables: DEGREE; Select Cases: GROUP = 3)
    a. Create a bar chart showing the highest degree 2010 GSS young adults had earned by the time of the survey. Have the chart show the valid percent associated with each degree. What percent of 2010 GSS young adults had
       i. not earned a high school degree?
       ii. earned a high school degree? (Assume persons with higher educational degrees had also earned a high school degree.)
       iii. earned at least a bachelor's degree? (Assume persons with graduate degrees had also earned a bachelor's degree.)
    b. [Figure 3.8 shows for the 1980 GSS young adults that 13.5% lacked a high school degree, 86.5% had a high school degree, and 14.3% had a bachelor's degree.] Summarize in a few well-written sentences totaling 50 words or less the similarities and/or differences in the highest degrees earned by the time of the survey by the 1980 and 2010 GSS young adults.

16. (*2010 GSS young adults*) This problem looks at the number of siblings (including full siblings, stepsiblings, adopted siblings, and deceased siblings) reported by the twentysomethings who took part in the 2010 GSS. (Variables: SIBLINGS; Select Cases: GROUP = 3)
    a. Create a histogram showing the number of siblings 2010 GSS young adults had. The histogram should show the frequency associated with each bin.
       i. What is the most common number of siblings reported by 2010 GSS young adults?
       ii. What percent of 2010 GSS young adults had no siblings? (You will have to calculate the percent.)
    b. [Figure 3.9 shows for the 1980 GSS young adults that 2 was the most frequently reported number of siblings and 1.8% had no siblings.] Summarize in a few well-written sentences totaling 50 words or less the similarities and/or differences in the number of siblings reported by the 1980 and 2010 GSS young adults.

17. Here are some interesting comparisons you might conduct using other variables introduced in this chapter. Remember that information about the 1980 GSS young adults can be found in the chapter.
    a. RACE (Be sure to review the section in the chapter that explains how the GSS measured race in 1980 and in 2010.)
       i. (1980 GSS young adults and 2010 GSS young adults)
       ii. (1980 GSS young adults and 2010 GSS middle-age adults)
    b. PLACE16
       i. (1980 GSS young adults and 2010 GSS young adults)
       ii. (1980 GSS middle-age adults and 2010 GSS young adults)
    c. WORKSTAT
       i. (1980 GSS young adults and 2010 GSS young adults)
       ii. (1980 GSS middle-age adults and 2010 GSS middle-age adults)
    d. MARITAL
       i. (1980 GSS young adults and 2010 GSS young adults)
       ii. (1980 GSS young adults and 2010 GSS middle-age adults)

Questions and Tools for Answering Them
(Chapter 4)

Univariate Descriptive	Univariate Inferential

Univariate Descriptive

Questions:

- What were the cases like on the variable?
- What was the most common answer?
- What score did the middle case have?
- What was the average?
- What was the lowest score? The highest?
- How far apart were the low and the high?
- The middle half scored between what and what?
- Did most people score close to the average?

Statistics:

- mode
- median
- mean
- percent distribution
- minimum
- maximum
- range
- percentiles
- variance
- standard deviation

SPSS Procedures:

- *Frequencies*
- *Descriptives*
- *Explore*

Data Management

Multivariate Descriptive

Multivariate Inferential

Central Tendency and Dispersion

4

In this chapter, you can learn

- how the values of the cases on a single variable can be summarized using measures of central tendency and measures of dispersion;
- how the central tendency can be described using statistics such as the mode, median, and mean;
- how the dispersion of scores on a variable can be described using statistics such as a percent distribution, minimum, maximum, range, and standard deviation along with a few others; and
- how a variable's level of measurement determines what measures of central tendency and dispersion to use.

Schooling, Politics, and Life After Death

Once again, we will use some questions about 1980 GSS young adults as opportunities to explain and demonstrate the statistics introduced in the chapter:

- Among the 1980 GSS young adults, are there both believers and nonbelievers in a life after death? Which is the more common view?
- On a seven-attribute political party allegiance variable anchored at one end by "strong Democrat" and at the other by "strong Republican," what was the most Democratic attribute used by any of the 1980 GSS young adults? The most Republican attribute? If we put all 1980

GSS young adults in order from the strongest Democrat to the strongest Republican, what is the political party affiliation of the person in the middle?

- What was the average number of years of schooling completed at the time of the survey by 1980 GSS young adults? Were most of these twentysomethings pretty close to the average on schooling completed, or were there large differences in amounts of school completed?

Once the data analysis techniques have been explained, evidence to answer the following questions will be quickly presented at the chapter's end:

- If we put the 1980 GSS young adults in line from the most conservative to the most liberal, what was the political orientation of the person in the middle?
- How low was the lowest social class reported by 1980 GSS young adults? How high was the highest social class? Putting them in order by social class, what did the person in the middle of the line say his or her social class was?
- How important did they think hard work was for success in life? How important was luck?
- How happy were they with their life? How healthy did they feel they were?
- How did the years of schooling completed thus far by 1980 GSS young adults compare to their fathers' schooling? Their mothers' schooling? And for those currently married, their spouses' schooling?
- Yes, they were all in their 20s when they took part in the GSS, but what was their average age?
- They were baby boomers, so did they have lots of siblings? What's the largest number of siblings any of them had?
- How many children did they have so far?
- How much on average did 1980 GSS young adults earn in the year prior to the survey?
- How much TV did the 1980 GSS young adults typically watch each day?

SPSS TIP

To Duplicate the Examples in This Chapter

To duplicate the examples in this chapter, use the *fourGroups.sav* data set. Before doing any of the statistical procedures, set the select cases condition to GROUP = 1.

Overview

This chapter takes you beyond frequency tables. On many occasions, you will not have the time, the space, or the desire to present and discuss all of the information in a frequency table, particularly when variables have many attributes. You want a way to summarize the data.

Think about when you come to class the day after an exam and someone asks the instructor how the grades were. Do you really want to know what percent of the grades were 100s, what percent 99s, what percent 98s, and so on? You want to know the average because that gives you a sense of the center of the grade distribution, and you might want to know the low grade and the high grade because they give you a sense of how spread out or concentrated the grades were. Those are the kinds of statistics this chapter discusses: measures of central tendency and measures of dispersion. <u>Central tendency</u> gets at the typical score on the variable, while **dispersion** <u>gets at how much variety there is in the scores.</u>

When describing the scores on a single variable, it is customary to report on both the central tendency and the dispersion. Not all measures of central tendency and not all measures of dispersion can be used to describe the values of cases on every variable. What choices you have depend on the variable's level of measurement. Table 4.1 gives you the "big picture" for this chapter. The statistics you gain as you move from nominal to ordinal to interval/ratio are in boldface in the table.

Table 4.1   Measures of Central Tendency and Dispersion by Level of Measurement

Level of Measurement	Measures of Central Tendency	Measures of Dispersion
nominal	mode	percent distribution
ordinal	median mode	minimum and maximum range percentiles percent distribution
interval/ratio	mean median mode	variance standard deviation minimum and maximum range percentiles percent distribution

[Handwritten annotations: "Low" next to mode; "med" next to median; "High" next to mean; "mode / Low ↑ | median ↓ Hight mean" diagram at right; "Best more Ques. flexibity" at bottom right]

<u>Modes and percent distributions</u> are relatively simple in nature and <u>only require that the attributes that make up a variable be different.</u> That is a property that the attributes of nominal, ordinal, and interval/ratio variables all have. Therefore, you can calculate modes and percentage distributions for all three levels of measurement.

Medians, minimums, maximums, ranges, and percentiles provide more information about the scores on variables, but these statistics only make sense if the attributes of a variable have rank order. Since rank order is a property possessed by the attributes of ordinal and interval/ratio variables but not nominal variables, you may only calculate medians, minimums, maximums, ranges, percentiles, and interquartile ranges for ordinal and interval/ratio variables.

Means, variances, and standard deviations provide still more information about the scores on variables, but these statistics require the attributes of the variable to form a numeric scale with a fixed unit of measurement. Since only interval/ratio variables have this property, means, variances, and standard deviations may only be calculated for interval/ratio variables.

Statistics are often referred to by the lowest level of measurement for which they can legitimately be calculated. For example, the mode would be described as a nominal measure of central tendency or the range as an ordinal measure of dispersion. Understand, however, that any measure that can be calculated for a nominal-level variable can also be calculated for ordinal and interval/ratio and that any statistic that can be calculated for an ordinal-level variable can also be calculated for an interval/ratio level of measurement.

When you have several measures of central tendency or several measures of dispersion from which to choose, how do you decide which one to use? Usually, you should use a statistic that makes the fullest use of the information packed into the variable's attributes. That means, for example, that in describing scores on an interval/ratio-level variable, you would normally choose a mean over a median or a mode because the mean makes use of the fact that the attributes on the variable not only are different and rank-ordered but also constitute a numeric scale. Using a median or a mode ignores some of those properties of the attributes. As you will see in this chapter, however, there are times when a statistic that does not use all the information contained in the variable is the better statistic!

Most of the chapter will be devoted to describing the individual statistics and what information each conveys. Requesting SPSS to calculate the various statistics is easy and can be quickly described in the final pages of the chapter. Most of the SPSS output in this chapter was generated using the *Frequencies* procedure.

CONCEPT CHECK

Without looking back, can you answer the following questions:

- What is the difference between central tendency and dispersion?
- What are three measures of central tendency? What are three measures of dispersion?
- What measures of central tendency and dispersion become available only at the interval/ratio level of measurement?

If not, go back and review before reading on.

Nominal Measures

Participants in the GSS were asked to indicate with a yes or a no if they believe there is life after death. Figure 4.1 shows the answers given by 1980 GSS young adults.

Statistics

POSTLIFE

N	Valid	294
	Missing	33
Mode		1

POSTLIFE

		Frequency	Percent	Valid Percent	Cumulative Percent
Valid	0 no	64	19.6	21.8	21.8
	1 yes	230	70.3	78.2	100.0
	Total	294	89.9	100.0	
Missing	8 don't know	31	9.5		
	9 no answer	2	.6		
	Total	33	10.1		
Total		327	100.0		

Figure 4.1   *Frequencies* Output for POSTLIFE for 1980 GSS Young Adults

Mode — occurs most often

The **mode** is the attribute of a variable that occurs most often in the data set. It is the most common valid answer. System-missing or user-defined missing values are usually not eligible to be the mode.

There are several ways of finding the mode for a variable. You could look at the valid percent column (or the frequency column or the percent column) in a frequency table and find the row among the valid values that has the highest percent (or frequency). The value that that row represents is the mode for that variable. In Figure 4.1, the most common answer to the question about life after death is yes. In other words, the mode is "yes." This attribute was coded "1" when the data set was created, and it is technically correct to say that the mode is 1; however, it is more informative when an attribute has a label to report the label rather than the numeric code. After all, the value label was added because the numeric code was not self-explanatory.

If you ask SPSS to calculate the mode, then the value of the mode will be included in the box of statistics that precedes the frequency table. As you can see in Figure 4.1, SPSS unfortunately only reports the numeric code for the mode and not the value label.

RESEARCH TIP

The Mode Is an Attribute, Not a Frequency or a Percent

A common mistake when identifying the mode from a frequency table is to report the largest frequency or the largest percent as the mode. The correct mode for the variable "belief in life after death" (Figure 4.1) is "yes." If a person reported the mode as 78.2% or as 230, she would be wrong! You only locate the largest valid percent or the largest frequency so that you can identify the attribute that is the mode. The mode is not the frequency or the percentage; the mode is the attribute.

It is always possible that two or more attributes may tie as the most common value in the data set. Watch for ties when you scan a frequency table looking for the mode. If SPSS is identifying the mode for you, it will tell you if there is more than one mode. Having informed you of that fact, it will report only the first mode it located. You would have to examine a frequency table to identify the other mode or modes.

Any distribution with more than one mode can be described as **multimodal.** A distribution with two modes, however, is usually referred to as **bimodal.** A distribution with three or more modes is just referred to as multimodal.

RESEARCH TIP

Multimodal Distributions That Are Not Really

Technically speaking, two or more attributes must exactly tie for most common in order for a distribution to be multimodal. In fact, however, the terms *bimodal* and *multimodal* are often used in a looser sense to describe when cases tend to cluster around two or more different attributes. For example, on a test in which there were 3 Fs, 13 Ds, 2 Cs, 20 Bs, and 5 As, the professor might describe the distribution as bimodal. Technically, it is not. The mode is B. But the instructor seeks to highlight the fact that many more students got Ds and Bs than got Fs, Cs, or As. This looser meaning of bimodal or multimodal is sufficiently common that you need to be aware of it

The mode is a nominal measure of central tendency, which means it can be legitimately reported for nominal, ordinal, or interval/ratio variables.

Percent Distribution

So, now you know that yes was the most common answer to the question about believing in life after death. But what other answers were given, and how frequently were each of the answers given? These are questions about dispersion; they are asking not about central tendency but about variation in the data. To answer questions such as these, you need to see a **percent distribution,** specifically, a valid percent distribution.

You can see in Figure 4.1 that yes was by far the more common answer (75.2%) but that about a fourth (24.8%) of 1980 GSS young adults said no.

Percent distributions can be calculated for nominal, ordinal, or interval/ratio variables.

RESEARCH TIP

The Mighty Percent Distribution—in Moderation

Although percent distributions are one of the simplest types of statistics, they are often the most effective way of describing the dispersion of scores on a variable. But reporting a long list of percents can deaden even the most interested audience. If you want the reader or listener to be aware of the valid percents for more than four categories, include the percent table in the presentation or paper and refer the reader to it.

Ordinal Measures

The GSS asked respondents to politically identify themselves on a 7-point scale from strong Democrat to strong Republican. The 7 points of the scale and the answers given by 1980 GSS young adults appear in Figure 4.2. The variable is named PARTYID. Being politically independent was placed in the middle of the scale. There was a user-missing code for persons who belonged to a political party other than Democrat or Republican, and one 1980 GSS young adult used that category.

Because the seven attributes are different from one another and can be put in order from least Republican (which would be the strong Democrat category) to most Republican (the strong Republican category) but do not form a numeric scale (remember, assigning numeric codes doesn't make a variable a numeric scale), PARTYID is an ordinal variable. We can still use the mode ("Democrat but not strong") to describe the central tendency and the percent distribution (the largest categories were "Democrat but not strong" [28.0%] and "independent" [21.2%], and the smallest categories were "strong Republican" [3.1%] and "strong Democrat" [6.2%]) to describe the dispersion, but we can also use some statistics that make use of the natural order among the attributes.

The ordinal measures of central tendency and dispersion are easiest to understand if you imagine the cases in your data set put in line based on their attribute on the variable: First we have all the "strong Democrats," then the "Democrats but not strong," then the "independents but nearly Democrat," and so on until finally the "strong Republicans" join the line.

Median

The **median** is a measure of central tendency. It identifies the value of the middle case when the cases have been placed in order or in line from low to high. The middle of the line is as far from

Statistics

PARTYID

N	Valid	325
	Missing	2
Median		3.00
Mode		1
Range		6
Minimum		0
Maximum		6
Percentiles	25	1.00
	50	3.00
	75	4.00

PARTYID

		Frequency	Percent	Valid Percent	Cumulative Percent
Valid	0 strong Democrat	20	6.1	6.2	6.2
	1 Democrat but not strong	91	27.8	28.0	34.2
	2 independent, nearly Democrat	49	15.0	15.1	49.2
	3 independent	69	21.1	21.2	70.5
	4 independent, nearly Republican	37	11.3	11.4	81.8
	5 Republican but not strong	49	15.0	15.1	96.9
	6 strong Republican	10	3.1	3.1	100.0
	Total	325	99.4	100.0	
Missing	7 other party	1	.3		
	9 no answer	1	.3		
	Total	2	.6		
Total		327	100.0		

Figure 4.2   *Frequencies* Output for PARTYID for 1980 GSS Young Adults

being extreme as you can get. There are as many cases in line in front of the middle case as behind the middle case. The median is the attribute used by that middle case. When you know the value of the median, you know that at least half the cases had that value or a higher value, while at least half the cases had that value or a lower value.

Be careful, here. The median is not about putting the *attributes* in order from low to high and identifying the middle attribute. It is about putting the *cases* in order from low to high based on their attributes and identifying the attribute used by the middle case. For an ordinal variable with seven attributes, the median won't necessarily be the fourth attribute. It might be, but it could be any of the seven attributes. It depends on how the cases are distributed across the attributes.

Figure 4.2 shows there were 325 valid answers on political party identification for the 1980 GSS young adults. The middle of a line with 325 cases is the 163rd case. Counting from the beginning of the line ("strong Democrats"), the 163rd case comes in the group of "independents." Therefore, the median for this variable is "independent." While "independent" happens to be the middle attribute on this seven-attribute variable, "independent" is the median because that was the attribute used by the middle case.

As with the mode, use the attached value label, if there is one, rather than the numeric code when reporting the value of the median. It is more informative to say the median is "independent" than to say the median is "3."

If the exact middle had fallen between two cases in different categories, the best way to report the median is to say that the median falls between the attributes _____ and _____.

The cumulative percent column in a frequency table can be used to quickly identify the median. As long as the rows of the table correspond to the natural order of the attributes, simply go down the cumulative percent column, stopping at the first row with a cumulative percent of 50.0 or higher. The attribute whose row you stopped at is the median. Try it on the frequency table in Figure 4.2. The first cumulative percent of 50.0 or higher is 70.5. The attribute represented by that row is "independent," so that is the median. (In the rare case where the cumulative percent is exactly 50.0, then the median is between the attributes represented by that row and the next row.)

An even easier way of getting the median is to ask SPSS to identify it. The box labeled "Statistics" in Figure 4.2 reports the median to be 3.00, which is the numeric code for the attribute "independent." If the median falls between two different attributes, SPSS will report as the median the average of the numeric codes for the two attributes (e.g., 2.50). While that is acceptable if the variable is interval/ratio, it is not appropriate when the variable is ordinal. In that case, it is better to report the two attributes between which the median falls.

The median is an ordinal measure of central tendency. It can be legitimately reported for ordinal- and interval/ratio-level variables. It is not appropriate for nominal variables because the attributes of a nominal variable lack rank order. A word of caution: SPSS will report medians for nominal variables as long as they are numeric-type variables. It is up to you to recognize that a median makes no sense for nominal variables.

Minimum and Maximum

What was the lowest attribute used by any case? That value is the **minimum**. What was the highest attribute used by any case? That value is the **maximum**. The minimum is the category with the lowest numeric code that was actually used by at least one person, and the maximum is the category with the highest numeric code that was actually used by at least one person. If we put the cases in line from low to high, the minimum is the attribute used by the first person in line, and the maximum is the attribute used by the last person. For 1980 GSS young adults, the minimum was "strong Democrat," and the maximum was "strong Republican."

When you know the value of the minimum and the maximum, you know that all of the cases had scores somewhere between those two values. For the 1980 GSS young adults, the answers went from strong Democrat to strong Republican. If in some other group the answers went only from "Democrat but not strong" to "independent but nearly Republican," then there would be less dispersion (less difference) in that group's political affiliations than among the 1980 GSS young adults.

While SPSS can identify the minimum and maximum values for you, you can certainly spot them yourself from a frequency table. If the rows are organized in order of ascending attributes, the minimum is the attribute represented by the first row of the valid values, and the maximum is the attribute represented by the last row of the valid values.

RESEARCH TIP

What Minimums and Maximums Aren't

The minimum and the maximum will not necessarily be the lowest available attribute and the highest available attribute. On a test, for example, no one may get a 100 and no one, hopefully, will get a 0. The maximum would be the highest score anyone actually got, and the minimum would be the lowest score actually received.

Furthermore, the minimum and the maximum will not necessarily be the attributes with the lowest and the highest frequencies. On a test in which there were 3 Fs, 13 Ds, 2 Cs, 20 Bs, and 5 As, the value of the minimum is F and the value of the maximum is A. That C was the least common grade and B the most common does not matter in identifying the minimum and the maximum.

min + max =
ordinal

Minimum and maximum are ordinal-level measures of dispersion, so they can be reported for ordinal- and interval/ratio-level variables since variables at both those levels of measurement have attributes with a natural order.

Range

The distance between the minimum and the maximum is called the **range.** The larger the value of the range, the more dispersed the cases are on the variable; the smaller the value of the range, the less dispersed (the more concentrated) the cases are on the variable.

Since the calculation of the range makes use of the minimum and the maximum, the range is an ordinal measure of dispersion. The interpretation of the range for ordinal variables is slightly different than for interval/ratio variables.

For ordinal variables, the range indicates how many attributes apart the minimum and the maximum are. For example, in Figure 4.2, "strong Republican" is six attributes away from "strong Democrat." Even if some of the intervening categories were empty, the range would still be 6. You count the number of attributes away the maximum is from the minimum, including both used and unused attributes. If consecutive numeric codes have been used to represent the attributes of the ordinal variable, you simply subtract the code representing the minimum from the code representing the maximum.

For these 1980 GSS young adults, the range on political party affiliation is 6. The maximum is six attributes from the minimum. If the minimum had been "Democrat but not strong" and the maximum had been "independent but nearly Republican," the range would have been 3 because the maximum is just three categories away from the minimum. A smaller range means there is less dispersion in the answers. If everyone in the data set had the same attribute on a variable, the range would be 0 (and the variable could correctly be described as a constant).

For interval/ratio variables, the range represents the distance on a numeric scale from the minimum to the maximum. You calculate the range by subtracting the minimum value from the maximum value.

$$range = maximum - maximum$$

If the maximum grade was 100 and the minimum was 55, the range would be 45.

If the range of final grade point averages is 0.50 for graduating criminal justice majors and 1.50 for graduating social work majors, then there is more dispersion in the final grade point averages of social work majors than of criminal justice majors. Note that this only tells you that there are greater differences among social work majors than among criminal justice majors. It does not tell you which group had the higher average GPA or which group included more students.

RESEARCH TIP

The Statistical Range Is a Single Number

Do not make the common mistake of reporting the range as *"the value of the minimum to the value of the maximum."* Simply putting the word *to* between the minimum and the maximum values does not make it the range. The range is a single number. The range for the political party affiliation is not "strong Democrat" to "strong Republican." The range is 6.

RESEARCH TIP

Ranges Are Never Negative

Remember that the range is *the maximum minus the minimum*. Do the subtraction in the wrong order and you will get a different answer—the wrong answer. If you get a negative number for the value of the range, you have done the subtraction incorrectly!

Percentiles

To understand percentiles, go back to the image of the cases in line from lowest to highest. To get the value of the median, you started at the low end of the line and walked 50% of the way down the line, turned to that case, and recorded its value. That value was the value of the median. Another name for the median is the 50th percentile. If you walked just 25% of the way down the line, turned to that case, and recorded its value, you would have the value of the 25th percentile. If you walked 98% of the way down the line, turned to that case, and recorded its value, that would be the 98th percentile. Percentiles are like milestones that mark certain points in the distribution of cases on a variable.

The 50th percentile is important because it marks the middle of the distribution. Other percentiles are usually reported in sets. For example, a researcher might want the values of the 25th, 50th, and 75th percentiles. These are called quartiles. Knowing them allows the researcher to divide the cases into four equal-size groups. A fourth of the cases have values between the minimum and the 25th percentile, a fourth have values between the 25th and 50th percentiles, a fourth have values between the 50th and 75th percentiles, and a fourth have values between the 75th percentile and the maximum.

In generating the *Frequencies* output for political party affiliation in Figure 4.2, the values for the quartiles (the 25th, 50th, and 75th percentiles) were requested. The values appear in the statistics box. The 25th percentile is "Democrat but not strong." The 50th percentile is "independent," and the 75th percentile is "independent, nearly Republican." So, what does that tell us? Since the 50th percentile is "independent," we know the middle person in the group identifies himself or herself as an independent. But that is one person. What if we want to know about the whole middle part of the group? Sometimes researchers wish to exclude the more extreme respondents on a variable and look at where the middle part of the distribution is—where what you might call the middle-of-the roaders or the nonextremists are. By looking at the values of the 25th and 75th percentiles together, you see where the middle 50% of the respondents stand on the question. For these 1980 GSS young adults, the middle 50% ranged from "Democrat but not strong" to "independent, nearly Republican." No one in the middle half of the group identified as a Republican! If you compared the 20th and 80th percentiles, you would see where the middle 60% are; the 10th and 90th percentiles tell you about the middle 80%.

Percentiles require that the cases be capable of being put in order from least to most. This can be done with ordinal and interval/ratio variables.

Interval/Ratio Measures

The GSS asked respondents how many years of formal schooling they had completed thus far. Since this is an interval/ratio variable, you can still ask the nominal-level questions (what is the most common years of schooling completed, and what percent of respondents reported various years of schooling completed?) and the ordinal-level questions (what is the fewest years of schooling completed, what is the greatest, how much difference is there between the greatest and the fewest, and how many years of schooling did the person in the middle of the distribution have?). You can also ask some interval/ratio-level questions: What is the average years of schooling completed? Were most persons pretty close to or pretty far from the average number of years of schooling completed? Figure 4.3 shows the SPSS results.

Mean

Our third and final measure of central tendency is the **mean.** (The technical name is the arithmetic mean to distinguish it from other means that we will not cover here.) The mean is what in

Statistics

EDUC

N	Valid	327
	Missing	0
Mean		12.79
Median		12.00
Mode		12
Std. Deviation		2.139
Variance		4.576
Skewness		.265
Std. Error of Skewness		.135
Range		12
Minimum		7
Maximum		19
Percentiles	25	12.00
	50	12.00
	75	14.00

EDUC

		Frequency	Percent	Valid Percent	Cumulative Percent
Valid	7	5	1.5	1.5	1.5
	8	4	1.2	1.2	2.8
	9	9	2.8	2.8	5.5
	10	14	4.3	4.3	9.8
	11	14	4.3	4.3	14.1
	12	154	47.1	47.1	61.2
	13	26	8.0	8.0	69.1
	14	36	11.0	11.0	80.1
	15	13	4.0	4.0	84.1
	16	37	11.3	11.3	95.4
	17	8	2.4	2.4	97.9
	18	5	1.5	1.5	99.4
	19	2	.6	.6	100.0
	Total	327	100.0	100.0	

Figure 4.3   *Frequencies* Output for EDUC for 1980 GSS Young Adults

everyday conversation is called the average. It is calculated by simply adding the values of all the valid cases together and dividing by the number of valid cases.

$$\text{mean} = \frac{\sum X_i}{N}$$

In this formula, X represents the variable we are working with. The X with a subscript i refers to each case's value on X. Putting the uppercase sigma ($\sum$) in front of the X_i indicates to sum all the individual values. After summing the values, you divide by N, which is the number of valid cases.

For example, a data set consists of just three cases. One of the variables is exam grade. The three scores on exam grade are 60, 90, and 90. To get the mean, you add the individual values (60 + 90 + 90 = 240) and divide that sum by the number of cases (240/3 = 80). The mean is 80.

The statistics in Figure 4.3 show that 1980 GSS young adults had a mean of 12.79 years of schooling completed at the time of the survey. You could calculate the mean by adding the 327 valid answers and then dividing the sum by 327. (Thank heaven for computers!)

The mean is an interval/ratio measure of central tendency. Its calculation requires that the attributes of the variable represent a numeric scale.

Variance

If someone tells you that the mean annual income of university graduates 10 years after graduation is $45,000, he is telling you about central tendency. But are all the graduates' incomes clustered right around $45,000, or are they actually quite different from each other? After all, you could get a mean of $45,000 in many different ways. If absolutely every graduate made $45,000, that would make the mean $45,000, but so would if half the grads were making $90,000 and half were making nothing. When you want information about the variety of scores or their spread, you are asking about dispersion.

An important measure of dispersion is the **variance**. The calculation of the variance requires the attributes of a variable to form a numeric scale. Thus, it is an interval/ratio-level measure of dispersion.

The variance indicates how close to or far from the mean are most of the cases for a particular variable. The smaller the value of the variance, the more the cases are concentrated around the value of the mean; the larger the value of the variance, the more spread out away from the mean are the cases.

The variance is not the simplest or easiest to understand measure of dispersion for interval/ratio variables. The reason why statisticians prefer it is because it provides an excellent basis for some very important multivariate statistics. One of the things that make the variance a bit tricky is that it does not look at simple distance of cases from the mean; instead, it looks at the squared distance of cases from the mean.

The formula for the variance is

$$\text{variance} = \frac{\sum (X_i - \bar{X})^2}{N - 1}.$$

To calculate the variance, you must first calculate the mean. (The mean is represented in the variance formula by $\bar{X}$. A bar over a variable is a common way of representing the mean.) Then, for each case in the data set, take the value of the case and subtract the mean. Take the result of each subtraction and square it (multiply it by itself). Now add up all those squared values. Finally, divide that sum by the number of cases in the data set minus 1. The result is the variance.

Table 4.2 illustrates the calculation of the variance using a data set of just three cases. The cases have the values 2, 4, and 6.

Table 4.2   Illustrating the Calculation of the Variance

Step 1	$\bar{X} = (2 + 4 + 6)/3 = 12/3 = 4$		
Step 2	X_i	$(X_i - \bar{X})$	$(X_i - \bar{X})^2$
	2	$2 - 4 = -2$	$-2 \times -2 = 4$
	4	$4 - 4 = 0$	$0 \times 0 = 0$
	6	$6 - 4 = 2$	$2 \times 2 = 4$
Step 3	$\sum (X_i - \bar{X})^2 = 4 + 0 + 4 = 8$		
Step 4	$\sum (X_i - \bar{X})^2 / (N - 1) = 8/(3 - 1) = 8/2 = 4$		

In Step 1, you calculate the mean. In Step 2, for each case, you subtract the mean from the value of the case and square that result. In Step 3, you add together the squared results from the previous step. In Step 4, you take the result from the previous step and divide by the number of cases minus 1.

What the variance tells you is the approximate average squared distance of cases from the mean. If that doesn't excite you, remember the big advantage of the variance is that it will provide a foundation for some very powerful multivariate statistics. The variance would be telling you the exact average squared distance of cases from the mean had it been divided by N rather than by $(N - 1)$. The reason for dividing by $(N - 1)$ is because social scientists so often work with sample data, which tends to underestimate the variance in the population. The $(N - 1)$ corrects for this underestimate. Technically, what we are calculating is the "sample variance," but, like SPSS, we will refer to it simply as the variance.

The important thing to remember is that the larger the variance is, the more spread out or dispersed the cases are; the smaller the variance is, the less spread out or dispersed the cases are. In the extreme situation that every case has the same value, the variance equals 0, which makes sense since there is no variability or dispersion in the data.

For 1980 GSS young adults, the variance for years of schooling completed is 4.576. The approximate average squared distance of cases from the mean is between 4 and 5 years of schooling. By itself, that is not very useful information. If you were comparing the years of schooling completed by different generations, however, you could compare the variances to see which generations had more uniformity in schooling and which had more variability.

Standard Deviation

Because people do not usually think in terms of squared distances, many researchers choose to report the **standard deviation** instead of the variance. The standard deviation tells you the approximate average distance of cases from the mean. This is easier to comprehend than the squared distance of cases from the mean.

The standard deviation is directly related to the variance. If you know the value of the variance, you can easily figure out the value of the standard deviation. The reverse is also true. If you know the value of the standard deviation, you can easily calculate the value of the variance.

The standard deviation is the square root of the variance.

$$\text{standard deviation} = \sqrt{\text{variance}}$$

In turn, the variance is equal to the value of the standard deviation squared.

$$\text{variance} = \text{standard deviation}^2$$

If you know the value of the variance and want the value of the standard deviation, take the square root of the variance. If the variance is 25, the standard deviation must be 5. If you know the value of the standard deviation and want the value of the variance, just square the standard deviation. If the standard deviation is 3, the variance would be 9.

Just like for the variance, the larger the standard deviation is, the more dispersed the cases are; the smaller the standard deviation is, the more concentrated around the mean the cases are. If all the cases had the same value on a variable, the standard deviation, like the variance, would have a value of 0.

Recall that the mean years of schooling completed by 1980 GSS young adults was 12.79 years. From Figure 4.3, you know the standard deviation is 2.139. That tells you something about how the cases clustered around that mean. On average, cases were about 2.139 years away from the mean value. Some cases were closer to the mean than that; some were further away. Is that a lot of dispersion or a little? Well, it certainly suggests a lot of these twentysomethings must have had 10 to 15 years of schooling, but, like the variance, the standard deviation is most useful when you can compare the standard deviations for different groups.

CONCEPT CHECK

Without looking back, can you answer the following questions:

- If an ordinal variable has nine attributes, is the fifth attribute always the median?
- If the value of the 25th percentile for household income is $20,000 and the value of the 75th percentile is $80,000, what do you know about the distribution of household incomes?

> - If the mean on an exam was 75 and the standard deviation was 5, what do you know about the distribution of exam grades around the mean?
>
> If not, go back and review before reading on.

[handwritten: Skip mean go to median]

[handwritten: + positive / Right skewed]

Which Measure to Use?

[handwritten diagram: F, median, (more than median) with mean > median, Right skewed positive; Left skewed Neg. (less than median)]

Researchers rarely report every possible measure of central tendency and measure of dispersion. So which ones should you report? Usually, you would use the measures that make the greatest use of the information packed into the attributes of the variable. For an interval/ratio variable, you use interval/ratio measures; for an ordinal variable, you use ordinal measures; and, of course, for a nominal variable, you can only use nominal measures.

If a researcher has time to describe only a few things about each variable, here are the standard approaches: For a nominal variable, report the mode and just a few valid percents. For an ordinal variable, report the median, the minimum, and the maximum. For an interval/ratio variable, report the mean and the standard deviation.

There are two exceptions to the standard reporting packages that occur frequently enough for you to be aware of them. Both exceptions deal with interval/ratio variables. First, it is often the case that the minimum and maximum will also be reported along with the mean and standard deviation. A standard deviation does not give most persons a sense of the dispersion of the cases the way a minimum and maximum do.

The second exception has to do with interval/ratio variables whose distributions are badly skewed. A skewed distribution occurs when there are a few extreme scores on a variable but only in one direction. For example, when all but a few students score in the 80s and 90s on an exam but those few others score below 50, the grade distribution is negatively skewed. Or when most employees in a company receive annual salaries between $25,000 and $50,000 but a few executives receive salaries in excess of $250,000, the salary distribution is positively skewed. The extreme cases pull the mean in their direction. The result is that the mean, although mathematically correct, is not a good measure of central tendency. The median, however, is not so sensitive to extreme values. The addition of one or two extreme cases has only a minor effect on the median, but they have a major effect on the mean. Therefore, report the median instead of the mean when the distribution is badly skewed.

RESEARCH TIP

What Constitutes a Badly Skewed Distribution?

The **skewness coefficient** is a statistic that indicates how skewed an interval/ratio variable's distribution is. When most of the cases are clustered above the mean but a few cases are far below the mean, the skewness coefficient will be negative. The further below zero the skewness coefficient is, the more negatively skewed (the more out of balance) the distribution is.

(Continued)

(Continued)

When most of the cases are clustered below the mean but a few cases are far above the mean, the skewness coefficient will be positive. The further above zero the skewness coefficient is, the more positively skewed (the more out of balance) the distribution is. The closer to zero the value of the skewness coefficient is, the greater the balance in the distribution of cases above and below the mean.

Ask your instructor for his or her suggestion for identifying badly skewed distributions, but here is one possible guideline: If the skewness coefficient is equal to or less (lower on the number line) than −2.00 or equal to or greater than +2.00, report the median instead of or in addition to the mean. Not many distributions have skewness coefficients at or below −2, and not many have skewness coefficients at or above +2, but those that do are pretty severely skewed. (The skewness coefficient is easy to obtain from SPSS.)

You might notice that government agencies often report the median on variables such as years of schooling, income, and age. Although these variables are typically interval/ratio and could support the calculation of a mean, they are often positively skewed in the population. That is the reason government statisticians prefer reporting medians. Housing prices are also often positively skewed and, therefore, better summarized by the median than the mean.

Table 4.3 summarizes the standard packages for describing the distribution of cases on a variable. As always, you have to know the variable's level of measurement before proceeding.

Table 4.3   Usual Statistics Reported When Describing the Distribution of Cases on a Variable

Variable's Level of Measurement	Usual Measure of Central Tendency	Usual Measures of Dispersion
Nominal	Mode	1 to 4 valid percents
Ordinal	Median	Minimum, maximum
Interval/ratio (not seriously skewed)	Mean	Standard deviation, minimum, maximum
Interval/ratio (seriously skewed)	Median	Standard deviation, minimum, maximum

Getting SPSS to Calculate Statistics

Several SPSS procedures will calculate the measures of central tendency and dispersion discussed in this chapter. Here are three. You have already seen *Frequencies*. The two new procedures are *Descriptives* and *Explore*.

Frequencies

The *Frequencies* procedure was discussed in Chapter 3. In addition to frequency tables and charts, this procedure can provide a variety of univariate statistics. The initial *Frequencies* procedure dialog (see Figure 3.1) includes a "Statistics" button. When it is clicked, a dialog similar to Figure 4.4 appears with its menu of statistics.

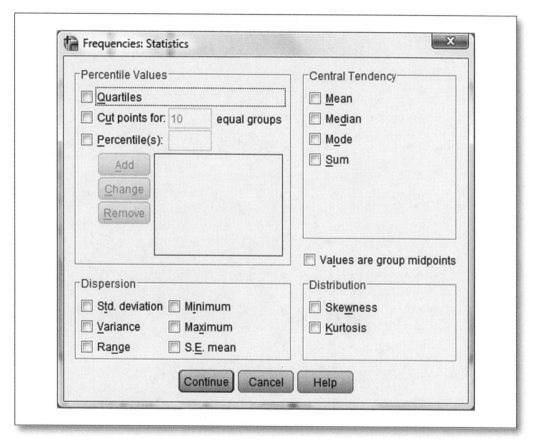

Figure 4.4   *Frequencies* Dialog for Selecting Univariate Statistics

Check as many or as few statistics as you want to appear in your output. When you click the "Continue" button, this dialog will disappear, and you will be back at the initial dialog for the *Frequencies* procedure.

Sometimes, all you want from the *Frequencies* procedure are the statistics and not the frequency table itself. For continuous variables with a large number of attributes, suppressing the actual frequency table is a good idea. You can tell SPSS not to print the frequency table by unchecking the "Display frequency tables" message on the initial *Frequencies* dialog (see Figure 3.1).

Descriptives

The *Descriptives* procedure is a simple method for displaying univariate statistical information for interval/ratio variables. To select the procedure, pull down the *Analyze* menu, move the cursor to *Descriptive Statistics,* and click *Descriptives.*

Analyze | Descriptive Statistics | Descriptives

A dialog similar to Figure 4.5 appears.

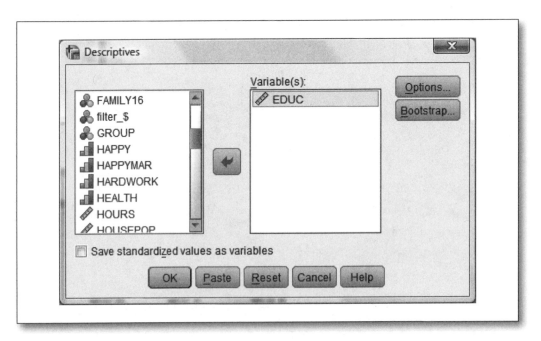

Figure 4.5   Dialog for *Descriptives* Procedure

Move the variables you want the statistical information for into the "Variable(s)" list, and then click "Options" to see the menu of available statistics. A dialog similar to Figure 4.6 will appear.

Make your choices and click "Continue" to return to the primary dialog. Click OK to generate the output. The output is straightforward and compact in format. An example appears in Figure 4.7. The

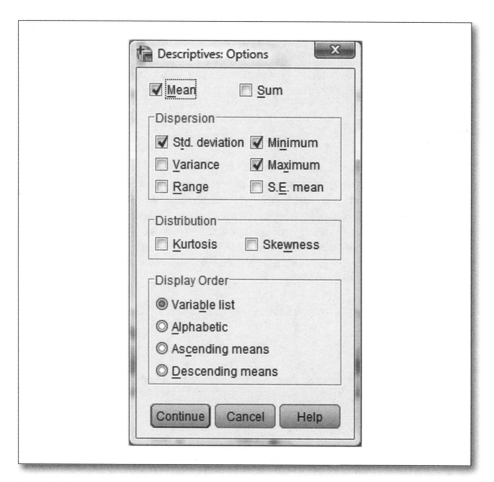

Figure 4.6   *Descriptives* Dialog for Selecting Univariate Statistics

Descriptive Statistics

	N	Minimum	Maximum	Mean	Std. Deviation
EDUC	327	7	19	12.79	2.139
Valid N (listwise)	327				

Figure 4.7   *Descriptives* Output for EDUC for 1980 GSS Young Adults

final line, which is labeled "Valid N (listwise)," tells you the number of cases with valid information on all of the variables appearing in the table. When you run the *Descriptives* procedure on several variables and those variables have differing amounts of missing data, it is sometimes useful to know how many cases had complete data, that is, valid values on all the variables included in the procedure. That is what that last line of the output is telling you.

Explore

The *Explore* procedure gives you a package of frequently used univariate statistics. The only statistical choice you have is whether or not you want percentiles included in the package. *Explore,* like *Frequencies,* provides charts to visually display your data. If you choose to have charts, you can get a boxplot, a stem-and-leaf plot, and a histogram for each variable. All these charts assume your data are interval/ratio. Although neither boxplots nor stem-and-leaf plots are discussed in this book, the SPSS *Help* functions can help you with them.

To access the *Explore* procedure, pull down the *Analyze* menu, move your cursor to *Descriptive Statistics,* and click on *Explore.*

Analyze | Descriptive Statistics | Explore

A dialog similar to Figure 4.8 appears.

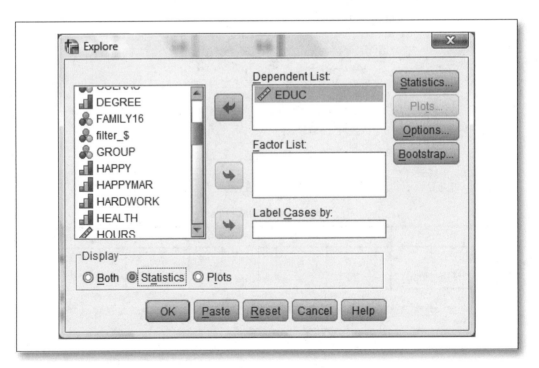

Figure 4.8   Initial Dialog for *Explore* Procedure

Move the variables you want statistical information for into the "Dependent List." If you only want the statistics and not the plots, set the display in the lower left part of the dialog to "Statistics." If you want percentiles, click on "Statistics" near the upper right of the dialog. In the dialog (not shown here) that opens, leave "Descriptives" checked but also check "Percentiles." Click "Continue" to return to the initial dialog. Click OK to generate your output. Figure 4.9 is an example of the statistical output generated by *Explore* when percentiles have not been requested.

Descriptives

			Statistic	Std. Error
EDUC	Mean		12.79	.118
	95% Confidence Interval for Mean	Lower Bound	12.56	
		Upper Bound	13.02	
	5% Trimmed Mean		12.79	
	Median		12.00	
	Variance		4.576	
	Std. Deviation		2.139	
	Minimum		7	
	Maximum		19	
	Range		12	
	Interquartile Range		2	
	Skewness		.265	.135
	Kurtosis		.570	.269

Figure 4.9   *Explore* Statistical Output for EDUC for 1980 GSS Young Adults

What Is Available Where?

Table 4.4 shows which statistics discussed in this chapter are available in which procedures. As you have seen, it's easy to request statistics from SPSS. It is up to you to know the level of measurement of your variables and which statistics are legitimate and which are not.

CONCEPT CHECK

Without looking back, can you answer the following questions:

- What univariate statistics are usually used to describe the distribution of cases on a nominal variable?

(Continued)

(Continued)

- What univariate statistics are usually used to describe the distribution of cases on an ordinal variable?
- What univariate statistics are usually used to describe the distribution of cases on an interval/ratio variable that is not badly skewed?

If not, go back and review before reading on

Table 4.4   Available Univariate Statistics From SPSS Procedures

	Frequencies	Descriptives	Explore
Mode	X		
Median	X		X
Mean	X	X	X
Percent distribution	X		
Minimum and maximum	X	X	X
Range	X	X	X
Percentiles	X		X
Variance	X	X	X
Standard deviation	X	X	X
Skewness	X	X	X

More Univariate Results

Several of the questions asked at the beginning of the chapter about the 1980 GSS young adults can be answered with the *Frequencies* output in Figure 4.10 for the variables POLVIEWS, CLASS, HARDWORK, HAPPY, and HEALTH. All five variables have small numbers of attributes, so their frequency tables are fairly short. They are all ordinal variables, so we want to be sure to note their medians, minimums, and maximums. While we could ask SPSS to report the values for those statistics, it is easy to pick those values out directly from the frequency tables. The minimum is the first valid attribute in the table, the maximum is the last valid attribute, and the median is the first valid attribute to have a cumulative percent of 50.0 or higher.

POLVIEWS

		Frequency	Percent	Valid Percent	Cumulative Percent
Valid	1 liberal	126	38.5	38.7	38.7
	2 moderate	115	35.2	35.3	73.9
	3 conservative	85	26.0	26.1	100.0
	Total	326	99.7	100.0	
Missing	8 don't know	1	.3		
Total		327	100.0		

CLASS

		Frequency	Percent	Valid Percent	Cumulative Percent
Valid	1 lower class	18	5.5	5.5	5.5
	2 working class	187	57.2	57.4	62.9
	3 middle class	114	34.9	35.0	97.9
	4 upper class	7	2.1	2.1	100.0
	Total	326	99.7	100.0	
Missing	8 don't know	1	.3		
Total		327	100.0		

HARDWORK

		Frequency	Percent	Valid Percent	Cumulative Percent
Valid	1 luck/help more important	30	9.2	9.2	9.2
	2 both equally important	82	25.1	25.2	34.4
	3 hard work more important	214	65.4	65.6	100.0
	Total	326	99.7	100.0	
Missing	8 don't know	1	.3		
Total		327	100.0		

HAPPY

		Frequency	Percent	Valid Percent	Cumulative Percent
Valid	1 not too happy	46	14.1	14.1	14.1
	2 pretty happy	185	56.6	56.6	70.6
	3 very happy	96	29.4	29.4	100.0
	Total	327	100.0	100.0	

HEALTH

		Frequency	Percent	Valid Percent	Cumulative Percent
Valid	1 poor	3	.9	.9	.9
	2 fair	40	12.2	12.2	13.1
	3 good	154	47.1	47.1	60.2
	4 excellent	130	39.8	39.8	100.0
	Total	327	100.0	100.0	

Figure 4.10   *Frequencies* Output for 1980 GSS Young Adults

The GSS asked respondents to politically identify themselves as extremely conservative, conservative, slightly conservative, moderate, slightly liberal, liberal, or extremely liberal. The variable POLVIEWS combines the three conservative answers into a single conservative category and the three liberal categories into a single liberal category. The variable was collapsed into just three categories to simplify some of the analyses in future chapters.

Respondents were asked to identify their social class as lower class, working class, middle class, or upper class. They were also asked, "Some people say that people get ahead by their own hard work, others say that lucky breaks or help from other people are more important. Which do you say is most important?" The responses of 1980 GSS young adults to these two questions are the variables CLASS and HARDWORK.

The variable HAPPY is based on this question in the GSS: "Taken all together, how would you say things are these days—would you say that you are very happy, pretty happy, or not too happy?" And the variable HEALTH comes from the following GSS question: "Would you say your own health, in general, is excellent, good, fair, or poor?"

Figure 4.11 shows the output from a *Descriptives* procedure for several other variables relevant to the chapter's opening questions about 1980 GSS young adults. All of the variables are interval/ratio, so we would usually report for each its mean, standard deviation, minimum, and maximum. The output also includes the skewness coefficient. This is not usually reported when presenting results but is useful for checking if the variable is badly skewed. If it is, then the median should be reported in place of or in addition to the mean.

Descriptive Statistics

	N	Minimum	Maximum	Mean	Std. Deviation	Skewness	
	Statistic	Statistic	Statistic	Statistic	Statistic	Statistic	Std. Error
MAEDUC	301	0	20	11.41	2.868	-.888	.140
PAEDUC	256	0	20	11.59	3.665	-.431	.152
SPEDUC	169	5	19	12.72	2.185	.233	.187
AGE	327	20	29	24.69	2.891	-.034	.135
SIBLINGS	327	0	20	3.96	2.756	1.668	.135
CHILDREN	327	0	6	.78	1.043	1.551	.135
INCOME86	244	755	139297	15182.60	14605.817	5.330	.156
TVHOURS	324	0	18	3.12	2.622	2.048	.135
Valid N (listwise)	98						

Figure 4.11   *Descriptives* Output for 1980 GSS Young Adults

Figure 4.11 begins with information about the years of schooling completed by the mothers, fathers, and spouses of 1980 GSS young adults. Only respondents who were currently married were asked about their spouse's years of schooling. That is why the N for SPEDUC is low.

Next appears information about the age of 1980 GSS young adults. Since this group should consist only of persons in their 20s, any ages younger than 20 or older than 29 would signal that a mistake was made in creating the file.

The GSS asks about SIBLINGS in the following way: "How many brothers and sisters did you have? Please count those born alive, but no longer living, as well as those alive now. Also include stepbrothers and stepsisters, and children adopted by your parents." The variable CHILDREN comes from the question, "How many children have you ever had? Please count all that were born alive at any time (including any you had from a previous marriage)."

INCOME86 records a respondent's income the year prior to the survey after converting it into the equivalent amount of 1986 dollars. By converting the incomes of both 1980 and 2010 GSS respondents into 1986 dollars, the effect of inflation is eliminated and comparisons can be made across different survey years. Persons who had no income during the previous year received a missing value code for INCOME86, which largely explains the lower number of valid cases for INCOME86. For the 1980 GSS young adults, INCOME86 was badly positively skewed. A few persons in the data set had incomes much higher than everyone else. These very high scores pulled the mean higher and made it less representative of the data set as a whole. This is a common problem with income data. Since the skewness is severe, the median should be reported. The median income for 1980 GSS young adults who had income in the previous year is $13,595. (The median can be obtained using the *Frequencies* or *Explore* procedures.)

RESEARCH TIP

The GSS and the Variable INCOME86

Income is always a difficult variable to measure well. A few things need to be noted about the income data reported by the GSS. First, respondents are asked only about their income from work. That means that other income, such as interest from savings, rent from property, or dividends from stock, is not included.

Second, the income data are for the calendar year prior to when the survey was conducted. Since people typically think of total income in terms of calendar years, that makes sense.

Third, because income can be a sensitive topic to some individuals and because exact income amounts are often difficult to recall, the GSS asks respondents to report their income using a set of categories. In their original form, these categories represent an ordinal scale. The GSS then recodes these categories, assigning the midpoint dollar amount of each category to each respondent who chose that category. This converts the variable to an interval/ratio level of measurement, and it also explains why, if you were to look at a frequency table for this variable, certain income amounts seem to be reported so frequently while other amounts are reported not at all.

Finally, TVHOURS is based on the GSS question, "On the average day, about how many hours do you personally watch television?" TVHOURS is also badly skewed but not as severely as INCOME86. The median number of hours of television watched daily by the 1980 GSS young adults is 3 hours.

1980 GSS Young Adults

The chapter began with some questions about 1980 GSS young adults. On the basis of our analyses, what do we now know?

- Most 1980 GSS young adults believed in life after death. Believers outnumbered nonbelievers by a ratio of almost 4 to 1.
- The political party affiliations of the 1980 GSS young adults ranged from strong Democrat to strong Republican. Democrats outnumbered Republicans, but the median reported affiliation was independent.
- At the time of the survey, 1980 GSS young adults had an average of one year of college (mean = 12.79 years). While completed years of schooling ranged from just 7 years to as high as 19 years, most had education levels fairly close to the average (standard deviation = 2.139 years). A lot of 1980 GSS young adults had just a high school education or only a few years of college completed at the time of the survey.
- Among 1980 GSS young adults, liberals outnumbered conservatives, but the median political orientation was moderate.
- Very few 1980 GSS young adults described themselves as upper class. Slightly more said they were lower class, but by far, most described themselves as either working class or middle class. Working class was the most commonly reported class. It was also the median.
- 1980 GSS young adults largely believed that success was primarily due to hard work. Almost two thirds said hard work was more important, while less than a tenth said luck was more important. The remainder believed hard work and luck were equally important.
- The median responses of 1980 GSS young adults were that their life was pretty happy and their health good. More described their life as very happy than as not too happy, and far more described their health as excellent than as poor or fair.
- Both the mothers and the fathers of 1980 GSS young adults averaged less than a complete high school education, which means that 1980 GSS young adults on average had already surpassed by more than a year the average educational levels of their parents. 1980 GSS young adults who were currently married had spouses who averaged almost the same schooling as themselves.
- 1980 GSS young adults ranged in age from 20 to 29 and had an average age of 24.69 years, which is very near the middle of the age range.
- 1980 GSS young adults averaged 3.96 siblings. Although some had no siblings, at least one person reported 20 siblings. If the average seems high and the maximum seems very high, remember that this was the baby boom generation and that stepsiblings and adopted siblings are included in the count.
- At the time of the survey, 1980 GSS young adults averaged less than one child. Of course, for most, their fertility was not yet complete, and for many, it had not yet begun.
- About three fourths of 1980 GSS young adults reported income from a job during the previous calendar year. Of those that did, the median income expressed in 1986 dollars was $13,595. While this may seem low, remember that this includes persons who may have

worked only part-time or part of the year and that those 1986 dollars purchased more than current dollars.

- 1980 GSS young adults watched quite a bit of television each day. Their median daily television viewing was 3 hours.

Important Concepts in the Chapter

bimodal	minimum
central tendency	mode
Descriptives procedure	multimodal
dispersion	percent distribution
Explore procedure	percentile
Frequencies procedure	range
maximum	skewness coefficient
mean	standard deviation
median	variance

Practice Problems

1. Explain what central tendency means. What are the measures of central tendency presented in this chapter?

2. Explain what dispersion means. What are the measures of dispersion presented in this chapter?

3. What is the lowest level of measurement for which it is permissible to calculate each of the following statistics?
   a. mean
   b. standard deviation
   c. variance
   d. minimum
   e. percentiles

4. When reporting on the central tendency and dispersion of an interval/ratio variable, what statistics are usually reported along with the mean and standard deviation because they give a person a quick sense of the dispersion?

5. When reporting on the central tendency of an interval/ratio variable, when is the median reported along with or in place of the mean?

6. Five students have the following number of TV shows they watch regularly: 0, 2, 3, 10, 10. Compute each of the following statistics based on these values:
   a. mean
   b. median
   c. mode
   d. maximum
   e. minimum
   f. range

7. A researcher takes a sample of three students from a large class and asks each of them how many years of formal schooling they have completed thus far and how many sisters they have. Calculate the variance for each variable.
   a. When asked how many sisters they have, the students' answers were 0, 0, and 3.
   b. When asked how many years of formal schooling they have completed thus far, the students' answers were 15, 15, and 15.

8. A variable has a standard deviation of 3.00. What is the value of its variance?

9. A variable has a variance of 36. What is the value of the standard deviation?

10. A variable has a variance of 36. What is the approximate average distance of cases from the mean for this variable?

11. You want to know the value of the middle case when the cases are arranged from low to high. Which statistic should you calculate?

12. The range for household incomes in Canon City is $400,000. The range for household incomes in Cripple Creek is $250,000.
    a. Which city has more dispersion in household incomes: Canon City, Cripple Creek, or is there insufficient information to tell?
    b. Which city has a higher mean household income: Canon City, Cripple Creek, or is there insufficient information to tell?

Problems Requiring SPSS and the *fourGroups.sav* Data Set

13. (*2010 GSS young adults*) This problem looks at the belief in life after death of the twentysomethings who took part in the 2010 GSS. (Variables: POSTLIFE; Select Cases: GROUP = 3)
    a. What percent believed in life after death?
    b. Summarize in a few well-written sentences totaling 50 words or less what you found out about the belief in life after death of 2010 GSS young adults.

14. (*2010 GSS middle-age adults*) This problem looks at the belief in life after death of the fiftysomethings who took part in the 2010 GSS. (Variables: POSTLIFE; Select Cases: GROUP = 4)

a. What percent believed in life after death?

b. [Figure 4.1 shows that 78.2% of the 1980 GSS young adults believed in life after death.] Summarize in a few well-written sentences totaling 50 words or less the similarities and/or differences in belief in life after death of these two groups of baby boomers—the 1980 young adults and the 2010 GSS middle-age adults.

15. (*2010 GSS middle-age adults*) This problem looks at the political party identification of the fiftysomethings who took part in the 2010 GSS. (Variables: PARTYID; Select Cases: GROUP = 4)

   a. For these 2010 GSS middle-age adults

      i. What was their modal political party identification?

      ii. What was their median political party identification?

      iii. What percent identified as Democrat? (Include both "strong Democrat" and "Democrat but not strong" but exclude "independent, nearly Democrat.")

   b. Summarize in a few well-written sentences totaling 50 words or less what you found out about the political party identification of 2010 GSS middle-age adults.

16. (*2010 GSS young adults*) This problem looks at the political party identification of the twentysomethings who took part in the 2010 GSS. (Variables: PARTYID; Select Cases: GROUP = 3)

   a. For these 2010 GSS young adults

      i. What was their modal political party identification?

      ii. What was their median political party identification?

      iii. What percent identified as Democrat? (Include both "strong Democrat" and "Democrat but not strong" but exclude "independent, nearly Democrat.")

   b. [Figure 4.2 shows for the 1980 GSS young adults a modal identification of "Democrat but not strong," a median identification of "independent," and 34.2% identifying as Democrat.] Summarize in a few well-written sentences totaling 50 words or less the similarities and/or differences in political party identification of the 1980 and 2010 GSS young adults.

17. (*2010 GSS young adults*) Which, if any, of the following interval/ratio variables are "badly skewed" in the data from the 2010 GSS young adults: EDUC, MAEDUC, PAEDUC, SPEDUC, AGE, SIBLINGS, CHILDREN, INCOME86, and TVHOURS? (See the text or your instructor for a definition of "badly skewed.") (Select Cases: GROUP = 3)

18. (*2010 GSS young adults*) This problem looks at the years of schooling completed by the time of the survey by the twentysomethings who took part in the 2010 GSS. (Variables: EDUC; Select Cases: GROUP = 3)

   a. For years of schooling for these 2010 GSS young adults,

      i. What is the value of the mean?

      ii. What is the value of the median?

      iii. What is the value of the skewness coefficient?

      iv. What is the value of the standard deviation?

      v. What is the value of the minimum and the maximum?

   b. [Figures 4.3 and 4.9 both show for years of schooling completed by the 1980 GSS young adults a mean of 12.79, a median of 12, a skewness coefficient of .265, a standard deviation of 2.139, a minimum of 7, and a maximum of 19.] Summarize in a few well-written sentences totaling 50 words or less the similarities and/or differences in the years of schooling completed by the time of the survey by the 1980 and 2010 GSS young adults. (If either group's data are badly skewed, base your comparison of central tendencies on the medians, otherwise the means.)

19. (*1980 GSS middle-age adults* and *2010 GSS middle-age adults*) This problem compares the years of schooling completed by the time of the survey by the fiftysomethings who took part in the 1980 GSS and the fiftysomethings who took part in the 2010 GSS. Unlike persons in their 20s, most persons in their 50s have obtained all the formal schooling they will ever get.
    a. For years of schooling for the 1980 GSS middle-age adults (Variables: EDUC; Select Cases: GROUP = 2),
        i. What is the value of the mean?
        ii. What is the value of the median?
        iii. What is the value of the skewness coefficient?
        iv. What is the value of the standard deviation?
        v. What is the value of the minimum and the maximum?
    b. For years of schooling for the 2010 GSS middle-age adults (Variables: EDUC; Select Cases: GROUP = 4),
        i. What is the value of the mean?
        ii. What is the value of the median?
        iii. What is the value of the skewness coefficient?
        iv. What is the value of the standard deviation?
        v. What is the value of the minimum and the maximum?
    c. Summarize in a few well-written sentences totaling 50 words or less the similarities and/or differences in the years of schooling completed by these two groups of fiftysomethings—the 1980 middle-age adults and the 2010 GSS middle-age adults. (If either group's data are badly skewed, base your comparison of central tendencies on the medians, otherwise the means.)

20. (*1980 GSS middle-age adults* and *2010 GSS middle-age adults*) This problem compares the number of children of the fiftysomethings who took part in the 1980 GSS and the fiftysomethings who took part in the 2010 GSS. Since persons in their 50s have generally had all the children they will have, this is a comparison of completed fertility.
    a. For number of children of the 1980 GSS middle-age adults (Variables: CHILDREN; Select Cases: GROUP = 2),
        i. What is the value of the mean?
        ii. What is the value of the median?
        iii. What is the value of the skewness coefficient?
        iv. What is the value of the standard deviation?
        v. What is the value of the minimum and the maximum?
    b. For number of children of the 2010 GSS middle-age adults (Variables: CHILDREN; Select Cases: GROUP = 4),
        i. What is the value of the mean?
        ii. What is the value of the median?
        iii. What is the value of the skewness coefficient?

iv. What is the value of the standard deviation?

v. What is the value of the minimum and the maximum?

c. Summarize in a few well-written sentences totaling 50 words or less the similarities and/or differences in number of children of these two groups of fiftysomethings—the 1980 middle-age adults and the 2010 GSS middle-age adults. (If either group's data are badly skewed, base your comparison of central tendencies on the medians, otherwise the means.)

21. Here are some comparisons you might conduct using other variables introduced in this chapter:

a. POLVIEWS

i. (1980 GSS young adults and 2010 GSS young adults)

ii. (1980 GSS young adults and 2010 GSS middle-age adults)

b. CLASS

i. (1980 GSS young adults and 2010 GSS young adults)

ii. (1980 GSS young adults and 2010 GSS middle-age adults)

c. HARDWORK

i. (1980 GSS young adults and 2010 GSS young adults)

ii. (1980 GSS young adults and 2010 GSS middle-age adults)

d. HEALTH

i. (1980 GSS young adults and 2010 GSS young adults)

ii. (1980 GSS young adults and 2010 GSS middle-age adults)

e. TVHOURS

i. (1980 GSS young adults and 2010 GSS young adults)

ii. (1980 GSS young adults and 2010 GSS middle-age adults)

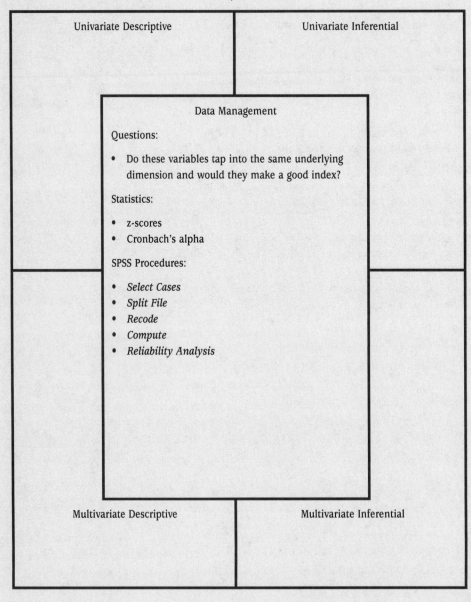

Questions and Tools for Answering Them
(Chapter 5)

Univariate Descriptive	Univariate Inferential

Data Management

Questions:

- Do these variables tap into the same underlying dimension and would they make a good index?

Statistics:

- z-scores
- Cronbach's alpha

SPSS Procedures:

- *Select Cases*
- *Split File*
- *Recode*
- *Compute*
- *Reliability Analysis*

Multivariate Descriptive	Multivariate Inferential

Creating New Variables 5

In this chapter, you can learn

- how to limit your analysis to just one group of cases,
- how to repeat your analysis for separate groups of cases,
- how to change the coding of a variable,
- how to create a new variable from the variables already in the data set,
- how to express scores on interval/ratio variables as standard deviations from the mean,
- how to see if several variables are all measuring the same underlying dimension, and
- how to combine scores on several variables into a single overall score or index.

Academic Freedom and Abortion

Just a few more variables in our data set need to be introduced. We'll do that in this chapter as we answer these questions:

- How willing were 1980 GSS young adults to allow controversial persons to teach in colleges or universities? Give public speeches? Have their books in the public library?
- Who were 1980 GSS young adults most willing to let teach college: someone who is against all churches and religions, someone who claims all blacks are inferior, a Communist, someone who advocates eliminating all elections and letting the military run the country, or an acknowledged homosexual? Which were they least willing to let teach?
- How willing were 1980 GSS young adults to allow legal abortions?

> **SPSS TIP**
>
> *To Duplicate the Examples in This Chapter*
>
> To duplicate the examples in the "Creating an Index and Checking Its Reliability" section of this chapter, use the *fourGroups.sav* data set and set the select cases condition to GROUP = 1.

Overview

After you have created your data set, you may want to change how some variables are coded or you may want to create a new variable that is a combination of one or more variables already in the data set. These are data management tasks easily handled by SPSS.

This chapter shows you how to do things like that and more. Before learning how to recode old variables and create new ones, however, you will get a more detailed description of the *Select Cases* procedure, which you have already been using, and you will be shown how to quickly repeat the same analysis on different groups of cases in your data set.

Select Cases

This procedure was first described in Chapter 3 and has been used in every chapter since then. To limit the analyses to just 1980 GSS young adults, we selected only those cases with a value of 1 on the variable GROUP. To do many of the practice problems in the last three chapters, you had to select only those cases with a 2 (for 1980 GSS middle-age adults) or a 3 (for 2010 GSS young adults) or a 4 (for 2010 GSS middle-age adults) on GROUP.

By default, SPSS includes all the valid cases in the data set in any analysis you conduct. Sometimes, however, you only want an analysis performed for a group of cases. For example, you may want to analyze only 2010 GSS young adults or only Protestants or only whites who are liberal. If you can describe the group you want to examine in terms of variables already in the data set, then SPSS lets you limit the analysis to just those cases.

Pull down the *Data* menu and click on *Select Cases*.

Data | *Select Cases*

A dialog similar to Figure 5.1 appears. By default, "All cases" is selected. There are several options for selecting a subset of cases. When you choose "If condition is satisfied," the "If" button below that option becomes active.

If you click the "If" button, a dialog similar to Figure 5.2 opens up.

All you need to do is enter the condition that describes the cases you want included in the analysis. You can key in numbers and symbols yourself or use the keypad provided in the dialog.

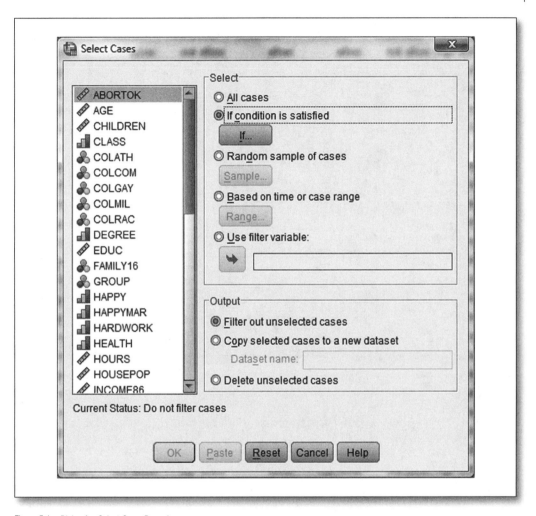

Figure 5.1   Dialog for *Select Cases* Procedure

Whenever you need to include a variable name in the condition, select it from the list and move it into the condition you are constructing or type the name in yourself. SPSS also has some built-in mathematical functions you can use in your condition. Using these built-in functions can save you time. The complete list of available functions appears in the lower right area of the dialog when you click "All" in the "Function group" list. To understand what any of those functions do, click on the function name. A brief explanation appears just below the keypad area.

In Figure 5.2, the analysis is being limited to cases that satisfy the condition that they have a value of 1 for the variable GROUP. Cases with any other code, including any type of missing code, would be excluded.

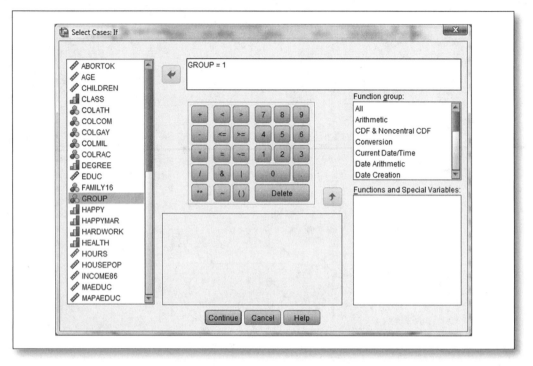

Figure 5.2   Dialog for Setting Condition for *Select Cases*

If you want to restrict an analysis to persons with two or more children, the condition you would specify would be

$$CHILDREN >= 2$$

You can use the conjunction *and* to specify two conditions that must both be met for a case to be included. If we wanted to restrict the analysis to just 1980 GSS young adults with two or more children, the condition would be

$$GROUP = 1 \text{ and } CHILDREN >= 2$$

You can also use the conjunction *or* to indicate that a case needs meet only one of two conditions to be included.

After you have specified the condition, click "Continue" to return to the initial *Select Cases* dialog (Figure 5.1). Notice the area in the lower right part of this dialog labeled "Output." There are three output choices. "Filter out unselected cases" is the default choice and what you usually want. With this choice, the cases that do not meet your condition are temporarily excluded from your analyses but can be once again included if you return to this "Select Cases" dialog and change your condition or return to analyzing "All cases."

The second output choice creates a new data set with just the cases that met your condition but leaves your present data set unaffected. The third choice deletes from the data set those cases that did not meet your condition.

Once you have made your output choice, which most often will be the default to simply filter out the unselected cases, click OK. The cases that meet your condition are selected for analysis. If you look at data view, you will see a slash through the row numbers of the cases that did not meet the condition.

SPSS TIP

Adding Notes to Output

Unfortunately, SPSS does not automatically insert a message in your output reminding you that at this point you selected a subgroup of cases for analysis. Since SPSS doesn't do it, you ought to. You should insert a message into your output whenever you change the criterion for including cases in an analysis. This can be done quite simply when you have the output screen in front of you. Pull down the *Insert* menu and click on *New Text*.

Insert | New Text

A box will open up in your output into which you can type a message. If the box isn't visible, click on the "Text" entry in the outline on the left to get the box to appear and then double-click in the box. When you are done entering your text, click outside the box. The message becomes part of your output.

The select cases criterion you created remains in effect until you change it or until you open a new data set. Whenever you want to change the selection criterion or return to analyzing all the cases in the data set, you have to go back to *Select Cases* and either choose "All Cases" or change the condition for a case to be selected.

Split File

You may want to divide your cases into groups and then perform the same analysis but separately on each group. You can do this by pulling down the *Data* menu and clicking on *Split File*.

Data | Split File

When you do this, a dialog like Figure 5.3 opens up.

The default choice for SPSS is "Analyze all cases, do not create groups." If you want to perform the same analysis on different groups of cases within your data set, choose "Compare groups." The "Groups Based on" list now becomes active. Move the variable whose attributes will define your groups from the list on the left to the "Groups Based on" list. Then click OK.

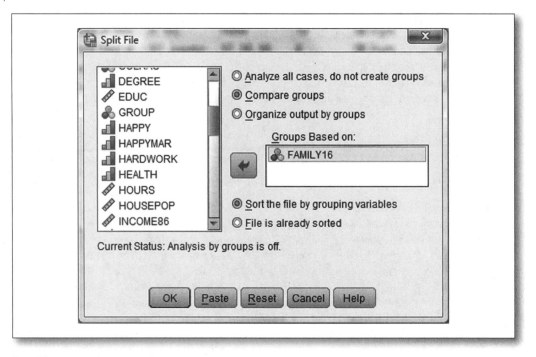

Figure 5.3   Dialog for *Split File* Procedure

For example, you want to see a separate frequency distribution on strength of religious affiliation (RELINTEN) for persons raised in different types of family situations. You could do that using *Split File* by selecting "Compare groups" and moving FAMILY16 into the "Groups Based on" field. Once you click OK, every analysis you request will be done four times—once for each category of FAMILY16 (raised by both parents, raised by a parent and a stepparent, raised by a single parent, and raised in some other arrangement) until you turn this split file function off by returning to *Split File* and selecting "Analyze all cases, do not create groups."

SPSS TIP

Be Careful When You Split Files

Usually you split a file based on a variable with a small number of attributes. Remember that for any analysis you request when you have split the file, SPSS will repeat that analysis for each and every attribute of the variable, including system-missing and user-defined missing attributes. If you split a file based on a variable with 100 different attributes and then asked for some frequency table, you would get 100 separate frequency tables—one for each attribute of the variable you used to split the file. Be careful what you ask for!

Like *Select Cases, Split File* remains in effect until you return to the split file dialog and either specify a different variable as the basis for your groups or choose "Analyze all cases, do not create groups." Unlike *Select Cases,* it is easy to remember when *Split File* is in effect. Your output will show which analyses are based on which groups.

Recode

Now comes the heart of this chapter: creating new variables. *Recode* is one of several SPSS procedures that can create new variables in your data set. There are two common reasons why analysts use the *Recode* procedure. One is to collapse or reduce the number of attributes that make up a variable. For example, our political party affiliation variable currently has seven categories, but you want to reduce it to just three categories: Democrat, Independent, and Republican. The second common reason for using *Recode* is to reorder the coding of a variable. For example, our political orientation variable currently has liberals coded 1 and conservatives coded 3, but you want to reverse the coding so that conservatives are coded 1 and liberals 3.

In neither of these situations is it necessary on a case-by-case basis to change values or enter new values. *Recode* can do all the work for you.

Pull down the *Transform* menu and move your cursor to *Recode.* You now have a choice. Do you want to recode into the *Same Variables* or into *Different Variables?* When you recode into the same variable, your new coding scheme replaces the old coding scheme. When you recode into a different variable, the original variable with the original coding remains in the data set, but you create a new variable with the new coding scheme. Recoding into the same variable is sometimes quicker, but it is also riskier. If you make a mistake with your recoding instructions, you have to open a new copy of the original data file in order to start again with the original coding. For persons just learning SPSS, recoding into a different variable is strongly recommended.

Transform | *Recode* | *Into Different Variables*

When you click on *Into Different Variables,* a dialog similar to Figure 5.4 appears.

Begin by finding the original variable in the list at the left of the box and move it to the "Numeric Variable — > Output Variable" list. Next, key in the name of the new variable in the "Name" field. After you have keyed in the variable name, you may enter a variable label in the "Label" field. Then click "Change" to connect the new variable to the old variable.

Now click "Old and New Values" A dialog similar to Figure 5.5 appears. This is where you will indicate how SPSS should create the values for the new variable.

In this dialog, you are essentially telling SPSS to "take cases with particular values on the old variable and give them certain values on the new variable." SPSS provides several ways of referring to values on the old variable. You can refer to a single value, system-missing value, both system and user-missing values, a range of values, or all the values on the old variable that have not been recoded yet. Once you have identified which value(s) on the old variable you are talking about, you can assign cases with those old values a different value on the new variable, a system-missing value, or the same value they had on the old variable. Once you have indicated the old and new values, click "Add" to put the recode into your list of recodes. Then you can describe the next old value(s)

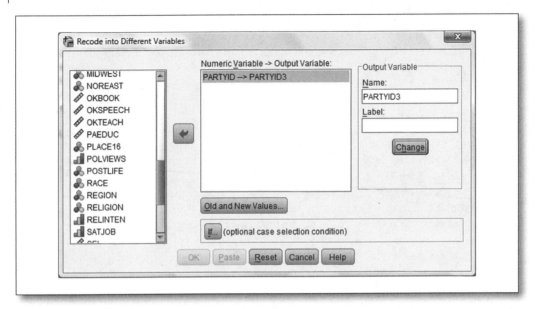

Figure 5.4   Initial Dialog for *Recode Into Different Variables* Procedure

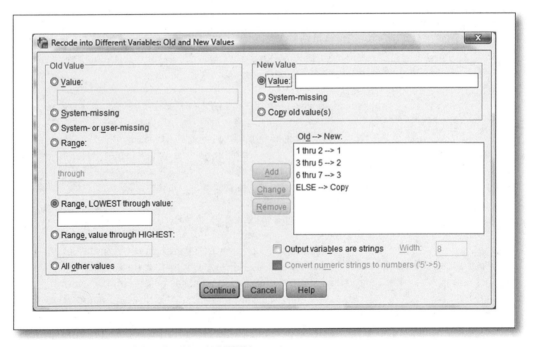

Figure 5.5   Dialog for Specifying Old and New Values for PARTYID3

you want recoded into a new value or, if your list of recodes is complete, you can click "Continue." Upon returning to the original dialog, click OK to perform the recode.

If you look at data view, you will see your new variable as the last variable in the data set. Your work is not done yet, however. If you look at variable view, you will see that neither the value labels nor the user-defined missing values information transferred from the old variable to the new variable. You must reenter that information if you want value labels and if you want certain values besides empty cells recognized as missing values.

Figure 5.5 shows the recodes you would use to convert the original political party variable, which had seven valid codes, into a new variable called PARTYID3 with just three valid codes. The old Democrat codes (1 and 2) were given a code of 1 on the new variable, the old independent codes (3, 4, and 5) were given a code of 2, and the old Republican codes (6 and 7) were given a code of 3. All the other old codes, which included the user-missing codes (8 and 9), were assigned the same codes on the new variable. But SPSS does not know that 8 and 9 are user-missing values on PARTYID3, nor does it have any value labels for PARTYID3. You will have to define those things using variable view.

Figure 5.6 shows the recodes you would use to reorder the coding on POLVIEWS into the new variable LIBERAL. The last recode, "ELSE —> Copy," ensures that the old values of 2, 8, and 9 remain the same on the new variable, but, as before, you would have to use variable view to assign value labels and user-missing values to the new variable.

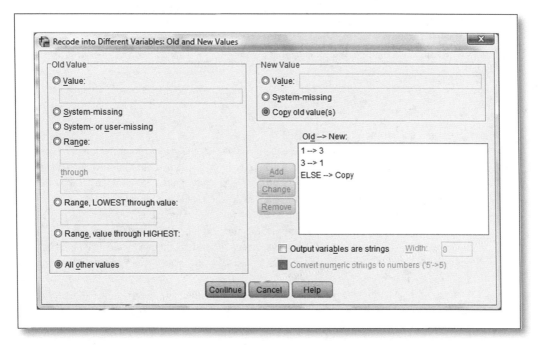

Figure 5.6   Dialog for Specifying Old and New Values for LIBERAL

SPSS TIP

Getting Recodes Right

Sometimes, the hardest part of collapsing or reversing codes is not getting confused yourself. It helps to jot down the recodes on a piece of paper and then methodically do them with SPSS. Doing a frequencies procedure for both the old and the new variable can also show if you have done the recode properly.

Make sure no old values were overlooked when recoding into a different variable. If they were, they get recoded as system-missing, which may not be what you wanted. Also, carefully check to make sure any user-missing values made it through the recode correctly. If you are collapsing a continuous variable into a variable with just a few categories, make sure the cases at the edges of your intervals get recoded into the correct categories.

Compute

Compute uses the values of one or more existing variables to calculate the values of a new variable. The *Compute* procedure is very versatile. Among other possibilities, you can add, subtract, multiply, and divide a case's values on one or more variables to calculate that case's value on a new variable.

To compute a new variable, pull down the *Transform* menu and click on *Compute Variable*.

Transform | *Compute Variable*

A dialog similar to Figure 5.7 appears.

In the "Target Variable" field, enter the name of the variable you are going to create. You can use the name of an existing variable, but that would mean that variable's old values will be replaced by the values resulting from your compute procedure. In the "Numeric Expression" field, enter the calculation that SPSS should perform to obtain each case's value on this new variable. Just like with *Select Cases,* you can use the keypad and built-in mathematical functions to simplify the process. To enter the names of any existing variables into the numeric expression, find them in the variable list and move them into the expression. You may notice that when you move a variable name into the expression, it still also remains in the variable list. That is because you may need a variable to appear more than once in an expression.

Once you have the target variable named and are satisfied with the numeric expression, click OK. If you now go to data view, you will find an additional column in your data set. These are the values for each case on your new variable. This new variable can be used like any other variable in the data set.

SPSS TIP

No Automatic Recalculations

A new variable created with the *Recode* or *Compute* procedures does not stay associated with the original variable(s) from which it was calculated. If after you created a new variable you discovered and corrected an error in one of the variables used to create that new variable, the values on the new variable would not be automatically adjusted. Hopefully, you will discover any data entry errors before you compute new variables, but if you do not discover them until later, you must re-compute those new variables.

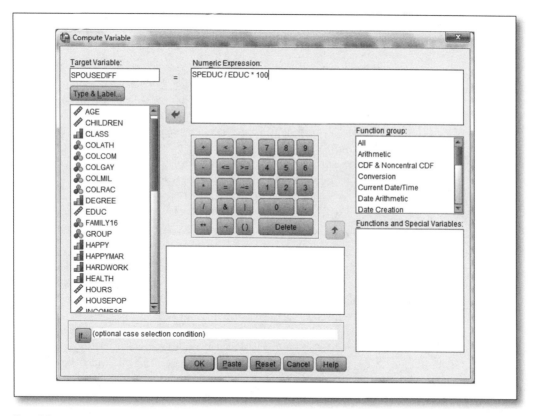

Figure 5.7   Dialog to Create SPOUSEDIFF Using the *Compute* Procedure

For example, let's say you want to create a new variable called SPOUSEDIFF that, for currently married respondents, expresses their spouse's years of schooling as a percent of the respondent's years of schooling. If they have identical years of schooling, the new variable's value should be 100; if the spouse has twice as much schooling, the value would be 200; if the spouse has half as much schooling, the value would be 50. Figure 5.7 shows the numeric expression you would use. The spouse's years of schooling would be divided by the respondent's years of schooling, and the result would be multiplied by 100. If any cases in the data set have missing values on any of the variables in the numeric expression used in the *Compute* procedure, those cases receive a system-missing value for the new variable. (Since persons not currently married have a missing value for spouse's years of schooling, persons not currently married receive a system-missing value on SPOUSEDIFF. Any respondents who have a 0 on EDUC will also receive a system-missing value on SPOUSEDIFF since division by 0 is mathematically undefined.)

SPSS TIP

The Order of Arithmetic Operations

In constructing numeric expressions, it is important to understand the order in which SPSS performs mathematical operations. Unless otherwise directed, SPSS first does any exponentiation (e.g., squares and square roots) that appears in the expression, and if there is more than one instance of exponentiation in the expression, it does them moving from left to right. Second, it does any multiplication and division in the expression, again moving from left to right. Keep in mind that multiplication does not have priority over division. They have the same priority and are done in the same sweep across the expression. Finally, SPSS does any addition and subtraction moving from left to right. Addition does not have priority over subtraction. They have the same priority.

An exception to this order is that anything placed within parentheses will be done first.

Here is a second example. It describes how an actual variable in your data set, MAPAEDUC, was computed. The variable is the average years of schooling of each respondent's parents. If a respondent knows both his mother's and father's years of schooling, the new variable is the average of those two amounts. If a respondent knows only the years of schooling of one parent, then that parent's years of schooling is used as the value of MAPAEDUC. Figure 5.8 shows the *Compute* dialog. One of the functions built into SPSS, the "Mean" function, was used to create the new variable. The "Mean" function can be inserted into the numeric expression by clicking "All" within the "Function group" list and then double-clicking "Mean" within the "Functions and Special Variables" list. The variables you want averaged then only need to be put inside the parentheses separated by commas.

But what if one or both of the values for MAEDUC or PAEDUC are missing for a case? Doesn't SPSS assign a system-missing value to the new variable? Several functions built into SPSS are exceptions to that rule. For the "Mean" function, as long as at least one variable within the parentheses has a valid value, a mean will be calculated and used as the value of the new variable. If all the variables within the parentheses have missing values, however, then the new variable is coded as system missing.

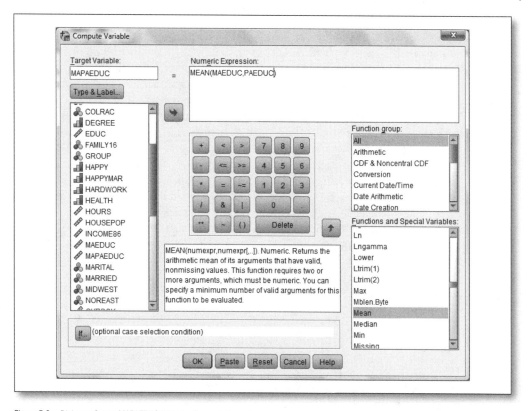

Figure 5.8   Dialog to Create MAPAEDUC With the *Compute* Procedure

z-Scores

Scores on interval/ratio variables can be stated in two ways: as raw scores or as *z*-scores. They are usually reported as raw scores. These are the actual scores cases have on variables. A student gets a 75 on the exam. A faculty member says that she has 3 children, 0 pets, and 4 computers. These are all raw scores. A second way to state them is as **z-scores** (also called standardized scores). A *z*-score describes a case's score in terms of how many standard deviations above or below the mean it is. A *z*-score of zero means the raw score perfectly matched the mean for that variable. A positive *z*-score means the raw score is above the mean. A standardized score of 2 means the raw score is two standard deviations above the mean; a *z*-score of 0.5 means the raw score is a half standard deviation above the mean. A negative *z*-score indicates the raw score is below the mean. For example, a *z*-score of –3 means the raw score is three standard deviations below the mean.

When a raw score is expressed as a *z*-score, you are given information about how that case's score fits into the overall distribution of scores on that variable. The student who got the 75 on the exam might be quite pleased if the corresponding z-score was 4, which means she not only beat the class average but beat it by four standard deviations. On the other hand, she might be quite disappointed if the corresponding z-score was –2.

Standardized scores give you a basis for comparing scores on different variables. For example, a student receives a 75 on the first exam, a 75 on the second exam, and a 75 on the third exam. His dad asks how he did on the three exams, and the student reports that he got three 75s. His dad, who happens to be a statistician, says, "That is interesting, but what are your z-scores?" The son reports that they are –1.5 (at which the dad expresses disappointment), 0 (at which the dad remarks that at least he caught up with the class), and 2 (at which the dad beams "That's my son!").

Standardized scores even let you compare scores on variables that initially appear quite different from one another. For the faculty member with 0 pets, 3 children, and 4 computers, you might ask on which dimension she is most typical of the faculty at her institution and on which dimension she is the most unusual. When her scores are expressed as raw scores, you cannot say. When her values are expressed as standardized scores, comparison becomes easy. Her z-scores are –2 for pets, 0.5 for children, and 3.3 for computers. She is most typical (closest to the mean) on children and least typical (furthest from the mean) on computers.

If you know the mean and standard deviation of a variable and you know a case's raw score, you can calculate the z-score. Simply take the case's raw score, subtract the mean, and divide the resulting difference by the standard deviation.

$$z\text{-score}_i = \frac{(X_i - \bar{X})}{\text{stdev}}$$

where z-score$_i$ is the case's z-score, X_i is the case's raw score, $\bar{X}$ is the variable's mean, and stdev is the variable's standard deviation. Calculating the case's raw score if you know the case's z-score and the variable's mean and standard deviation is equally easy. The formula is

$$\text{raw score}_i = (z\text{-score}_i \times \text{stdev}) + \bar{X}$$

You multiply the case's z-score by the value of the standard deviation and to this product add the value of the mean.

Transforming a case's raw score into a z-score is useful because it indicates where in the distribution of cases on the variable this case occurs. However, an even greater benefit of z-scores is their ability to make comparisons across different variables. No matter whether the original variables are measured in inches, dollars, persons per square mile, or grade points, when these original variables are transformed into standardized variables, these transformed variables are all expressed in the same units: standard deviations. (When someone tells you that a case's z-score was 2, for example, you do not have to ask "2 what?" because you know it means 2 standard deviations. Standardized scores always refer to standard deviations above or below the mean, which is another way of saying standardized variables all have the same metric.) These standardized variables share something else in common. Standardized variables all have the same value for their mean and the same value for their standard deviation. The value of the mean for standardized variables is always zero, and the value for the standard deviation (and the variance) is always 1.

Some of the multivariate techniques you will see later in the book make use of standardized variables to compare the effects of different variables (often originally measured in different metrics) on a dependent variable (probably originally measured in still another metric). Converting these variables into standardized variables converts them all to the same metric, which makes comparisons of their effects possible.

You could use the *Compute* procedure to create a standardized variable in your data set. Before doing so, you would need to find out the original variable's mean and standard deviation. Then go to *Compute* and use $(X_i - \overline{X})\,/\,\mathrm{stdev}$ for your "Numeric Expression," substituting the name of the interval/ratio variable that you want to standardize for X_i, the actual value of the variable's mean for $\overline{X}$, and the actual value of the variable's standard deviation for *stdev.*

However, there is an easier way of adding a standardized variable to your data set. The dialog for the *Descriptives* procedure (see Figure 4.5) includes a checkbox labeled "Save standardized values as variables." When that box is checked, a standardized variable is added to your data set for every variable run through the *Descriptives* procedure.

CONCEPT CHECK

Without looking back, can you answer the following questions:

- When would you use *Select Cases* and when would you use *Split File?*
- What are the two most common reasons for recoding a variable?
- When would you use *Recode* and when would you use *Compute?*
- Why are *z*-scores useful?

If not, go back and review before reading on.

Creating an Index and Checking Its Reliability

The GSS asked respondents if each of the following types of persons should be allowed to teach at a college: someone who is against all churches and religions, a Communist, an acknowledged homosexual, someone who advocates eliminating all elections and letting the military run the country, and someone who claims all blacks are inferior. Each question is coded 0 for the answer "not allow" and 1 for the answer "allow." The variable names are COLATH, COLCOM, COLGAY, COLMIL, and COLRAC. Figure 5.9 shows how 1980 GSS young adults responded to these questions.

Since all five variables seem to be getting at a similar idea, a person's willingness to let possibly controversial persons teach college, you might want to combine the five answers a person gave into a single score.

COLATH

		Frequency	Percent	Valid Percent	Cumulative Percent
Valid	0 not allow	107	32.7	33.5	33.5
	1 allow	212	64.8	66.5	100.0
	Total	319	97.6	100.0	
Missing	8 don't know	8	2.4		
Total		327	100.0		

COLCOM

		Frequency	Percent	Valid Percent	Cumulative Percent
Valid	0 not allow	143	43.7	45.8	45.8
	1 allow	169	51.7	54.2	100.0
	Total	312	95.4	100.0	
Missing	8 don't know	15	4.6		
Total		327	100.0		

COLGAY

		Frequency	Percent	Valid Percent	Cumulative Percent
Valid	0 not allow	97	29.7	30.1	30.1
	1 allow	225	68.8	69.9	100.0
	Total	322	98.5	100.0	
Missing	8 don't know	5	1.5		
Total		327	100.0		

COLMIL

		Frequency	Percent	Valid Percent	Cumulative Percent
Valid	0 not allow	157	48.0	48.8	48.8
	1 allow	165	50.5	51.2	100.0
	Total	322	98.5	100.0	
Missing	8 don't know	5	1.5		
Total		327	100.0		

COLRAC

		Frequency	Percent	Valid Percent	Cumulative Percent
Valid	0 not allow	152	46.5	48.3	48.3
	1 allow	163	49.8	51.7	100.0
	Total	315	96.3	100.0	
Missing	8 don't know	12	3.7		
Total		327	100.0		

Figure 5.9 *Frequencies* Output for College-Teaching Variables for 1980 GSS Young Adults

Index Construction

Often researchers measure a concept by gathering several items of information for each case and combining the items together to form an overall score. If the items being combined are all assumed to be of approximately equal importance in measuring the underlying concept, the resulting measure is called an **index**. For example, a researcher might use 10 questions to ask persons if they have ever used each of 10 illegal drugs. A researcher who only cares about how many drugs have been used might simply add up the number of affirmative answers and assign that score to the person. That would be an index score.

If the items being combined are themselves thought to possess some internal structure so that the items could be ranked in terms of how strongly they reflect the underlying concept, the resulting measure is usually referred to as a **scale**. For example, the researcher might differentiate the 10 drugs based on just how illegal they are (perhaps based on the severity of the punishment for their possession). Each person might receive a score not based on the number of drugs used but on the most illegal drug the person has ever used. That would be a scale score.

Indexes (or indices) are much more common than scales in the social sciences. Even when there may be an underlying order or structure to the items being combined, researchers may simply choose not to explore that structure and treat the combined score as an index. In this book, only the creation and evaluation of indexes will be considered.

RESEARCH TIP

The Terms Index and Scale

This text is using the more common definitions of *index* and *scale*. Regrettably, these terms are not used consistently in the social sciences. Researchers will sometimes refer to what are being described here as indexes as scales and sometimes refer to what are being described here as scales as indexes. So, try to find out what an author really means when one of these terms is used.

Making matters worse, the term *scale* is sometimes used to refer to the set of attributes that make up a variable. For example, a set of attributes such as strongly disagree, moderately disagree, slightly disagree, slightly agree, moderately agree, and strongly agree is often referred to as a Likert scale, named for Rensis Likert, who popularized the idea of presenting survey respondents with a set of statements and measuring their agreement or disagreement with each. All that can be done is to repeat the advice: Try to find out what an author really means when one of these terms is used.

Since the items composing the index are usually averaged or summed, the *Compute* procedure can be very useful. As you know, SPSS includes in its list of functions available for the *Compute* procedure a "Mean" function. It also includes a "Sum" function. To use these functions, simply find the function you want, move it into the "Numeric Expression" field, and insert the names of the variables to be summed or averaged between the parentheses. Here is an example of a numeric expression if you wanted the values for three variables (VAR1, VAR2, and VAR3) averaged:

MEAN(VAR1,VAR2,VAR3)

and here is what the numerical expression would be if you wanted the values summed:

SUM(VAR1,VAR2,VAR3).

The "Mean" and "Sum" functions work a little differently than if you actually put the formula for the mean or the sum into the numeric expression field. The difference has to do with missing cases. If you want a sum calculated and you specify in the numeric expression VAR1 + VAR2 + VAR3 and a case has a missing value on any of these variables, that case will have a system-missing value for the new variable. However, if you specify in the numeric expression field SUM(VAR1,VAR2,VAR3) and a case has a missing value on any of these variables, you will not get a system-missing value. Instead, you will get the sum of those variables that are not missing. You will get a system-missing value only if all three variables have missing values. Similarly, the "Mean" function will give you a result as long as at least one of the component variables has a valid value.

Fortunately, SPSS provides the capability to customize both the "Mean" and "Sum" functions. You can insert a period and a number just before the left parenthesis to indicate the number of variables that must have valid values in order for the function to calculate a value for the new variable. Thus, MEAN.2(VAR1,VAR2,VAR3) will only report a value if a case has valid values on at least two of the component variables, and SUM.3(VAR1,VAR2,VAR3) will only report a value if a case has valid values on all three component variables.

So, you see, there is a decision to make when creating an index: How much missing data for a case can you accept before you say that is too much and the resulting index score would be invalid? Of course, you hope you have no missing data, but the reality is that you probably will have some. While a 2-item index might be meaningless for a case if 1 of the items is missing, a 10-item index might still be useful if 1 or 2 items are not answered.

When every case you are analyzing has complete data (either because there are no missing data or you exclude a case from analysis even if one component variable is missing), it makes no difference whether you create your index by summing or averaging the component variables. However, if you are including cases in your analysis that are missing one or more items in an index, then you should average the items. The averages for cases with some missing data can be compared to cases with no missing data, but the sums for cases with some missing data should not be compared to cases with no missing data because the sums for cases with some missing data are artificially capped.

The variable OKTEACH in your data set represents an index score. It was created using the following *Compute* expression:

OKTEACH = SUM.5(COLATH, COLCOM, COLGAY, COLMIL, COLRAC).

The ".5" after SUM means that only persons who answered all five of the individual questions received a valid score on OKTEACH. Since each of the individual questions was coded 0/1, OKTEACH simply counts how many of these possibly controversial persons the respondent would allow to teach in college. Valid scores on OKTEACH can go from 0 if the respondent would not permit any of them to teach in college to 5 if the respondent would allow all of them.

But is this a good index? Does it really make sense to combine these five items? Are they all tapping into a single underlying dimension? One way to tell is to check the index's reliability.

Reliability Analysis

As noted in Chapter 1, reliability refers to consistency. Are you using a measurement procedure that repeatedly yields the same score if it repeatedly measures the same object? When it comes to indexes, the most common measure of reliability is a statistic called alpha. It is often referred to as **Cronbach's alpha,** in recognition of the statistician who developed it; it is also sometimes referred to as coefficient alpha. It looks at the internal consistency of the items that make up the index. Alpha is based on the correlations of the items in the index with each other. Alpha ranges in value from 0 to 1. The closer to 1, the greater is the reliability of the index.

Alpha values of .70 or higher are generally considered adequate in the social sciences. However, alpha values should be well above .90 for indexes on which important client decisions are to be made such as diagnostic indexes on which treatment decisions will be based.

Usually, the more items included in an index, the higher its alpha value tends to be. However, removing a single item from an index when that item correlates very badly with the other items can also improve an index's reliability.

SPSS provides an easy way of checking the internal consistency of an index using alpha. Pull down the *Analyze* menu and move the cursor to *Scale.* Click on *Reliability Analysis.*

Analyze | Scale | Reliability Analysis

A dialog similar to Figure 5.10 appears.

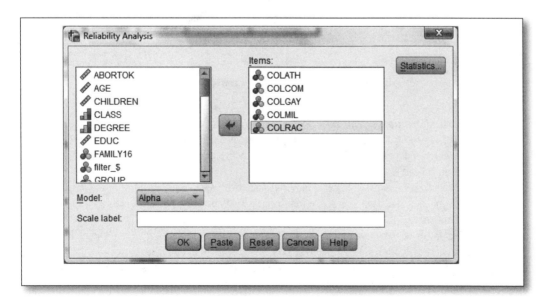

Figure 5.10   Dialog for Checking the Reliability of an Index

Begin by moving the variables to be included in the index from the variable list into the "Items" list. Clicking OK at this point would get you the value of Cronbach's alpha, but clicking on "Statistics" opens up a dialog similar to Figure 5.11 where you can ask for additional output.

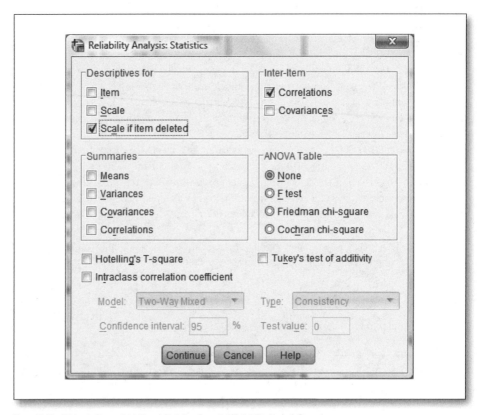

Figure 5.11   Dialog to Request Additional Statistics From the *Reliability Analysis* Procedure

Under "Descriptives for," check "Scale if item deleted," and under "Inter-item," check "Correlations." Then click "Continue," and finally click OK. Figure 5.12 shows some of the output this procedure produces when the index consists of the five items about allowing particular persons to teach in college.

The value of alpha is .794, which indicates adequate reliability. Furthermore, the last column in the "Item-Total Statistics" shows that removing any variable from the index would weaken its internal consistency.

Having evidence that OKTEACH is a good index, we can now look at what it shows. Figure 5.13 presents the output from a *Frequencies* procedure. While the modal score was 5, which indicates allowing all five persons to teach, there were quite a few 1980 GSS young adults at every level of the index. The mean index score was 2.97.

Reliability Statistics

Cronbach's Alpha	Cronbach's Alpha Based on Standardized Items	N of Items
.794	.794	5

Inter-Item Correlation Matrix

	COLATH	COLCOM	COLGAY	COLMIL	COLRAC
COLATH	1.000	.363	.377	.578	.578
COLCOM	.363	1.000	.424	.484	.321
COLGAY	.377	.424	1.000	.425	.322
COLMIL	.578	.484	.425	1.000	.485
COLRAC	.578	.321	.322	.485	1.000

Item-Total Statistics

	Scale Mean if Item Deleted	Scale Variance if Item Deleted	Corrected Item-Total Correlation	Squared Multiple Correlation	Cronbach's Alpha if Item Deleted
COLATH	2.29	2.147	.637	.461	.736
COLCOM	2.42	2.231	.515	.298	.775
COLGAY	2.27	2.328	.499	.263	.778
COLMIL	2.44	2.044	.666	.456	.724
COLRAC	2.44	2.173	.559	.374	.760

Figure 5.12   *Reliability Analysis* Output for College-Teaching Variables for 1980 GSS Young Adults

Other Indexes

The GSS asked respondents not only if they would permit these five possibly controversial persons to teach college but also if they would permit these persons to give public speeches or have their books in the public library. Your data set does not include the answers the respondents gave to the individual questions, but it does include the index scores that were created from these questions. These indexes were named OKSPEECH and OKBOOK. Like OKTEACH, they range from 0 to 5 depending on how many persons a respondent would permit to publicly speak and have their books in the library. Also like OKTEACH, index scores were computed only for respondents who answered all five questions. Frequency tables and means for OKSPEECH and OKBOOK appear in Figure 5.14.

Statistics

OKTEACH

N	Valid	296
	Missing	31
Mean		2.97
Std. Deviation		1.802
Skewness		-.313
Std. Error of Skewness		.142

OKTEACH

		Frequency	Percent	Valid Percent	Cumulative Percent
Valid	0	39	11.9	13.2	13.2
	1	39	11.9	13.2	26.4
	2	42	12.8	14.2	40.5
	3	40	12.2	13.5	54.1
	4	45	13.8	15.2	69.3
	5	91	27.8	30.7	100.0
	Total	296	90.5	100.0	
Missing	System	31	9.5		
Total		327	100.0		

Figure 5.13   *Frequencies* Output for OKTEACH for 1980 GSS Young Adults

Respondents were also asked their opinions about abortion. Specifically, they were presented with six different reasons why a woman might want an abortion and then asked for each if they thought legal abortion should be available. The six reasons were the following: if there is a strong chance of serious defect in the baby, if she is married and does not want any more children, if the woman's own health is seriously endangered by the pregnancy, if the family has a very low income and cannot afford any more children, if she became pregnant as a result of rape, and if she is not married and does not want to marry the man.

Your data set includes the index ABORTOK, which is a count of the number of times a respondent said legal abortion should be available. The index scores range from 0 to 6, and only respondents who answered all six questions received a score on the index. Descriptive statistics for ABORTOK also appear in Figure 5.14.

Statistics

		OKBOOK	OKSPEECH	ABORTOK
N	Valid	306	315	296
	Missing	21	12	31
Mean		3.73	3.60	4.23

OKBOOK

		Frequency	Percent	Valid Percent	Cumulative Percent
Valid	0	22	6.7	7.2	7.2
	1	28	8.6	9.2	16.3
	2	21	6.4	6.9	23.2
	3	32	9.8	10.5	33.7
	4	39	11.9	12.7	46.4
	5	164	50.2	53.6	100.0
	Total	306	93.6	100.0	
Missing	System	21	6.4		
Total		327	100.0		

OKSPEECH

		Frequency	Percent	Valid Percent	Cumulative Percent
Valid	0	28	8.6	8.9	8.9
	1	19	5.8	6.0	14.9
	2	31	9.5	9.8	24.8
	3	45	13.8	14.3	39.0
	4	42	12.8	13.3	52.4
	5	150	45.9	47.6	100.0
	Total	315	96.3	100.0	
Missing	System	12	3.7		
Total		327	100.0		

ABORTOK

		Frequency	Percent	Valid Percent	Cumulative Percent
Valid	0	20	6.1	6.8	6.8
	1	10	3.1	3.4	10.1
	2	26	8.0	8.8	18.9
	3	60	18.3	20.3	39.2
	4	23	7.0	7.8	47.0
	5	23	7.0	7.8	54.7
	6	134	41.0	45.3	100.0
	Total	296	90.5	100.0	
Missing	System	31	9.5		
Total		327	100.0		

Figure 5.14 *Frequencies* Output for Other Indexes for 1980 GSS Young Adults

CONCEPT CHECK

Without looking back, can you answer the following questions:

- How can missing data be handled when constructing an index?
- Why would an analyst want to know the value of Cronbach's alpha?
- What is the lowest level of Cronbach's alpha for an index to be considered to have acceptable reliability in the social sciences?

If not, go back and review before reading on.

1980 GSS Young Adults

The chapter began with some questions about 1980 GSS young adults. On the basis of our analyses, what do we now know?

- Although there were some 1980 GSS young adults who would completely prohibit controversial persons from teaching in college, giving public speeches, and having their books in the library, most expressed much more willingness to permit freedom of speech. In fact, the modal or most common answer pattern was to always permit controversial persons to teach, speak, and have their writings in the public library. However, 1980 GSS young adults did express less tolerance for controversial persons teaching college than for their publicly speaking or having their books in the library.
- The 1980 GSS young adults were most willing to allow the gay individual to teach and least willing to allow the advocate of rule by the military. For each controversial figure, more than half but less than three fourths of 1980 GSS young adults would allow the individual to teach college.
- For the six reasons for abortion presented in the GSS, 1980 GSS young adults would allow legal abortion in an average of 4.23 of them. Individual 1980 GSS young adults ranged from permitting abortion in none of the situations to permitting it in all. Permitting it in all was the modal response.

Important Concepts in the Chapter

Compute procedure

Cronbach's alpha

index

Recode procedure

Reliability Analysis procedure

scale

Select Cases procedure   *z*-scores

Split File procedure

Practice Problems

1. Which SPSS procedure would you use to do each of the following?
   a. limit an analysis to just those cases in a data set that meet a particular condition
   b. combine categories of a variable so you end up with a variable with fewer attributes
   c. divide the cases in a data set into separate groups to perform the same statistical procedure on each group
   d. change the numeric codes assigned to a variable's attributes
   e. create a new variable by performing mathematical operations on one or more of the variables already in the data set

2. A researcher uses the *Compute* procedure to create a variable called NEW.
   a. If its numeric expression is NEW = (VARA + 10)/VARB, what is the value of NEW for the following two cases?
      i. case #1   VARA = 6   VARB = 2
      ii. case #2   VARA = 10   VARB = 10
   b. If its expression is NEW = VARA + 10/VARB, what is the value of NEW for the following two cases?
      i. case #1   VARA = 6   VARB = 2
      ii. case #2   VARA = 10   VARB = 10

3. You have a data set in which every person works two jobs. You already have in the data set their weekly pay from each job (JOB1PAY and JOB2PAY). You want to use the *Compute* procedure to calculate a new variable called YEARPAY, which is the amount they make from both jobs over 52 weeks. State the numeric expression you would use to calculate the new variable.   YEARPAY = _____

4. Standardized scores (*z*-scores) require what level of measurement?

5. Calculate the *z*-score or raw score for each of the following cases:
   a. A variable has a mean of 20 and a standard deviation of 2.
      i.   case #1   raw score = 40   z-score = _____
      ii. case #2   raw score = 10   z-score = _____
      iii. case #3   z-score = 2   raw score = _____
      iv. case #4   z-score = −1   raw score = _____
   b. A variable has a mean of 10 and a standard deviation of 5.
      i.   case #1   raw score = 40   z-score = _____
      ii. case #2   raw score = 10   z-score = _____
      iii. case #3   z-score = 0   raw score = _____
      iv. case #4   z-score = −1   raw score = _____

6. Once all the raw scores on a variable have been converted into z-scores, the mean becomes _____ and the variance becomes _____ .

7. Where in the distribution of scores on a variable do cases with each of the following z-scores fall?
    a. a z-score of 2.5
    b. a z-score of -8
    c. a z-score of 0

8. You are creating an index based on four variables in your data set: VAR1, VAR2, VAR3, and VAR4. One of the cases in your data set has valid values for VAR1, VAR2, and VAR3 but has missing data for VAR4. For each of the following *Compute* commands, indicate if SPSS would report a valid value or a missing value for this case on the index.
    a. index = VAR1 + VAR2 + VAR3 + VAR4
    b. index = (VAR1 + VAR2 + VAR3 + VAR4)/4
    c. index = SUM(VAR1,VAR2,VAR3,VAR4)
    d. index = MEAN(VAR1,VAR2,VAR3,VAR4)
    e. index = SUM.4(VAR1,VAR2,VAR3,VAR4)
    f. index = MEAN.3(VAR1,VAR2,VAR3,VAR4)

9. You find the following statements in the methods section of an article you are reading. For each statement, indicate if the index in question has at least minimally acceptable reliability.
    a. "the loyalty index was found to have an alpha of .94"
    b. "Cronbach's alpha for integration into the group was .65"
    c. "self-efficacy was measured using 12 items (alpha = .75)"
    d. "coefficient alpha for our measure of test anxiety was .49"

Problems Requiring SPSS and the *fourGroups.sav* Data Set

10. (*2010 GSS young adults*) For 2010 GSS twentysomethings who were working full-time, what was the mean number of hours worked in the week prior to the survey? (Variables: HOURS; Select Cases: GROUP = 3 and WORKSTAT = 1)

11. (*1980 GSS middle-age adults* and *2010 GSS middle-age adults*) What percent of fiftysomethings (include both the 1980 and the 2010 GSS middle-age adults) reported their health as "excellent"? (Variables: HEALTH; Select Cases: GROUP = 2 or GROUP = 4)

12. (*all four groups*) This problem looks at what the GSS respondents thought it took to get ahead. (Variables: HARDWORK; Split File: GROUP)
    a. What percent said hard work was more important than luck
        i.   among the 1980 GSS young adults?
        ii. among the 1980 GSS middle-age adults?
        iii. among the 2010 GSS young adults?
        iv. among the 2010 GSS middle-age adults?

b. Summarize in a few well-written sentences totaling 50 words or less what you found out about these four groups' beliefs about the importance of hard work for getting ahead.

13. (*all four groups*) This problem looks at the percent of women reporting their primary work activity as "keeping house." Recall that for this question in the GSS, "keeping house" means keeping house and *not* being employed, *not* looking for employment, and *not* being in school. (Variables: WORKSTAT; Select Cases: SEX = 1; Split File: GROUP)

a. What percent reported their primary work activity as keeping house
   i. among the 1980 GSS young women?
   ii. among the 1980 GSS middle-age women?
   iii. among the 2010 GSS young women?
   iv. among the 2010 GSS middle-age women?

b. Summarize in a few well-written sentences totaling 50 words or less what you found out about the percent of women in these four groups who were primarily keeping house.

14. (*2010 GSS young adults*) Recode the variable HOURS into the variable HOURS4 using the specifications that follow. The old value of 97 was a user-defined missing value indicating the question was not asked because the person was not employed, but you will recode it to a 0 and treat it as a valid value. Be sure to specify value labels after you do the recode. (Variables: HOURS)

Old Value on HOURS	New Value on HOURS4	Value Label
97	0	Worked 0 hours
1–34	1	Worked 1 to 34 hours
35–44	2	Worked 35 to 44 hours
45–89	3	Worked 45 or more hours
All other values	System missing	

a. What percent of 2010 GSS young adults in the week before the survey (Select Cases: GROUP = 3)
   i. worked 0 hours?
   ii. worked 1 to 34 hours?
   iii. worked 35 to 44 hours?
   iv. worked 45 or more hours?

b. Summarize in a few well-written sentences totaling 50 words or less what you found out about the working hours of 2010 GSS young adults in the week before the survey.

15. (*1980 GSS young adults* and *2010 GSS young adults*) Compute a new variable called INSCHOOL using the following numeric expression:

$$EDUC/AGE * 100.$$

This variable describes the percent of a respondent's life she or he has been in school. (Variables: EDUC, AGE)
  a. What is the mean on INSCHOOL for 1980 GSS young adults? (Select Cases: GROUP = 1)
  b. What is the mean on INSCHOOL for 2010 GSS young adults? (Select Cases: GROUP = 3)
  c. Summarize in a few well-written sentences totaling 50 words or less the similarities and/or differences in percentage of their lives 1980 and 2010 GSS young adults spent in school.

16. (*2010 GSS young adults*) This problem looks at the willingness of the 2010 GSS twentysomethings to let each of five possibly controversial persons teach college. (Variables: COLATH, COLCOM, COLGAY, COLMIL, COLRAC; Select Cases: GROUP = 3)
  a. List the five persons in order from the one 2010 GSS young adults were most willing to allow teach college to the one they were least willing to allow teach college. Next to each, indicate the percent of 2010 GSS young adults who would let that person teach college.
  b. [Figure 5.9 shows the percent of 1980 GSS young adults who would allow each to teach college: the gay (69.9%), the atheist (66.5%), the Communist (54.2%), the racist (51.7%), and the militarist (51.2%).] Summarize in a few well-written sentences totaling 50 words or less the similarities and/or differences in how the 1980 and 2010 GSS young adults ranked the five persons.

17. (*2010 GSS young adults*) Check the reliability for the twentysomethings who took part in the 2010 GSS of an index made up of the five "willing to let teach college" variables. (Variables: COLATH, COLCOM, COL-GAY, COLMIL, COLRAC; Select Cases: GROUP = 3)
  a. What is the value of Cronbach's alpha?
  b. Do the five items form an index with sufficient reliability?

18. (*2010 GSS middle-age adults*) Create an index called OKTEACH3, which is the mean of only these three variables: COLATH, COLCOM, and COLRAC. As long as a case has valid answers for at least two of the variables, SPSS should compute the new variable. (Variables: COLATH, COLCOM, COLRAC; Select Cases: GROUP = 4)
  a. How many 2010 GSS middle-age adults have valid values on OKTEACH3?
  b. What is the mean for 2010 GSS middle-age adults on OKTEACH3?

19. (*2010 GSS young adults*) This problem looks at the tolerance of the twentysomethings who took part in the 2010 GSS. (Select Cases: GROUP = 3)
  a. Of those five possibly controversial persons, what was the average number 2010 GSS young adults would
    i. allow to teach college? (Variable: OKTEACH)
    ii. allow to give public speeches? (Variable: OKSPEECH)
    iii. allow to have books in libraries? (Variable: OKBOOK)
  b. [Figures 5.13 and 5.14 show averages for the 1980 GSS young adults on OKTEACH of 2.97, on OKSPEECH of 3.60, and on OKBOOK of 3.73.] Summarize in a few well-written sentences totaling 50

words or less the similarities and/or differences in these two groups of twentysomethings, the 1980 GSS young adults and the 2010 GSS young adults, in letting persons teach college, give speeches, and have books in the library.

20. (*2010 GSS middle-age adults*) This problem looks at the tolerance of the fiftysomethings who took part in the 2010 GSS. (Select Cases: GROUP = 4)

   a. Of those five possibly controversial persons, what was the average number 2010 GSS middle-age adults would

      i. allow to teach college? (Variable: OKTEACH)

      ii. allow to give public speeches? (Variable: OKSPEECH)

      III. allow to have books in libraries? (Variable: OKBOOK)

   b. [Figures 5.13 and 5.14 show averages for the 1980 GSS young adults on OKTEACH of 2.97, on OKSPEECH of 3.60, and on OKBOOK of 3.73.] Summarize in a few well-written sentences totaling 50 words or less the similarities and/or differences in these two groups of baby boomers, the 1980 GSS young adults and the 2010 GSS middle-age adults, in letting persons teach college, give speeches, and have books in the library.

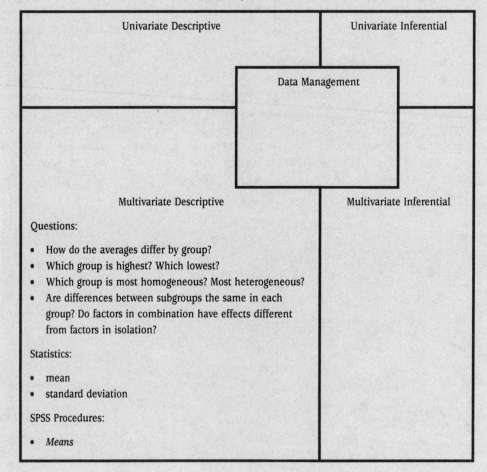

Questions and Tools for Answering Them
(Chapter 6)

Univariate Descriptive

Univariate Inferential

Data Management

Multivariate Descriptive

Multivariate Inferential

Questions:

- How do the averages differ by group?
- Which group is highest? Which lowest?
- Which group is most homogeneous? Most heterogeneous?
- Are differences between subgroups the same in each group? Do factors in combination have effects different from factors in isolation?

Statistics:

- mean
- standard deviation

SPSS Procedures:

- *Means*

Comparing Group Means 6

In this chapter, you can learn

- how groups formed by the attributes of one variable can then be compared in terms of their mean or standard deviation on some other variable,
- how those groups can themselves be subdivided based on the attributes of still another variable,
- how to judge the size of an independent variable's effect on the mean of a dependent variable, and
- how to see if the size and possibly even the direction of the effect of one independent variable on the mean of the dependent variable is influenced by another independent variable.

Differences by Region, Race, and Sex

Now that you know what the GSS groups were like on individual variables, it's time to start looking at the relationships between variables.

- How big were the regional differences in the willingness of 1980 GSS young adults to let controversial persons teach college? 1980 GSS young adults in which region expressed the greatest willingness? The least willingness?
- How did whites and blacks compare on years of schooling? How did women and men compare? And was the gender difference in schooling the same for blacks and for whites?

SPSS TIP

To Duplicate the Examples in This Chapter

To duplicate the examples in this chapter, use the *fourGroups.sav* data set. For the example in "Groups Based on One Variable," set the *Select Cases* condition to GROUP = 1. For the example in "Groups Based on More Than One Variable," set the *Select Cases* condition to GROUP = 1 and AGE >=25.

Overview

This chapter begins the multivariate descriptive section of the book. While our intent is still to describe only the cases for which we have data, the focus shifts from describing single variables to describing relationships between two or more variables. While the SPSS procedure introduced in this chapter provides only univariate statistics, the procedure requires two variables to work and labels them as dependent and independent variables.

The first examples in the chapter use the attributes of a single independent variable to create groups of cases and then compare these groups on a dependent variable. In this way, we can see how large or small the group differences are on the dependent variable. If all the groups have the same mean on the dependent variable, we say there's no relationship between the variables. If there are group differences, the variables are said to be related. Later in the chapter, we subdivide the groups based on the attributes of a second independent variable and again compare means on the dependent variable. With two independent variables, we can see if either or both are related to the dependent variable and if the relationship between one of the independent variables and the dependent variable actually changes depending on the value of the other independent variable.

The scores of the groups on the dependent variable can be compared using statistics other than the mean. For example, group comparisons based on standard deviations show which groups have greater internal differences on the dependent variable and which have less.

Remember that the existence of a statistical relationship between two variables does not prove there is a causal relationship. As noted in Chapter 1, a statistical relationship is only one of the three things that must be shown before you can say you have found a causal relationship.

Groups Based on One Variable

The SPSS procedure that compares group means is appropriately named *Means*. To use it, pull down the *Analyze* menu, move the cursor over *Compare Means*, and click on *Means*.

Analyze | Compare Means | Means

A box similar to Figure 6.1 will appear.

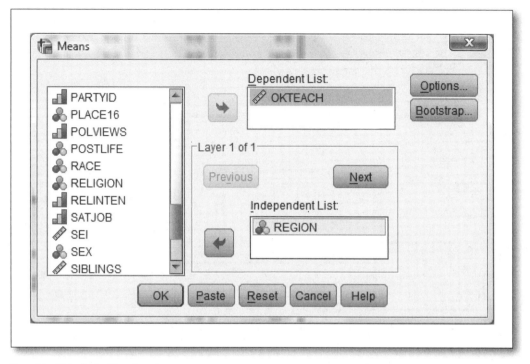

Figure 6.1   Dialog for the *Means* Procedure

You can begin by moving a variable into the "Dependent List." This will be the variable on which the groups will be compared. Since each group's mean on this variable will be calculated, this variable must be interval/ratio. In this example, the dependent variable will be the individual's score on the index OKTEACH. This is the index described in the last chapter. Scores range from 0 to 5, reflecting how many controversial persons the individual would let teach college.

Next, move a variable into the "Independent List." The attributes of the independent variable create the groups that will be compared. Independent variables in the *Means* procedure are sometimes referred to as factors. For this example, the independent variable or factor will be REGION. (REGION records the current place of residence of the GSS respondent. It is a nominal variable consisting of four categories: Northeast, Midwest, South, and West.) Although the variables moved into the "Independent List" field can be any level of measurement since it is only being used to create groups, analysts usually create groups using nominal or ordinal variables. When both independent and dependent variables are interval/ratio, there are usually better ways of looking at the relationship than the *Means* procedure. No matter what level of measurement variable is used to create groups, the variable should be discrete rather than continuous. Continuous variables typically use many attributes with just a few cases in each attribute. This results in an overly large number of groups. When this happens, the *Means* procedure produces statistically correct but practically useless output because there are so many small groups to compare.

If you click "Options," you will see the statistics SPSS can produce for each group. By default, SPSS shows the number of cases in each group and each group's mean and standard deviation on the dependent variable. Among the statistics available are each group's median, minimum, maximum, range, variance, and skewness.

Figure 6.2 shows the resulting output when 1980 GSS young adults from the four regions are compared on willingness to let controversial persons teach college.

Case Processing Summary

	Cases					
	Included		Excluded		Total	
	N	Percent	N	Percent	N	Percent
OKTEACH * REGION	296	90.5%	31	9.5%	327	100.0%

Report

OKTEACH

REGION	Mean	N	Std. Deviation
1 Northeast	3.25	60	1.723
2 Midwest	3.03	80	1.684
3 South	2.64	106	1.908
4 West	3.22	50	1.788
Total	2.97	296	1.802

Figure 6.2   *Means* Output for OKTEACH by REGION for 1980 GSS Young Adults

The "Case Processing Summary" provides information about valid and missing cases. Of the 1980 GSS young adults, 296 of 327 had valid data on both variables used in this analysis. There were 31 cases missing information on one or both variables and, therefore, excluded from the analysis.

The "Report" describes each of the groups separately and, in the row labeled "Total," all 296 cases combined. Looking over the means for the groups tells you a lot about the differences and similarities between regions. Keeping in mind that the index scores can range from 0 to 5, all four regions are fairly close together. The group means range from 2.64 to 3.25, a difference of just 0.61.

The 1980 GSS young adults in the Northeast and West were the most willing to let persons with possibly unpopular ideas teach college, followed by the Midwest, followed by the South.

The standard deviations, which are measures of dispersion, show that persons in the South were in more disagreement with one another on academic freedom than persons in the other regions, but once again, the regions do not show large differences here. The standard deviations for the regions are relatively similar.

RESEARCH TIP

Does Group Size Affect the Mean or Standard Deviation?

No, the value of the mean or the standard deviation is not affected by the size of the group. A small group can have a high or low mean just as easily as can a large group. A small group, as long as it has at least two members, can have a high or low standard deviation just as easily as can a large group.

RESEARCH TIP

Is It OK to Compare Different-Size Groups?

The size of the groups in Figure 6.2 varies considerably, with 106 persons from the South but only 50 persons from the West. Is it legitimate to compare groups of differing sizes? Yes, it is perfectly acceptable. There is no need to have equal-size groups when making comparisons!

CONCEPT CHECK

Without looking back, can you answer the following questions:

- The dependent variable in a *Means* procedure must be what level of measurement?
- Which column in the *Means* report gives you information about central tendency?
- Which column in the *Means* report gives you information about dispersion?

If not, go back and review before reading on.

Groups Based on More Than One Variable

The *Means* procedure and its logic can be taken further. Groups created from the attributes of one independent variable can then be divided into subgroups based on the attributes of a second independent variable. SPSS gives the name *layering* to this process of subdividing groups.

To illustrate, we will use highest year of school completed as the dependent variable, and we will layer the analysis first by race and then by gender. Since many persons in their early 20s are still in school, we will limit the analysis to persons age 25 and older. This is accomplished through the *Select Cases* procedure, which for this analysis selects cases if

$$GROUP = 1 \ and \ AGE >= 25.$$

Since the 1980 GSS young adults include persons only in their 20s, this *Select Cases* condition limits the analyses to those between the ages of 25 and 29.

Years of schooling completed is the dependent variable. The cases will first be divided by race; then each racial group will be further divided by gender. EDUC goes into the dependent list, and the variable RACE goes into the independent list. Notice the phrase "Layer 1 of 1," which appears above and to the left of the independent list. When you enter the variable that creates the first set of groups, the "Next" button becomes active. If you click on that button, the independent list becomes blank, and the phrase above that list changes to "Layer 2 of 2." Now you can enter the name of the variable that will subdivide the initial groups into subgroups. For this example, that variable is SEX. You can use "Previous" and "Next" to navigate between the layers of groups and subgroups. Once the dependent variable and all the layers of independent variables have been specified and the desired statistics selected, click OK. Figure 6.3 shows the results.

Note how the report is organized. The attributes of the variable that represents the first layer are listed at the left. To the right of those attributes are the attributes of the variable that forms the second layer. Look closely at that second column. Not only are there rows for white males and for white females, but those two rows are followed by a total row for whites. This row provides a summary for all the white 1980 GSS young adults, combining men and women together. The same sequence of male-female-total occurs for blacks. In the last part of the report, there are rows for total males and total females. These rows provide a summary for all the male respondents, combining both races together, and a summary for all the female respondents, again combining both races together. Next there is a row that could be described as a grand total. The last row in a *Means* procedure report always provides information on all of the respondents included in the analysis, which, in this case, combines both races and both genders.

When two or more independent variables have been layered, the *Means* procedure report contains lots of information if you know where to look for it. You get a description of all of the cases combined together (the total/total row), a description of the groups created by each independent variable separately (the white/total and black/total rows for RACE, the total/male and total/female rows for SEX), and a description of the subgroups created by combining the independent variables (the white/male, white/female, black/male, and black/female rows).

Report

EDUC

RACE	SEX	Mean	N	Std. Deviation
1 white	0 male	13.42	62	2.486
	1 female	13.07	85	2.267
	Total	13.22	147	2.360
2 black	0 male	11.50	4	2.517
	1 female	12.67	12	2.188
	Total	12.38	16	2.247
Total	0 male	13.30	66	2.511
	1 female	13.02	97	2.250
	Total	13.13	163	2.356

Figure 6.3   *Means* Output for EDUC by RACE by SEX for 1980 GSS Young Adults

RESEARCH TIP

Is It OK to Report Statistics for Small Groups?

Is it appropriate to report statistics based on just a few cases? After all, there are just 4 black males and 12 black females. Yes, it is appropriate if you are doing descriptive statistics.

As long as you really want to describe only the cases in your data set, then go ahead and describe them. If there are just 4 black males and their mean education is 11.50 years, then that is their mean, and there is nothing wrong with reporting it.

Now, if you want to draw conclusions about some larger population and your data are a sample, then you would have good reason to hesitate basing your conclusions about black males on just 4 cases or black females on just 12 cases, but when you are drawing conclusions about a larger population based on a sample, you are doing inferential statistics. We will take up inferential statistics in the last part of the book.

A number of questions can be answered from the information in Figure 6.3. From the very last line in the report, the grand total line, we see that 25- to 29-year-old 1980 GSS young adults averaged 13.13 years of schooling. (That is higher than the mean of 12.79 we saw in Chapter 4, but that earlier mean included the 20- to 24-year-old 1980 GSS young adults.)

The report also shows that overall, men averaged more schooling than women, and whites averaged more schooling than blacks. Among blacks, however, women had more schooling than men.

The standard deviations in Figure 6.3 indicate how much variability in educational level there was within the groups and subgroups. Overall, there was slightly more variability in schooling among whites than among blacks and more variability among males than among females.

When you are comparing group and subgroup means, you can talk about main effects and interaction effects. A **main effect** is the difference in means that you see when you create groups based on the attributes of just one variable. An **interaction effect** is the difference that you see in the size and/or direction of the effect of one of the independent variables on the dependent variable depending on the value of the other independent variable. Think of a drug interaction. A particular drug has one kind of effect on your health when you are not taking some other drug, but it has a very different effect on your health when you are taking that other drug. That is what is meant by an interaction.

In Figure 6.3, there is a main effect of gender on schooling because all the males combined have a different average education than all the females combined (compare the total/male and the total/female means). There is also a main effect of race because there are differences in the average education of all whites compared to all blacks (compare the white/total and the black/total means).

Furthermore, gender and race have an interaction effect because the size and direction of the gender gap in educational attainment differ by race (compare the difference in mean schooling between white/males and white/females to the difference between black/males and black/females). That same interaction is evidenced by the fact that the size of the race gap differs by gender (compare the difference in mean schooling between white/males and black/males to the difference between white/females and black/females).

An interaction effect does not require that both the direction and the size of subgroup differences differ between groups. A difference in either the direction or the size constitutes an interaction effect.

In some analyses, the main and interaction effects will be larger than you see here; in some analyses, smaller. Nevertheless, as long as there is some difference in group means, there is a main effect as far as descriptive statistics are concerned, and as long as there is some group difference in subgroup differences, there is an interaction effect as far as descriptive statistics are concerned.

Could there be no interaction effect present in an analysis? Yes. For example, had the gender gap been the same in each race or the racial differences the same in each gender, there would be no interaction effect. Could there be no main effect present in an analysis? Also, yes. Had each of the races, or each of the genders, the same average educational attainment, there would be no main effect present. These situations are rare in descriptive statistics, but they can happen. As long as there are even small differences, we can talk of main effects or interaction effects in the data. Whether those small differences are substantively important is not a statistical judgment but a substantive judgment best made by persons knowledgeable in the substantive area.

For most researchers, interaction effects trump main effects. That is, the presence of an interaction effect means the world is too complicated to describe in terms of simple main effects. In the previous example, does gender matter in regards to amount of schooling and, if so, how much?

The main effect tells you it does, but the interaction effect tells you that the nature of the effect of gender varies by race. To simply say that males on average have 0.28 more years of schooling ignores the fact that the magnitude and even the direction of the gender effect differ by race. Similarly, race matters in regards to the amount of schooling, but the presence of an interaction effect means a simple comparison of races is simplistic since the magnitude of the racial gap differs by gender.

Would you have gotten the same results in the problem if you had made SEX the first layer variable and RACE the second layer? Figure 6.4 shows the results when the *Means* procedure is set up this alternate way. SPSS gives you the same statistical information. The only difference is in layout. When SEX is the first layer, the first column in the report is the attributes of gender, and the second column is the attributes of race.

Report

EDUC

SEX	RACE	Mean	N	Std. Deviation
0 male	1 white	13.42	62	2.486
	2 black	11.50	4	2.517
	Total	13.30	66	2.511
1 female	1 white	13.07	85	2.267
	2 black	12.67	12	2.188
	Total	13.02	97	2.250
Total	1 white	13.22	147	2.360
	2 black	12.38	16	2.247
	Total	13.13	163	2.356

Figure 6.4 *Means* Output for EDUC by SEX by RACE for 1980 GSS Young Adults

Which layout is better depends on whether you want to focus on gender differences within race (in which case, Figure 6.3 is easier to use) or race differences within gender (in which case, Figure 6.4 is easier to use).

You are not limited to just two layers when constructing *Means* analyses. SPSS can take up to 10 layers. Obviously, the subgroups become quite numerous as you increase the number of layers. Correspondingly, interaction effects are not limited to the effect of two independent variables. A three-way interaction is when the effect of one independent variable on the dependent variable depends on the values of two other independent variables, a four-way interaction is when the effect of one independent variable on the dependent variable depends on the values of three other independent variables, and so on. The more variables involved in an interaction, the more difficult it becomes to understand and to describe to others.

CONCEPT CHECK

Without looking back, can you answer the following questions:

- What does layering independent variables do?
- What is a main effect?
- What is an interaction effect?

If not, go back and review before reading on.

1980 GSS Young Adults

The chapter began with some questions about 1980 GSS young adults. On the basis of our analyses, what do we now know?

- The four regions were relatively similar in their average willingness to let controversial persons teach college. 1980 GSS young adults in the Northeast and West were the most willing, while 1980 GSS young adults in the South were the least willing.
- Among 1980 GSS young adults ages 25 to 29, whites averaged more schooling than blacks. This white advantage was considerably larger among men than among women. Among whites, men averaged more schooling than women, but among blacks, it was women who averaged more schooling.

Important Concepts in the Chapter

interaction effect	main effect
layering	*Means* procedure

Practice Problems

1. What is the lowest level of measurement permissible in the *Means* procedure
   a. For the dependent variable, that is, the variable that is averaged for each group or subgroup?
   b. For the independent variables, that is, the variables whose attributes are used to create the groups and subgroups?

2. Which column in the *Means* procedure report would you check to find out which group
   a. Had the highest average on the dependent variable?
   b. Had the greatest internal differences on the dependent variable?
   c. Was most homogeneous in their scores on the dependent variable?
   d. Disagreed with one another the most on the dependent variable?
   e. Had the least variability on the dependent variable?
   f. Had the fewest cases?

3. When comparing groups,
   a. Will larger groups always have greater variance?
   b. Will larger groups always have greater means?

4. Explain each of the following:
   a. a main effect
   b. an interaction effect

5. (*2010 GSS middle-age adults*) Use this *Means* procedure output, which reports on willingness to allow controversial persons to give speeches, to answer the following questions about the fiftysomethings in the 2010 GSS:

Report

OKSPEECH

POLVIEWS	Mean	N	Std. Deviation
1 liberal	4.23	53	1.171
2 moderate	3.52	93	1.646
3 conservative	3.94	71	1.511
Total	3.83	217	1.519

   a. For the 2010 GSS middle-age adults,
      i. what was the mean for liberals?
      ii. what was the standard deviation for moderates?
      iii. how many conservatives were in the analysis?
      iv. what was the overall mean?

   b. Were the liberals, the moderates, or the conservatives
      i. most willing to let controversial persons give speeches?
      ii. least willing to let controversial persons give speeches?
      iii. most homogeneous in their opinions about letting controversial persons give speeches?
      iv. most heterogeneous in their opinions about letting controversial persons give speeches?

6. (*2010 GSS young adults*) Use this *Means* procedure output, which reports on willingness to allow the books of controversial persons to be in the library, to answer the following questions about the twentysomethings in the 2010 GSS:

Report

OKBOOK

REGION	SEX	Mean	N	Std. Deviation
1 Northeast	0 male	3.50	10	1.716
	1 female	4.17	18	1.098
	Total	3.93	28	1.359
2 Midwest	0 male	4.00	21	1.581
	1 female	4.53	30	1.042
	Total	4.31	51	1.304
3 South	0 male	3.56	25	1.609
	1 female	3.89	47	1.507
	Total	3.78	72	1.540
4 West	0 male	3.91	23	1.621
	1 female	3.65	23	1.695
	Total	3.78	46	1.645
Total	0 male	3.77	79	1.601
	1 female	4.05	118	1.407
	Total	3.94	197	1.490

a. What was the mean
   i. for 2010 GSS young women living in the Northeast?
   ii. for 2010 GSS young men (combining all regions together)?
b. What was the standard deviation
   i. for 2010 GSS young men living in the South?
   ii. for 2010 GSS young adults living in the West (combining men and women together)?
c. In which region (combining men and women together) was there the highest mean?
d. In which region(s) were men more varied than women?

7. (*2010 GSS middle-age adults*) Use this *Means* procedure output, which reports the number of hours worked for persons who worked the week prior to the survey, to answer the following questions about 2010 GSS middle-age adults:

Report

HOURS

REGION	SEX	Mean	N	Std. Deviation
1 Northeast	0 male	47.73	22	11.801
	1 female	39.86	21	13.108
	Total	43.88	43	12.934
2 Midwest	0 male	47.69	26	14.279
	1 female	42.25	36	15.015
	Total	44.53	62	14.841
3 South	0 male	45.57	46	12.799
	1 female	43.02	52	11.741
	Total	44.21	98	12.252
4 West	0 male	44.59	22	13.525
	1 female	40.25	28	9.505
	Total	42.16	50	11.529
Total	0 male	46.27	116	12.995
	1 female	41.77	137	12.435
	Total	43.83	253	12.867

a. Is there a main effect of region on number of hours worked? If so, describe it.
b. Is there a main effect of gender on number of hours worked? If so, describe it.
c. Is there an interaction effect of region and gender on number of hours worked? If so, describe it.

Problems Requiring SPSS and the *fourGroups.sav* Data Set

8. (*2010 GSS middle-age adults*) This problem looks at 2010 GSS fiftysomething regional differences in willingness to allow controversial persons to teach college. (Variables: OKTEACH, REGION; Select Cases: GROUP = 4)
   a. 2010 GSS middle-age adults in which region were
      i. most willing to allow controversial persons to teach? What was their mean?
      ii. least willing to allow controversial persons to teach? What was their mean?
   b. How large was the difference in means between the most and the least willing regions?
   c. Summarize in a few well-written sentences totaling 100 words or less what you found out about regional differences in willingness to allow controversial persons to teach college among the 2010 GSS middle-age adults.

9. (*1980 GSS young adults* and *2010 GSS young adults*) This problem compares the 1980 and 2010 GSS young adult regional differences in willingness to allow controversial persons to teach college. Use two layers for your *Means* procedure. (Variables: OKTEACH, GROUP, REGION; Select Cases: GROUP = 1 or GROUP = 3)
   a. What was the average number of controversial persons GSS young adults would let teach college
      i. in 1980?
      ii. in 2010?
   b. In which regions were GSS young adults
      i. more tolerant in 2010 than in 1980?
      ii. less tolerant in 2010 than in 1980?
   c. Summarize in a few well-written sentences totaling 100 words or less how willingness to let controversial persons teach college changed overall and by region between 1980 and 2010 for GSS young adults.

10. (*2010 GSS young adults*) This problem looks at differences in education by race among 25- to 29-year-olds who took part in the 2010 GSS. (Variables: EDUC, RACE; Select Cases: GROUP = 3 and AGE >= 25)
   a. Which racial group of 2010 GSS young adults has
      i. the highest mean years of schooling?
      ii. the lowest mean years of schooling?
      iii. the greatest variability in years of schooling?
   b. Summarize in a few well-written sentences totaling 100 words or less what you found out about the racial differences in education among 2010 GSS young adults.

11. (*2010 GSS young adults*) This problem looks at the gender gaps in education within races among 25- to 29-year-olds who took part in the 2010 GSS. (Variables: EDUC, RACE, SEX; Select Cases: GROUP = 3 and AGE >= 25)
   a. How large and in what direction (who is higher and who is lower) is the gender gap in years of schooling
      i. among white 2010 GSS young adults?
      ii. among black 2010 GSS young adults?
      iii. among 2010 GSS young adults who belong to some other race?
   b. [Figure 6.3 shows a gender gap in education of 0.35 years favoring males among white 1980 GSS young adults and a gender gap of 1.17 years favoring females among black 1980 GSS young adults.] Summarize in a few well-written sentences totaling 100 words or less the similarities and/or differences between the 1980 and 2010 young adults in the white gender gap in education and the similarities and/or differences between the 1980 and 2010 young adults in the black gender gap in education.

12. (*2010 GSS middle-age adults*) This problem looks at the effects of race and sex on education for the fiftysomethings in the 2010 GSS. (Variables: EDUC, RACE, SEX; Select Cases: GROUP = 4)
   a. Is there a main effect of race on years of schooling? If so, describe it.
   b. Is there a main effect of sex on years of schooling? If so, describe it.
   c. Is there an interaction effect of race and sex on years of schooling? If so, describe it.

13. (*2010 GSS middle-age adults*) Persons in their 50s have had just about all the children they are going to have. This problem looks at religious differences in number of children for the fiftysomething baby boomers in the 2010 GSS. (Variables: CHILDREN, RELIGION; Select Cases: GROUP = 4)
   a. 2010 GSS middle-age adults in which religion category
      i. have the largest average number of children? What is that average?
      ii. have the smallest average? What is that average?

b. How large is the difference between the religion category with the lowest and the highest averages?

c. In which religion category
    i. is there the largest variability in number of children?
    ii. is there the smallest variability?

d. Summarize in a few well-written sentences totaling 100 words or less what you found out about the religious differences in childbearing among 2010 GSS middle-age adults.

14. (*2010 GSS middle-age adults*) This problem looks at the relationship between educational degree and occupational prestige for the fiftysomethings in the 2010 GSS. Occupational prestige, the dependent variable, is measured using the SEI (socioeconomic index). Respondents are assigned an SEI score based on their current or most recent job. (Variables: SEI, DEGREE; Select Cases: GROUP = 4)

a. Summarize in a few well-written sentences totaling 100 words or less what you found out about the relationship between educational degree and occupational prestige for 2010 GSS middle-age adults.

15. (*2010 GSS middle-age adults*) This problem looks at the effects of educational degree and sex on occupational prestige for the fiftysomethings in the 2010 GSS. Occupational prestige is measured using the SEI (socioeconomic index). Respondents are assigned an SEI score based on their current or most recent job. (Variables: SEI, DEGREE, SEX; Select Cases: GROUP = 4)

a. Is there a main effect of educational degree on occupational prestige? If so, describe it.

b. Is there a main effect of sex on occupational prestige? If so, describe it.

c. Is there an interaction effect of educational degree and sex on occupational prestige? If so, describe it.

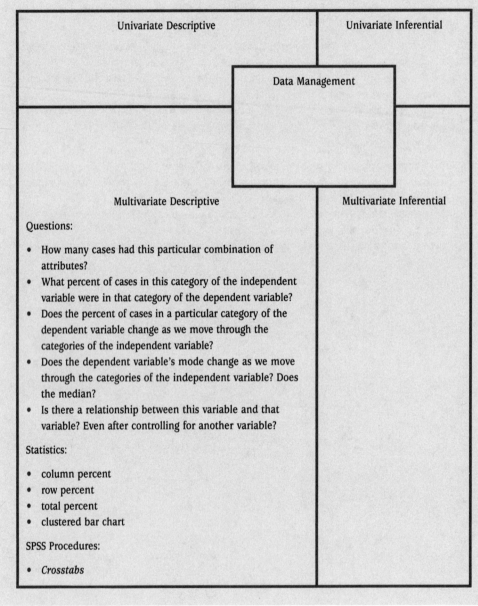

Questions and Tools for Answering Them
(Chapter 7)

Univariate Descriptive

Univariate Inferential

Data Management

Multivariate Descriptive

Questions:

• How many cases had this particular combination of attributes?
• What percent of cases in this category of the independent variable were in that category of the dependent variable?
• Does the percent of cases in a particular category of the dependent variable change as we move through the categories of the independent variable?
• Does the dependent variable's mode change as we move through the categories of the independent variable? Does the median?
• Is there a relationship between this variable and that variable? Even after controlling for another variable?

Statistics:

• column percent
• row percent
• total percent
• clustered bar chart

SPSS Procedures:

• *Crosstabs*

Multivariate Inferential

Crosstab Tables 7

In this chapter, you can learn

- how to create a table that classifies your cases based on each case's values on two or more variables;
- how to find out what percent of the cases in a column, in a row, or in the entire table are in a particular cell;
- how to determine if a case's value on the dependent variable is related to its value on the independent variable; and
- how to see how the relationship between two variables changes when controlling for a third variable.

Health and Happiness

In Chapter 4, we looked at the self-reported health of 1980 GSS young adults and at their overall happiness. This chapter asks some questions about the relationship between their health and happiness:

- Were 1980 GSS young adults who were in better health more likely to be very happy?
- Did happiness require at least "fair" health?
- Was the relationship between health and happiness the same for women and men?

SPSS TIP

To Duplicate the Examples in This Chapter

To duplicate the examples in this chapter, use the *fourGroups.sav* data set. Before doing any of the statistical procedures, set the select cases condition to GROUP = 1.

Overview

Crosstab tables, also known as crosstabulations or contingency tables, give you a way of looking at the relationship between two discrete variables. The attributes of one variable form the columns of the table, and the attributes of the other variable form the rows.

Crosstab tables are a common device for examining the relationship between two variables. As you will see in coming chapters, crosstab tables also form the basis for many other statistical tools. The variables used to create crosstab tables are always discrete and usually nominal or ordinal. Continuous variables have too many attributes to work well in crosstab tables, and interval/ratio variables, even when they are discrete, are usually analyzed using other statistical techniques.

Constructing Crosstab Tables

To construct a simple crosstab table, pull down the *Analyze* menu, move the cursor to *Descriptive Statistics,* and click *Crosstabs.*

Analyze | Descriptive Statistics | Crosstabs

A dialog similar to Figure 7.1 appears.

For a simple crosstab, you just move the variable whose attributes will define the columns into the "Column" list and the variable whose attributes will define the rows into the "Row" list. Once the column and row variables are specified, click OK.

If you are thinking of one of the variables as the independent variable and the other as the dependent variable, *develop the habit of making the independent variable the column variable and the dependent variable the row variable.* Most data analysts usually create crosstab tables in this way, and so does this book. Consistently making the independent variable the column variable makes it easier to interpret crosstabs, particularly when you are first learning data analysis. Realize, however, that SPSS doesn't care whether you make the independent variable the column or row variable, and crosstab tables you see outside of this book may have the independent variable's attributes defining either the columns or the rows.

For the first crosstab example, HEALTH is the independent variable and, therefore, the column variable; HAPPY is the dependent variable and, therefore, the row variable. Although how happy a person is may affect his or her health, the more common or greater influence probably flows from health to happiness. Figure 7.2 shows the output generated by the dialog in Figure 7.1.

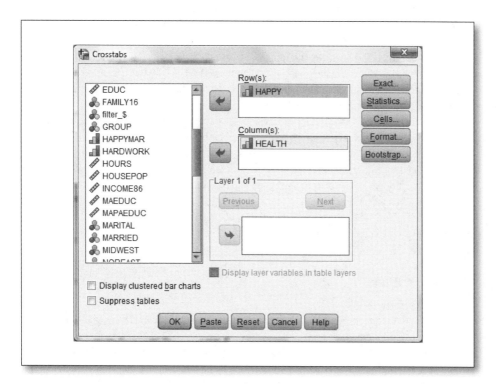

Figure 7.1   Dialog for Creating a Crosstab Table

HAPPY * HEALTH Crosstabulation

Count

		HEALTH				Total
		1 poor	2 fair	3 good	4 excellent	
HAPPY	1 not too happy	2	11	18	15	46
	2 pretty happy	1	22	93	69	185
	3 very happy	0	7	43	46	96
Total		3	40	154	130	327

Figure 7.2   *Crosstabs* Output for HAPPY by HEALTH for 1980 GSS Young Adults

The categories of HEALTH, the column variable, define the columns. The categories of the row variable, HAPPY, define the rows. The inside of the table is made up of cells. A cell is where a column and a row cross one another. Since there are four columns (do not count the one labeled "Total") and three rows (again, do not count the one labeled "Total"), there are 12 cells ($4 \times 3 = 12$). The column labeled "Total" and the row labeled "Total" are referred to as marginals because they occur on the margin or edge of the table.

The number in each cell shows the number of cases in the data set with that *combination* of attributes. For example, the 2 in the upper-left cell indicates that exactly two cases said "poor" when asked about their health and "not too happy" when asked about their general happiness. The numbers in the right-hand marginal are the total number of cases in each row, and the numbers in the bottom marginal are the total number of cases in each column. The number that appears in the bottom-right corner of the table is the total number of cases in the table.

So, which groups of respondents are most likely and least likely to say they are not too happy? The health category with the most persons saying "not too happy" was "good" health with 18, while the health category with the least not too happy persons was "poor" health with just 2, but that is 18 persons out of a group of 154 and 2 persons out of a group of 3. To answer questions about most likely, least likely, and simply how likely, you need percents. While you could calculate the percents yourself from the cell counts and marginals, SPSS can do the work for you.

Adding Percents

The initial *Crosstabs* dialog (Figure 7.1) includes a button labeled "Cells." When you click it, a dialog similar to Figure 7.3 appears.

SPSS can include many things in each cell of a crosstab table. By default, only the observed count (the number of cases with that combination of attributes) is shown. For now, just look at the options listed on the left under "Percentages." For each cell in the crosstabs, SPSS can calculate three different percents. You can ask for one, two, or all three of these by checking "Row," "Column," or "Total."

Row percents show the percent of cases in that row that are in that cell. The formula for calculating a row percent is

$$\text{row percent} = \frac{\text{cell count}}{\text{row total}} \times 100$$

Column percents show the percent of cases in that column that are in that cell. The formula for calculating a column percent is

$$\text{column percent} = \frac{\text{cell count}}{\text{column total}} \times 100$$

Total percents show the percent of cases in the entire table that are in that cell. The formula for calculating a total percent is

$$\text{total percent} = \frac{\text{cell count}}{\text{table total}} \times 100$$

The row total, the column total, and the table total are all in the marginals of the table.

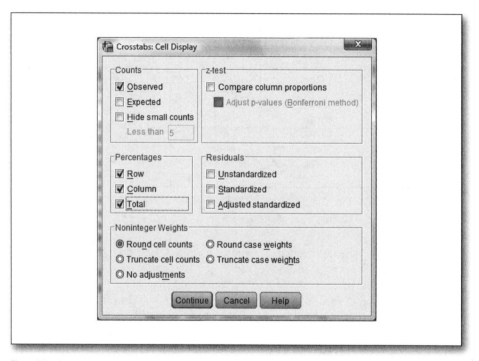

Figure 7.3   *Crosstabs* Dialog to Add Cell Percents

SPSS TIP

Total Percents

New SPSS users might assume a request for "total percents" is a request to calculate all of the available percents. It is not. Total percents refer to a specific calculation. They tell you of all the cases in the table what percent are in that cell.

Figure 7.4 shows the output for the crosstab table when all three percents have been requested.

			HEALTH				
			1 poor	2 fair	3 good	4 excellent	Total
HAPPY	1 not too happy	Count	2	11	18	15	46
		% within HAPPY	4.3%	23.9%	39.1%	32.6%	100.0%
		% within HEALTH	66.7%	27.5%	11.7%	11.5%	14.1%
		% of Total	.6%	3.4%	5.5%	4.6%	14.1%
	2 pretty happy	Count	1	22	93	69	185
		% within HAPPY	.5%	11.9%	50.3%	37.3%	100.0%
		% within HEALTH	33.3%	55.0%	60.4%	53.1%	56.6%
		% of Total	.3%	6.7%	28.4%	21.1%	56.6%
	3 very happy	Count	0	7	43	46	96
		% within HAPPY	.0%	7.3%	44.8%	47.9%	100.0%
		% within HEALTH	.0%	17.5%	27.9%	35.4%	29.4%
		% of Total	.0%	2.1%	13.1%	14.1%	29.4%
Total		Count	3	40	154	130	327
		% within HAPPY	.9%	12.2%	47.1%	39.8%	100.0%
		% within HEALTH	100.0%	100.0%	100.0%	100.0%	100.0%
		% of Total	.9%	12.2%	47.1%	39.8%	100.0%

HAPPY * HEALTH Crosstabulation

Figure 7.4   *Crosstabs* Output With Row, Column, and Total Percents for HAPPY by HEALTH for 1980 GSS Young Adults

The cells become easier to identify because more horizontal lines have been added. However, each cell now contains not only the observed count but also that cell's row, column, and total percents. Which percent is which? SPSS tells you, but it can still be a bit tricky to figure out. Look at the information just to the left of the cells. The first label is "Count," so the first entry in each cell is the observed count. The second label is "% within HAPPY." HAPPY is the row variable, so SPSS is telling you that the second entry in each cell is the row percent. The third label is "% within HEALTH." Since HEALTH is the column variable, the third entry in each cell is the column percent. The fourth label is "% of Total," which obviously tells you that the fourth entry in each cell is the total percent.

RESEARCH TIP

Which Percent Answers the Question?

If someone asks the following questions about the crosstab table in Figure 7.4, would you know which cell to go to and which percent to report?

- Of those in excellent health, what percent are very happy?
- Of those who are very happy, what percent are in excellent health?
- Of all the cases in the analysis, what percent are both in excellent health and very happy?

You probably know to go to the cell where the column labeled excellent and the row labeled very happy overlap, which is the cell with a count of 46, but which percent would you want: row, column, or total? The key is in the "of" phrase of the question. That phrase tells you if you are interested in a row, a column, or the entire table.

The first question includes the phrase "of those in excellent health." Persons in excellent health are represented by a column in this table, so you want column percents. The second question includes the phrase "of those who are very happy." Persons who are very happy are represented by a row in this table, so you want row percents. The third question's "of" phrase talks about all the cases in the analysis, which means you want total percents.

Describing Relationships Using Crosstab Tables

Do persons at different levels of health report different levels of happiness? To find out, you want to compare the happiness of persons in poor health, fair health, good health, and excellent health. Since those persons are respectively in the first, second, third, and fourth columns of the table, you will need to compare columns to see how happiness differs by health status. Row percents and total percents aren't relevant for examining the influence of the column (independent) variable on the row (dependent) variable and don't need to appear in the table. The table in Figure 7.5 will be easier to work with because row and total percents were not requested.

Here are three simple ways to illustrate the relationship between the independent and dependent variables as that relationship appears in a crosstab table. Later chapters will introduce more statistically precise ways of describing a relationship, but even then you often want to illustrate the relationship by using one of these simple methods.

HAPPY * HEALTH Crosstabulation

			HEALTH				
			1 poor	2 fair	3 good	4 excellent	Total
HAPPY	1 not too happy	Count	2	11	18	15	46
		% within HEALTH	66.7%	27.5%	11.7%	11.5%	14.1%
	2 pretty happy	Count	1	22	93	69	185
		% within HEALTH	33.3%	55.0%	60.4%	53.1%	56.6%
	3 very happy	Count	0	7	43	46	96
		% within HEALTH	.0%	17.5%	27.9%	35.4%	29.4%
Total		Count	3	40	154	130	327
		% within HEALTH	100.0%	100.0%	100.0%	100.0%	100.0%

Figure 7.5   *Crosstabs* Output With Column Percents for HAPPY by HEALTH for 1980 GSS Young Adults

Comparing Percents

The most common way of illustrating a relationship in a crosstab table is to examine how the column percent for a particular row changes as you move through the categories of the independent variable. For example, the percent of persons reporting they are "very happy" with their life overall is 0.0% for persons in poor health, 17.5% for persons in fair health, 27.9% for those in good health, and 35.4% for those in excellent health. The difference between the largest and smallest column percent in the row gives you a sense of the magnitude of the independent variable's effect on the dependent variable. In this case, there is a difference of 35.4 percentage points.

But which row do you use to compare the column percents of the independent variable categories? In some rows, the difference between the largest and smallest column percent may be small, but in other rows of the same table, the difference may be large. Reporting the difference in column percents for every row is usually more detail than most readers or listeners want. So, what row or rows do you select?

If certain categories of the dependent variable are of particular theoretical or substantive interest, report on those rows. Or you might report on the row with the largest differences in column percents and note that this was the largest difference and on the row with the smallest difference, noting that this was the category where the independent variable made the least difference.

If the dependent variable is ordinal or interval/ratio, most analysts will compare column percents using the first or the last category of the dependent variable. Comparing column percents for a middle category of a dependent variable with rank order is usually a bit frustrating for a reader or listener because the person is left wondering if most of the cases not in the reported category are in a higher or lower category. Reporting on the lowest ranking or highest ranking attribute of the dependent variable eliminates that problem.

RESEARCH TIP

Using the Correct Percents

If you want to know the influence of the independent variable on the dependent variable using percents, you must examine the correct percents. If you construct the crosstab following the guideline of making the independent variable the column variable, then you should be looking at column percents. Looking at row percents when the independent variable is the column variable will usually lead you to an incorrect conclusion. (If for some reason you make the independent variable the row variable, only then should you be looking at row percents.) A hopefully easy rule to remember is "Wherever you put your independent variable, those are the kind of percents you should be examining."

Comparing Modes

Another way of illustrating the relationship in a crosstab table is to note how the mode of the dependent variable changes as you move across the categories of the independent variable. This is a relatively crude method of comparison that is not as sensitive to small differences as a comparison of percents, but it is simple to do, and sometimes the simplest method has the greatest impact. It is also a method of comparison that can be done whatever the dependent variable's level of measurement.

Identifying the mode for each category of the independent variable is as simple as finding in each column the row with the largest column percent, which will also be the row with the largest observed count. Remember that the mode is an attribute of the dependent variable and not the value of the column percent or the cell count. In Figure 7.5, the mode for persons in poor health is "not too happy," whereas the modes for persons in fair, good, and excellent health are all "pretty happy."

If all the categories of the independent variable have the same mode on the dependent variable, then the independent variable must not exert great influence on the dependent variable. If the mode changes depending on the category of the independent variable, then the independent variable makes more of a difference.

Comparing Medians

If the attributes of the dependent variable have rank order, you could illustrate the relationship by noting how the dependent variable's median changes as you move through the categories of the independent variable. Like comparing modes, comparing medians tends to be less sensitive to small differences than comparing percents, but for ordinal and interval/ratio dependent variables, it does make use of the natural order present in the categories of the dependent variable—something a comparison of modes ignores.

A comparison of medians takes a bit more work on your part. Starting at the top of each column, add the column percents until they total 50% or more. The category whose percent first gets you to 50 or higher contains the median or middle case. (What you are doing is calculating cumulative percents just as they would appear in a frequency table.) Remember that if in totaling the column percents you hit 50% exactly, then the median is between that category of the dependent variable and the next category.

As when comparing modes, unchanging medians suggest at most only a weak relationship between the independent and dependent variables, whereas changing medians suggest a stronger relationship. Using Figure 7.5, you can see that 1980 GSS young adults in poor health had a median level of happiness of "not too happy," while 1980 GSS young adults in fair, good, and excellent health all had "pretty happy" as their median. This suggests a relationship between health and happiness but not a particularly strong one.

If the dependent variable were interval/ratio, could we compare means for the different categories of the independent variable? Sure! But doing that from crosstabs output requires more calculation than comparing medians, and besides, comparing means for the categories of the independent variable is exactly what the *Means* procedure does.

CONCEPT CHECK

Without looking back, can you answer the following questions:

- What is the difference between a column percent and a row percent?
- Why are column percents more useful than row percents for seeing if the column (independent) variable affects the row (dependent) variable?
- How can comparing percents indicate the independent variable's effect on the dependent variable?
- How can you use column percents to identify the median?

If not, go back and review before reading on.

Clustered Bar Charts

The *Crosstabs* procedure provides an easy way to request a chart to visually display the information in a crosstab table. A **clustered bar chart** can be requested by simply checking the box on the initial *Crosstabs* procedure dialog (Figure 7.1). A clustered bar chart is like several small bar charts (see Chapter 3) combined into a single graphic. Figure 7.6 shows a clustered bar chart for the relationship between health and happiness for 1980 GSS young adults. There is a small bar chart for each category of health. You can see how persons in poor health, fair health, good health, and excellent health answered the happiness question.

The bar charts are much bigger for persons in good health and excellent health because many more 1980 GSS young adults reported being in good or excellent health. More important, as far as the relationship between the variables is concerned, you can see for each health group how they answered the overall happiness question. It is easy to spot the modal level of happiness for each health group since the mode is the tallest bar in each cluster. In fact, you can rank the levels of happiness from most to least common for each health group.

Chart Builder, which appears in the *Graphs* pull-down menu, is an SPSS procedure not covered in this book but certainly worth investigating. It allows you to customize clustered bar charts to show specific aspects of the relationship between variables. For example, the height of the bars can be set to correspond to column percents, thereby giving visual impact to the comparison of percents. The clustered bar chart option built into the *Crosstabs* procedure is not so versatile. The height of the bars corresponds to the observed counts in the crosstab table and cannot be converted to column percents.

An even more serious limitation of the clustered bar chart function built into *Crosstabs* is that it creates small bar charts for each category of the row variable. It is comparing the rows in the crosstab! Since the custom in the social sciences is to make the independent variable the column variable,

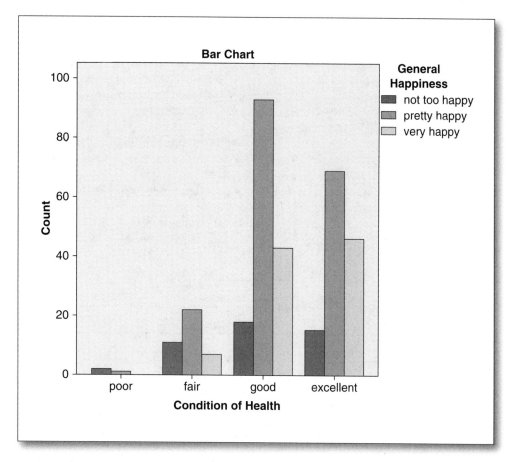

Figure 7.6   Clustered Bar Chart of HAPPY by HEALTH for 1980 GSS Young Adults

the *Crosstabs* clustered bar chart function is initially grouping cases based on the wrong variable. We want to compare columns, not rows, because it is the columns that represent different categories of the independent variable.

To overcome this limitation, you should do a second *Crosstabs* procedure if, after looking at a crosstab table, you decide you want a clustered bar chart. For this second *Crosstabs* procedure, (1) check "Display clustered bar charts" on the initial *Crosstabs* dialog, (2) check "Suppress tables" on that same dialog, and (3) make your independent variable your row variable and your dependent variable your column variable. That is how the clustered bar chart in Figure 7.6 was created. *Making the independent variable the row variable and the dependent variable the column variable violates our previous guideline for constructing crosstabs and only should be done for these clustered bar charts!*

Layering

You can layer a crosstab analysis just like you layer a *Means* analysis. Below the "Column(s)" list on the initial *Crosstabs* dialog is a field within a box labeled "Layer 1 of 1." Putting a variable in that field produces a separate crosstab table for each category of your layering variable. Figure 7.7 shows the output produced when HEALTH is the column variable, HAPPY is the row variable, and SEX is the Layer 1 variable.

The output actually consists of three entirely separate crosstabs. The first crosstab includes only males, the second includes only females, and the third combines males and females. The statistics in each crosstab are based just on the cases in that table.

Layering a crosstab allows you to examine the relationship between the independent and dependent variables for separate groups of cases. This is one way of introducing a control variable into the analysis.

Imagine you tell someone based on a comparison of percents or modes or medians that a person's health affects his or her happiness, and the person responds that the relationship between

HAPPY * HEALTH * SEX Crosstabulation					HEALTH				
SEX				1 poor	2 fair	3 good	4 excellent	Total
0 male	HAPPY	1 not too happy	Count	1	2	9	6	18
			% within HEALTH	50.0%	18.2%	13.6%	11.1%	13.5%
		2 pretty happy	Count	1	7	41	33	82
			% within HEALTH	50.0%	63.6%	62.1%	61.1%	61.7%
		3 very happy	Count	0	2	16	15	33
			% within HEALTH	.0%	18.2%	24.2%	27.8%	24.8%
	Total		Count	2	11	66	54	133
			% within HEALTH	100.0%	100.0%	100.0%	100.0%	100.0%
1 female	HAPPY	1 not too happy	Count	1	9	9	9	28
			% within HEALTH	100.0%	31.0%	10.2%	11.8%	14.4%
		2 pretty happy	Count	0	15	52	36	103
			% within HEALTH	.0%	51.7%	59.1%	47.4%	53.1%
		3 very happy	Count	0	5	27	31	63
			% within HEALTH	.0%	17.2%	30.7%	40.8%	32.5%
	Total		Count	1	29	88	76	194
			% within HEALTH	100.0%	100.0%	100.0%	100.0%	100.0%
Total	HAPPY	1 not too happy	Count	2	11	18	15	46
			% within HEALTH	66.7%	27.5%	11.7%	11.5%	14.1%
		2 pretty happy	Count	1	22	93	69	185
			% within HEALTH	33.3%	55.0%	60.4%	53.1%	56.6%
		3 very happy	Count	0	7	43	46	96
			% within HEALTH	.0%	17.5%	27.9%	35.4%	29.4%
	Total		Count	3	40	154	130	327
			% within HEALTH	100.0%	100.0%	100.0%	100.0%	100.0%

Figure 7.7 *Crosstabs* Output for HAPPY by HEALTH by SEX for 1980 GSS Young Adults

health and happiness is spurious, that is, false. This person asserts that what really determines happiness is a person's gender. He claims that if you control for gender, the apparent relationship between health and happiness would disappear. The critic suggests the only reason there seems to be a relationship between health and happiness is because females are happier than males and females also happen to be healthier than males. The critic claims that if you just compare males to one another or just compare females to one another, persons at different health levels will appear equally happy.

By layering the crosstab with the variable SEX, you are able to look separately at males and females. If your critic is correct, there should be no relationship between health and happiness among males or among females when each gender is examined separately.

Overall, the evidence from Figure 7.7 does not support the critic. The relationship between health and happiness remains essentially the same even after controlling for gender. For men and women, the percent saying they are very happy goes up and the percent saying they are not very happy goes down as health improves. The pattern of modes and medians is the same as we saw before with the sole exception that the happiness of males in poor health is bimodal with a median that falls between not very happy and pretty happy.

The statistical relationship between health and happiness is not explained away by taking gender into account. However, fighting off one challenge to the authenticity of the relationship between health and happiness does not conclusively prove that the relationship is nonspurious. It still may be spurious. We may simply not have controlled for the right other variable(s). Perhaps the relationship disappears if age or education or some other variable is controlled. Nevertheless, our confidence in the relationship between health and happiness is at least slightly strengthened by showing that the relationship remains even when we control for gender.

When layering crosstabs, be careful what you ask for. Introducing a layering variable increases the number of tables you get but decreases the number of cases in each table. When the layering variable is a dichotomy, it produces just two tables plus a total table, but if the layering variable has eight categories, you would get eight tables plus a total table. If you specify a second layer variable, you get a separate crosstab for every combination of attributes for the first and second layer variables. As the number of crosstabs increases, the number of cases in each crosstab decreases, making it more difficult to determine the effect of the control variable(s) on the original relationship.

CONCEPT CHECK

Without looking back, can you answer the following questions:

- In a clustered bar chart, why should the cases first be clustered by categories of the independent variable?
- How can layering reveal if the relationship between the original two variables was spurious or not?

If not, go back and review before reading on.

1980 GSS Young Adults

The chapter began with some questions about 1980 GSS young adults. On the basis of our analyses, what do we now know?

- The better the self-reported health of the 1980 GSS young adults, the more likely they were to say they were very happy and the less likely they were to say they were not too happy. However, the relationship between health and happiness does not appear to be very strong. Whether persons were in fair, good, or excellent health, pretty happy was their mode and their median.
- No one in poor health said they were very happy. It should be noted, however, that only three 1980 GSS young adults described themselves as being in poor health.
- The relationship between health and happiness for 1980 GSS young adults was very similar for men and women. The better one's health, the happier one's life.

Important Concepts in the Chapter

clustered bar chart

column percent

control variable

column variable

Crosstabs procedure

dependent variable

independent variable

layering variable

row percent

row variable

total percent

Practice Problems

1. For a *Crosstabs* procedure, what is the lowest level of measurement permissible for
   a. a column variable?
   b. a layer variable?
   c. a row variable?

2. A crosstab is created with the independent variable as the column variable and the dependent variable as the row variable. To determine the effect of the independent variable on the dependent variable, should you use column percents, row percents, total percents, or doesn't it matter which percents you use?

3. (*2010 GSS young adults*) Calculate the missing values in this crosstab table.

POSTLIFE * RACE Crosstabulation

| | | | RACE | | | |
			1 white	2 black	3 other	Total
POSTLIFE	0 no	Count	40	4	9	53
		% within POSTLIFE	aaaa%	7.5%	17.0%	100.0%
		% within RACE	bbbb%	6.3%	25.0%	17.7%
		% of Total	cccc%	1.3%	3.0%	17.7%
	1 yes	Count	161	59	27	dddd
		% within POSTLIFE	65.2%	23.9%	10.9%	100.0%
		% within RACE	80.1%	93.7%	75.0%	82.3%
		% of Total	53.7%	19.7%	9.0%	82.3%
Total		Count	201	63	36	eeee
		% within POSTLIFE	67.0%	21.0%	12.0%	100.0%
		% within RACE	100.0%	100.0%	100.0%	100.0%
		% of Total	67.0%	21.0%	12.0%	100.0%

a. aaaa = ?

b. bbbb = ?

c. cccc = ?

d. dddd = ?

e. eeee = ?

4. (*2010 GSS middle-age adults*) Use this crosstab table to answer the following questions about 2010 GSS fiftysomethings:

CHILDREN * RACE Crosstabulation

| | | | RACE | | | |
			1 white	2 black	3 other	Total
CHILDREN	0	Count	52	5	6	63
		% within RACE	17.3%	8.8%	28.6%	16.7%
	1	Count	48	13	3	64
		% within RACE	16.0%	22.8%	14.3%	16.9%
	2	Count	109	11	8	128
		% within RACE	36.3%	19.3%	38.1%	33.9%
	3	Count	48	17	1	66
		% within RACE	16.0%	29.8%	4.8%	17.5%
	4	Count	23	6	1	30
		% within RACE	7.7%	10.5%	4.8%	7.9%
	5	Count	13	3	1	17
		% within RACE	4.3%	5.3%	4.8%	4.5%
	6	Count	3	1	0	4
		% within RACE	1.0%	1.8%	.0%	1.1%
	7	Count	1	0	0	1
		% within RACE	.3%	.0%	.0%	.3%
	8 eight or more	Count	3	1	1	5
		% within RACE	1.0%	1.8%	4.8%	1.3%
Total		Count	300	57	21	378
		% within RACE	100.0%	100.0%	100.0%	100.0%

   a. What percent
     i. of whites have had no children?
     ii. of blacks have had no children?
     iii. of others have had no children?
   b. What is the modal number of children
     i. for whites?
     ii. for blacks?
     iii. for others?
   c. What is the median number of children
     i. for whites?
     ii. for blacks?
     iii. for others?

5. (*2010 GSS young adults*) Does this table support the claim that for 2010 GSS young adults, blacks tend to be more strongly affiliated to a religion than whites? State a verbal conclusion. Then state the numerical information in the table that justifies your answer:

RELINTEN * RACE Crosstabulation

			RACE			
			1 white	2 black	3 other	Total
RELINTEN	0 no religion	Count	66	15	13	94
		% within RACE	30.6%	21.7%	37.1%	29.4%
	1 not very strong	Count	97	28	10	135
		% within RACE	44.9%	40.6%	28.6%	42.2%
	2 strong	Count	53	26	12	91
		% within RACE	24.5%	37.7%	34.3%	28.4%
Total		Count	216	69	35	320
		% within RACE	100.0%	100.0%	100.0%	100.0%

6. (*1980 GSS middle-age adults*) Summarize in a few sentences totaling less than 100 words what this clustered bar chart reveals about the strength of affiliation to a religion of male and female GSS fiftysomethings in 1980.

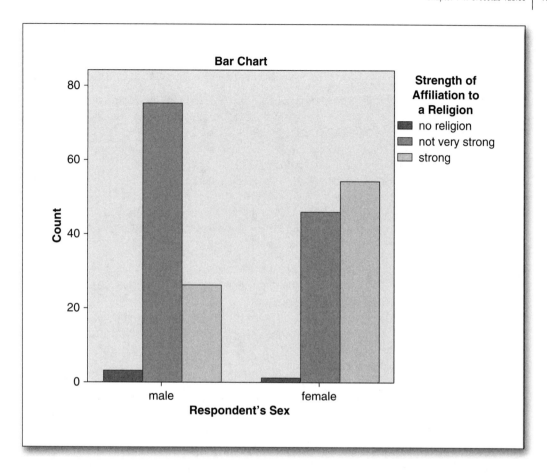

Bar Chart

Problems Requiring SPSS and the *fourGroups.sav* Data Set

7. *(2010 GSS young adults)* This problem looks at the relationship between health and happiness for the 2010 GSS twentysomethings. Health is the independent variable. (Variables: HEALTH, HAPPY; Select Cases: GROUP = 3)
   a. What percent of 2010 GSS young adults
      i. in excellent health reported being very happy?
      ii. in poor health reported being very happy?
   b. How large is the difference in percent very happy between those in excellent health and those in poor health?
   c. Do a separate *Crosstabs* procedure to create a clustered bar chart for 2010 GSS young adults with the cases clustered by level of health and, within each cluster, bars to represent the levels of happiness.

d. [Figure 7.5 shows for the 1980 GSS young adults that 35.4% of those in excellent health were very happy but 0.0% of those in poor health were very happy. This is a difference of 35.4 percentage points.] Summarize in a few well-written sentences totaling 100 words or less the similarities and/or differences in the relationship between health and happiness for the 1980 and 2010 GSS young adults.

8. (*2010 GSS young adults* and *2010 GSS middle-age adults*) This problem compares the relationship between health and happiness for the 2010 GSS twentysomethings and the 2010 GSS fiftysomethings. Health is the independent variable. (Variables: HEALTH, HAPPY, GROUP; Select Cases: GROUP = 3 or GROUP = 4)
   a. What percent of the 2010 GSS young adults in excellent health reported being very happy? What percent in poor health reported being very happy? How large is the difference?
   b. What percent of 2010 GSS middle-age adults in excellent health reported being very happy? What percent in poor health reported being very happy? How large is the difference?
   c. Summarize in a few well-written sentences totaling 100 words or less what you found out about differences in the relationship between health and happiness for 2010 GSS twentysomethings and fiftysomethings.

9. (*2010 GSS middle-age adults*) This problem looks at the relationship between religious affiliation and happiness for the 2010 GSS fiftysomethings. Religious affiliation is the independent variable. (Variables: RELIGION, HAPPY; Select Cases: GROUP = 4)
   a. As you move through the five religious groups (include "none" as a religious affiliation group),
      i. does the percent saying they are very happy change?
      ii. does the modal level of happiness change?
      iii. does the median level of happiness change?
   b. Do a separate *Crosstabs* procedure to create a clustered bar chart for 2010 GSS middle-age adults with the cases clustered by religious affiliation and, within each cluster, bars to represent the levels of happiness.
   c. Summarize in a few well-written sentences totaling 100 words or less what you found out about the relationship between religious affiliation and happiness for 2010 GSS middle-age adults.

10. (*2010 GSS young adults*) This problem looks at the relationship between political orientation and happiness for the 2010 GSS twentysomethings. Political orientation is the independent variable. (Variables: POLVIEWS, HAPPY; Select Cases: GROUP = 3)
   a. As you move through the political orientations,
      i. does the percent saying they are very happy change?
      ii. does the modal level of happiness change?
      iii. does the median level of happiness change?
   b. Do a separate *Crosstabs* procedure to create a clustered bar chart for 2010 GSS young adults with the cases clustered by political orientation and, within each cluster, bars to represent the levels of happiness.
   c. Summarize in a few well-written sentences totaling 100 words or less what you found out about the relationship between political orientation and happiness for 2010 GSS young adults.

11. (*2010 GSS middle-age adults*) This problem looks at the relationship between marital status and happiness for the 2010 GSS fiftysomethings. Marital status is the independent variable. Be sure to use the variable MARRIED. (Variables: MARRIED, HAPPY; Select Cases: GROUP = 4)
   a. As you move through the three marital status categories,
      i. does the percent saying they are very happy change?
      ii. does the modal level of happiness change?
      iii. does the median level of happiness change?

b. Do a separate *Crosstabs* procedure to create a clustered bar chart for 2010 GSS middle-age adults with the cases clustered by marital status and, within each cluster, bars to represent the levels of happiness.

c. Summarize in a few well-written sentences totaling 100 words or less what you found out about the relationship between marital status and happiness for 2010 GSS middle-age adults.

12. (*2010 GSS middle-age adults*) This problem looks at the relationship between marital status and happiness controlling for sex for the 2010 GSS fiftysomethings. Marital status is the independent variable. Be sure to use the variable MARRIED. (Variables: MARRIED, HAPPY, SEX; Select Cases: GROUP = 4)

a. Males in which marital status are most likely to say they are very happy? Males in which marital status are least likely to say they are very happy? How large is the percentage point difference?

b. Females in which marital status are most likely to say they are very happy? Females in which marital status are least likely to say they are very happy? How large is the percentage point difference?

c. Summarize in a few well-written sentences totaling 100 words or less what you found out about gender differences in the relationship between marital status and happiness for 2010 GSS middle-age adults.

13. (*all four groups*) This problem compares the political orientations of 1980 and 2010 young and middle-age GSS groups. Group is the independent variable. (Variables: GROUP, POLVIEWS; Select Cases: all cases)

a. Which GSS group had the highest percent

    i. conservative?

    ii. moderate?

    iii. liberal?

b. Summarize in a few well-written sentences totaling 100 words or less the similarities and/or differences in the political orientations of these four GSS groups.

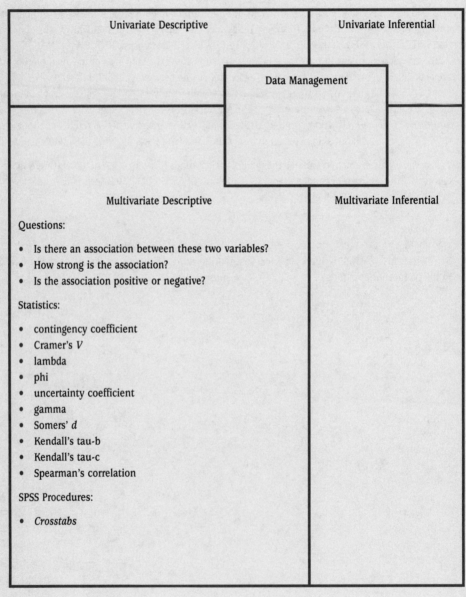

Questions and Tools for Answering Them
(Chapter 8)

Univariate Descriptive

Univariate Inferential

Data Management

Multivariate Descriptive

Multivariate Inferential

Questions:

- Is there an association between these two variables?
- How strong is the association?
- Is the association positive or negative?

Statistics:

- contingency coefficient
- Cramer's V
- lambda
- phi
- uncertainty coefficient
- gamma
- Somers' d
- Kendall's tau-b
- Kendall's tau-c
- Spearman's correlation

SPSS Procedures:

- *Crosstabs*

Nominal and Ordinal Measures of Association

In this chapter, you can learn

- how the relationship between variables in a crosstab table can be summarized by a measure of association,
- how to describe the strength of an association,
- how to describe the direction of an association, and
- how selecting an appropriate measure of association depends on the level of measurement.

Work and Gender, Degree and Happiness

In this chapter, we continue to see how the characteristics of 1980 GSS young adults are related:

- How much more likely were men than women to be working full-time? How much more likely were women than men to be keeping house? Overall, how strong was the association between gender and primary work activity?
- Were persons with bachelor degrees happier than persons with just high school degrees? In general, was there a positive association between educational degree and happiness? How strong was the association?

SPSS TIP

To Duplicate the Examples in This Chapter

To duplicate the examples in this chapter, use the *fourGroups.sav* data set. Before doing any of the statistical procedures, set the select cases condition to GROUP = 1.

Overview

In Chapter 6, the *Means* procedure was used to describe the relationship between two variables, and in Chapter 7, percentages, medians, and modes from *Crosstabs* were used to describe the relationship between two variables. Those ways of describing a relationship involve comparing categories of the independent variable. They all go something like this: "Cases in this category of the independent variable have this mean (or median or mode or percent giving this answer) on the dependent variable, but cases in this other category of the independent variable have this other mean (or median or mode or percent) on the dependent variable." If there is no difference in the means or medians or modes or percents, the two variables are said to be not related. If there are differences, they are related. The bigger the differences are, the greater is the relationship between the two variables.

Describing relationships in that way provides a sense of what is going on between the variables but has some real limitations. Depending on what part of the crosstab table you focus on, the relationship between two variables may look quite different. For example, there could be only small differences among health groups in the percent saying they are not too happy but much larger differences in the percent saying they are very happy. Or the difference may be large between the region with the highest average respect for academic freedom and the region with the lowest, implying that regional differences are sizable, but it may be just one region that is really different from all the others, which are quite similar. While all of these complications can be explained to readers or listeners, it takes time.

Data analysts want a concise way of describing as much of the relationship between two variables as possible. The measures of association described in this and the next chapter are their solution. A **measure of association** is a single number that describes the strength of the relationship between two variables. If both variables are at least ordinal, the measure of association describes both the strength and the direction of the relationship.

About Measures of Association

Many Choices

Statisticians over the decades have developed many different measures of association. Each of them in a slightly different way mathematically measures the relationship between variables. This chapter introduces some of the most frequently used measures. You should become familiar with every measure introduced in this chapter. You could easily encounter any one of them in reading reports or research articles in your professional field.

There is no "perfect" statistical measure of association. If there were a perfect measure, there would not be dozens of options. Each measure of association is designed to detect a certain type of mathematical association. That means that each measure has blind spots, certain types of relationships that it does not detect. Usually, these blind spots are small but not always. Some of the more important limitations will be pointed out in the discussion of particular statistics.

RESEARCH TIP

Choosing Which Measure of Association to Use

As this chapter explains, the level of measurement of your variables limits your choice of a measure of association, but it usually does not limit it to only one. In most situations, there will be more than one measure of association you could use.

It is unethical for a researcher to calculate many different measures of association for a particular relationship and then only report the measure of association that comes closest to what the researcher hoped the relationship would be. Researchers should decide which measure of association they will use before they see the actual value of the statistic.

When a single measure of association is needed in this text, Cramer's *V* will be used if a nominal measure of association is called for, Kendall's tau-b if an ordinal measure of association, and Pearson's *r* if an interval/ratio measure of association. (Cramer's *V* and Kendall's tau-b are discussed in this chapter, Pearson's *r* in the next.) Ask your instructor which measures of association you should use.

Levels of Measurement

Choosing a measure of association to describe the relationship between two variables depends on the level of measurement of the two variables. Some measures of association only assume that the attributes that make up each of the variables are different. These are referred to as **nominal measures of association**. **Ordinal measures of association** assume that the attributes that make up each of the variables are not only different but have rank order. Finally, **interval/ratio measures of** association assume that the attributes that make up each of the variables are different, have rank order, and represent a numerical scale.

So, to decide which measure of association to use, or to decide if someone else has chosen a measure of association correctly, you must know the level of measurement of the two variables involved in the relationship. In particular, you need to know the lower level of measurement of the two variables. It is the lower level of measurement that determines which measure of association you use. If one of the two variables is nominal, then you must use a nominal measure of association regardless of the other variable's level of measurement. If neither variable is nominal but one or both of the variables is ordinal, you use an ordinal measure of association. Only if both variables are interval/ratio do you use an interval/ratio level of measurement.

Nominal and ordinal measures of association are explained in this chapter. An interval/ratio measure of association will be presented in the next chapter.

Strength of a Relationship

All measures of association indicate the strength of the relationship between the two variables. When two variables are strongly related to one another, the probability of a case having a certain attribute on the second variable varies quite a bit depending on the case's attribute on the first variable. When the relationship between two variables is strong, knowing a case's score on the first variable substantially improves accuracy in predicting its score on the second variable. For example, most married couples are quite similar to one another in age. If you have a data set in which the cases represent married couples and one variable in the data set is husband's age and another variable is wife's age, you would probably find a strong relationship between those two variables.

When two variables are weakly related, however, the probability of a case having a particular attribute on the second variable is about the same regardless of what its attribute is on the first variable. Knowing a case's score on the first variable does not typically improve the accuracy of a guess about its score on the second variable. Although married couples resemble one another on many things, they probably do not resemble one another on day of the week on which they were born. Society does not give much importance to that trait. So, if you also have in that data set of married couples a variable for day of the week on which the husband was born and day of the week on which the wife was born, you would probably find at most only a very weak statistical relationship between the two.

For almost all measures of association, the closer the value of the statistic to zero, the weaker the relationship between the two variables, and the further from zero, the stronger the relationship. Another way of saying the same thing is the greater the absolute value of the measure of association, the greater the strength of the relationship between the two variables. Most nominal measures of association range from 0.00 to 1.00. Most ordinal and interval/ratio measures of association range from –1.00 to 1.00.

MATH TIP

Absolute Value

The absolute value of a number is its distance from zero on the number line. For positive numbers, the absolute value is the number itself. For example, the absolute value of 5 is 5. For negative numbers, the absolute value is the number without the negative sign. For example, the absolute value of –3 is 3.

So, what constitutes a strong relationship? What constitutes a weak relationship? If the value of a measure of association is 0.37, is that strong? Is that weak? Unfortunately, there are no accepted guidelines for what constitutes strong or weak. Analysts differ in their use of those adjectives. In part, it is a matter of personal preference, but it is also a matter of how large previously discovered relationships in the substantive area have been. For example, if no previously reported predictor of job satisfaction correlated with job satisfaction at more than 0.20 and you find a predictor that correlates at 0.37, you would be inclined to call it a strong relationship. However, if several previously reported predictors of job satisfaction correlated with job satisfaction in the 0.60 to 0.70 range, you should think twice before calling your 0.37 relationship strong.

Even though no consensus exists among data analysts about how to describe the strength of associations, communication in this book will be clearer and your task of learning data analysis will be easier if a set of standards is adopted for describing strength. Table 8.1 shows the criteria used for this text. Your instructor may provide different guidelines.

Table 8.1   Guide for Describing the Strength of a Relationship

If the Absolute Value of a Measure of Association Is:	The Relationship Will Be Described As:
.000	No relationship
.001 to .199	Weak
.200 to .399	Moderate
.400 to .599	Strong
.600 to .999	Very strong
1.000	Perfect relationship

Direction of a Relationship

Ordinal and interval/ratio measures of association indicate not only the strength of a relationship but also its direction. Relationships between ordinal and interval/ratio variables are either positive or negative. When two variables are positively related, high scores on one variable tend to coincide with high scores on the other variable, medium scores on one variable go with medium scores on the other, and low scores go with low scores. Put differently, when two variables are positively related, an increase in a case's score on one variable results in an increase in that case's score on the second variable, whereas a decrease in a case's score on the first variable results in a decrease in its score on the second variable. An example of two variables that most instructors believe are positively related would be hours spent studying for a test and test grade. Persons who study more get higher grades; persons who study less get lower grades. The important thing to understand when two variables are positively related is that scores on the two variables tend to go together.

When two variables are negatively related, high scores on one variable tend to coincide with low scores on the other variable, medium scores on one variable go with medium scores on the other, and low scores on the first variable go with high scores on the second. When two variables are negatively related, an increase in a case's score on one variable results in a decrease in that case's score on the second variable, whereas a decrease in a case's score on the first variable results in an increase in its score on the second variable. An example of two variables that most instructors believe are negatively related would be number of class absences and test grade. Persons who miss many classes get lower grades; persons who miss few classes get higher grades. Another name for a negative relationship is an inverse relationship.

It is easy to tell from the value of an ordinal or interval/ratio measure of association if a relationship is positive or negative. If the value of the statistic is negative, then the relationship is negative (or inverse). If the value of the statistic is positive, then the relationship is positive.

Remember that nominal measures of association only indicate strength—not direction. That is because the relationship between two variables does not have direction if one or both of the variables in the relationship is nominal. For a relationship to have direction, the attributes of both variables must have rank order. If the attributes of even one of the variables lack a high end and a low end, then you cannot tell if high scores on one variable go with high or low scores on the other. So, be careful when talking about nominal measures of association. While it makes sense to report on the strength and direction of ordinal and interval/ratio measures of association, it makes no sense to talk about the direction of a nominal measure of association. The values of nominal measures of association are always positive numbers, but that does not mean the relationships they describe are positive. They are positive numbers because the statistic cannot take on negative values. The relationship between a nominal variable and some other variable can be described in terms of its strength, but it has no direction.

Symmetric and Asymmetric Measures

A last characteristic of measures of association to describe before looking at the measures themselves is symmetry. Some measures of association require you to identify the independent and dependent variables. Depending on which variable is independent and dependent, you may get different values for the statistic. Measures of association that result in different values depending on which variable is independent and dependent are **asymmetric measures** of association. Other measures of association do not care which variable is which. For these measures, you get the same statistical value regardless of which variable is independent and dependent. These measures of association are called **symmetric**. You need to know which measures are symmetric and asymmetric and, when using asymmetric ones, be sure the correct variables are identified as independent and dependent.

CONCEPT CHECK

Without looking back, can you answer the following questions:

- Do nominal measures of association indicate the strength of a relationship? Do ordinal? Do interval/ratio?
- Do nominal measures of association indicate the direction of a relationship? Do ordinal? Do interval/ratio?
- What is the difference between a symmetric and an asymmetric measure of association?
- How do you decide for a pair of variables whether you need a nominal, an ordinal, or an interval/ratio measure of association?

If not, go back and review before reading on.

Nominal Measures of Association

SPSS gives you easy access to five nominal measures of association. They are the contingency coefficient, Cramer's V, lambda, phi, and the uncertainty coefficient. Table 8.2 shows each measure's range and whether it is symmetric or asymmetric.

Table 8.2 Nominal Measures of Association

Nominal Measure of Association	Range	Symmetric or Asymmetric
Contingency coefficient	0.00 to approximately 1.00	Symmetric
Cramer's V	0.00 to 1.00	Symmetric
Lambda	0.00 to 1.00	Symmetric and asymmetric versions
Phi	In 2 × 2 tables, range is −1.00 to 1.00; in larger tables, range is 0.00 to approximately 1.00.	Symmetric
Uncertainty coefficient	0.00 to 1.00	Symmetric and asymmetric versions

Contingency Coefficient

The contingency coefficient can have a value as low as 0.00. That would indicate that it detects no statistical relationship between the two variables. The higher the value of the statistic, the stronger the relationship it found. However, the contingency coefficient can never quite attain a value of 1.00, no matter how strong the relationship between the variables. How close it can get to 1.00 depends on the size of the crosstab table under examination.

The contingency coefficient is a symmetric measure. Mathematically, the contingency coefficient is based on a statistic called chi-square (χ^2). Chi-square is an inferential statistic and not itself a measure of association. We will be looking more closely at chi-square in the inferential statistics part of the book. Because chi-square is such a widely used inferential statistic, many measures of association are based on it. The contingency coefficient is one such measure.

Cramer's V

Cramer's V has a range from 0.00 to 1.00 and is a symmetric measure of association. Like the contingency coefficient, it is chi-square based.

Lambda

Lambda (λ) has a range from 0.00 to 1.00. It comes in both symmetric and asymmetric forms. When you ask SPSS for lambda, it outputs three values: the value for the symmetric statistic, the value if the row variable is the dependent variable, and the value if the column variable is the dependent variable. SPSS also gives you the values for Goodman and Kruskal's tau when you ask for lambda. This is a nominal measure of association closely related to lambda. Goodman and Kruskal's tau is an asymmetric measure, so you get a value if the row variable is the dependent variable and a value if the column variable is the dependent variable.

Lambda is a proportional reduction in error (PRE) statistic. PRE statistics are actually very easy to interpret—easier than chi-square-based statistics. The statistic tells you how helpful the independent variable is in predicting cases' scores on the dependent variable. If the value of lambda is 0.35, for example, that means you would make 35% fewer errors in guessing cases' scores on the dependent variable if you are first told each case's independent variable score than you would if you had to guess without knowledge of the independent variable. A lambda of .75 means you would make 75% fewer errors. A lambda of 0.00 means you would make 0% fewer errors—in other words, knowing cases' scores on the independent variable does not help at all. A lambda of 1.00 means you would make 100% fewer errors—in other words, you would guess every case right. It is very easy to understand what "the strength of a relationship" means for PRE measures.

The calculation of lambda is related to how the dependent variable's mode changes as you move across the categories of the independent variable. That actually makes lambda's calculation quite easy to understand, but it does blind lambda to relationships that don't affect the mode.

Phi

Phi (Φ) is a symmetric, chi-square-based statistic. What is most notable about it is its peculiar range. In 2×2 tables (i.e., tables with two rows and two columns), it has a range from –1.00 to 1.00. How can a nominal measure of association have a negative value if nominal relationships do not have direction? Essentially, phi is treating each of the dichotomous variables as if they were interval/ratio. (Chapter 1 noted that dichotomies are sometimes treated as interval/ratio variables.) In tables where one or more of the variables has more than two attributes, the lower limit of phi is 0.00 (there are no longer any negative values), but the upper limit of the statistic can slightly exceed 1.00.

Uncertainty Coefficient

The final nominal measure of association is the **uncertainty coefficient**. Like lambda, it comes in both symmetric and asymmetric forms. It has a range of possible values from 0.00 to 1.00 and, like lambda, is a proportional reduction in error measure.

Nominal Measures of Association With SPSS

Nominal measures of association can be requested from the *Crosstabs* procedure. Click "Statistics" in the initial *Crosstabs* dialog (see Figure 7.1). A dialog similar to Figure 8.1 appears.

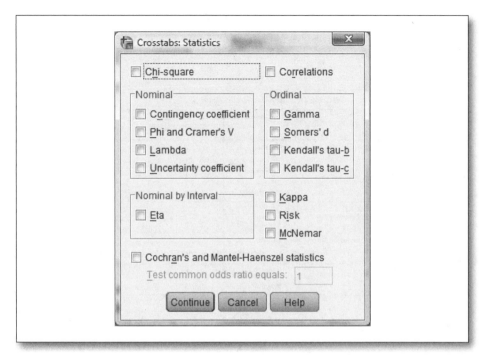

Figure 8.1   *Crosstabs* Dialog for Requesting Measures of Association

In the "Nominal" section of the dialog, check the measures of association you want. Phi and Cramer's *V* come together. You cannot get one without the other. (Although not covered in this text, SPSS can also report the value of eta—a measure of association for a nominal independent variable and an interval/ratio dependent variable.) Click "Continue" to return to the initial *Crosstabs* dialog.

SPSS TIP

If You Just Want the Statistics and Not the Crosstab

Sometimes analysts are only interested in the measures of association or other extras you can get from the *Crosstabs* procedure and do not really want to see the crosstab table itself. Notice that on the initial *Crosstabs* dialog (Figure 7.1), you can check "Suppress tables." When that is checked, you get no crosstab tables.

There is a similar option on the *Frequencies* dialog. Sometimes researchers only want the univariate statistics or other extras and do not need the frequency tables themselves.

So, how much does gender influence whether 1980 GSS young adults are working for pay, unemployed, going to school, or keeping house? In other words, how strongly are gender and work status related? Figure 8.2 shows a crosstab for gender and main task. Gender is the independent variable, so it

WORKSTAT * SEX Crosstabulation

			SEX 0 male	SEX 1 female	Total
WORKSTAT	1 working full-time	Count	92	95	187
		% within SEX	69.2%	49.0%	57.2%
	2 working part-time	Count	11	21	32
		% within SEX	8.3%	10.8%	9.8%
	3 employed but not currently working	Count	3	6	9
		% within SEX	2.3%	3.1%	2.8%
	4 unemployed but looking for work	Count	12	4	16
		% within SEX	9.0%	2.1%	4.9%
	6 in school	Count	12	11	23
		% within SEX	9.0%	5.7%	7.0%
	7 keeping house	Count	2	56	58
		% within SEX	1.5%	28.9%	17.7%
	8 other	Count	1	1	2
		% within SEX	.8%	.5%	.6%
Total		Count	133	194	327
		% within SEX	100.0%	100.0%	100.0%

Directional Measures

			Value	Asymp. Std. Error[a]	Approx. T[b]	Approx. Sig.
Nominal by Nominal	Lambda	Symmetric	.033	.023	1.410	.159
		WORKSTAT Dependent	.000	.000	[c]	[c]
		SEX Dependent	.068	.046	1.410	.159
	Goodman and Kruskal tau	WORKSTAT Dependent	.047	.013		.000[d]
		SEX Dependent	.149	.025		.000[d]
	Uncertainty Coefficient	Symmetric	.092	.019	4.879	.000[e]
		WORKSTAT Dependent	.070	.014	4.879	.000[e]
		SEX Dependent	.136	.028	4.879	.000[e]

a. Not assuming the null hypothesis.
b. Using the asymptotic standard error assuming the null hypothesis.
c. Cannot be computed because the asymptotic standard error equals zero.
d. Based on chi-square approximation.
e. Likelihood ratio chi-square probability.

Symmetric Measures

		Value	Approx. Sig.
Nominal by Nominal	Phi	.386	.000
	Cramer's V	.386	.000
	Contingency Coefficient	.360	.000
N of Valid Cases		327	

Figure 8.2 *Crosstabs* Output for WORKSTAT by SEX for 1980 GSS Young Adults

is the column variable. Column percentages are included. Since gender and work status are both nominal variables, nominal measures of association were requested. Normally, a researcher decides which one measure of association will be used and requests only that one measure. In this case, however, all the nominal measures of association were requested so you can see how they appear in the output.

A glance at the cells of the crosstab makes it clear that these 1980 GSS young adult women and men differ in the jobs they are doing. Although the modal activity for both women and men is working full-time, men are more likely to report this than women (69.2% vs. 49.0%). Men are also more likely than women to report being unemployed or going to school. Women, on the other hand, are much more likely than men to report keeping house as their principal task (28.9% vs. 1.5%). The percent of men and women working part-time or employed but not currently at work is quite similar. Clearly, there is a relationship between gender and work status since the percent distributions for men and women differ. Measures of association can tell us how strong that relationship is.

SPSS separates the measures that have asymmetric versions from those that are only symmetric. The measures that have asymmetric forms are grouped together under the label "Directional Measures." The value of symmetric lambda is reported first, followed by the two asymmetric versions of lambda, followed by the two asymmetric versions of Goodman and Kruskal's tau, followed by the symmetric uncertainty coefficient and the two asymmetric uncertainty coefficients. For the symmetric measures, phi leads off, followed by Cramer's V and the contingency coefficient.

For right now, the only numerical information to pay attention to are the numbers under the column labeled "Value." If you had decided beforehand to use asymmetric lambda (with WORKSTAT as the dependent variable) as your measure of association, you would report that there is no relationship between gender and work status with the value of lambda being 0.000. If you had decided beforehand to use Cramer's V, you would report a moderate relationship between gender and work status with the value of Cramer's V being 0.386.

You can see from this example that the measure of association you choose can make a real difference in the apparent strength of the relationship. That is why it is important to understand the differences between the measures and to decide before looking at the results which measure of association you will use.

Ordinal Measures of Association

SPSS gives you quick access to five ordinal measures of association. An ordinal measure of association is appropriate when neither of the variables in the relationship is nominal and at least one is ordinal. Ordinal measures of association indicate both the strength and the direction of the relationship. Table 8.3 provides an overview of the measures introduced in this section.

Classifying Pairs of Cases

The property of rank order is what is gained at the ordinal level of measurement, and all of the ordinal measures of association are based in one way or another on comparing how cases rank on the two variables whose relationship is being examined. Gamma, Somers' d, Kendall's tau-b, and

Table 8.3   Ordinal Measures of Association

Ordinal Measure of Association	Range	Symmetric or Asymmetric
Gamma	−1.00 to 1.00	Symmetric
Somers' *d*	−1.00 to 1.00	Symmetric and asymmetric versions
Kendall's tau-b	In square tables, −1.00 to 1.00; otherwise, approximately −1.00 to 1.00	Symmetric
Kendall's tau-c	In square tables, −1.00 to 1.00; otherwise, approximately −1.00 to 1.00	Symmetric
Spearman's correlation	−1.00 to 1.00	Symmetric

Kendall's tau-c rank cases on the two variables a pair of cases at a time, whereas Spearman's correlation ranks cases on the two variables the whole data set at a time.

To calculate the value of gamma, Somers' *d*, Kendall's tau-b, and Kendall's tau-c, every pair of cases in the data set must be placed in one of five categories. The total numbers of pairs in each category then become the components in the calculation of the statistic. Here is a very simple illustration of how pairs of cases are classified.

Imagine a data set consisting of two variables and five cases. Both variables are ordinal. The first is social class, and its attributes are lower class, working class, middle class, and upper class. The second variable is importance of hard work for getting ahead. Its attributes are getting ahead depends mostly on luck, equally on luck and hard work, and mostly on hard work. Table 8.4 shows the values for each of the five cases. (Gamma, tau-b, and tau-c are symmetrical measures of association and do not care which variable might be considered independent and dependent. Somers' *d*, however, does come in an asymmetric form. For this illustration, consider the second variable, importance of hard work, to be the dependent variable.)

To begin, you have to identify every possible pair of cases. There are 10 pairs in a data set of five cases. For each pair, you ask two questions: Which of the two cases is higher on the first variable? And which of the two cases is higher on the second variable? For each question, there are only three possible answers: The first case is higher, the second case is higher, or the cases are tied. The answers to the two questions enable you to classify the pair as concordant (if the same case is higher on both variables), discordant (if one case is higher on one variable but the other case is higher on the other variable), tied on just the first variable, tied on just the second variable, or tied on both variables. Table 8.5 shows the results from this data set.

Table 8.4   Data Set for Illustrating Types of Pairs

	Social Class	Importance of Hard Work
Case 1	Lower class	Equally luck and hard work
Case 2	Middle class	Mostly hard work
Case 3	Middle class	Mostly luck
Case 4	Upper class	Equally luck and hard work
Case 5	Upper class	Equally luck and hard work

Table 8.5   Pairs of Cases Classified by Type

Pairs	Which Case Is Higher		Type of Pair
	On Social Class?	On Importance of Hard Work?	
Case 1 and Case 2	2	2	Concordant
Case 1 and Case 3	3	1	Discordant
Case 1 and Case 4	4	Tied	Tied on second variable
Case 1 and Case 5	5	Tied	Tied on second variable
Case 2 and Case 3	Tied	2	Tied on first variable
Case 2 and Case 4	4	2	Discordant
Case 2 and Case 5	5	2	Discordant
Case 3 and Case 4	4	4	Concordant
Case 3 and Case 5	5	5	Concordant
Case 4 and Case 5	Tied	Tied	Tied on both variables

All that remains to be done before calculating the values of the measures of association is to count the number of pairs of each type in the data set. Table 8.6 shows these results.

Table 8.6   Number of Different Types of Pairs

Type of Pair	Number in the Data Set
Concordant	3
Discordant	3
Tied on first variable	1
Tied on second variable	2
Tied on both variables	1

Gamma

Gamma is a symmetric measure of association whose values range from –1.00 to 1.00. Gamma is based solely on the number of concordant and discordant pairs in the data set. It ignores any tied pairs. Gamma has positive values when concordant pairs outnumber discordant pairs, and that happens when cases that are high on one variable also tend to be high on the second variable, while cases that are low on the first variable also tend to be low on the second variable. Gamma has negative values when discordant pairs outnumber concordant pairs, and that happens when cases that are high on one variable tend to be low on the second variable, while cases that are low on the first variable tend to be high on the second variable. The more one type of pair outnumbers the other, the stronger the relationship reported by gamma. If the number of concordant pairs and discordant pairs is equal, gamma is 0.00.

Somers' *d*

If many pairs of cases have different values on the first or independent variable but the same values on the second or dependent variable, **Somers'** *d* sees that as an indication that the relationship between the independent and dependent variable is weak. After all, if it were a strong relationship, then different values on the independent variable should result in different values on the dependent variable. Somers' *d*, therefore, includes in its calculation the number of concordant pairs, the number of discordant pairs, and the number of pairs only tied on the second variable. Somers' *d* was originally developed as an asymmetric measure of association, but a symmetric version of the statistic has been developed and is included in the output from SPSS. The possible values of Somers' *d* range from –1.00 to 1.00.

Kendall's tau-b

Like Somer's *d*, **Kendall's tau-b** includes in its calculation pairs tied only on the second variable, but it also includes pairs tied only on the first variable. The logic for including pairs tied only on the first variable is that cases that have the same value on the first variable should have the same value on the second variable if the relationship were strong. Tau-b, therefore, includes in the calculation of the statistic the number of concordant pairs, the number of discordant pairs, the number of pairs tied only on the first variable, and the number of pairs tied only on the second variable. Because of the way it is calculated, tau-b can only possibly reach values of −1.00 and 1.00 in square tables. It is a symmetric measure of association.

Kendall's tau-c

Kendall's tau-c, like gamma, does not use the number of tied pairs of any type in its calculation. It does, however, make use of the size of the crosstab table and the number of cases to make the statistic more comparable across different-size tables and different-size data sets. Like tau-b, tau-c cannot reach values of −1.00 and 1.00 in all size tables, but it does come closer than tau-b in this regard. Tau-c is a symmetric measure of association.

Spearman's Correlation

Spearman's correlation, also known as Spearman's rank-order correlation or Spearman's rho, is not based on an analysis of pairs of cases. Rather, all the cases in the analysis are placed in order on the first variable and assigned a numeric rank. The case with the lowest value is assigned a rank of 1, the case with the second lowest value is assigned a rank of 2, and so on. If several cases had the same value, then their positions or ranks in line would be averaged, and each case would be assigned that averaged rank. Once every case was assigned a rank based on the first variable, each case would also be assigned a rank based on the second variable.

Once the two ordinal variables have been transformed into rank scores, the correlation between the two sets of rank scores is calculated. Spearman's correlation is calculated using the same formula as Pearson's r, which is discussed in the next chapter. Pearson's r is an interval/ratio measure of association and, as such, is not appropriate for measuring the association between ordinal variables. However, when the ordinal variables have both been converted to a numeric scale representing rank, the formula for Pearson's r becomes justified but is known as Spearman's correlation. The important thing to understand when you use or read about Spearman's correlation is that it is an ordinal measure of association in which the original values of the variables have been converted into rank scores. Spearman's correlation is a symmetric measure whose possible values range from −1.00 to 1.00.

Ordinal Measures of Association With SPSS

Figure 8.6 shows *Crosstabs* output for highest degree by happiness for 1980 GSS young adults. All five ordinal measures of association can be requested from the same *Crosstabs* dialog (see Figure 8.1) used to request nominal measures of association. Gamma, Somers' *d*, Kendall's tau-b, and Kendall's tau-c can each be individually requested in the "Ordinal" section of the dialog. Spearman's correlations are obtained by checking "Correlations," which provides both Spearman's and Pearson's *r* correlations. The output in Figure 8.3 shows all five ordinal measures, but normally a researcher would request just one.

HAPPY * DEGREE Crosstabulation

| | | | DEGREE | | | | | |
			0 less than HS degree	1 high school degree	2 associate's degree	3 bachelor degree	4 graduate degree	Total
HAPPY	1 not too happy	Count	12	29	1	4	0	46
		% within DEGREE	27.3%	13.1%	6.7%	9.5%	.0%	14.1%
	2 pretty happy	Count	23	127	9	24	2	185
		% within DEGREE	52.3%	57.5%	60.0%	57.1%	40.0%	56.6%
	3 very happy	Count	9	65	5	14	3	96
		% within DEGREE	20.5%	29.4%	33.3%	33.3%	60.0%	29.4%
Total		Count	44	221	15	42	5	327
		% within DEGREE	100.0%	100.0%	100.0%	100.0%	100.0%	100.0%

Directional Measures

			Value	Asymp. Std. Error[a]	Approx. T[b]	Approx. Sig.
Ordinal by Ordinal	Somers' d	Symmetric	.129	.050	2.525	.012
		HAPPY Dependent	.138	.054	2.525	.012
		DEGREE Dependent	.122	.048	2.525	.012

a. Not assuming the null hypothesis.
b. Using the asymptotic standard error assuming the null hypothesis.

Symmetric Measures

		Value	Asymp. Std. Error[a]	Approx. T[b]	Approx. Sig.
Ordinal by Ordinal	Kendall's tau-b	.129	.050	2.525	.012
	Kendall's tau-c	.105	.041	2.525	.012
	Gamma	.237	.090	2.525	.012
	Spearman Correlation	.142	.055	2.578	.010[c]
Interval by Interval	Pearson's R	.136	.054	2.477	.014[c]
N of Valid Cases		327			

a. Not assuming the null hypothesis.
b. Using the asymptotic standard error assuming the null hypothesis.
c. Based on normal approximation.

Figure 8.3   *Crosstabs* Output for HAPPY by DEGREE for 1980 GSS Young Adults

An examination of the crosstab suggests a positive relationship between degree and happiness (the percent very happy goes from 20.5% for less than a high school degree to 60.0% for graduate degree) but not a very strong one (the modes and the medians for the first four degree groups are identical: pretty happy). The ordinal measures of association confirm this. All are positive, but none point to a strong relationship. They range from .10 (Kendall's tau-c) to .24 (gamma). While the value of gamma falls within what we would describe as moderate strength, all the others indicate a weak relationship.

CONCEPT CHECK

Without looking back, can you answer the following questions:

- What is the typical range of nominal measures of association? Ordinal measures of association? Interval/ratio measures of association?
- What are the names of two nominal measures of association? Two ordinal measures of association?
- What is the difference between a concordant pair of cases and a discordant pair of cases?

If not, go back and review before reading on.

1980 GSS Young Adults

The chapter began with some questions about 1980 GSS young adults. On the basis of our analyses, what do we now know?

- Gender and primary work activity were moderately related (Cramer's $V = .386$). Men were more likely to be employed full-time. Women were much more likely to be not employed but keeping house.
- A weak positive relationship existed between highest educational degree and happiness (Kendall's tau-b = .129). While persons with bachelor degrees were more likely than persons with just high school degrees to report being very happy, pretty happy was the modal and median response for both groups.

Important Concepts in the Chapter

asymmetric measure

contingency coefficient

concordant pair

Cramer's V

Crosstabs procedure

direction of a relationship

discordant pairs	ordinal measure of association
gamma	phi
interval/ratio measure of association	Somers' d
Kendall's tau-b	Spearman's correlation
Kendall's tau-c	strength of a relationship
lambda	symmetric measure
measure of association	tied pair
nominal measure of association	uncertainty coefficient

Practice Problems

1. For each of the following, name a pair of variables not previously mentioned that you suspect
   a. have a strong relationship
   b. have a weak relationship
   c. have a positive relationship
   d. have a negative relationship

2. Which of the following is a nominal measure of association: gamma, Kendall's tau-b, lambda, or Spearman's correlation?

3. Which of the following is an ordinal measure of association: Cramer's V, gamma, lambda, or uncertainty coefficient?

4. Which of the following measures of association comes in an asymmetric form: Cramer's V, gamma, Kendall's tau-b, or lambda?

5. Which of the following is most appropriate for measuring the relationship between an ordinal variable and a nominal variable: Cramer's V, Kendall's tau-b, or Spearman's correlation?

6. Which of the following is most appropriate for measuring the relationship between two ordinal variables: Cramer's V, gamma, or lambda?

7. The value of gamma is −.85. This indicates what kind of relationship: weak and negative, moderate and negative, strong and positive, or very strong and negative?

8. The value of Cramer's V is .65. This indicates what type of relationship: strong, strong and positive, very strong, or very strong and positive?

9. The value of gamma for variables A and B is −.40. The value of gamma for variables C and D is .60. Which pair of variables is more strongly related: variables A and B, variables C and D, the relationships are of equal strength, or gamma does not indicate strength?

closest to 1 = Highest

10. Which of the following Kendall's tau-b values indicates the strongest relationship: -0.75, -0.10, 0.00, or 0.45?

11. Which of the following values for a statistic is clearly incorrect because it is outside the statistic's range: Cronbach's alpha = .50, Cramer's V = .45, gamma = $-.50$, or Kendall's tau-c = 1.25?

12. The value of Spearman's correlation for variables D and E is .95. Which is true about cases that have a high value on D: likely to have a low value on E, likely to have a high value on E, or equally likely to have a high or low value on E?

Problems Requiring SPSS and the *fourGroups.sav* Data Set

13. (*2010 GSS young adults*) Calculate a measure of association for the relationship between gender and work status for 2010 GSS young adults. Also, produce a crosstab. Gender is the independent variable. (Variables: SEX, WORKSTAT; Select Cases: GROUP = 3)
    a. Which measure of association did you use? What is its value? Describe the strength of the relationship using the guide in this chapter. *— NOM -B*
    b. To further describe the relationship:
       i. What is the modal work status of 2010 GSS young men? Of 2010 GSS young women?
       ii. Select a category of the dependent variable. What percent of 2010 GSS young men are in that category? Of 2010 GSS young women?
    c. [Figure 8.2 shows for the 1980 GSS young adults a moderate relationship between gender and work status. The value of Cramer's V is .386.] Summarize in a few well-written sentences totaling 100 words or less the similarities and/or differences in the relationship between gender and work status for the 1980 and 2010 GSS young adults. *Both.*

14. (*2010 GSS middle-age adults*) Calculate a measure of association for the relationship between gender and work status for 2010 GSS middle-age adults. Also, produce a crosstab. Gender is the independent variable. (Variables: SEX, WORKSTAT; Select Cases: GROUP = 4)
    a. Which measure of association did you use? What is its value? Describe the strength of the relationship using the guide in this chapter.
    b. To further describe the relationship:
       i. What is the modal work status of 2010 GSS middle-age men? Of 2010 GSS middle-age women?
       ii. Select a category of the dependent variable. What percent of 2010 GSS middle-age men are in that category? Of 2010 GSS middle-age women?
    c. [Figure 8.2 shows for the 1980 GSS young adults a moderate relationship between gender and work status. The value of Cramer's V is .386.] Summarize in a few well-written sentences totaling 100 words or less the similarities and/or differences in the relationship between gender and work status of these two groups of baby boomers—the 1980 young adults and the 2010 GSS middle-age adults.

15. (*2010 GSS young adults*) Calculate a measure of association for the relationship between highest educational degree and happiness for 2010 GSS twentysomethings. Also, produce a crosstab. Degree is the independent variable. (Variables: DEGREE, HAPPY; Select Cases: GROUP = 3)
    a. Which measure of association did you use? What is its value? What is the direction of the relationship? How would you describe the strength of the relationship using the guide in this chapter?

    b. To further describe the relationship, as you move through the five degree groups
       i. Does the percent saying they are very happy change?
      ii. Does the modal level of happiness change?
     iii. Does the median level of happiness change?

    c. [Figure 8.3 shows for the 1980 GSS young adults a weak positive relationship between degree and happiness. The value of Kendall's tau-b is .129.] Summarize in a few well-written sentences totaling 100 words or less the similarities and/or differences in the relationship between degree and happiness for the 1980 and 2010 GSS young adults.

The rest of the problems revisit practice problems from the previous chapter, adding measures of association to the previous analysis. For each problem, answer these questions:

- *Which measure of association did you use?*
- *What is its value?*
- *How would you describe the strength of the relationship using the guide in this chapter?*
- *If appropriate, what is the direction of the relationship?*

16. (*2010 GSS young adults*) Calculate a measure of association for the relationship between race and belief in life after death for 2010 GSS twentysomethings. Race is the independent variable. (Variables: RACE, POSTLIFE; Select Cases: GROUP = 3)

17. (*2010 GSS middle-age adults*) Calculate a measure of association for the relationship between race and number of children for 2010 GSS fiftysomethings. Race is the independent variable. (Variables: RACE, CHILDREN; Select Cases: GROUP = 4)

18. (*2010 GSS young adults*) Calculate a measure of association for the relationship between race and strength of religious affiliation for 2010 GSS twentysomethings. Race is the independent variable. (Variables: RACE, RELINTEN; Select Cases: GROUP = 3)

19. (*1980 GSS middle-age adults*) Calculate a measure of association for the relationship between gender and strength of religious affiliation for 1980 GSS fiftysomethings. Gender is the independent variable. (Variables: SEX, RELINTEN; Select Cases: GROUP = 2)

20. (*2010 GSS young adults*) Calculate a measure of association for the relationship between health and happiness for 2010 GSS twentysomethings. Health is the independent variable. (Variables: HEALTH, HAPPY; Select Cases: GROUP = 3)

21. (*2010 GSS young adults*) Calculate a measure of association for the relationship between health and happiness for 2010 GSS twentysomethings separately for men and for women. Health is the independent variable. Use SEX as a layering variable. (Variables: HEALTH, HAPPY, SEX; Select Cases: GROUP = 3)

22. (*2010 GSS middle-age adults*) Calculate a measure of association for the relationship between religious affiliation and happiness for 2010 GSS fiftysomethings. Religious affiliation is the independent variable. (Variables: RELIGION, HAPPY; Select Cases: GROUP = 4)

23. (*2010 GSS young adults*) Calculate a measure of association for the relationship between political orientation and happiness for 2010 GSS twentysomethings. Political orientation is the independent variable. (Variables: POLVIEWS, HAPPY; Select Cases: GROUP = 3)

24. (*2010 GSS middle-age adults*) Calculate a measure of association for the relationship between marital status and happiness for 2010 GSS fiftysomethings. Marital status is the independent variable. Be sure to use the variable MARRIED. (Variables: MARRIED, HAPPY; Select Cases: GROUP = 4)

25. (*2010 GSS middle-age adults*) Calculate a measure of association for the relationship between marital status and happiness for 2010 GSS fiftysomethings separately for men and for women. Marital status is the independent variable. Use SEX as a layering variable. Be sure to use the variable MARRIED. (Variables: MARRIED, HAPPY, SEX; Select Cases: GROUP = 4)

26. (*all four groups*) Calculate a measure of association for the relationship between GSS group and political orientation. GSS group is the independent variable. (Variables: GROUP, POLVIEWS; Select Cases: all cases)

Questions and Tools for Answering Them
(Chapter 9)

Univariate Descriptive	Univariate Inferential

Data Management

Multivariate Descriptive	Multivariate Inferential

Questions:

- Is there a correlation between these two variables? How strong is it? Is it positive or negative?
- Changing a case's value on the independent variable produces how much of a change in the dependent variable?
- How well does the independent variable explain the differences among the cases on the dependent variable?
- What would we predict a case's score on the dependent variable to be? How close is our prediction to the case's actual score?

Statistics:

- Pearson's r (correlation)
- scatterplot
- unstandardized coefficient (slope, b)
- regression residual
- multiple correlation coefficient (R)
- coefficient of determination (R^2)
- coefficient of alienation

SPSS Procedures:

- *Bivariate Correlations*
- *Linear Regression*

Pearson's Correlation and Bivariate Regression

In this chapter, you can learn

- how the strength and direction of an association between two interval/ratio variables can be described by a single number,
- how the relationship between two interval/ratio variables can be illustrated on a two-dimensional graph,
- how the equation for a straight line can summarize that relationship between interval/ratio variables,
- how that straight-line equation can be used to predict a case's score on the dependent variable, and
- how a single number can indicate how well an independent variable does in explaining the variation among cases on the dependent variable.

Education, Spouse's Education, and Income

In this chapter, we consider the following questions:

- Do opposites really attract when it comes to schooling and marriage? Looking first at the parents of the 1980 GSS twentysomethings, how closely did the years of schooling of the dads and moms of these baby boomers match?
- Did the baby boomers reject the customs of their parents when it came to choosing marriage partners? For those 1980 GSS twentysomethings who were already married by the time of the survey, how closely do their and their spouses' years of schooling match?

- Were 1980 GSS young adults who had more schooling making more money?
- How much was an additional year of schooling worth in terms of annual income?
- What proportion of the differences in annual income among 1980 GSS young adults could be explained simply by their differences in education?

SPSS TIP

To Duplicate the Examples in This Chapter

To duplicate the examples in this chapter, use the *fourGroups.sav* data set. For Figures 9.1 through 9.4, set the select cases condition to GROUP = 1. For Figure 9.5, set the select cases condition to GROUP = 1 and AGE >= 25. For all other examples, set the select cases condition to GROUP = 1 and AGE >= 25 and WORKSTAT = 1 and INCOME86 < 139297.

Overview

This chapter begins with Pearson's r, a measure of association for interval/ratio variables. It then explains scatterplots, which are visual representations of relationships between two interval/ratio variables. Scatterplots illustrate the relationship but don't provide a precise summary of the relationship. For that we turn to linear regression.

Using the best-fitting straight line through data points, linear regression describes several things: how much change in the dependent variable typically results from a change in the independent variable, the strength and direction of the independent variable's effect on the dependent variable, and the proportion of the variation among the cases on the dependent variable that is explained by differences among the cases on the independent variable. This chapter looks only at bivariate linear regression, which is the effect of a single independent variable on a dependent variable. The next chapter will consider more interesting regression examples using multiple independent variables.

Interval/Ratio Measures of Association

Pearson's r

While different researchers prefer different nominal measures of association and different ordinal measures of association, there is near unanimity regarding interval/ratio measures of association. **Pearson's r** is far and away the most commonly used interval/ratio measure of association. It is sometimes referred to as Pearson's correlation. If you see a reference to a correlation or a correlation coefficient with no other identifying information, the author is probably referring to Pearson's r.

Pearson's *r* is a symmetric measure of association. It has a possible range of values from −1.00 to 1.00.

Interval/Ratio Measures of Association With SPSS

To demonstrate Pearson's *r*, we use data for 1980 GSS young adults on several school-related variables: mother's years of schooling, father's years of schooling, the respondent's own years of schooling completed at the time of the survey, and, if the respondent was married at the time of the survey, his or her spouse's years of schooling.

As you saw in the previous section, you can get the value of Pearson's *r* from the *Crosstabs* procedure. However, a more versatile method for obtaining Pearson's *r* is to pull down the *Analyze* menu, move the cursor to *Correlate,* and click on *Bivariate.*

Analyze | Correlate | Bivariate

A dialog similar to Figure 9.1 appears.

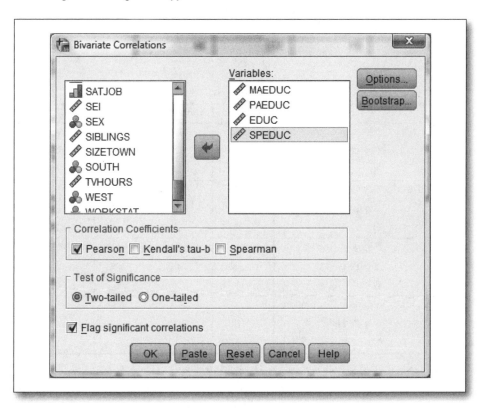

Figure 9.1 Dialog for Obtaining Bivariate Correlations

To get Pearson correlation coefficients, simply move interval/ratio variables from the list on the left to the "Variables" list on the right. At a minimum, you want to move two variables into the "Variables" list. By default, this procedure calculates values for Pearson's *r*. However, you can also (or instead) request values for Kendall's tau-b or Spearman's correlation. If you are requesting one of these ordinal measures of association, then you could move both interval/ratio and ordinal variables into the variables field.

While a researcher might be interested only in the association between a particular pair of variables, often she wants to see the values of a measure of association for many different pairs of variables. That is no problem because you can move any number of variables into the variables list. The output in Figure 9.2 resulted from moving four variables into the variables field. While we are primarily interested in the correlation between mother's and father's schooling and between the respondent's schooling and his or her spouse's schooling, the correlation matrix will show us the correlation between each variable and every other variable. In fact, it gives us each of these correlations twice!

The *Bivariate Correlations* procedure always produces a correlation matrix. The results come in a rectangular table where the variables included in the procedure define the columns and also the rows. To find the value of Pearson's *r* for any pair of variables, simply locate one of the variables in the column headings and move down that column until you come to the row representing the other variable. In most cells of the table, there are three pieces of information. The first number is

Correlations

		MAEDUC	PAEDUC	EDUC	SPEDUC
MAEDUC	Pearson Correlation	1	.539**	.325**	.248**
	Sig. (2-tailed)		.000	.000	.002
	N	301	246	301	155
PAEDUC	Pearson Correlation	.539**	1	.371**	.344**
	Sig. (2-tailed)	.000		.000	.000
	N	246	256	256	132
EDUC	Pearson Correlation	.325**	.371**	1	.389**
	Sig. (2-tailed)	.000	.000		.000
	N	301	256	327	169
SPEDUC	Pearson Correlation	.248**	.344**	.389**	1
	Sig. (2-tailed)	.002	.000	.000	
	N	155	132	169	169

**. Correlation is significant at the 0.01 level (2-tailed).

Figure 9.2 *Bivariate Correlations* Output for MAEDUC, PAEDUC, EDUC, and SPEDUC for 1980 GSS Young Adults

the value of the measure of association. (Ignore any asterisks for now. They have to do with inferential statistics.) The second number in the cell also deals with inferential statistics and can be ignored for the time being. The third number is N, that is, the number of cases in the data set available for calculating the correlation.

A few things about the matrix may seem strange. First, the cells in the diagonal (going from the top left to the bottom right) all have a value for Pearson's r of 1. A 1.00 indicates a perfect positive correlation, but don't get too excited. Those cells represent the correlation of a variable with itself. Any variable correlated with itself yields a correlation of 1.00. These 1s are neither surprising nor noteworthy. Second, every cell (other than those on the diagonal) appears twice in the matrix. For example, you can find the correlation between MAEDUC and PAEDUC in the second cell of the first row, but you can find the same information in the first cell of the second row. It does not matter which cell you use.

A third thing you might notice about the matrix is that the N on which the correlations are based differs. That's because different variables in a data set often have different amounts of missing data. As a result, the number of cases with data on the two variables involved in a specific correlation differs depending on which two variables are involved. You can tell from the cells in the diagonal how many cases (out of the 327 young adults in the 1980 GSS) had valid values for each of the four variables.

Figure 9.2 shows a strong positive correlation between how many years of schooling the dad and mom had. Pearson's r is .539. On many traits, Americans tend to marry persons similar to themselves. Social scientists call this homogamy. Years of schooling is one of those traits. Those 1980 GSS young adults who were married at the time of the survey also show homogamy on schooling. Their correlation is not quite as strong as between the respondents' parents; it is just .389—a moderate positive association. Of course, many of these twentysomethings are not done with their schooling, and many are not yet married. When they are older and more have married and more have completed their schooling, their level of homogamy may match or even exceed their parents' level.

This is a good time to introduce the distinction between **pairwise** and **listwise** deletion of missing data. By default, the *Bivariate Correlations* procedure uses pairwise deletion of missing data. That means a case that might have valid information on the variables EDUC, MAEDUC, and SPEDUC but not on PAEDUC would be included in the calculation of correlations between EDUC, MAEDUC, and SPEDUC but not included in the calculation of any correlations involving PAEDUC. Pairwise deletion of cases makes the maximum use of the valid data available. However, it makes comparisons between correlations problematic because the different correlations are based on different groups of cases. In a large correlation matrix with substantial missing data, it is possible to have two correlations that have few or even no cases in common. Listwise deletion of missing cases is an alternative available on many SPSS procedures. Like the name implies, listwise deletion removes a case from the entire matrix if it is missing data on any of the variables represented in the matrix. Listwise deletion lowers the number of cases on which correlations are based but ensures that every correlation in the matrix is based on the same cases.

If you click "Options" in the initial *Bivariate Correlations* dialog, a dialog similar to Figure 9.3 appears.

By default, "Exclude cases pairwise" is selected but you can switch to "Exclude cases listwise" by simply clicking that phrase.

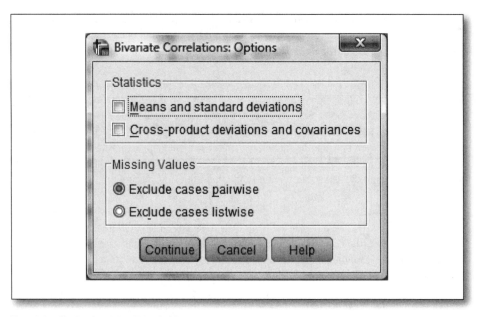

Figure 9.3   *Bivariate Correlations* Dialog for Missing Values Handling

Scatterplots

Although drawn somewhat differently, the **scatterplot** is essentially the Cartesian graph you first used in elementary school. The scatterplot, like the Cartesian graph, is based on two axes or number lines. One is horizontal and is often referred to as the X axis; the other is vertical and is often referred to as the Y axis. On the X axis, larger numbers are found to the right; on the Y axis, larger numbers are found higher up. In a Cartesian graph, the two number lines or axes cross at the zero point on both number lines.

Any point in the graph can be identified by two coordinates: the X coordinate and the Y coordinate. The X coordinate indicates where the point is relative to the X axis; the Y coordinate indicates where the point is relative to the Y axis. Points in the upper right quarter (or quadrant) of the graph have positive X and Y coordinates, points in the upper left quadrant have negative X coordinates but positive Y coordinates, points in the lower left quadrant have negative X and Y coordinates, and points in the lower right quadrant have positive X coordinates but negative Y coordinates.

Since the attributes of interval/ratio variables represent numeric scales, they can be represented by number lines. Two interval/ratio variables can be represented by two number lines, and if those number lines are positioned to form a Cartesian graph, then any case's values on the two number lines can be represented by a point in the Cartesian graph. If every case in the data set that has valid values on the two variables is represented by its own point in the Cartesian graph, then the graph gives you a visual image of the relationship between the two variables. That is exactly what a scatterplot does. (The scatterplots in this chapter were created using *Chart Builder,* which is included in the *Graphs* pull-down menu.)

The scatterplot in Figure 9.4 illustrates the strong positive correlation of .539 between mother's and father's years of schooling for the 1980 GSS young adult. While not every mother and father have identical years of schooling, it is visually clear that as mother's years of schooling goes up, father's schooling also rises. (Since spouses choose one another, the variables in this example are not thought of as independent and dependent. If they were, however, the independent variable would be the horizontal or *X* axis variable, and the dependent variable would be the vertical or *Y* axis variable.)

The scatterplot is shown as an enclosed area with the number lines at the bottom and left edges of the area rather than the more traditional representation of a Cartesian graph with the two axes crossing at their zero points forming four quadrants. Nevertheless, the *X* and *Y* coordinates of points in the scatterplot are easy to identify.

There is a straightforward relationship between Pearson's *r* and the distribution of points in a scatterplot. The closer the points in a scatterplot correspond to a straight line, the stronger the correlation between the two variables. And if the straight line that the points approximate rises as the

[handwritten margin note: independent variable = X axis. Dependent - Y axis]

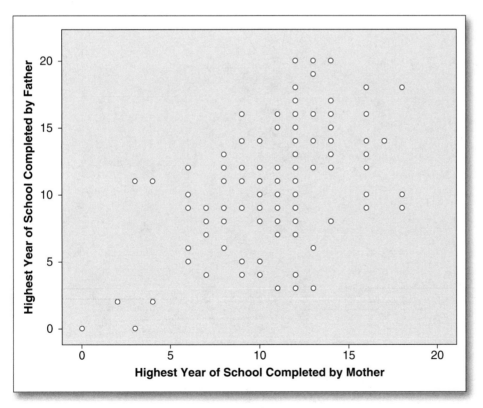

Figure 9.4   Scatterplot of MAEDUC and PAEDUC for 1980 GSS Young Adults

line moves to the right, the value of Pearson's r will be positive. If the straight line falls as it moves to the right, Pearson's r will be negative. How steep the rise or sharp the fall in that line, however, has no impact on the value of Pearson's r.

Wherever you see a data point in a scatterplot, you know there is at least one case in the data set with that combination of coordinates, but there could be many more than one—particularly when your variables are discrete rather than continuous. Both of the variables in Figure 9.4 are discrete. That is why the data points line up in straight vertical columns and horizontal rows. In fact, the data set has dozens of persons whose parents both had exactly 12 years of schooling. Unfortunately, those dozens of persons are represented by just a single data point in Figure 9.4.

Figure 9.5 shows a scatterplot that overcomes this limitation. The size of the data points corresponds to the number of cases they represent. SPSS calls this a bin scatterplot. Figure 9.5 illustrates

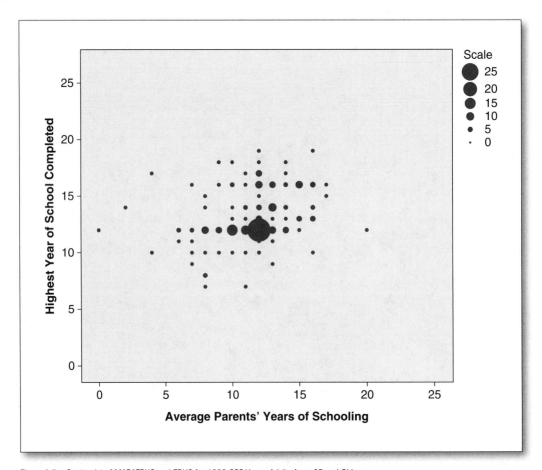

Figure 9.5   Scatterplot of MAPAEDUC and EDUC for 1980 GSS Young Adults Ages 25 and Older

the relationship between years of schooling and average parental years of schooling for the 1980 GSS young adults who were at least 25 years old. Since parents' schooling typically precedes children's schooling, parents' schooling is the independent variable and is reported along the horizontal axis. This bin scatterplot makes clear the large number of parents and children with exactly 12 years of schooling. The tendency of cases to be higher in the scatterplot the further to the right you look can just be made out. The value of Pearson's r for this relationship is .291, a moderate positive relationship.

CONCEPT CHECK

Without looking back, can you answer the following questions:

- Which number line represents the independent variable in a scatterplot?
- How does a scatterplot indicate the strength of the relationship between two variables?
- How does a scatterplot indicate the direction of the relationship between two variables?

If not, go back and review before reading on.

Bivariate Linear Regression

Linear regression uses the equation for a straight line to summarize the relationship between interval/ratio variables illustrated by a scatterplot—thus, the name *linear* regression. (Any references to regression in this book will be to linear regression. Other kinds of regression are not covered here.) Regression using just a single independent variable is referred to as **bivariate regression**; regression using more than one independent variable is termed **multiple regression**. Multiple regression is discussed in the next chapter. We start here with bivariate regression. All the principles of bivariate regression also apply to multiple regression.

Equation for a Straight Line

Almost all lines can be uniquely described (i.e., differentiated from every other possible line) by two numbers. The first number is the line's Y intercept and describes where the line crosses the Y axis on a Cartesian graph. The second number is the line's slope and describes the direction and rate at which the line rises or falls as it moves to the right. (Not *all* lines can be described in this way. Perfectly vertical lines cannot be mathematically described by means of a Y intercept and slope. This exception can be safely ignored for the purposes in this book.)

Y intercept

slope

A straight line can be described using the following formula:

$$Y = a + b(X)$$

The *a* represents the *Y* intercept, and the *b* represents the slope. In the equation for a specific line, the *a* and the *b* are replaced by numbers, for example, $Y = 10 + 3X$. The *Y* and the *X* are variables and represent the coordinates of all the points in the chart that lie right on the line.

The *Y* intercept is quite simple to interpret. It tells you where the line crosses the *Y* axis. Since straight lines are straight, they can only cross the *Y* axis once. The *Y* intercept tells you where that crossing is.

The slope packs more information. It describes the direction and rate at which the line rises or falls as it moves to the right. If the slope is a positive number, the line is rising as it moves to the right; if it is a negative number, the line is falling. The magnitude, or absolute value, of the slope indicates the rate at which it is rising or falling. Specifically, the slope tells you how many units higher or lower as measured by the *Y* axis the line will be when the line is one unit further to the right as measured along the *X* axis. Since straight lines are straight, they have the same slope everywhere along the line.

MATH TIP

Examples of Straight-Line Equations

Here are three examples of equations describing specific straight lines:

$$Y = 0 + 15(X)$$
$$Y = 12 - 0.01(X)$$
$$Y = -2.5 + 0(X)$$

For the first line, the *Y* intercept of 0 tells you the line crosses the *Y* axis at 0, and the slope of 15 tells you the line rises 15 units for every 1 unit it moves to the right. For the second line, the *Y* intercept of 12 tells you the line crosses the *Y* axis at 12, and the slope of −0.01 tells you the line falls 1/100th of a unit for every 1 unit it moves to the right. For the third line, the *Y* intercept of −2.5 tells you the line crosses the *Y* axis at −2.5, and the slope of 0.00 tells you the line is perfectly horizontal, neither rising nor falling as it moves to the right.

"Best-Fitting" Straight Line

So, the points in a scatterplot can be represented by a straight line, and a straight line can be uniquely defined by specifying the line's *Y* intercept and its slope. But which line will be selected to represent the points in a scatterplot? An infinite number of straight lines could be drawn on a scatterplot. Some rise as they move to the right; others fall. Some rise or fall rapidly; others gradually. Since the points in a scatterplot rarely form a perfectly straight line, some criterion is needed to identify what will be called the "best-fitting" straight line.

The criterion used by statisticians employs the notion of vertical distance of points from a line— but not simple vertical distance. The best-fitting straight line is defined as the line that minimizes the sum of the *squared* vertical distance of points from the line.

Notice the similarity between this criterion for the best-fitting straight line and the formula for the variance. Both make use of the squared distance of cases from something. The variance looks at the squared distance of cases from the mean. This best-fitting criterion looks at the squared distance of cases from a line. In fact, the best-fitting straight line could be defined as the line that minimizes the variance of the points around the line.

Bivariate Regression With SPSS

All of the regression examples in this chapter use income as the dependent variable and years of schooling as the independent variable.

RESEARCH TIP

Methodological Note About Income and Years of Schooling

As noted in Chapter 4, the GSS measure of income only includes earnings from employment, is based on the entire previous year, is adjusted for inflation to what the income was worth in 1986 dollars, and was originally measured in categories and then converted into an interval/ratio measure.

The regression analysis in this chapter is limited to persons 25 and older since these individuals are more likely to have completed all or almost all of their schooling. The analysis is further limited to the eighty-eight 1980 GSS young adults age 25 and older who reported working full-time in the week prior to the survey and who reported at least some income in the previous year.

Income for these 88 individuals is severely skewed by a single person with a very high income. One 1980 GSS young adult reported an income of $139,297 (the midpoint of the income category the individual selected), while the next highest incomes were just $56,647. Since the reason for this exceptionally high income is likely to also be exceptional and different from the usual factors affecting the incomes of most 1980 GSS young adults, this outlying case has been excluded from the regression analysis. This was done by only selecting cases with incomes less than $139,297. With this case dropped from the analysis, the data are no longer severely skewed.

To get SPSS to provide the Y intercept and slope of the best-fitting straight line through the scatterplot of two interval/ratio variables, pull down the *Analyze* menu, move the cursor over *Regression,* and click *Linear.*

Analyze | Regression | Linear

A dialog similar to Figure 9.6 appears. Move the dependent variable into the "Dependent" list, move the independent variable into the "Independent(s)" list, and click OK.

As Figure 9.7 shows, just those few steps produce a lot. Some of the output from the regression procedure will not be used in this book, other parts will be explained in later chapters, and still other parts will be explained later in this chapter. For now, only the last box of the output, the "Coefficients" box, is of interest. It has the Y intercept and the slope for the best-fitting straight line.

The Y intercept appears in the row labeled "(Constant)," and the slope appears in the row that has the name of the independent variable. The values for the Y intercept and the slope are both in the column headed "B," which is under the larger heading "Unstandardized Coefficients." These coefficients are unstandardized because the variables in the equation are measured in terms of raw scores. In the next chapter, we will discuss the standardized coefficients that result from a regression when all variables have been converted to z or standardized scores. Unstandardized coefficients are sometimes referred to by the lowercase letter b, although SPSS uses an uppercase B for the heading. And one other matter of terminology: In the context of regression, the equation for the best-fitting straight line is usually referred to as the regression equation.

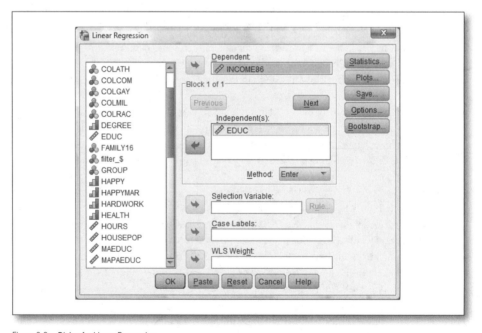

Figure 9.6   Dialog for Linear Regression

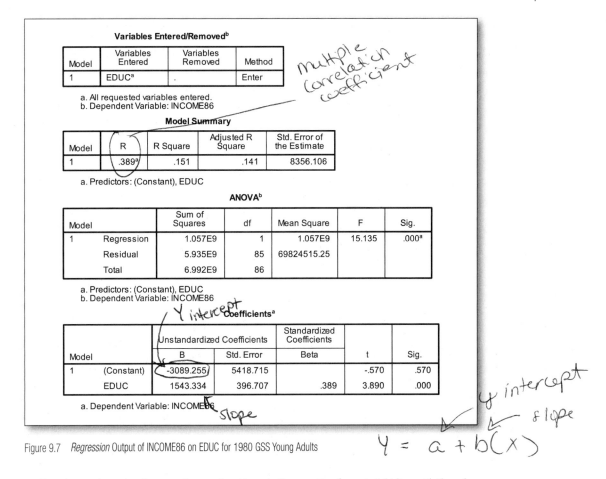

Variables Entered/Removed[b]

Model	Variables Entered	Variables Removed	Method
1	EDUC[a]	.	Enter

a. All requested variables entered.
b. Dependent Variable: INCOME86

multiple correlation coefficient

Model Summary

Model	R	R Square	Adjusted R Square	Std. Error of the Estimate
1	.389[a]	.151	.141	8356.106

a. Predictors: (Constant), EDUC

ANOVA[b]

Model		Sum of Squares	df	Mean Square	F	Sig.
1	Regression	1.057E9	1	1.057E9	15.135	.000[a]
	Residual	5.935E9	85	69824515.25		
	Total	6.992E9	86			

a. Predictors: (Constant), EDUC
b. Dependent Variable: INCOME86

Y intercept

Coefficients[a]

Model		Unstandardized Coefficients		Standardized Coefficients	t	Sig.
		B	Std. Error	Beta		
1	(Constant)	-3089.255	5418.715		-.570	.570
	EDUC	1543.334	396.707	.389	3.890	.000

a. Dependent Variable: INCOME86

slope

y intercept
slope

$Y = a + b(X)$

Figure 9.7   *Regression* Output of INCOME86 on EDUC for 1980 GSS Young Adults

To write out the regression equation, replace the *a* in the equation for a straight line with the value of the *Y* intercept, −3089.255, and replace the *b* in the equation with the value of the unstandardized coefficient, 1543.334. The variables *X* and *Y* remain in the equation. So, the regression equation is

$$Y = -3089.255 + 1543.334(X)$$

Sometimes, analysts substitute the variable names or the variable labels that *X* and *Y* represent for the *X* and the *Y* in the equation. These are just different ways of representing the variables. Thus, when describing the regression equation, you would also be correct to state

$$INCOME86 = -3089.255 + 1543.334(EDUC)$$

or

$$Annual\ income = -3089.255 + 1543.334(years\ of\ education)$$

Figure 9.8 shows the bin scatterplot for years of education and income with the regression line drawn in. The line crosses the Y axis at −3089.255. It rises as it moves to the right. More specifically, for every one-unit increase in X, the line rises 1543.334 units along the Y axis. (The meaning of the phrase "R^2 Linear = 0.151," which appears at the right of the scatterplot, will be explained later in the chapter.)

The Y intercept and unstandardized coefficient become more interesting when we talk about them in substantive terms. The Y intercept says a person with no schooling would hypothetically earn −$3,089. We'll skip a discussion of what negative income would mean since no cases in the scatterplot actually have less than 8 years of schooling. What the Y intercept is really doing is providing a baseline from which we can calculate the effect of schooling. Since the unstandardized coefficient for years of schooling is positive, each additional year of schooling typically results in additional income. Specifically, for every additional year of education, income increases above the baseline amount by approximately $1,543.

If one of the 1980 GSS young adults had 1 year more schooling than another 1980 GSS young adult, we would expect that first person to have $1,543 more income than the other. If one 1980 GSS young adult had 10 years more schooling than another, we would expect that first person to have an annual income $15,433 more than the other. (The unstandardized coefficient of 1543.334 is for a

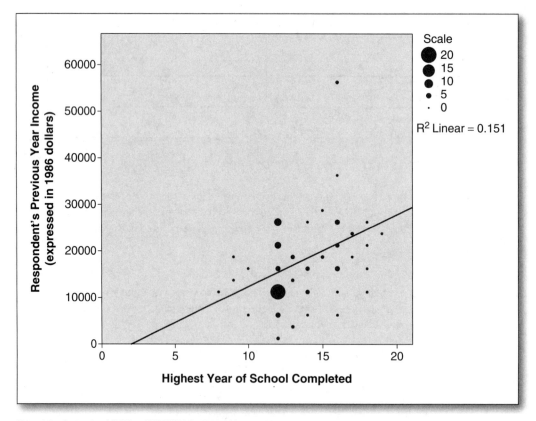

Figure 9.8   Scatterplot of EDUC and INCOME86 for 1980 GSS Young Adults

1-year difference in schooling. To see the effect of a 10-year difference in schooling, multiply the unstandardized coefficient by 10.) If one 1980 GSS young adult had 5 years less schooling than someone else, we would expect that first person to have $7,717 less income than the other. (To calculate the effect of a 5-year disadvantage in schooling, multiply the unstandardized coefficient by −5.)

The regression equation provides a much more precise description of the relationship between variables than could be obtained by just eyeballing a scatterplot. However, it should be remembered that not all points in the scatterplot fall exactly on the line. That means that one additional year of education did not translate into $1,543 more income for every 1980 GSS twentysomething. Some individuals received more income than expected given their schooling; others received less than expected. Nevertheless, the best overall description for the data set of how years of schooling are converted into income is indicated by the unstandardized coefficient, 1543.334.

While the unstandardized coefficient indicates how much of a change in Y typically occurs for every one-unit change in X, it does not indicate the strength of the relationship between the independent and dependent variables. Because independent and dependent variables, even though they are interval/ratio, have different means, have different variances and standard deviations, and often are measured on different numeric scales (e.g., years, dollars, inches, number of persons, number of cars), the unstandardized coefficients have no fixed range. While Pearson's r, for example, can range only from −1.00 to 1.00, unstandardized coefficients can be huge positive or negative numbers. Do not interpret the magnitude of the unstandardized coefficient as an indicator of strength, and do not apply the guidelines of weak, moderate, strong, or very strong when describing an unstandardized coefficient.

Predicted Values and Regression Residuals

With the regression equation, it becomes possible to predict a case's score on the dependent variable. Simply substitute its score on the independent variable for the X in the regression equation and do the math on the right side of the equation. The result is the **predicted value** for the dependent variable. While a case's actual score on the dependent variable is represented by Y, a case's predicted score is usually represented by $\hat{Y}$.

For example, return to the regression equation for income and years of education. The equation is

$$Y = -3089.255 + 1543.334(X)$$

If a person had 12 years of schooling, what is that person's predicted income? In place of the X in the equation, insert 12; multiply 12 by 1543.334, and then take that product and subtract 3089.255. The result, $15,430.75, is the predicted income for that person. Stated differently, $\hat{Y} = \$15,430.75$.

Of course, cases do not always have the values on the dependent variable that the regression equation predicted for them. If they did, all the points on the scatterplot would fall exactly on the regression line. The difference between a case's actual score on the dependent variable and that case's predicted score based on the regression equation is known as the **regression residual**. To calculate the regression residual, simply take the actual score on the dependent variable and subtract the predicted score.

$$\text{regression residual} = Y - \hat{Y}$$

Using our bivariate regression equation for income, a person with 8 years of schooling would have a predicted income of $9,257.42. If the person actually had an income of $15,000, the regression residual would be $5,742.58 (i.e., $15,000 minus $9,257.42). On the other hand, if the person had an income only of $8,000, the regression residual would be –$1,257.42 (i.e., $8,000 minus $9,257.42).

Any case that has an actual score on the dependent variable greater than its predicted score will have a positive residual. All the points in the scatterplot that fall above the regression line have positive residuals. Any case that has an actual score less than its predicted score will have a negative residual. These are the points on the scatterplot below the regression line. And any cases whose actual scores perfectly match their predicted scores will have regression residuals of 0. These are the points on the scatterplot that fall exactly on the regression line.

An examination of regression residuals can serve several purposes. Occasionally, researchers discover that cases with large regression residuals had those large residuals because the original data were entered into the data matrix incorrectly. In such cases, the solution is to correct the data set and rerun the analysis.

More often, analyzing regression residuals enables researchers to improve their theory of why certain things happen. The cases with large residuals, either large negative or large positive residuals, are particularly useful. For the cases with small residuals, the independent variable would appear to be doing a good job of predicting the dependent variable. But clearly, the independent variable is not doing such a good job in predicting the dependent variable for cases with large residuals. A researcher might want to find out more about those cases with large residuals. What other things besides years of schooling might be accounting for their unexpectedly high or unexpectedly low income? Perhaps some of the persons with large negative residuals come from very large families or some of the persons with large positive residuals were born to particularly well-connected families. If that's true, it would appear that income is influenced not only by how much schooling the person gets but also by number of siblings and social class origin. If these variables are in the researcher's data set, adding them as additional independent variables should increase the explanatory power of the regression model while decreasing the size of the residuals.

Multiple Correlation Coefficient (R)

Look back at the regression output in Figure 9.7. Two statistics in the box labeled "Model Summary" summarize the overall relationship between the dependent variable and the set of independent variables. The first is the multiple correlation coefficient.

The **multiple correlation coefficient**, sometimes represented as R, can be described in two ways: statistically and substantively. Statistically, it is the correlation between the values the cases in the data set have on the dependent variable (Y) and their predicted values on the dependent variable ($\hat{Y}$). Substantively, the multiple correlation represents the association between the set of independent variables and the dependent variable. Note that it can be thought of as the association between a single variable (the dependent variable) and a set of variables (the independent variables). In bivariate regression, there is just a single independent variable, so the set of independent variables includes just one variable. That situation will quickly change when multiple independent variables are introduced into the regression equation in the next chapter.

Do not confuse Pearson's r with the multiple correlation coefficient. Both are measures of association, and their strength can be described using the scale presented in Chapter 8. However, there are three important differences. First, Pearson's r is usually represented by a lowercase r, whereas the multiple correlation is usually represented by an uppercase R. Second, while Pearson's r describes the association between two variables, the multiple correlation describes the association between a variable and a *set* of variables. Third, Pearson's r can range from −1.00 to 1.00, but the multiple correlation ranges only from 0.00 to 1.00. It never takes on negative values. At worst, the predicted values from a regression equation will have no relationship to the actual values on the dependent variable, in which case the correlation would be 0.00. At best, the predicted values will perfectly match the actual values, which would result in a correlation of 1.00. The predicted values will never correlate negatively with the actual values on the dependent variable.

The value of the multiple correlation coefficient appears in the Model Summary box under the heading "R." The value of the multiple correlation when INCOME86 is regressed on EDUC for 1980 GSS young adults is .389. In terms of strength, this is a moderate relationship. Since the multiple correlation ranges only from 0.00 to 1.00, it is neither necessary nor appropriate to describe its direction.

RESEARCH TIP

The Relationship Between Pearson's r and the Regression Coefficients

If you were to calculate Pearson's r for income and education for 1980 GSS young adults, remembering to limit the analysis to full-time workers age 25 and older with some income in the previous year but less than $139,297, you would get a value of .389, the same as the value of the multiple correlation. Standardized coefficients will be discussed in the next chapter, but a quick peek at the standardized coefficient for years of schooling in Figure 9.4 reveals it to also be .389.

As you might guess, the identical values of these statistics are not a coincidence. For bivariate regression and only for bivariate regression, the standardized regression coefficient always equals the value of Pearson's r, and if the value of Pearson's r is positive, the multiple correlation will also equal the value of Pearson's r. If the value of Pearson's r had been negative (i.e., −.389), the standardized regression coefficient would also be −.389. The multiple correlation, however, would still be .389. Its value would not have changed. The direction of the relationship between the independent and dependent variables does not matter for the multiple correlation since R does not indicate direction.

Coefficient of Determination (R^2)

The second useful summary statistic in the "Model Summary" box of the regression output appears right next to the value of R. This statistic goes by many names: R square, R^2, and **coefficient of determination**. Like the multiple correlation, it has both a statistical and substantive definition. The statistical definition of the coefficient of determination is quite simple. It is the value of the multiple correlation squared.

$$\text{coefficient of determination} = R^2$$

Substantively, the coefficient of determination shows how much of the variability initially observed in the scores on the dependent variable can be explained or accounted for by the independent variable(s) in the regression equation.

Like lambda in Chapter 8, the coefficient of determination is a proportional reduction in error (PRE) statistic. The statistic indicates how much better you do in predicting scores on the dependent variable when you know about the independent variable(s). The coefficient of determination is a proportion— the proportion of the variability in the dependent variable that is explained by the independent variable(s). As with most proportions, it ranges from 0.00 to 1.00. Most people find it easier to talk about percentages than about proportions. By multiplying the coefficient of determination by 100, you convert the proportion of variability explained into the percent of variability explained.

An R^2 of .00 means basing predictions of dependent variable scores on the regression equation is just as bad as always guessing the mean of the dependent variable. None of the original variability is explained by the independent variable(s). On the other hand, an R^2 of 1.00 means predictions of dependent variable scores based on the regression equation are perfect. You eliminate all the original error you had when you were just guessing based on the mean of the dependent variable. The regression equation explains all the original variability in the dependent variable. Of course, R^2 values of .00 or 1.00 are rare. They are usually somewhere in between. The closer R^2 is to .00, the poorer the independent variable(s) is in explaining differences in scores on the dependent variable. The closer R^2 is to 1.00, the better the explanation of the dependent variable provided by the independent variable(s).

Figure 9.7 shows the value of R^2 to be .151. (The same information appears to the right of the scatterplot of income by years of schooling in Figure 9.8.) Differences in years of schooling account for 15.1% of the differences in income. This does not mean the predicted levels of income are exactly right for 15.1% of the cases. It means the amount of error in the initial guesses of persons' income is reduced by 15.1% when predictions are based on their years of schooling and the regression equation.

R^2 can serve as a handy guide for comparing alternative explanations for differences in a dependent variable. One analyst believes education is the best explanation for differences in income among 1980 GSS young adults; another analyst believes the best explanation is differences in number of siblings. Who is right? Run two bivariate regressions, one with education as the independent variable and one with number of siblings as the independent variable. Which equation has the larger R^2? In the next chapter, additional independent variables are added to the regression equation. How can an analyst tell if those additional variables improve the ability to account for differences in the dependent variable? Look at how R^2 changes when the additional variables are added.

A companion statistic to the coefficient of determination is the coefficient of alienation. The coefficient of determination states the proportion of variance in the dependent variable explained by the independent variable(s). The **coefficient of alienation** states the proportion of variance in the dependent variable *not* explained by the independent variable(s). Although not reported in the SPSS output, the coefficient of alienation is easily calculated. Simply subtract the coefficient of determination from 1.00.

$$\text{coefficient of alienation} = 1 - R^2$$

If the proportion of variability in income explained by education is .151, then the proportion *not* explained is .849 (i.e., 1 − .151). The coefficient of alienation, like the coefficient of determination, can also be expressed as a percent.

Some Limitations to Remember

Regression Does Not Prove Causality

Regression statistics (b, R, R^2, $1-R^2$, and others to be introduced in later chapters) are only describing the statistical relationships between the variables. Statistical relationships alone do not prove causality. Even an R^2 of 1.00 does not prove that the independent variable caused the dependent variable unless there is also evidence of temporal sequence and nonspuriousness.

Linear Means Only Linear

Figure 9.9 shows a scatterplot with its best-fitting straight line. The best-fitting straight line may come as a surprise. It is apparent that a relationship exists between pretest scores and posttest scores. Both low pretest scores and high pretest scores go with low posttest scores while midrange pretest scores go with high posttest scores. Furthermore, the relationship appears to be pretty strong. Nevertheless, Pearson's r indicates a relationship so weak it is almost nonexistent, and the regression line seems to be missing what is obviously going on.

Statistics summarize data by looking for certain patterns, but that inevitably means they are not looking for other kinds of patterns. Both Pearson's r and linear regression are designed to detect linear relationships between variables. Linear relationships are those that resemble a straight line when graphed. Not all relationships are linear, however. Figure 9.9 is an example of a curvilinear relationship. The scatterplot resembles an inverted-U shape.

Do not automatically assume relationships between interval/ratio variables are linear. If possible, examine scatterplots. Look for patterns in residuals.

[handwritten margin note: Pearson's r + linear regression are designed to detect linear relationships bW variables]

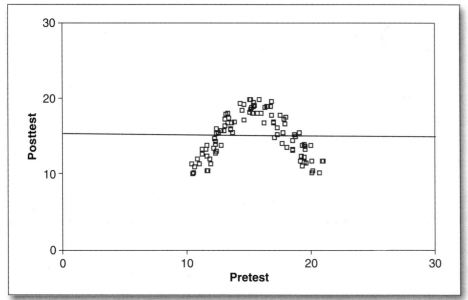

Figure 9.9   A Nonlinear Relationship (Pearson's $r = -.01$)

CONCEPT CHECK

Without looking back, can you answer the following questions:

- What information does an unstandardized coefficient provide?
- What information does a regression residual provide?
- What information does a multiple correlation coefficient provide?
- What information does a coefficient of determination provide?

If not, go back and review before reading on.

1980 GSS Young Adults

The chapter began with some questions about 1980 GSS young adults. On the basis of our analyses, what do we now know?

- When it comes to schooling and marriage, opposites clearly do not attract, or at least not marry. There was a strong positive relationship (Pearson's $r = .539$) between the educational levels of the mothers and fathers of the 1980 GSS young adults. In that parental generation, married partners resembled one another when it came to schooling.
- While many 1980 GSS twentysomethings had not yet married or finished their schooling, those who had married showed initial signs of resembling their parents when it comes to mate selection and schooling. There was a moderate positive relationship (Pearson's $r = .389$) between the respondent's years of schooling and his or her spouse's years of schooling. 1980 GSS twentysomethings with lots of schooling were marrying persons with lots of schooling; 1980 GSS twentysomethings with little schooling were marrying persons with little schooling.
- For 1980 GSS young adults, there was a moderately strong relationship between schooling and income ($R = .389$).
- Not controlling for other variables, each additional year of schooling typically resulted in $1,543 more annual income.
- About 15% of the differences in annual income among 1980 GSS young adults can be explained by differences in years of schooling. While 15% is noteworthy, it is clear that other things besides years of schooling played a part in the income differences.

Important Concepts in the Chapter

best-fitting straight line

Bivariate Correlations procedure

bivariate regression

coefficient of alienation

coefficient of determination (R^2)

interval/ratio measure of association

Linear Regression procedure

listwise deletion

multiple correlation coefficient (R)

pairwise deletion

Pearson's r

predicted value

regression equation

regression residual

scatterplot

unstandardized coefficient (slope, b)

Y intercept

Practice Problems

1. Which of the following Pearson's r values indicates the weakest relationship: $-.82$, $-.29$, $.10$, or $.65$?

2. The value of Pearson's r for variables A and B is $-.80$.
   a. Which is true about cases that have a high value on A: likely to have a low value on B, likely to have a high value on B, or equally likely to have a low or high value on B?
   b. Which is true about cases that have a low value on A: likely to have a low value on B, likely to have a high value on B, or equally likely to have a low or high value on B?

3. The value of Pearson's r for variables C and D is $-.56$, the value of Pearson's r for variables E and F is $.00$, and the value of Pearson's r for variables G and H is $.37$. Which pair of variables has the strongest association?

4. Which axis of a scatterplot, the horizontal axis or the vertical axis,
   a. represents the values of the independent variable?
   b. represents the values of the dependent variable?

5. If an independent variable's unstandardized regression coefficient is positive, do increases in the independent variable result in increases or decreases in the predicted score on the dependent variable?

6. If the value of R^2 for a regression equation is $.60$,
   a. How much of the variability in the dependent variable is accounted for by the independent variables?
   b. How much of the variability in the dependent variable is *not* accounted for by the independent variables?

7. What would each of these residuals tell you about a case's actual value on the dependent variable compared to the case's predicted value based on the regression equation?
   a. a negative residual
   b. a positive residual
   c. a residual of exactly zero

8. Here's a regression equation: PRICE = 10000 + 20000(ROOMS).
   a. For each additional room that a house has, how much does the predicted price increase?
   b. A six-room house would be predicted to sell for what price?

9. An analyst is interested in the relationship between hours spent preparing for an exam (the independent variable) and exam grade (the dependent variable). She regresses exam grade on hours spent studying. Here is the regression equation: GRADE = 60 + 5(HOURS).
   a. For every additional hour spent studying, what happens to the predicted grade?
   b. One student studied 5 hours. What was that student's predicted grade?

c. If one student studied 0 hours and received a grade of 50, what was that student's regression residual?
d. Does the best-fitting straight line through the scatterplot rise or fall as it moves to the right?

10. (*2010 GSS middle-age adults*) The following figure shows the results of regressing OKTEACH (an index ranging from 0 to 5 with higher scores indicating more willingness to let controversial persons teach college) on EDUC (years of schooling) for 2010 GSS middle-age adults. Answer the questions that follow the figure.

Model Summary

Model	R	R Square	Adjusted R Square	Std. Error of the Estimate
1	.250[a]	.062	.058	1.612

a. Predictors: (Constant), EDUC

Coefficients[a]

Model		Unstandardized Coefficients		Standardized Coefficients	t	Sig.
		B	Std. Error	Beta		
1	(Constant)	1.420	.545		2.606	.010
	EDUC	.145	.039	.250	3.727	.000

a. Dependent Variable: OKTEACH

a. What is the regression equation?
b. For every additional year of schooling, what happens to the predicted score on OKTEACH?
c. What proportion of the variability in willingness to let controversial persons teach college is explained by years of schooling?
d. What is the predicted score on OKTEACH for someone with 20 years of schooling?
e. If that person with 20 years of schooling actually has a score of 5 on OKTEACH, what is the regression residual?

Problems Requiring SPSS and the *fourGroups.sav* Data Set

11. (*2010 GSS young adults*) Calculate a measure of association for the relationship between years of schooling and spouse's years of schooling for the 2010 GSS twentysomethings. (Variables: EDUC, SPEDUC; Select Cases: GROUP = 3)
a. Which measure of association did you use? What is its value? What is the direction of the relationship? How would you describe the strength of the relationship using the guide in the last chapter?
b. Did 2010 GSS young adults with many years of schooling tend to marry persons with many or few years of schooling?
c. Summarize in a few well-written sentences totaling 100 words or less what you found out about the relationship between education and spouse's education for 2010 GSS young adults.

12. (*2010 GSS middle-age adults*) Calculate a measure of association for the relationship between years of schooling and spouse's years of schooling for the 2010 GSS fiftysomethings. (Variables: EDUC, SPEDUC; Select Cases: GROUP = 4)

    a. Which measure of association did you use? What is its value? What is the direction of the relationship? How would you describe the strength of the relationship using the guide in the last chapter?

    b. Did 2010 GSS middle-age adults with many years of schooling tend to marry persons with many or few years of schooling?

    c. [Figure 9.2 shows for the 1980 GSS young adults a moderate positive relationship between education and spouse's education. The value of Pearson's *r* is .389.] Summarize in a few well-written sentences totaling 100 words or less the similarities and/or differences in the relationship between education and spouse's education for these two groups of baby boomers—the 1980 young adults and the 2010 GSS middle-age adults.

13. (*2010 GSS young adults*) Regress income on years of schooling for 2010 GSS twentysomethings who were at least 25 years old, had some income in the previous year, and were working full-time the week before they took part in the GSS. (Variables: INCOME86, EDUC; Select Cases: GROUP = 3 and AGE >= 25 and WORKSTAT = 1)

    a. What is the regression equation?

    b. For each additional year of schooling, what happens to predicted income?

    c. Using the guide in the last chapter, how strong is the multiple correlation between income and the independent variable?

    d. What proportion of the variability in income is explained by education?

    e. [Figure 9.7 shows for the 1980 GSS young adults that education explained 15.1% of the differences in income.] Summarize in a few well-written sentences totaling 100 words or less the similarities and/or differences in the relationship between education and income for the 1980 and 2010 GSS young adults.

14. (*2010 GSS middle-age adults*) Regress SEI, which is a measure of occupational prestige on years of schooling, for the 2010 GSS fiftysomethings. (Variables: SEI, EDUC; Select Cases: GROUP = 4)

    a. What is the regression equation?

    b. For each additional year of schooling, what happens to predicted occupational prestige?

    c. Using the guide in the last chapter, how strong is the multiple correlation between occupational prestige and the independent variable?

    d. What proportion of the variability in occupational prestige is explained by education?

    e. Summarize in a few well-written sentences totaling 100 words or less what you found out about the relationship between occupational prestige and education for 2010 GSS middle-age adults.

15. (*2010 GSS middle-age adults*) Regress years of schooling on parental years of schooling for 2010 GSS middle-age adults. (Variables: EDUC, MAPAEDUC; Select Cases: GROUP = 4)

    a. What is the regression equation?

    b. For each additional year of parental schooling, what happens to the predicted years of schooling?

    c. Using the guide in the last chapter, how strong is the multiple correlation between years of schooling and the independent variable?

    d. What proportion of the variability in years of schooling is explained by parental years of schooling?

    e. Summarize in a few well-written sentences totaling 100 words or less what you found out about the relationship between education and parental education for 2010 GSS middle-age adults.

Questions and Tools for Answering Them
(Chapter 10)

Univariate Descriptive	Univariate Inferential

Data Management

Multivariate Descriptive	Multivariate Inferential

Questions:

- Changing a case's values on the independent variables produces how much of a change in the dependent variable?
- How well does the set of independent variables explain the differences among the cases on the dependent variable?
- What would we predict a case's score on the dependent variable to be? How close is our prediction to the case's actual score?
- What effect does an independent variable have on the dependent variable after controlling for the effect of other variables?
- Which of the independent variables has the strongest net effect on the dependent variable? Which has the weakest?

Statistics:

- unstandardized coefficient (slope, b)
- standardized coefficient (beta, β)
- regression residual
- multiple correlation coefficient (R)
- coefficient of determination (R^2)
- coefficient of alienation

SPSS Procedures:

- *Linear Regression*

Multiple Regression

10

In this chapter, you can learn

- how the equation for a straight line can summarize the relationship between an interval/ratio dependent variable and several independent interval/ratio variables,
- how that straight-line equation can be used to predict a case's score on the dependent variable,
- how to determine the strength and direction of an independent variable's effect on the dependent variable after controlling for the effects of other variables,
- how to assess how well a set of independent variables do in explaining the variation among cases on the dependent variable, and
- how ordinal and even nominal variables can be used as independent variables in regression.

Income, Education, Age, Gender, and Region

This chapter's questions about 1980 GSS young adults all relate to income:

- Does education still have an effect on income after other factors are controlled for?
- Controlling for other factors, did older 1980 GSS young adults have greater incomes than younger 1980 GSS young adults?
- Controlling for other factors, was there an income penalty for being female and, if so, how much?
- Controlling for other factors, did the region where the person lived help explain why some incomes were higher than others? If so, where were incomes highest?

- When other factors are being controlled, what had the greatest effect on income: years of schooling, age, gender, or region?
- How well do education, age, gender, and region together do in explaining the differences in income among 1980 GSS twentysomethings?

SPSS TIP

To Duplicate the Examples in This Chapter

To duplicate the examples in this chapter, use the *fourGroups.sav* data set. Set the select cases condition to GROUP = 1 and AGE >= 25 and WORKSTAT = 1 and INCOME86 < 139297.

Overview

In the last chapter, we saw the result of regressing income (the dependent variable) on years of schooling (the independent variable). This chapter introduces multiple regression by adding other independent variables to our explanation of income differences. With multiple independent variables, we can talk about each independent variable's net effect on the dependent variable, that is, its effect after controlling for other variables that might also be affecting the dependent variable. Because linear regression easily handles multiple independent variables and provides such useful information about the relationships between the variables, multiple regression is one of the most frequently used data analysis techniques.

Multiple Linear Regression

By including multiple independent variables, it is possible to construct more complete and powerful explanations for why cases differ on the dependent variable. For example, we can certainly come up with better models of why young adults differ in income if we are not limited to single-variable explanations. While how much schooling a person has helps explain income differences, other factors undoubtedly also play a part (as the modest coefficient of determination in the last chapter made apparent). Multiple regression enables you to assess the combined effectiveness of several independent variables in explaining differences on a dependent variable while it also identifies the unique contribution each independent variable makes to that overall explanation.

That unique contribution is the independent variable's net effect. Net effects are a way of controlling for other factors. For example, when you ask, "Does a person's gender still influence his or her income even after taking into account differences in education, age, and region of residence?" you are asking about gender's net effect.

Adding Independent Variables With SPSS

As in the last chapter, when regressing income on education for 1980 GSS young adults, the cases are limited to persons 25 and older who reported working full-time in the week prior to the survey and who reported some but less than $139,297 income in the previous year.

To get SPSS to do a multiple regression problem, follow the same steps as for a bivariate regression but move more than one variable into the "Independent(s)" list in the linear regression dialog. It is as simple as that.

Figure 10.1 shows the regression output when the dependent variable INCOME86 is regressed on the independent variables EDUC, AGE, and SEX for 1980 GSS young adults. Recall that this last variable is a dichotomy with males coded 0 and females coded 1.

Variables Entered/Removed[b]

Model	Variables Entered	Variables Removed	Method
1	SEX, AGE, EDUC	.	Enter

a. All requested variables entered.
b. Dependent Variable: INCOME86

Model Summary

Model	R	R Square	Adjusted R Square	Std. Error of the Estimate
1	.558[a]	.312	.287	7613.747

a. Predictors: (Constant), SEX, AGE, EDUC

ANOVA[b]

Model		Sum of Squares	df	Mean Square	F	Sig.
1	Regression	2.180E9	3	7.268E8	12.538	.000[a]
	Residual	4.811E9	83	57969144.55		
	Total	6.992E9	86			

a. Predictors: (Constant), SEX, AGE, EDUC
b. Dependent Variable: INCOME86

Coefficients[a]

Model		Unstandardized Coefficients B	Std. Error	Standardized Coefficients Beta	t	Sig.
1	(Constant)	-8142.153	17406.391		-.468	.641
	EDUC	1650.831	362.486	.416	4.554	.000
	AGE	267.101	609.235	.040	.438	.662
	SEX	-7174.415	1636.085	-.400	-4.385	.000

a. Dependent Variable: INCOME86

Figure 10.1 Output From Regressing INCOME86 on EDUC, AGE, and SEX for 1980 GSS Young Adults

The first box, which is labeled "Variables Entered/Removed," indicates that all three of the independent variables were entered into the regression model. Some regression techniques enter independent variables into the regression model in stages and, under certain circumstances, remove independent variables that have previously been entered. Those techniques are not used in this book.

The "ANOVA" box will continue to be skipped over for now since it deals with inferential statistics. As with bivariate regression, the boxes labeled "Model Summary" and "Coefficients" are the ones of interest.

Similarities to Bivariate Regression

The things you learned about bivariate regression also apply to multiple regression. The interpretation of regression statistics remains essentially the same whether there is one independent variable or more than one.

Unstandardized Coefficients

In the "Coefficients" box, the numbers under the "B" are the values of the Y intercept and unstandardized coefficients for the regression equation. The general form for a regression equation with multiple independent variables is

$$Y = a + b_1(X_1) + \ldots + b_n(X_n)$$

This is still the equation for a straight line, but it is a straight line through multidimensional space. As you add variables to the problem, you add dimensions. Each of the independent variables (X_1 through X_n) has its own unstandardized coefficient (b_1 through b_n). Each independent variable and unstandardized coefficient are given a numeric subscript just to keep straight which is which. There is still just one Y intercept.

As before, the regression equation is written by substituting the values of the Y intercept and unstandardized coefficients for their symbols in the general equation:

$$Y = -8142.153 + 1650.831(X_1) + 267.101(X_2) - 7174.415(X_3)$$

As before, the names or labels of the variables can be used instead of the Y and the Xs:

$$INCOME86 = -8142.153 + 1650.831(EDUC) + 267.101(AGE) - 7174.415(SEX)$$

What do the Y intercept and unstandardized coefficients say about the effect of the independent variables on the dependent variable? Starting from a baseline of −$8,142.15 (the Y intercept), each year of education typically increases income by $1,650.83, each year of age typically increases income by $267.10, and being female (which was coded 1 on SEX) rather than male (coded 0) typically decreases income by $7,174.41. The effect of being female is a decrease in income because the unstandardized coefficient is negative.

Predicted Values and Residuals

As before, the regression equation can be used to predict a case's value on the dependent variable, and the case's actual value on the dependent variable can be compared to its predicted value to get its residual. If a person in the data set had 12 years of schooling (EDUC = 12), was 25 years old (AGE = 25), and was male (SEX = 0), those values can be plugged into the regression equation to produce a predicted income of $18,345.34. If a second person had 12 years of schooling (EDUC = 12) and was 25 years old (AGE = 25) but was female (SEX = 1), her predicted income would be $11,170.93. The second person's predicted income is $7,174.41 lower than the first person's income, which coincides exactly with the unstandardized coefficient for SEX, which makes sense since that is the only difference between the two persons.

If the first person's actual income was $19,000 and the second person's actual income was $10,000, then the regression residual for the first person would be $654.66 ($19,000 minus $18,345.34), and the regression residual for the second would be −$1,170.93 ($10,000 minus $11,170.93).

If two people were of identical age and gender but the first person had 4 more years of schooling than the second person, the first person's predicted income would be $6,603.32 more than the second person's income. The only difference between the two is that the first person has 4 more years of schooling. Since we know from the unstandardized coefficient that each additional year of schooling increases income by $1,650.83, we can simply multiply that unstandardized coefficient by 4 to see what an increase of 4 years of schooling would mean. (Notice that we did not need to know the age or gender of the persons to solve this problem. All we needed to be told was that the two persons were of the same age and the same gender.)

Multiple Correlation

The interpretation of the multiple correlation (R) in multiple regression is the same as in bivariate regression. It is the correlation between the actual scores on the dependent variable and the scores predicted by the regression equation. The multiple correlation of .558 in Figure 10.1 indicates there is a strong correlation between income and the set of independent variables, which includes years of schooling, age, and gender. No mention should be made of the direction of the multiple correlation because R does not indicate direction.

Coefficients of Determination and Alienation

As with bivariate regression, the coefficient of determination (R^2) indicates how much of the variability initially observed in income can be explained by the set of independent variables, and the coefficient of alienation ($1 - R^2$) indicates how much cannot be explained by the set of independent variables. For 1980 GSS young adults, education, age, and gender account for 31.2% of the observed differences in income, leaving 68.8% unexplained.

RESEARCH TIP

Why Data Analysts Don't Think They Know It All

The two regression examples we have seen thus far have explained 15% and then 31% of the observed differences in income among the persons in the data set. That is not spectacular, but don't be surprised when you observe coefficients of determination that are even lower than these. The fact is that social behavior is very difficult to explain. Even when you incorporate several independent variables into the explanation, R^2 often reveals that you are explaining only a small proportion of the observed differences in what you hoped to explain. Data analysts tend to be humble in making claims about what causes certain kinds of behavior. Not only do they know how difficult it is to prove causality, but they have also seen too many low coefficients of determination. The next time you hear someone making claims about how one or two variables completely explain something, be suspicious. Withhold judgment about the completeness of their explanation until you have seen the results of an empirical test.

Of course, the upside of low coefficients of determination is that there is still plenty to discover about how the social world works. Small coefficients of determination mean large coefficients of alienation. The world still awaits your discoveries!

Standardized Coefficients

In addition to its unstandardized coefficient or slope, each independent variable in the regression equation has a **standardized coefficient** (also known as **beta** and sometimes represented by β). It appears in the "Coefficients" box of the output in a column labeled "Beta" under the heading "Standardized Coefficients." The direction of a variable's unstandardized coefficient and the direction of its standardized coefficient are always the same. If one is positive, the other is positive; if one is negative, the other is negative. But while the direction of the two coefficients is always the same, the size of the two coefficients certainly is not.

The standardized coefficients represent a recalculation of the regression equation after all of the values on each variable, dependent and independent, have been transformed into standardized or z-scores. SPSS is actually solving the regression problem twice. First, it solves the problem using the actual values in the data set for the dependent and independent variables. Second, it transforms all the variables in the regression problem into standardized variables and solves the problem again. The first solution gives us the unstandardized coefficients; the second gives us the standardized coefficients.

Both solutions provide unique and valuable information. While both sets of coefficients show the direction of each independent variable's effect on the dependent variable, only the unstandardized coefficients show the relationship between the variables in their actual metrics. We learn, for example, how much more income results from one more year of age. On the other hand, only the standardized coefficients show the strength of each independent variable's effect on the dependent variable. We can see, for example, that the effect of education on income is slightly stronger than the effect of gender, even though gender has a larger unstandardized coefficient. (Recall that the direction of a relationship matters not at all when discussing the strength of a relationship.)

While we could not apply the criteria for weak, moderate, strong, and very strong to the unstandardized coefficients, we can to the standardized coefficients. Both schooling and gender have strong effects on income, with the effect of education being slightly stronger. Age, however, has only a weak effect on income for these 1980 GSS young adults, which may not be surprising given that we have narrowed our data set to only those between the ages of 25 and 29.

Net Effects

It often happens that independent variables are correlated with other independent variables. For example, what if older 1980 GSS young adults tend to have more schooling than younger 1980 GSS young adults? That would make it more difficult to identify the specific effect of being older on income. Do older 1980 GSS young adults have greater income because they are older or because they have more schooling? Similarly, it creates a problem in identifying the specific effect of education on income. Do better educated 1980 GSS young adults tend to have more income because they are better educated or simply because they are older?

What we need is a way to separate the effect of an individual independent variable from the effects of the other independent variables. What we need is a way to see the net effect of each independent variable on the dependent variable. It is called the net effect because it is the effect that is left after the effects of the other independent variables have been removed.

One way to eliminate the effect of other variables is to hold them constant. For example, if we were studying a group of 1980 GSS young adults who were identical on age and gender but differed on years of education and we found a statistical relationship between education and income, we would know that the effect education is having on income is not because education is related to age or because education is related to gender because age and gender have been controlled by being held constant.

For most types of research, limiting an analysis to cases that are identical on all but the independent and dependent variables is impractical. Fortunately, an alternative method of controlling for other variables exists. Several multivariate statistical techniques, including linear regression, estimate the net effect of independent variables on dependent variables based on the observed interrelationships between the variables in the data set. Both the standardized and the unstandardized coefficients in linear regression are net effects. They show how much effect each independent variable has on the dependent variable when the other independent variables are controlled or statistically held constant. When you see an independent variable having an effect on the dependent variable, it is not because that independent variable is related to one or more of the other independent variables. What you are seeing are the net effects.

Imagine someone saying, "Yes, sure, better educated 1980 GSS young adults have more income than less educated 1980 GSS young adults, but that is only because the better educated twentysomethings are older. How long a person stays in school just does not matter if you take into account their gender and their age." The regression equation proves this critic wrong! The regression coefficients for education are not reduced to zero when age and gender are included in the equation. Education has a strong, positive effect even after age and gender are taken into account.

Of course, we still have not proven that differences in education cause differences in income. It is still possible that the relationship between education and income is spurious and would disappear if the right variables were controlled for. For example, some other critic might claim that the apparent effect of education on income is really due to geographic region. That wages are higher in some regions than in others, and once region is taken into account, the apparent effect of education will disappear. It is impossible to statistically control for all possible other factors. The best an analyst can do is to control for the more likely other factors. For now, we know the effect of education is not due to age and gender. We will leave the second critic's claim about region for later.

RESEARCH TIP

Which to Use: Pearson's r *or Beta?*

There are many times when you simply want to know what the correlation is between two interval/ratio variables. Regardless of whether the relationship is spurious or not, you just want to know how strongly associated the two variables are and in which direction. In that case, Pearson's *r* is what you want.

Other times, however, it is the net effect of one variable on another that you want to know. When you want to separate out the effect of one variable from the effect of other variables, beta is what you want.

CONCEPT CHECK

Without looking back, can you answer the following questions:

- What information does a standardized coefficient provide?
- What is a net effect?

If not, go back and review before reading on.

Multicollinearity

Multiple regression does have a problem, though, regarding net effects. When two or more of the independent variables are very strongly correlated with one another, it becomes very difficult to statistically separate each variable's net effect. An analogy might help. When two people do some things together but some things separately, you can still get a sense for how each acts apart from the other from the times you see them separately. But when two people do almost everything together, it is difficult to tell what each of them is like alone. It is the same thing with two variables. When two variables are weakly, moderately, or even strongly correlated, multiple regression still has enough separate occurrences of each variable to identify its net effect. But when the two variables are very strongly correlated, there are not enough separate occurrences to confidently measure their net effects.

The situation when two or more independent variables are very strongly related is called multicollinearity. (The guidelines in Chapter 4 for describing measures of association defined "very strongly related" as an association whose absolute value is .60 or higher.) Very strong negative correlations are just as much of a problem as very strong positive correlations. Multicollinearity is only concerned with correlations among the independent variables. A very strong correlation between an independent variable and the dependent variable is not a multicollinearity problem.

When multicollinearity occurs, you will still get unstandardized and standardized regression coefficients for the affected variables. The problem is that those specific coefficients are not stable. They are based on the very few cases in the data set where the very strongly correlated variables do not co-vary. If just a few of those cases had been different, the coefficients would have been dramatically different. Multicollinearity affects the regression coefficients. The values of the multiple correlation and the coefficient of determination are not affected.

You need to know if you have a multicollinearity problem before you do a multiple regression. SPSS will not warn you of the situation. The simplest way to spot multicollinearity is to examine a correlation matrix that includes all the independent variables in the regression problem and that is based on the same cases as are included in the regression problem. That exact correlation matrix can be requested when setting up the regression problem. In the linear regression dialog (see Figure 9.6), there is a "Statistics" button. When you click it, a dialog similar to Figure 10.2 opens. When it appears, leave everything as it is but also check "Descriptives"; then click "Continue."

Checking "Descriptives" adds two additional boxes of output. They actually precede the other regression output. Figure 10.3 shows these "Descriptives" boxes when income is regressed on schooling, age, and gender for 1980 GSS young adults.

Requesting descriptive statistics gets the mean and standard deviation for each of your regression variables along with a correlation matrix. An examination of the correlation matrix for this example shows no multicollinearity problem. Among the independent variables, the strongest correlation is the weak positive correlation between education and gender. There is no multicollinearity problem. Remember that the correlations between the independent variables and the dependent variable do not matter in terms of multicollinearity; only the correlations among the independent variables need to be checked.

What if multicollinearity is present? There are a few options. The first and most frequently used solution is to remove one of the very strongly correlated independent variables from the regression problem. Remove the variable that you are less interested in theoretically. A second choice would be to leave all the independent variables in the problem, make use of the multiple correlation and coefficient of determination, but ignore the individual regression coefficients. A third choice would be to drop both of the very strongly correlated independent variables from the regression problem but insert in their place a newly computed variable that is a combination of the very strongly correlated original variables. For example, the variable MAPAEDUC was described in Chapter 5. It is the average of mother's years of schooling and father's years of schooling. For the GSS 1980 middle-age adults, using both MAEDUC and PAEDUC as independent variables in a regression equation would create a multicollinearity problem. Using MAPAEDUC instead avoids the problem.

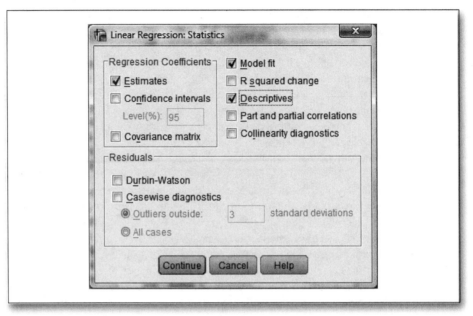

Figure 10.2 Regression Dialog to Request Descriptive Statistics

Descriptive Statistics

	Mean	Std. Deviation	N
INCOME86	17701.40	9016.697	87
EDUC	13.47	2.271	87
AGE	27.08	1.349	87
SEX	.51	.503	87

Correlations

		INCOME86	EDUC	AGE	SEX
Pearson Correlation	INCOME86	1.000	.389	.021	-.373
	EDUC	.389	1.000	-.039	.064
	AGE	.021	-.039	1.000	.008
	SEX	-.373	.064	.008	1.000
Sig. (1-tailed)	INCOME86	.	.000	.425	.000
	EDUC	.000	.	.360	.279
	AGE	.425	.360	.	.471
	SEX	.000	.279	.471	.
N	INCOME86	87	87	87	87
	EDUC	87	87	87	87
	AGE	87	87	87	87
	SEX	87	87	87	87

Figure 10.3 Descriptive Statistics From Regressing INCOME86 on EDUC, AGE, and SEX for 1980 GSS Young Adults

Levels of Measurement

Multiple regression is a very commonly used multivariate statistical procedure. It and analysis of variance, which is explained in the inferential section of the book, are the two real multivariate workhorses in statistical analysis. Because multiple regression so easily handles multiple independent variables and provides such a variety of information about the relationships among the variables, researchers have explored just how wide a range of problems multiple regression can handle.

One of the restrictions of multiple regression is that it was originally intended for use only with interval/ratio variables. Both the dependent and the independent variables are assumed to be interval/ratio. However, researchers have found that for some situations, the level of measurement requirement can be lowered or otherwise gotten around.

When it comes to the dependent variable, however, the original requirement holds. The dependent variable in a regression problem must be interval/ratio. Furthermore, it cannot be a dichotomy. While dichotomous variables are sometimes treated as interval/ratio (see Chapter 1), other multivariate techniques beyond the scope of this book should be used for dichotomous dependent variables.

The situation is more flexible when it comes to the independent variables. Of course, interval/ratio independent variables are fine. Ordinal independent variables are also acceptable. Statisticians have found that multiple regression is sufficiently robust (a statistical term for flexible) that it yields interpretable results when ordinal independent variables are included in the research problem. Generally, the more categories the ordinal variable has, the more meaningful the regression results are.

Nominal independent variables are a more complicated case. Ordinal variables at least have rank order; nominal variables do not. First consider the case of dichotomous nominal variables. As noted above, dichotomous variables cannot serve as regression dependent variables even if they are thought of as interval/ratio. As regression independent variables, however, dichotomous variables pose no problem. When including a dichotomous independent variable in a regression problem, the regression coefficients are easiest to interpret if the dichotomy is coded 0 and 1. In the previous multiple regression example, the variable SEX is a dichotomy with males coded 0 and females coded 1. When the dichotomy is coded 0 and 1, the unstandardized coefficient shows the net effect of being in the category coded 1. SEX had an unstandardized coefficient of -7174.415. For females (those with a code of 1 on SEX), the unstandardized coefficient is multiplied by 1 and has the effect of lowering predicted income by \$7,174.41. For males (those with a code of 0 on SEX), the unstandardized coefficient is multiplied by 0, which means the predicted income is not lowered by \$7,174.41.

Nominal variables with more than two categories are more of a problem. Nevertheless, they too can be included as independent variables in multiple regression but only after they have been converted into a series of dichotomous variables.

Dummy Variables

Nominal variables with three or more attributes must be converted into a series of dichotomous variables (called **dummy variables**) to be included in a multiple regression problem. The set of dichotomous variables *as a group* contains the same information that was originally contained in the single nominal variable. Converting the original information into dichotomous variables solves the problem of getting the original variable into the multiple regression analysis since dichotomous variables can be treated as interval/ratio and can be included in multiple regression as independent variables.

In the previous multiple regression, we were trying to understand why 1980 GSS young adults differed in income. Perhaps we want to include in our explanation region along with education, age, and gender. But REGION is a nominal variable consisting of four attributes: Northeast (coded 1), Midwest (coded 2), South (coded 3), and West (coded 4). We need to transform REGION into a series of dummy variables using the *Recode* procedure. Table 10.1 shows how this could be done.

Table 10.1 Converting REGION Into a Set of Dummy Variables

Original Variable		
REGION	Northeast = 1, Midwest = 2, South = 3, West = 4	
New Variables		
NOREAST	if REGION = 1, NOREAST = 1	otherwise NOREAST = 0
MIDWEST	if REGION = 2, MIDWEST = 1	otherwise MIDWEST = 0
SOUTH	if REGION = 3, SOUTH = 1,	otherwise SOUTH = 0
WEST	if REGION = 4, WEST = 1,	otherwise WEST = 0

All of the information in the original variable REGION is contained in the set of variables NOREAST, MIDWEST, SOUTH, and WEST. A person who is coded Northeast on REGION would be coded 1 on NOREAST, 0 on MIDWEST, 0 on SOUTH, and 0 on WEST. A person who is coded Midwest on REGION would be coded 0 on NOREAST, 1 on MIDWEST, 0 on SOUTH, and 0 on WEST. A person who is coded South on REGION would receive a code of 1 on SOUTH but 0 on each of the other variables, and a person coded West on REGION would be coded 1 on WEST but 0 on each of the others. Since NOREAST, MIDWEST, SOUTH, and WEST are dichotomies, they could be included as independent variables in a multiple regression.

However, the entire set of dummy variables should not be included in the regression equation. One should be omitted. This is because its information is actually unnecessary. Think about it. If you know a case's score on three of the regional dummy variables—for example, NOREAST, MIDWEST, and SOUTH—you know that case's score on the fourth dummy variable, WEST. If someone has a 1 on one of the first three variables, you know all the other variables, including WEST, must be 0. On the other hand, if someone has 0 on each of the first three variables, then this person must have a 1 on WEST. Just like you need only one dichotomy to convey the information in a two-category variable, you need only two dichotomies to convey the information in a three-category variable, three dichotomies to convey the information in a four-category variable, and so on. If you put all the dummy variables into the multiple regression, you actually create a type of multicollinearity problem for yourself since cases' scores on one of the independent variables could be perfectly predicted from scores on the other independent variables.

Thought needs be given to which dummy variable is omitted since the effect on the dependent variable of the dummy variables included in the regression equation will be compared to the effect of the omitted dummy variable. You want the effect of the omitted category to be relatively certain so the omitted dummy variable should be based on a category that has a substantial number of cases in it. If one of the categories represents the standard treatment or the typical situation and the other categories represent experimental treatments or less typical situations, omit the dummy variable that represents the standard treatment or the typical situation. This will make interpretation of your results easier.

Figure 10.4 shows the model summary and regression coefficients when income is regressed onto education, age, gender, and a series of regional dummy variables. MIDWEST is the omitted dummy variable.

Model Summary

Model	R	R Square	Adjusted R Square	Std. Error of the Estimate
1	.608[a]	.369	.322	7424.529

a. Predictors: (Constant), WEST, AGE, EDUC, SEX, NOREAST, SOUTH

Coefficients[a]

Model		Unstandardized Coefficients		Standardized Coefficients	t	Sig.
		B	Std. Error	Beta		
1	(Constant)	-8136.639	17004.221		-.479	.634
	EDUC	1459.651	361.261	.368	4.040	.000
	AGE	428.827	603.294	.064	.711	.479
	SEX	-8022.563	1659.835	-.447	-4.833	.000
	NOREAST	-1947.002	2472.013	-.094	-.788	.433
	SOUTH	-3551.716	2272.454	-.192	-1.563	.122
	WEST	2661.086	2652.157	.112	1.003	.319

a. Dependent Variable: INCOME86

Figure 10.4   Output From Regressing INCOME86 on EDUC, AGE, SEX, NOREAST, SOUTH, and WEST for 1980 GSS Young Adults

The multiple correlation and coefficient of determination are higher for this new regression equation. That means the regional variables add additional explanatory power.

The coefficients for the three regional variables should each be interpreted relative to the omitted category, which was Midwest. The unstandardized coefficients tell us that after controlling for education, age, and gender, Westerners typically earned $2,661 more than 1980 GSS young adults living in the Midwest, Northeasterners $1,947 less, and Southerners $3,552 less. Of the regional net effects, the negative effect on income of living in the South is strongest.

Controlling for region by including the regional dummy variables in the equation alters the net effects of the original independent variables, particularly education and sex. The net effect of education declines (beta = .37) while the effect of sex increases (beta = −.45). Some of what appeared to be the effect of education was apparently due to better educated individuals living in higher income areas, and some of the income penalty for being female was masked by employed women being in higher income regions. By controlling for region, the actual net effects of education and sex become clearer.

CONCEPT CHECK

Without looking back, can you answer the following questions:

- What is multicollinearity and why is it a problem?
- How can a nominal variable with three attributes be used as a regression independent variable?

If not, go back and review before reading on.

1980 GSS Young Adults

The chapter began with some questions about 1980 GSS young adults. On the basis of our analyses, what do we now know?

- The positive effect of years of schooling on income remains even after age, gender, and region are taken into account (beta = .368).
- Age has a weak positive effect on income even after controlling for education, gender, and region (beta = .064). The 1980 GSS young adults included in the analysis only ranged in age from 25 to 29, but even within this small range, older individuals typically earned more than younger individuals.
- Even after taking education, age, and region into account, being female had a strong negative effect on income (beta = − .447). Female 1980 GSS young adults typically made about $8,023 less than males from the same region with the same schooling and age.
- The effects of region on income are weak but present among 1980 GSS young adults (betas range from − .192 to .112). After controlling for schooling, age, and gender, 1980 GSS young adults living in the West had the highest typical incomes while 1980 GSS young adults living in the South had the lowest.
- When schooling, age, gender, and region are all included in the analysis, gender has the strongest net effect on income for 1980 GSS young adults. The net effect of schooling is next strongest.
- Education, age, gender, and region together account for more than a third of the differences in income among 1980 GSS young adults ($R^2 = .369$).

Important Concepts in the Chapter

coefficient of alienation

coefficient of determination (R^2)

dummy variable

Linear Regression procedure

multicollinearity

multiple correlation coefficient (R)

multiple regression

net effect

predicted value

regression equation

regression residual

standardized coefficient (beta, β)

unstandardized coefficient (slope, b)

Practice Problems

1. In the context of regression analysis, each of the following has at least one other name. State at least one of those other names:
   a. slope
   b. R
   c. R²
   d. beta

2. For each of the following, indicate if it gives you information about just the strength of a relationship, just the direction of a relationship, or both the strength and direction of a relationship:
   a. Pearson's r
   b. unstandardized regression coefficient
   c. standardized regression coefficient
   d. multiple correlation coefficient

3. For each of the following, indicate if it can be used as the *dependent* variable in regression.
   a. a dichotomy
   b. a nominal variable (with three or more attributes)
   c. an ordinal variable
   d. an interval/ratio variable

4. For each of the following, indicate if it can be used as an *independent* variable in regression.
   a. a dichotomy
   b. a nominal variable (with three or more attributes)
   c. an ordinal variable
   d. an interval/ratio variable

5. The regression coefficients for two independent variables that are very strongly related to one another may not be very stable. What is the name for this regression problem?

6. You want to do a multiple regression analysis in which the dependent variable is final course average and the independent variables are SAT score, year in college, and academic major. The problem is that academic major is a nominal variable with five attributes: criminal justice, political science, sociology, social work, and other. How could you proceed?

7. Here's a regression equation: PRICE = 10000 + 15000(ROOMS) − 1000(YEARS).
    a. For each additional room that a house has, how much does the predicted price increase?
    b. For each additional year since a house was built, how much does the predicted price decrease?
    c. A six-room house that is 10 years old would be predicted to sell for what price?

8. An analyst regresses exam grade on hours spent studying and number of children in the household. Here is the regression equation:

$$GRADE = 60 + 6(HOURS) - 2(CHILDREN).$$

    a. For every additional hour spent studying, what happens to the predicted grade? 6
    b. For every additional child in the household, what happens to the predicted grade? -2
    c. One student studied 5 hours. There are three children in his household. What was that student's predicted grade? $Y = 60 + 6 \times 5 - 2 \times 3 = 84$
    d. If one student studied 6 hours, has one child in her household, and received a grade of 100, what was that student's regression residual? $Y - predicted\ \hat{Y}\ (60 + 6 \times 6 - 2 \times 1) = 94) = 6$
       100

9. (2010 GSS young adults) The following figure shows the results of regressing hours of TV per day on hours of work per week, number of children, and gender. Gender was coded 0 for males and 1 for females. Answer the questions that follow the figure.

Model Summary

Model	R	R Square	Adjusted R Square	Std. Error of the Estimate
1	.256[a]	.066	.046	2.011

a. Predictors: (Constant), SEX, CHILDREN, HOURS

Coefficients[a]

Model		Unstandardized Coefficients		Standardized Coefficients	t	Sig.
		B	Std. Error	Beta		
1	(Constant)	2.589	.566		4.573	.000
	HOURS	-.011	.012	-.075	-.903	.368
	CHILDREN	.479	.163	.239	2.935	.004
	SEX	-.438	.344	-.106	-1.273	.205

a. Dependent Variable: TVHOURS

    a. What is the value of the multiple correlation?
    b. What proportion of the variability in hours of TV is explained by the set of independent variables?
    c. What is the regression equation?

d. For every additional child, how does the predicted score on TVHOURS change?

e. Two men both worked 40-hour weeks. One man had no children, and the other had two children. Which would you predict watched more TV? How much more?

f. Controlling for number of hours worked and number of children, which gender averaged more hours of TV? How much more?

g. Describe the strength of each independent variable's net effect.

10. (*2010 GSS middle-age adults*) The following figure shows the results of regressing years of schooling on parental years of schooling, number of siblings, and gender. Gender was coded 0 for males and 1 for females. Answer the questions that follow the figure.

Model Summary

Model	R	R Square	Adjusted R Square	Std. Error of the Estimate
1	.446[a]	.199	.193	2.592

a. Predictors: (Constant), SEX, MAPAEDUC, SIBLINGS

Coefficients[a]

Model		Unstandardized Coefficients B	Unstandardized Coefficients Std. Error	Standardized Coefficients Beta	t	Sig.
1	(Constant)	10.649	.604		17.629	.000
	MAPAEDUC	.323	.044	.372	7.416	.000
	SIBLINGS	-.140	.046	-.152	-3.016	.003
	SEX	-.067	.277	-.012	-.241	.810

a. Dependent Variable: EDUC

a. How would you describe the strength of the multiple correlation between years of schooling and the set of independent variables?

b. What proportion of the variability in years of schooling is explained by the set of independent variables?

c. What proportion of the variability in years of schooling is *not* explained by the set of independent variables?

d. What is the value of the coefficient of determination?

e. What is the regression equation?

f. For every additional year of parental schooling, how does the predicted score on EDUC change?

g. Controlling for parental schooling and gender, do persons with more siblings get more schooling or less schooling?

h. Describe the strength of each independent variable's net effect.

Problems Requiring SPSS and the *fourGroups.sav* Data Set

11. (*2010 GSS young adults*) Regress income on years of schooling, age, and gender for 2010 GSS twentysomethings who were at least 25 years old and were working full-time the previous week. (Variables: INCOME86, EDUC, AGE, SEX; Select Cases: GROUP = 3 and AGE >= 25 and WORKSTAT = 1)

    a. What is the regression equation?

    b. Net of other factors, identify for each of the following which 2010 GSS young adults tended to have higher incomes:

        i. persons with less schooling or with more schooling?

        ii. younger persons or older persons?

        iii. males or females?

    c. Which independent variable had the strongest effect on income? Which the weakest?

    d. What proportion of the variability in income is explained by the combination of education, age, and gender?

    e. [Figure 10.1 shows for the 1980 GSS young adults that education had a strong positive effect on income, age had a weak positive effect, and being female had a strong negative effect.] Summarize in a few well-written sentences totaling 100 words or less the similarities and/or differences in the effects of education, age, and gender on income for the 1980 and 2010 GSS young adults.

12. (*2010 GSS middle-age adults*) Regress income on years of schooling, age, gender, and the Northeast, South, and West dichotomies for 2010 GSS fiftysomethings who were working full-time the previous week. (Variables: INCOME86, EDUC, AGE, SEX, NOREAST, SOUTH, WEST; Select Cases: GROUP = 4 and WORKSTAT = 1)

    a. What proportion of the variability in income is explained by the combination of education, age, gender, and region?

    b. How strong is the net effect of

        i. years of schooling?

        ii. age?

        iii. gender?

    c. Controlling for other factors, 2010 GSS middle-age adults in which of the four regions typically had the highest income? The lowest income?

    d. [Figure 10.4 shows for the 1980 GSS young adults that education, age, gender, and region accounted for 36.9% of the differences in income.] Summarize in a few well-written sentences totaling 100 words or less the similarities and/or differences in the ability of education, age, gender, and region to explain income for these two groups of baby boomers—the 1980 GSS young adults and the 2010 GSS middle-age adults.

13. (*2010 GSS middle-age adults*) Regress SEI, which is a measure of occupational prestige, on years of schooling, age, and gender for 2010 GSS fiftysomethings. A person's SEI score is based on his or her current or most recent job. (Variables: SEI, EDUC, AGE, SEX; Select Cases: GROUP = 4)

    a. What is the regression equation?

    b. Net of other factors, identify for each of the following which 2010 GSS middle-age adults tended to be in higher prestige occupations:

  i. persons with less schooling or with more schooling?

  ii. younger persons or older persons?

  iii. males or females?

c. Which independent variable had the strongest effect on occupational prestige? Which the weakest?

d. What proportion of the variability in occupational prestige is explained by the combination of education, age, and gender?

e. Summarize in a few well-written sentences totaling 100 words or less what you found out about the effect of education, age, and gender on occupational prestige for the 2010 GSS middle-age adults.

14. (*2010 GSS young adults*) Regress willingness to allow legal abortion on years of schooling, gender, and strength of religious affiliation for 2010 GSS twentysomethings. (Variables: ABORTOK, EDUC, SEX, RELINTEN; Select Cases: GROUP = 3)

a. What is the regression equation?

b. Net of other factors, identify for each of the following which 2010 GSS young adults tended to have greater willingness to allow legal abortion:

  i. persons with less schooling or with more schooling?

  ii. males or females?

  iii. persons with weaker ties or stronger ties to religion?

c. Which independent variable has the strongest effect on willingness? Which the weakest?

d. What proportion of the variability in willingness is explained by the combination of education, gender, and strength of religious affiliation?

e. Summarize in a few well-written sentences totaling 100 words or less what you found out about the effect of education, gender, and strength of religious affiliation on willingness to allow legal abortion for 2010 GSS young adults.

15. (*2010 GSS middle-age adults*) Regress number of children on years of schooling, number of siblings, and strength of religious affiliation for 2010 GSS fiftysomethings. (Variables: CHILDREN, EDUC, SIBLINGS, RELINTEN; Select Cases: GROUP = 4)

a. What is the regression equation?

b. Describe the direction and strength of the net effect on number of children of

  i. years of schooling

  ii. number of siblings

  iii. strength of religious affiliation

c. Which independent variable has the strongest effect on number of children? Which the weakest?

d. What proportion of the variability in number of children is explained by the combination of education, siblings, and strength of religious affiliation?

e. Summarize in a few well-written sentences totaling 100 words or less what you found out about the effect of education, siblings, and strength of religious affiliation on number of children for the 2010 GSS middle-age adults.

PART III

INFERENTIAL STATISTICS

Answering Questions About Populations

Formulas Appearing in Part Three (Chapters 11–16):

$$\text{standard error} = \frac{\text{population stdev}}{\sqrt{\text{sample size}}}$$

$$\text{estimated standard error} = \frac{\text{sample stdev}}{\sqrt{\text{sample size}}}$$

one-sample t test: $df = N - 1$

one-sample t test: $N = df + 1$

paired-samples t test: $df = N - 1$

paired-samples t test: $N = df + 1$

one-way ANOVA: $df = (K - 1 \text{ and } N - K)$

one-way ANOVA: $K = df_1 + 1$

one-way ANOVA: $N = df_2 + K$

$$\text{expected count} = \frac{\text{row total} \times \text{column total}}{\text{table total}}$$

cell residual = observed count − expected count

$$\text{chi-square} = \sum \frac{\text{cell residual}^2}{\text{expected count}}$$

chi-square: $df = (\text{\# of rows} - 1) \times (\text{\# of columns} - 1)$

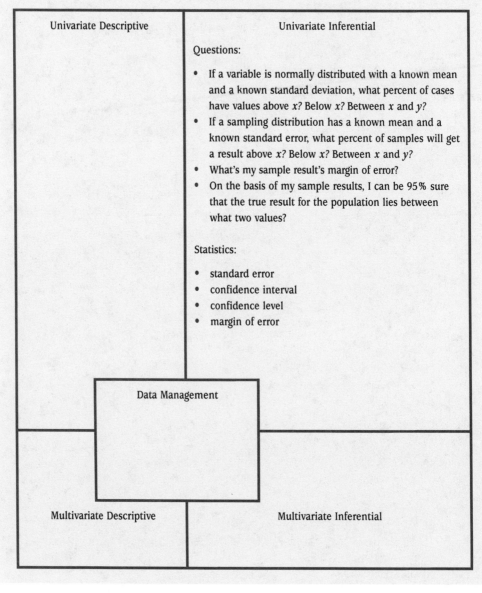

Questions and Tools for Answering Them
(Chapter 11)

Univariate Descriptive	Univariate Inferential
	Questions:
	• If a variable is normally distributed with a known mean and a known standard deviation, what percent of cases have values above x? Below x? Between x and y?
	• If a sampling distribution has a known mean and a known standard error, what percent of samples will get a result above x? Below x? Between x and y?
	• What's my sample result's margin of error?
	• On the basis of my sample results, I can be 95% sure that the true result for the population lies between what two values?
	Statistics:
	• standard error
	• confidence interval
	• confidence level
	• margin of error

Data Management

Multivariate Descriptive	Multivariate Inferential

Sampling Distributions and Normal Distributions

11

In this chapter, you can learn

- how statements about populations can be made from sample data;
- how the normal distribution can be used to answer questions about the percent of cases above, below, or between certain values;
- how sampling distributions can be used to answer questions about the percent of samples getting results above, below, or between certain values;
- how the margin of error of a sample result can be calculated; and
- how research decisions affect the size of a sample result's margin of error.

1980 GSS Young Adults Take a Break

Thus far in this book, any data analysis conclusions have been stated in such a way that it hopefully was clear the conclusion applied only to the persons actually included in the data set. Conclusions did not apply, for example, to all 1980 young adults but only to 1980 GSS young adults, that is, those twentysomethings in 1980 who participated in the GSS. Until now!

This chapter lays the groundwork for inferential statistics. Once that groundwork is laid, we return to our young adults and middle-age adults. But we use the data to make statements not just about the twentysomethings and fiftysomethings who took part in the GSS in 1980 or 2010 but about all twentysomethings and all fiftysomethings in 1980 and in 2010.

Overview

With inferential statistics, the focus shifts from describing the cases for which you actually have data to making statements about the population from which the cases in your data set came. The population is assumed to include more cases than were included in the data set. If data are available on every element in the population, then the data set constitutes a census, and only descriptive statistics are needed to describe the population since the population and the data set are identical.

But just because the data represent a sample from a larger population does not automatically mean inferential statistics can be used. The sample must be the result of a probability sampling technique such as simple random sampling, systematic random sampling, stratified random sampling, or cluster (multistage) random sampling. Nonprobability sampling techniques such as convenience sampling, purposive sampling, quota sampling, or snowball sampling offer real advantages such as speed, lower cost, and access to hard-to-identify populations but are unable to support inferential statistical techniques.

The discussion of inferential statistics in this text assumes that the sample was selected using a simple random sampling technique. Simple random sampling forms the basis of all probability sampling techniques. Some of the formulas for calculating inferential statistics change slightly when the data are from some other type of probability sampling procedure, but the logic of inferential statistics is the same regardless of which probability sampling procedure produced the sample.

Frequency Distributions

Imagine there is a college somewhere with exactly 1,000 currently enrolled students. A researcher creates a data set that includes 1,000 cases. Each case corresponds to one of the college's students. (Since the researcher has data on every element in the population, she is working with a census.) One of the variables is the number of courses in which the student is currently enrolled. Figure 11.1 shows both a frequency distribution for these data and a histogram.

When asked in how many courses they were currently enrolled, answers ranged from 1 to 10 with a mode of 5. The mean was 4.29 with a standard deviation of 1.58. The frequencies that are being reported are the number of cases with particular values: 100 cases had a value of 1, 60 cases had a value of 2, and so on.

We know that 4.29 is the true mean for this population of 1,000 students because data from every member of the population have been included in the calculation of the mean. Statisticians use the terms parameter and statistic to distinguish between characteristics of a population (those are parameters) and characteristics of a sample (those are statistics). The value of 4.29 for the mean is a parameter because it is based on the entire population.

Some Sampling Reminders

But what if the researcher was facing a deadline? She did not have the time to gather information on every currently enrolled student. Instead, she took a simple random sample of just 10 currently enrolled students, asked them in how many courses they were enrolled, and calculated a mean.

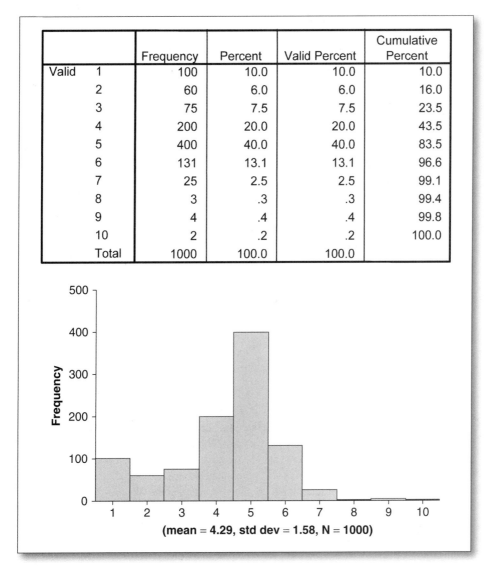

		Frequency	Percent	Valid Percent	Cumulative Percent
Valid	1	100	10.0	10.0	10.0
	2	60	6.0	6.0	16.0
	3	75	7.5	7.5	23.5
	4	200	20.0	20.0	43.5
	5	400	40.0	40.0	83.5
	6	131	13.1	13.1	96.6
	7	25	2.5	2.5	99.1
	8	3	.3	.3	99.4
	9	4	.4	.4	99.8
	10	2	.2	.2	100.0
	Total	1000	100.0	100.0	

(mean = 4.29, std dev = 1.58, N = 1000)

Figure 11.1   Frequency Distribution and Histogram for Number of Courses

Obviously, she is now dealing with sample results rather than census results. Before looking at the variety of sample results she might have obtained, note two things about sampling.

First, sample statistics do not always perfectly match population parameters. In fact, sample results rarely match the population value perfectly. When the researcher calculates her sample mean, it is unlikely to match the population parameter precisely. When a newspaper reports that an overnight poll found a certain percentage of eligible voters favored candidate Smith, readers should realize that a different result probably would have been obtained had a census of all eligible voters been taken instead. One hopes the sample result and the census result would not be far apart, but it would be foolish to believe the sample result hit the census result exactly on the head. This difference between the sample result and the census result is known as **sampling error.** Although it is called error, it does not imply that someone did something wrong, which caused the sample result and the census result to differ. Sampling error is a natural consequence of working with samples rather than censuses. Researchers who work with samples learn to live with sampling error, although they hope the amount of sampling error in their sample is small.

Second, samples of the same size from the same population can yield different results because elements in the sample are randomly selected. If a second researcher at the college took a simple random sample of 10 students from the same list of 1,000 students, asked them in how many courses they were enrolled, and calculated the mean, the second researcher's sample result is unlikely to perfectly match the first researcher's sample result. Once again, the discrepancy is not due to anyone doing anything wrong. Each researcher selected his or her own sample of just 10 persons from a population of 1,000 persons. Although possible, it is unlikely that any students at the college ended up in both samples. Because the researchers ended up with different students, it is very likely that their sample results will differ. The closer their results to each other, the more confidence we might have in the type of samples they took, but even with very sound sampling procedures, a perfect match between the sampling results would be unlikely. Furthermore, neither researcher's result is likely to perfectly match the true mean for the population.

Sampling Distributions

When our researcher takes her sample from the college population of 1,000 students, she will end up with a particular group of 10 students. The reason we can be quite sure that a second researcher following the same procedure would end up with a different sample is that there are so many different combinations of 10 students who could be selected from a population of 1,000. In fact, the number of different combinations is approximately 263,409,540,000,000,000,000,000. Furthermore, if simple random sampling is used to select the sample, any one of those 2.6×10^{23} combinations is as likely as any other combination to be the one selected.

Some of those combinations, however, will result in the same statistical value even though the group of 10 people making up the combination is different. A **sampling distribution** shows how frequently particular statistical results would occur if every possible sample of a particular size from a particular population were taken.

While a frequency distribution *compares cases* on their score for a particular variable, a sampling distribution *compares samples* on their value for a particular statistic. Although a histogram representing a frequency distribution and a histogram representing a sampling distribution may look similar, there is an important difference. A frequency distribution and its accompanying histogram counts how many cases have particular values on a variable; a sampling distribution and its accompanying histogram counts how many samples have a particular value on a statistic.

A complete sampling distribution for samples of size 10 from a population of 1,000 would tell you how many of those 2.6×10^{23} samples would give you a sample mean of 1.0 (which is the lowest possible sample mean), 1.1, 1.2, 1.3, and so on up to 8.7 (which is the highest possible sample mean). Figure 11.2 shows you a partial sampling distribution representing just 1,000 different samples from that college student population. Each of the samples consisted of 10 randomly selected students. The complete sampling distribution would obviously have much higher frequencies but would have approximately similar proportions.

Compare the frequency distribution in Figure 11.1 to the sampling distribution in Figure 11.2. One difference that is not particularly important but is certainly noticeable is that the bins are narrower in the sampling distribution. That is because the frequency distribution shows the values of cases, and the variable "number of courses in which enrolled" can take on only integer values. The sampling distribution, however, shows the values for the means of different samples. There are many more possible values for the mean than for the variable itself.

An important similarity between the frequency distribution and the sampling distribution has to do with their central tendencies; an important difference has to do with their dispersions. This similarity and this difference are the topics of the next two sections.

Central Tendency of Sampling Distributions

Keep in mind that the mean of a frequency distribution is calculated by averaging cases, while the mean of a sampling distribution is calculated by averaging sample results. The mean for Figure 11.1, the frequency distribution, is 4.29. Since the frequency distribution included every element in the population,

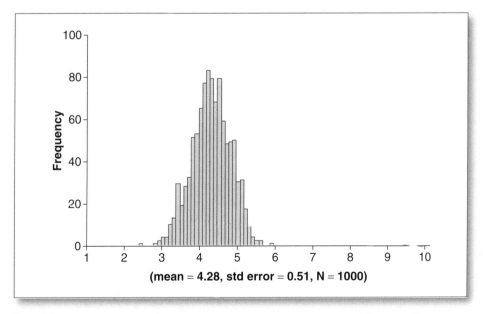

Figure 11.2   Histogram Representing a Sampling Distribution for 1,000 Samples of Size 10 for Number of Courses

that mean of 4.29 is the mean for the entire population—in other words, it is a parameter value. The mean for Figure 11.2, the partial sampling distribution, is 4.28. That is obviously pretty close to the parameter value of 4.29. And if Figure 11.2 were a complete sampling distribution and not the result of only 1,000 samples, the mean would have been exactly 4.29. Indeed, it can be proven that the mean of a complete sampling distribution always perfectly matches the mean of the population.

Now, no one recommends taking every possible sample of a particular size from a particular population to figure out the value of the population parameter. It would be a lot less work to take a census! What is important to remember, though, is that the mean of a sampling distribution corresponds exactly to the value of the population parameter. That fact will prove very useful later!

Dispersion of Sampling Distributions

An important difference between the frequency distribution and the sampling distribution is that the sample results in the sampling distributions are more concentrated together (less dispersed) than are the case values in the frequency distribution. Since the true mean in the population is 4.29, the fact that the sample results are clustered together around where 4.29 falls on the number line should be comforting to people who use samples and, therefore, must always worry about sampling error. Most samples were close, meaning they had only a small amount of sampling error.

In the frequency distribution, some cases had values as low as 1 or as high as 10. Since the samples represented in the sampling distribution are each composed of 10 randomly selected cases, there could have been a sample mean as low as 1.0 if all 10 randomly selected cases had values of 1, but because there were only 2 students in the population who were enrolled in 10 courses each, there could never be a sample mean as high as 10.0 as long as the sample is required to have 10 people. If by chance the 10 students with the highest number of courses all were selected in a single sample, that sample's mean would only be 8.7. In fact, though, the lowest sample mean to occur after 1,000 different samples was 2.4, and the highest was 5.9. While a sample of 10 could get a sample mean of less than 2.4 or more than 5.9, the probability of getting a sample of all low scores or one of all high scores is small. Samples were much more likely to end up with a mix of people in which the more common middle values of 4 or 5 courses were well represented.

The variance and standard deviation describe the dispersion in a frequency distribution. A statistic directly comparable to standard deviation exists to describe the dispersion in a sampling distribution. It is called standard error. The *standard deviation* indicates the average distance of cases from the mean; the *standard error* indicates the average distance of sample results from the population parameter. Just like standard deviation, the smaller the value of the standard error, the less dispersion (the more concentration), and the larger the value of the standard error, the more dispersion (the less concentration).

Standard Error

A large standard error means that different samples are getting very different results. A small standard error means that different samples are getting very similar results. A standard error of zero would mean all the sample results are identical. Not surprisingly, researchers like small standard errors because they mean that had the researcher by chance taken a different sample than she did, she still would have gotten a very similar result. Small standard errors, coupled with the fact noted earlier that sampling distributions are centered over the population parameter, make researchers very happy people!

RESEARCH TIP

Standard Deviation and Standard Error

The difference between standard deviation and standard error is important. Standard deviation measures the dispersion in a frequency distribution. Standard error measures the dispersion in a sampling distribution. When you read or hear someone talking about standard error, you should immediately realize that he or she is talking about a sampling distribution.

Calculating Standard Error

Figure 11.1 reports a standard deviation of 1.58 for the frequency distribution; Figure 11.2 reports a standard error of 0.51 for the sampling distribution. The smaller number for the standard error should come as no surprise since the sample results in the sampling distribution are more concentrated together than the values of the cases in the frequency distribution. In fact, there is a direct relationship between the standard deviation in a population and the standard error in a sampling distribution. It is expressed as follows:

$$\text{standard error} = \frac{\text{population stdev}}{\sqrt{\text{sample size}}}$$

To get the standard error for a sampling distribution, simply divide the standard deviation of the population by the square root of the size samples you are taking. In our example, the standard deviation in the population is 1.58, and the sampling distribution is built with samples of size 10.

$$\text{standard error} = \frac{1.58}{\sqrt{10}} = 0.50$$

The result is close to the 0.51 calculated by SPSS but not a perfect match! Rather than using the formula for standard error, SPSS calculated the standard error using the results of the 1,000 samples in the sampling distribution. But a sampling distribution based on 1,000 samples includes only a small fraction of the possible samples of size 10. Had the sampling distribution been complete—that is, included the results of all 2.6×10^{23} possible samples—it would have been a perfect match.

Factors Affecting Standard Error

Recall that researchers like small standard errors. Small standard errors mean that the results of different samples will be quite similar to one another, which means researchers will get pretty close to the same result regardless of which sample they happen to randomly select. The formula for the standard error reveals two factors that affect the size of the standard error: the standard deviation in the population and the size of the sample.

The larger the standard deviation in the population, the larger will be the standard error. The greater the dispersion of values in the population, the greater are the differences in possible sample results; and, of course, the less dispersion in the population, the smaller are the differences in possible sample results.

Think of two colleges. The first is the college we have been using for our example. The number of courses in which students are enrolled ranges from 1 to 10. Now imagine a second college. It also has exactly 1,000 students. At this college, though, students can enroll in only four or five courses per semester—nothing less than four and nothing more than five. There is less dispersion in this second college's population. If we were taking samples of size 10 from this second college's student population, there would still be 2.6×10^{23} possible samples, but no sample could have a sample mean less than 4.0 or greater than 5.0. The sampling distribution would have less dispersion; the standard error would be smaller. If we found a third college with 1,000 students where every student was absolutely required to register for five and only five courses, all of the samples of size 10 would have the same sample result, 5.0, and the standard error would be zero.

The less dispersion in the population, the smaller the standard error and the happier the researcher. Unfortunately, dispersion in the population is usually a factor beyond the researcher's control. Whatever the dispersion in the population, be it large or small, the researcher just has to work with it.

Sample size is a second factor that affects the size of the standard error, and this time a researcher may have more control. As the formula shows, standard error is inversely related to the square root of the sample size. The larger the sample size is, the smaller the standard error is; the smaller the sample size is, the larger the standard error is. If we constructed a sampling distribution based on samples of size 5, there would be more dispersion in the sample results than in Figure 11.2, whereas a sampling distribution based on samples of size 25 would have less dispersion than in Figure 11.2. Since researchers prefer small standard error, they should take large samples. Unfortunately, larger samples typically take more time and money to conduct, so a researcher must balance the desire for a small standard error against the time and monetary constraints under which she must work.

The fact that the square root of the sample size is in the denominator of the fraction means that larger sample size will always result in smaller standard error, but because it is the sample size's square root, the rate at which the standard error gets smaller slows down the larger the sample already is. Increasing a sample size from 100 to 200 gets you a much greater reduction in standard error than increasing a sample size that is already at 1,500 to 1,600.

Although it is not evident from the formula for standard error, a third factor that affects the size of the standard error is the type of probability sample being taken. Our formula for the standard error is for simple random sampling. Other types of probability sampling require different formulas for standard error. Sampling distributions based on stratified random sampling tend to have the smallest standard error, those based on cluster sampling tend to have the largest, and those based on simple or systematic random sampling tend to fall in between in regards to the size of the standard error.

Type of probability sample, like sample size, is at least somewhat within the researcher's control. For smaller standard errors, a researcher should do stratified sampling. However, time and money again enter the picture. Typically, stratified samples require the longest time and the most money to conduct, while cluster samples require the least time and money. So, once again, the desire for a smaller standard error must be weighed against the realities of limited time and limited money!

CONCEPT CHECK

Without looking back, can you answer the following questions:

- What is the difference between a frequency distribution and a sampling distribution?
- What is the difference between a standard deviation and a standard error?
- Why do researchers prefer sampling distributions with small standard errors?

If not, go back and review before reading on.

Normal Distributions

Understanding sampling distributions is essential for understanding inferential statistics, but so also is understanding the nature of **normal distributions**. A normal distribution is not an alternative to frequency and sampling distributions. Normal distribution refers to the shape of the distribution. Frequency distributions can be normal distributions or not. Sampling distributions can be normal distributions or not. The fact that normal distributions are called normal does not mean they are the norm, or that they are typical, or that distributions that are not normal are in some way defective. Normal is just a name given to distributions with certain mathematical properties.

You have probably heard references to things being normally distributed. The histogram for a normal distribution has a bell shape. In fact, normal distributions are sometimes referred to as bell curves. However, it takes more than an approximately bell-shaped histogram for a distribution to qualify as a normal distribution. A distribution must precisely meet a number of specific criteria to be a normal distribution. For our purposes, three criteria for a normal distribution are particularly important.

Symmetry

If a distribution is normal, then its histogram is perfectly symmetrical. The left side of the histogram perfectly matches the right side. If a normal distribution's histogram is folded over on itself, the two sides perfectly match. The symmetry of normal distributions is important because if something is true about one side of a normal distribution, then that same thing must be true about the other side since the two sides are identical.

Central Tendency

If a distribution is normal, then the values of the mean, median, and mode are identical. If the value of one of the measures of central tendency is known, then the values of the other two are also known since the mean, the median, and the mode all equal the same value. Since normal distributions are symmetrical, the middle case must occur at the center of the distribution. There have to be as many cases to the left of the center of the distribution as to the right—otherwise, the distribution would not be symmetrical. Since the median corresponds to the center of the distribution, so also must the mean and the mode since all three measures of central tendency have the same value. So, if you know where on the number line the center of the distribution occurs, you know the value of the mean, the median, and the mode.

Distributional Properties

Both frequency distributions and sampling distributions may qualify as normal distributions. The next few pages talk about normal frequency distributions; then the focus will shift to normal sampling distributions.

Not only must a distribution be symmetrical and its three measures of central tendency be identical for the distribution to be considered normal, but also the cases must be distributed around the mean (which is the center of the distribution) in exactly a certain way. It is these distributional requirements that give the distribution its bell shape. If a frequency distribution is a normal distribution,

- approximately 68% of all the cases must be within one standard deviation of the mean,
- approximately 95% of all the cases must be within two standard deviations of the mean, and
- approximately 99.7% of all the cases must be within three standard deviations of the mean.

The above statements mention the percent of cases within one, two, and three standard deviations of the mean in a normal distribution. In fact, the mathematical definition of a normal distribution specifies exactly what percent of cases must be within any distance from the mean. For our purposes, however, remembering the percents within one, two, and three standard deviations from the mean will be sufficient.

Each of the distributional criteria begins with the word *approximately*. This is because a small amount of rounding has been done to end up with numbers that are easier to remember.

Putting the Pieces Together

If you put together the fact that normal distributions are symmetrical, have identical values for their measures of central tendency, and must meet certain distributional properties, you actually know quite a bit about the percent of cases with certain values. Figure 11.3 illustrates just some of what can be deduced from the properties of a normal distribution.

The number line in Figure 11.3 corresponds to z-scores (first discussed in Chapter 5). Once a variable is transformed into z-scores, its mean becomes 0 and its standard deviation (and variance) equals 1. Figure 11.3 points out that for any variable that is normally distributed,

- 2.5% of the cases will have values more than two standard deviations below the mean,
- 13.5% of the cases will have values between one and two standard deviations below the mean,
- 34% of the cases will have values between the mean and one standard deviation below the mean,
- 34% of the cases will have values between the mean and one standard deviation above the mean,
- 13.5% of the cases will have values between one and two standard deviations above the mean, and
- 2.5% of the cases will have values more than two standard deviations above the mean.

Given the properties of normal distributions stated earlier, all of the percentage statements just made must be true.

Figure 11.3 could have been made even more detailed by drawing vertical lines corresponding to the z-scores −3.0 and 3.0 to subdivide the 2.5% of the cases in the left tail of the distribution and

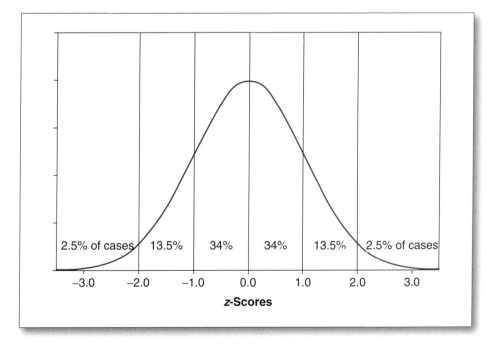

Figure 11.3   Distribution of Cases in a Normal Distribution

the 2.5% of cases in the right tail, but enough is enough. Just realize that the normal distribution continues even further to the left and right than you can see in Figure 11.3. Of course, very few cases fall that far from the center of a normal distribution, but some do.

Answering Questions With Normal Frequency Distributions

Some pretty interesting questions can be answered with just the elementary knowledge about normal distributions exhibited in Figure 11.3.

For example, a teacher tells a class that the grades on the last exam were normally distributed with a mean of 75 and a standard deviation of 5. Note that the students have been told three things: the mean, the standard deviation, and, very importantly, that the grades were normally distributed. Of course, since the grades were normally distributed and had a mean of 75, the median and the mode must also be 75. Knowing the mean and the standard deviation, the z-scores on the number line in Figure 11.3 could be converted into actual scores, thereby producing Figure 11.4.

With Figure 11.4, it should be easy to answer any of the following questions:

- What percent of students scored better than 85? (2.5%)
- What percent scored better than 80? (13.5 + 2.5 = 16.0%)
- What percent scored worse than 75? (2.5 + 13.5 + 34 = 50.0%)
- What percent scored between 65 and 85? (13.5 + 34 + 34 + 13.5 = 95%)

Take another hypothetical example. Someone states that length of life for men is normally distributed with a mean of 76 and a standard deviation of 7. Figure 11.3 can again be converted from z-scores into actual scores, thereby producing Figure 11.5.

With Figure 11.5, the following questions should be child's play:

- What percent of men will die before age 62? (2.5%)
- What percent of men will live past 83? (13.5 + 2.5 = 16.0%)
- What percent of men will die between the ages of 62 and 83? (13.5 + 34 + 34 = 81.5%)
- What is the median age at death for men? (76.0)

Of course, everything in the last two examples depends on the variables being normally distributed. If the exam mean is 75 and the standard deviation is 5 but the grades are not normally distributed, the median, the mode, and the percent of cases above, below, or between certain grades cannot be determined. The same would be true about male length of life. The properties of a normal distribution can only be applied to frequency distributions if the frequency distributions are stated to be normal. And here is the rub: Very few of the variables social scientists study in the real world are normally distributed!

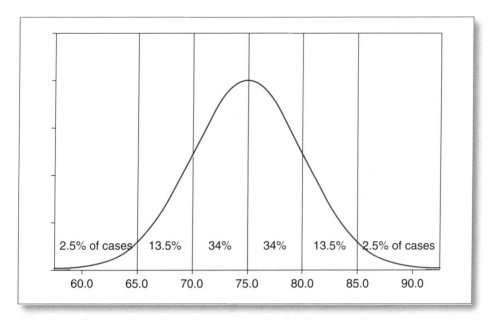

Figure 11.4   A Normal Distribution of Grades With a Mean of 75 and a Standard Deviation of 5

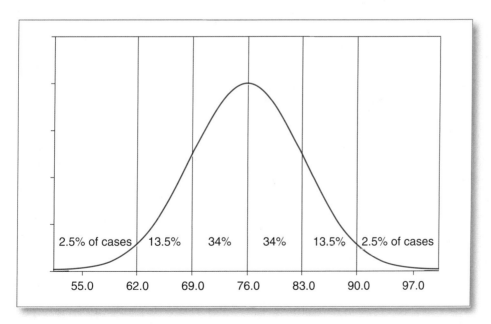

Figure 11.5   A Normal Distribution of Male Length of Life With a Mean of 76 and a Standard Deviation of 7

Central Limit Theorem

Feeling disappointed? Here you have all this knowledge about normal distributions and then are told you will find very few frequency distributions to which you can apply the knowledge. Fortunately, though, mathematicians have come to your rescue. While very few frequency distributions are normally distributed, most sampling distributions are normally distributed. Everything you learned about normal distributions can be routinely applied to sampling distributions.

The central limit theorem demonstrates that the larger the samples being taken, the closer the sampling distribution comes to being a normal distribution. And samples do not have to be very large before their sampling distribution closely approximates a normal distribution. Sampling distributions based on samples of 30 or more cases can be treated as normal distributions. Since social scientists are almost always dealing with samples of more than 30 subjects, a researcher can assume that the sampling distribution from which her one sample comes is a normal distribution.

Without the central limit theorem, most inferential statistics would be impossible. But with it, all the properties of normal distributions apply to sampling distributions.

- Sampling distributions are symmetrical.
- The mean of a sampling distribution equals the median equals the mode. The center of the sampling distribution corresponds to the mean, and, as noted earlier in the chapter, the mean of the sampling distribution corresponds exactly to the mean of the population. So the center of the sampling distribution corresponds to the population parameter—the very number the researcher is trying to infer from her sample data.
- Approximately 68% of all samples will produce a result within one standard error of the center of the sampling distribution, approximately 95% of all samples will produce a result within two standard errors of the center of the sampling distribution, and approximately 99.7% of all samples will produce a result within three standard errors of the center of the sampling distribution.
- And since the center of the sampling distribution corresponds to the population parameter, that means
  - approximately 68% of all samples will produce a result within one standard error of the true value in the population,
  - approximately 95% of all samples will produce a result within two standard errors of the true value in the population, and
  - approximately 99.7% of all samples will produce a result within three standard errors of the true value in the population.

That means that when a researcher takes a sample and calculates a sample statistic, she can be 99.7% sure that the true value in the population, the value she would have gotten if she did a census, is no more than three standard errors away from her sample result. Of course, whether that is encouraging or not depends on the value of the standard error. If the standard error is large, multiplying it by 3 results in a very large number, which means the sample result could be quite a distance from the population parameter, but if the standard error is very small, multiplying it by 3 does not produce a large number, which means the sample result is probably quite close to the true value. The key is the size of the standard error, and we saw earlier in the chapter what affects the size of the standard error: the variation in the population, the size of the sample, and the type of probability sample. The time, effort, and expense involved in doing a large stratified sample pay off in a smaller standard error, which means less sampling error, which means a sample result that is probably closer to the true value in the population.

Answering Questions With Sampling Distributions

Thanks to the central limit theorem, sampling distribution questions can be answered in a manner similar to how normal frequency distribution questions were answered. Like before, you will need to know where on the number line the center of the distribution (in this case, the sampling distribution) is. This may be communicated in many ways since the center of the sampling distribution could be correctly described as the mean of the sampling distribution, the median of the sampling distribution, the mode of the sampling distribution, or the population parameter.

While answering questions about normal frequency distributions requires the value of the standard deviation, answering questions about sampling distributions requires the value of the standard error. You might be directly told the value of the standard error or the value of the population standard deviation and the size of the samples on which the sampling distribution is based. Knowing those two things, the value of the standard error can be calculated using the formula for the standard error.

With frequency distributions, you need to be told that the distribution is normal. If you are not told that, you cannot apply the properties of normal distributions. However, you know from the central limit theorem that sampling distributions are normal distributions. Therefore, no one needs to tell you that the sampling distribution is normal. If it is a sampling distribution, you can assume that the properties of normal distributions apply.

Say that 1,000 data analysis students each take random samples of 500 persons from the adult population in Chicago and ask each person his or her total individual income last year. Also assume that the true mean adult income in Chicago last year was $23,000, and the standard error of the sampling distribution is $250. With that information, Figure 11.3 can be converted into Figure 11.6 by replacing z-scores with actual figures (substituting the value of the standard error for the value of the standard deviation in the formula that converts z-scores into actual scores).

The following questions can easily be answered using Figure 11.6.

- What percent of the samples got results between $22,750 and $23,250? (34 + 34 = 68%)
- What percent of the samples got results below $22,500? (2.5%)
- What percent of the samples missed the true mean by more than $250? (2.5 + 13.5 + 13.5 + 2.5 = 32%)
- What percent of the samples got results within $250 of the true mean? (34 + 34 = 68%)

This time a researcher is interested in the mean years of schooling of adults living in Texas. He hires 500 social science graduate students to each take a random sample of 1,600 adult Texans. Assume that in the Texas adult population, the actual average years of schooling is 15.0 and the standard deviation is 4.0.

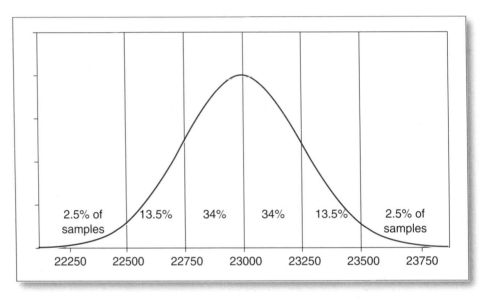

Figure 11.6   Sampling Distribution of Mean Income for Samples of Size 500 (Population Mean = $23,000 and Standard Error = $250)

For this example, the standard error must be calculated from the available information before converting Figure 11.3.

$$\text{standard error} = \frac{\text{population stdev}}{\sqrt{\text{sample size}}} = \frac{4.0}{\sqrt{1600}} = \frac{4.0}{40} = 0.1$$

Notice how much smaller the standard error is compared to the standard deviation! Replacing the z-scores in Figure 11.3 with actual figures produces Figure 11.7.

Once a chart like Figure 11.7 is drawn out, questions like the following become simple:

- What percent of the samples will miss the true value by more than 0.2 years? (2.5 + 2.5 = 5%)
- What percent of the samples will get results greater than 15.1 years? (13.5 + 2.5 = 16%)

- What percent of the samples will be within 0.1 years of the true value? (34 + 34 = 68%)
- What percent of the samples will be within 0.2 years of the true value? (13.5 + 34 + 34 + 13.5 = 95%)

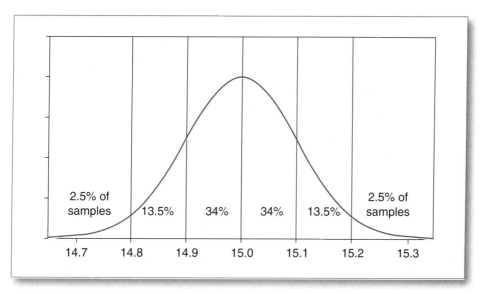

Figure 11.7   Sampling Distribution of Mean Years of Schooling for Samples of Size 1,600 (Population Mean = 15.0 Years and Standard Error = 0.1 Years)

RESEARCH TIP

Switching to Questions About Hypothetical Situations

Thus far, you have been told where on the number line the center of the distribution is. Now consider these questions. By beginning with "If the true average years of schooling is 15.0," you are being asked a question about a hypothetical situation.

- If the true average years of schooling is 15.0, what percent of the samples will miss that mean (either on the low or high side) by more than 0.1 years? (2.5 + 13.5 + 13.5 + 2.5 = 32%)
- If the true average years of schooling is 15.0, what percent of the samples will miss that mean by more than 0.2 years? (2.5 + 2.5 = 5%)

(Continued)

(Continued)

- If the true average years of schooling is 15.0, what percent of the samples will miss that mean by more than 1.0 years? (While this question cannot be answered from Figure 11.7, you should recognize that it will be a very small percent because the tails of the sampling distribution ten standard errors away from the center of the distribution must be extremely thin.)

Questions like these will be very important in later chapters when the true center of the sampling distribution is not known. Claims will be made about the location of the center of the sampling distribution, and you will be asked to evaluate those claims based on your sample results. If your sample result is very likely given the claimed center of the distribution, the claim will not be rejected. However, if your sample result is very unlikely given the claimed center of the distribution, the claim will be rejected.

Working With Results From a Single Sample

Now it is time to move a little closer to the world that researchers actually inhabit. In reality, researchers do not know the population parameters. For these examples, that means they do not know the value of the population mean or the population standard deviation. After all, if they knew the true mean in the population, why would they bother doing a sample? If they do not know the population mean or the population standard deviation, they do not know where the center of the sampling distribution is or what the standard error is. Further compounding the problem, the real-life researcher does not take repeated samples from a population to construct a sampling distribution. Researchers take just one sample.

What would a researcher know from just that one sample? He or she would know the sample mean and the sample standard deviation and, of course, the size of the sample that was taken. The other thing the researcher would know from having taken a data analysis course would be the properties of a sampling distribution. As you will soon see, armed just with those pieces of knowledge, the researcher can make some very useful probabilistic statements about the population from which his or her sample came.

Return to the example described earlier in this chapter. A researcher wants to know the mean number of courses students are taking at a college with 1,000 students. This time, though, the researcher does not know the true mean for the population or the actual standard deviation in the population. The researcher takes a single random sample of 10 students and asks each respondent the number of courses in which the respondent is currently enrolled. On the basis of those 10 answers, the researcher calculates for the sample the mean number of courses in which students are currently enrolled. As noted earlier, there are approximately 2.6×10^{23} different samples of size 10 from a population of 1,000. The researcher has taken one of those 2.6×10^{23} different samples but does not know if it was one of the many samples that provide a result quite close to the population mean or one of the few samples that provide a result quite far away from the population mean. The researcher does not know this because, while the value of the sample statistic is known, the value of the population parameter is not known.

RESEARCH TIP

A Sample of Just 10?

Since the central limit theorem applies only to sampling distributions based on large samples, we should be taking samples of at least 30 cases each. We will ignore that restriction this time to keep our example as simple as possible!

But the researcher does know some very important things. Approximately 68% of all the possible samples yield a sample result within one standard error of the population parameter. That means there is a 68% chance that the sample result is within one standard error of the true mean for the population. Since 95% of all sample results are within two standard errors of the population parameter and 99.7% are within three standard errors, there is a 95% chance this one sample result is within two standard errors of the population mean and a 99.7% chance that it is within three standard errors of the population mean.

If the researcher knew the actual value of the standard deviation for the population, he or she could calculate the value of the standard error; but it would require a census to determine the actual value of the standard deviation in the population, and doing a census would eliminate the need for doing a sample. The researcher does know the value of the standard deviation in the sample, however, and that can be used, at least for now, as an estimate for the standard deviation in the population. With just the results from the one sample, an estimate of the standard error can be calculated:

$$\text{estimated standard error} = \frac{\text{sample stdev}}{\sqrt{\text{sample size}}}.$$

Confidence Interval, Confidence Level, and Margin of Error

With what our researcher knows or can estimate from the results of just one sample, she can begin to make statements that are useful to the people who pay researchers to do sample research. She can build an interval around her sample result and state the probability that the true population parameter lies within that interval.

A **confidence interval** is a range of values within which a researcher has a certain level of confidence that the parameter lies. To create this interval, our researcher begins with the sample result. The sample result represents the center of the interval.

Next, she goes an equal distance out in both directions from her sample result. The distance she goes from the center of the interval to either end of the interval is what is known as the **margin of error.** How large the margin of error is depends on the **confidence level** she wants to have that the confidence interval contains the population parameter. If she wants a 68% level of confidence, the margin of error equals the standard error times 1. If she wants a 95% level of confidence, the margin of error equals the standard error times 2. If she wants a 99.7% level of confidence, the margin of error equals the standard error times 3.

Why does she go one, two, and three standard errors out in each direction to construct confidence intervals in which she has 68%, 95%, and 99.7% levels of confidence? Think about a complete sampling distribution with the results of all possible samples of a particular size from a population. Now think of arms extending exactly one standard error out to the left and right from each sample result. With arms extended out that long, what percentage of the sample results would be able to grab the center of the distribution, which, of course, corresponds to the population parameter? Approximately 68% would have arms long enough to reach the center of the distribution. If the arms were extended so they were exactly two standard errors long in each direction, approximately 95% of the sample results would now include the population parameter in their grasp. And if the arms were extended out three standard errors, approximately 99.7% of the sample results could include the population parameter in their grasp.

Answering Questions With Results From a Single Sample

If you know (or are told) the sample mean, the sample standard deviation, and the sample size, you can make statements similar to the ones made by experienced researchers when working with sample data. These statements tend to be of two types. This first statement is what frequently appears in the paper when the results of a voter preference poll are being reported.

The sample result was _____ with a margin of error of _____ (and a level of confidence of _____ percent).

Completing this statement simply requires you to insert the sample result in the first blank, the margin of error in the second, and the confidence level in the third. The last part of the statement appears in parentheses because it is often omitted. Whenever you are not told the confidence level used to calculate a margin of error or a confidence interval, you should assume the statement is being made with a 95% level of confidence. That is by far the most commonly used confidence level for reporting sample survey results.

Say an election is being held and the only two candidates are Kim and Kris. A researcher is hired by candidate Kim to find out what proportion of likely voters favor her. He takes a random sample of likely voters. In his sample, 56% favor Kim. On the basis of his sample results and the size of the sample, he calculates the standard error to be 2.5 percentage points. Keeping in mind that the margins of error for confidence levels of 68%, 95%, and 99.7% are, respectively, the standard error times 1, times 2, and times 3, he could report any of the following to Kim:

- In the sample, 56% favored you with a margin of error of 2.5 percentage points and a confidence level of 68%.

- In the sample, 56% favored you with a margin of error of 5.0 percentage points and a confidence level of 95%.
- In the sample, 56% favored you with a margin of error of 7.5 percentage points and a confidence level of 99.7%.

RESEARCH TIP

Standard Error of a Proportion

Until now, all of our examples have been about estimating population means. This example about estimating candidate Kim's voter support may appear different because it is about estimating a population proportion. In fact, however, the same procedures apply. The standard error of a proportion, like the standard error of a mean, is the standard deviation in the population (as estimated by the sample) over the square root of the sample size. The guidelines for making statements about confidence intervals, confidence levels, and margins of error are the same.

If Kim's campaign decides to report the sample results to the press, the newspaper story will probably report, "In a poll of 100 randomly selected likely voters, 56% favored Kim with a margin of error of 5.0 percentage points." Most newspaper readers have a general sense that the smaller the margin of error, the greater the confidence they should have in the poll result, but one wonders how many people really understand what the margin of error means and that it can only be interpreted in relation to a particular level of confidence.

This next type of statement is actually clearer, although you rarely see poll results reported this way. This is the type of statement a researcher might make when reporting the results to the person who commissioned the study.

I am _____ percent sure that the actual value lies between _____ and _____.

To complete this statement, you insert the level of confidence in the first blank and the lower and upper ends of the confidence interval in the second and third blanks.

For example, a researcher wants to know the average speed at which cars travel on a particular highway. She observes a random sample of 625 cars. For her sample, the average speed was 60 mph and the standard deviation was 10 mph. She calculates the estimated standard error to be 0.4 mph. Once she knows the standard error and has chosen a level of confidence, she calculates the margin of error and goes that distance below the sample result to get the lower end of the confidence interval and that same distance above the sample result to get the upper end of the confidence interval. Depending on the level of confidence she chooses, she could state the following:

- I am 68% sure that the true average speed of cars on this highway is between 59.6 and 60.4 mph.
- I am 95% sure that the true average speed of cars on this highway is between 59.2 and 60.8 mph.
- I am 99.7% sure that the true average speed of cars on this highway is between 58.8 and 61.2 mph.

Before finishing the chapter, return for a moment to candidate Kim as she receives the results of the poll. Being honest, she tells the researcher that she does not quite understand what margin of error means. The researcher then explains the results using this second format.

The researcher states that "I am 68% sure that the actual percent of eligible voters favoring you is between 53.5% and 58.5%." Kim replies that she is pleased that she appears to be in the lead but notes that 68% is not a huge amount of confidence. She asks the researcher if he can make a statement in which he has more confidence.

"No problem," replies the researcher. "I am 95% sure that the actual percent of eligible voters favoring you is between 51.0% and 61.0%." Kim likes the higher level of confidence and asks the researcher if he can make a statement about the actual percent of eligible voters favoring Kim in which he is absolutely certain.

The researcher replies, "While I can tell you that I am 100% sure that the actual percent of eligible voters favoring you is between 0 and 100 percent, that is not particularly useful information. I can tell you, however, that I am 99.7% sure that the actual percent of eligible voters favoring you is between 48.5% and 63.5%." Kim looks dissatisfied and remarks that every time the researcher increased his level of confidence, he widened the interval. "That last interval in which you were 99.7% sure is so wide I could lose in a close race or win by a landslide. Is there a statement you could make that would have a narrow confidence interval and a high confidence level?"

The researcher smiles, knowing that the only way to have a narrow confidence interval and a high level of confidence is to have a very small standard error. The researcher tells Kim, "Three things can get you that narrow confidence interval and high confidence level. I can increase the size of my sample, but that will increase my expenses. I can switch from a simple random sampling technique to a stratified random sampling technique, but that will also raise my expenses. Last, you could convince an even greater share of eligible voters that you are the better candidate. That would reduce the variability in the electorate regarding who they favor, which would result in a narrow confidence interval and a high confidence level, but to do that will probably increase your expenses." As Kim walked away, the last thing she was heard to say was "Money, money, money!"

CONCEPT CHECK

Without looking back, can you answer the following questions:

- What are the properties of a normal distribution?
- What does the central limit theorem say about sampling distributions?
- What are confidence intervals, confidence levels, and margins of error?

If not, go back and review before reading on.

Important Concepts in the Chapter

central limit theorem	probability sampling
confidence interval	sampling distribution
confidence level	sampling error
frequency distribution	standard deviation
margin of error	standard error
normal distribution	statistic
parameter	

Practice Problems

1. Why are inferential statistics called inferential?

2. What is sampling error?

3. Can the possibility of sampling error ever be eliminated from samples?

4. What is a sampling distribution?

5. How does a sampling distribution differ from a frequency distribution?

6. If you know the value of the population mean, what do you know about sampling distributions based on samples from that population?

7. What is a standard error?

8. How does a standard error differ from a standard deviation?

9. Do researchers prefer to work with sampling distributions with large standard errors or small standard errors? Why?

10. How are sampling error and standard error related?

11. What is the formula for the standard error?

12. A researcher is interested in knowing the average number of children baby boomers had. Assume the standard deviation for number of baby boomer children is 2.0. Our researcher plans to take a simple random sample of 400 baby boomers. What will the standard error of the sampling distribution be?

13. A researcher is interested in knowing the average income of members of the Republican Party. Assume the standard deviation for income among members of the Republican Party is $25,000. Our researcher plans to take a simple random sample of 2,500 Republicans.
    a. What will the standard error of the sampling distribution be?
    b. What could our researcher do to get a sampling distribution with a smaller standard error?

14. If someone tells you that income in a town is "normally distributed," what specific things about the distribution of income do you now know to be true?

15. Scores on a test were normally distributed. The most common score was 73.
    a. What was the mean score?
    b. What was the median score?
    c. What was the value of the skewness coefficient?

16. You are told county crime rates (number of crimes per 100,000 population) are normally distributed with a mean of 5,000 and a standard deviation of 250. What percent of counties have crime rates
    a. greater than 5,500?   y Frequency
    b. less than 4,750?
    c. between 4,750 and 5,250?
    d. less than 5,500?

17. Using the central limit theorem, what do you know about the properties of sampling distributions?

18. Suppose that based on census data, you know that the actual mean age of the U.S. population is 36.1 years.
    a. Where would the center of the sampling distribution be on the number line if you constructed a sampling distribution of random samples
        i. with each sample containing 1,500 persons?
        ii. with each sample containing 500 persons?
    b. Which sampling distribution would have the smaller standard error?

19. Assume that in the U.S. adult population, the mean cholesterol level is 200 and the standard deviation for cholesterol level is 60. One thousand medical researchers each take samples of 900 persons from the adult U.S. population and measure each person's cholesterol level.
    a. Is this question describing a normal frequency distribution or a sampling distribution?
    b. What percent of the researchers will get sample means
        i. between 198 and 202?
        ii. below 196?
        iii. more than 4 points from the population mean?

20. The number of pages in statistics textbooks is normally distributed with a mean of 450 and a standard deviation of 100.
    a. Is this question describing a normal frequency distribution or a sampling distribution?
    b. What percent of textbooks have
        i. more than 650 pages?
        ii. between 250 and 450 pages?

21. Define the following terms:
    a. confidence interval
    b. confidence level
    c. margin of error

22. A researcher takes a sample of 500 licensed social workers. In the sample, the average annual income for the social workers is $80,000. Our researcher estimates the value of the standard error to be $1,000. Complete the following statements:
    a. The sample result was _____ with a margin of error of _____ and a level of confidence of 95%.
    b. The sample result was _____ with a margin of error of _____ and a level of confidence of 68%.
    c. The sample result was _____ with a margin of error of _____ and a level of confidence of 99.7%.

23. A researcher takes a sample of 625 police officers. In the sample, the average annual income for the police officers is $80,000, and the standard deviation is $25,000. Complete the following statements:
    a. I am 68% sure that the true average annual income for police officers is between _____ and _____.
    b. I am 95% sure that the true average annual income for police officers is between _____ and _____.
    c. I am 99.7% sure that the true average annual income for police officers is between _____ and _____.

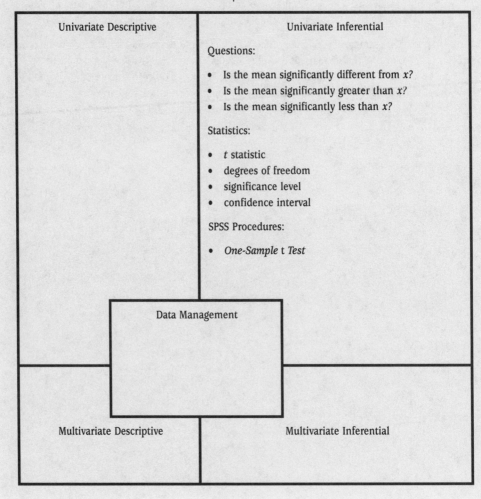

Questions and Tools for Answering Them
(Chapter 12)

Univariate Descriptive

Univariate Inferential

Questions:

- Is the mean significantly different from x?
- Is the mean significantly greater than x?
- Is the mean significantly less than x?

Statistics:

- t statistic
- degrees of freedom
- significance level
- confidence interval

SPSS Procedures:

- *One-Sample* t *Test*

Data Management

Multivariate Descriptive

Multivariate Inferential

Hypothesis Testing and One-Sample *t* Tests

12

In this chapter, you can learn

- how to form pairs of testable hypotheses,
- how to proceed through the four basic steps of hypothesis testing,
- how to tell if a result is statistically significant,
- what statistical significance actually means,
- whether or not to reject a claim that a population mean is equal to a particular value,
- whether or not to reject a claim that a population mean is equal to or less than a particular value, and
- whether or not to reject a claim that a population mean is equal to or greater than a particular value.

Household Size, Siblings, and Parents' Schooling

Starting with this chapter, the questions about the 1980 GSS young adults that lead off every chapter will look and be different. Each question will ask about a specific condition and whether it was statistically significant.

- Did the average household size of 1980 GSS young adults differ significantly from three?
- Defining siblings to include full-siblings, half-siblings, and adopted siblings, did 1980 GSS young adults average significantly more than four siblings?
- Did the parents of 1980 GSS young adults average significantly less than 12 years of schooling?

SPSS TIP

To Duplicate the Examples in This Chapter

To duplicate the examples in this chapter, use the *fourGroups.sav* data set. Before doing any of the statistical procedures, set the select cases condition to GROUP = 1.

Overview

There are two broad categories of inferential statistics. In the last chapter, we used a sample to estimate what percent of the population of eligible voters favored candidate Kim. We observed our sample result, estimated the standard error, selected a confidence level, computed the margin of error, and stated a range of values within which we had a particular level of confidence that the population value lay. That was an example of **interval estimation,** the first broad category of inferential statistics. Interval estimation requires no prior predictions by the researcher about the state of the population. The sample results are simply calculated and used as the basis for probabilistic statements about the population. Confidence intervals, confidence levels, and margins of error are all part of interval estimation.

A second category of inferential statistics is **hypothesis testing.** This is the more common of the two types of inferential statistics, and the remainder of this book describes various hypothesis testing techniques. Unlike interval estimation, hypothesis testing requires an explicit prediction about the population parameter. That prediction is then tested against the sample data.

This chapter presents the basics of hypothesis testing and then applies those basics to possibly the simplest type of hypothesis testing—a one-sample *t* test. A one-sample *t* test is used when a claim is made about the mean of one variable for one group. Later chapters will show how to test claims about means on more than one variable and for more than one group.

Hypothesis Testing

Hypotheses

A **hypothesis** is simply a prediction or a claim. You might make a prediction about a single person or event (e.g., that 5 years after you graduate, you will have an annual income over $50,000), but statisticians, particularly inferential ones, are more interested in predictions about populations (e.g., that 5 years after graduation, your college graduation class will have an average annual income over $50,000).

In fact, hypotheses used for inferential statistics are always about the population from which a sample was randomly selected. While descriptive statistics draw conclusions about the cases that make up the sample, inferential statistics go beyond those cases. Sometimes inferential hypotheses will explicitly state "in the population" and sometimes that will be left implicit, but inferential hypotheses are always claims about the population.

Hypotheses can be based on any number of things. They may be derived from previous research or based on logical deduction. They may be based on personal experience or even a hunch. Obviously, the probability that the data will support the hypothesis varies depending on the basis for the hypothesis, but from a data analysis perspective, the source of the hypothesis is irrelevant. All that is needed is a hypothesis.

The time to form hypotheses is before examining the data. A peek at the data to be used to test a hypothesis is *not* an acceptable or ethical basis for forming a hypothesis. A hypothesis based on an examination of present data could be tested on some other data set, but the same data set should not be the basis for both the hypothesis and the test of the hypothesis.

Actually, not one but two hypotheses are needed to do hypothesis testing. A researcher with a hypothesis about the population must then form a second hypothesis—a companion hypothesis. The two hypotheses must be carefully stated so that logically one of the hypotheses must be true (although the researcher does not know at the start which one is true), but they cannot both be true. With practice, forming these pairs of hypotheses becomes quite simple.

If one hypotheses is "in the population, the average annual household income is $38,000," then the companion hypothesis must be "in the population, the average annual household income is not $38,000." Consider these two hypotheses. One must be true, but they cannot both be true. The average annual household income either is or is not $38,000. It cannot at the same time both be and not be $38,000.

If one hypothesis is "in the population, there is no association (as measured by Cramer's *V*) between birth order and occupation," then the companion hypothesis must be "in the population, there is an association (as measured by Cramer's *V*) between birth order and occupation."

If one hypothesis is "in the population, there is a positive correlation (as measured by Pearson's *r*) between years of schooling and annual income," what is the companion hypothesis? Be careful here. If you said the companion hypothesis is "in the population, there is a negative correlation (as measured by Pearson's *r*) between years of schooling and annual income," you would be wrong. Why? Although both hypotheses cannot simultaneously be true, it is not the case that one must be true. They would both be false if there was no correlation between years of schooling and annual income. The correct companion hypothesis is "in the population, there is a negative correlation or no correlation (as measured by Pearson's *r*) between years of schooling and annual income." A shorter but less descriptive way of stating the companion hypothesis is "in the population, there is not a positive correlation (as measured by Pearson's *r*) between years of schooling and annual income."

If one hypothesis is "in the population, the average first-semester grade point average is less than 2.00," then the companion hypothesis must be "in the population, the average first-semester grade point average is 2.00 or higher." Once again, an alternative statement of the companion hypothesis could be "in the population, the average first-semester grade point average is not less than 2.00."

Null Hypothesis and Research Hypothesis

One of the pair of hypotheses is known as the null hypothesis; the other hypothesis goes by many different names. In this book, it will be called the research hypothesis, but it is also referred to as the alternative hypothesis or the scientific hypothesis.

The hypothesis that includes in its prediction a specific value for the parameter in question is the null hypothesis. The null hypothesis may actually include a variety of possibilities, but one of the possibilities is a specific number. The examples in Table 12.1 make this clearer.

For each pair, the null hypothesis is always the one that includes a specific number in its prediction. It is never the case that both hypotheses include specific numbers. If the pair of hypotheses was constructed correctly, only one can include a specific number, and that one is the null hypothesis.

The null hypothesis is even easier to spot if the hypotheses are stated mathematically. Not all hypotheses can be expressed using common mathematical symbols, but most can. In mathematical form, the null hypothesis is always the one that includes the equal sign. It might be an equal sign by itself (=) or an equal sign along with a greater than (≥) or a less than (≤) sign.

The specific number included in the null hypothesis is very important because it identifies a place on the number line to center the sampling distribution. The null hypothesis says the center of the sampling distribution is located at exactly that point. The sample result can then be

Table 12.1   Hypothesis Pairs Expressed Verbally and Mathematically

Type of Hypothesis	Verbal Statement	Mathematical Equivalent
Null	In the population, the average annual household income is $38,000.	$\overline{\text{INCOME}} = \$ 38,000$
Research	In the population, the average annual household income is not $38,000.	$\overline{\text{INCOME}} = \$ 38,000$
Null	In the population, there is no association (as measured by Cramer's V) between birth order and occupation.	Cramer's $V = 0.00$
Research	In the population, there is an association (as measured by Cramer's V) between birth order and occupation.	Cramer's $V \neq 0.00$
Research	In the population, there is a positive correlation (as measured by Pearson's r) between years of schooling and annual income.	$r > 0.00$
Null	In the population, there is a negative correlation or no correlation (as measured by Pearson's r) between years of schooling and annual income.	$r \leq 0.00$
Research	In the population, the average first-semester grade point average is less than 2.00.	$\overline{\text{GPA}} < 2.00$
Null	In the population, the average first-semester grade point average is 2.00 or higher.	$\overline{\text{GAP}} \geq 2.00$

examined, the standard error estimated, and an evaluation made of just how likely it would be to get a sample result that far from the center of the sampling distribution *if the center of the sampling distribution is where the null hypothesis claims.*

As will soon become evident, hypothesis testing is all about the null hypothesis. It is the null hypothesis that gets tested and ultimately rejected or not rejected. In a sense, the research hypothesis is only along for the ride.

The Four Steps in Hypothesis Testing

Hypothesis testing can be understood as a simple four-step process. The steps are illustrated in Figure 12.1. Get to know them well.

Step 1: State the research hypothesis and the null hypothesis.

Sometimes hypothesis testing begins with a null hypothesis; probably more often, the research hypothesis is thought of first. Whichever comes first, you must then formulate the companion hypothesis. The order in which the hypotheses are formed does not matter. Just be sure when you

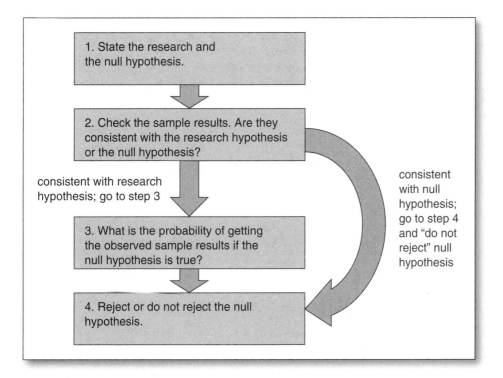

Figure 12.1   Four Steps of Hypothesis Testing

are given one hypothesis, you can correctly state the other hypothesis and correctly identify which is the null hypothesis and which is the research hypothesis. Remember that the two hypotheses should form a pair such that one must be true but both cannot be true.

The last pair of hypotheses from Table 12.1 can serve as an example as we move through the steps of hypothesis testing: The research hypothesis is "in the population, the average first-semester grade point average is less than 2.00." The null hypothesis is "in the population, the average first-semester grade point average is 2.00 or higher."

Step 2: Check the sample results. Are they consistent with the null hypothesis or the research hypothesis?

The hypotheses are making claims about the value of some parameter. The claims might be about the value for the population of a mean, a particular measure of association, a beta, or some other statistic. You do not have census data. If you did, you would know the true value of the parameter and know with certainty which hypothesis is true.

You do have sample data, however. Take a look at the value of the sample statistic—the mean, the measure of association, the beta, or whatever. The value of the sample statistic will be consistent with either the research hypothesis or the null hypothesis. It has to be consistent with one of them and cannot be consistent with both.

Remember that the goal of hypothesis testing ultimately is to reject or not reject the null hypothesis. Let's say, for our example, the sample mean grade point average is 1.95. That is clearly consistent with the research hypothesis that predicted a GPA below 2.00 and inconsistent with the null hypothesis prediction of a GPA of 2.00 or higher. But are you willing to reject the null hypothesis based on this evidence? Your answer should be no, and the reason is that you only have sample data and you know that sample results do not usually hit the true population value on the head. The situation might be that the true population mean is 2.00 or something higher than that, but sampling error caused the sample result to be below 2.00. Nevertheless, the initial evidence suggests there may be reason to reject the null hypothesis. The evidence against the null hypothesis is at least strong enough to go on to Step 3.

But what if the sample result is consistent with the null hypothesis? What if, for our example, the sample GPA is 2.01? That does not prove that the research hypothesis is wrong or that the null hypothesis is right. For example, sampling error might have gotten you a sample result of 2.01 when the true population mean is 1.98. However, the fact that the sample results favor the null hypothesis is enough to show that you do not have a strong case against the null hypothesis. If the sample results are consistent with the null hypothesis, then you proceed directly to Step 4 and do not reject the null hypothesis.

Step 3: What is the probability of getting the observed sample results if the null hypothesis is true?

If the null hypothesis is true, what is the probability that you would get the sample results you got? This is asking the kind of question you answered with sampling distributions in the last chapter.

If the center of the sample distribution is located where the null hypothesis says it is located, how likely is it to get the sample result you got?

This question is asked in terms of probabilities. Probabilities are usually expressed as numbers ranging from zero to 1. If the probability of something happening is exactly zero, there is no chance of it occurring. If the probability is exactly 1, then it is certain to happen. The closer the probability is to zero, the less likely something is to happen; the closer the probability is to 1, the more likely something is to happen.

Probabilities can also be described as fractions or as percentages. Table 12.2 shows some probabilities expressed in different ways.

SPSS output will always show probabilities, but you should be able to comfortably move between probabilities, fractions, and percentages as ways of expressing the likelihood of an event happening. For example, the sampling distribution examples in the previous chapter were asking what percent of samples would get certain results. If the answer was 16%, you could say the probability of getting those results was .16. If 5% of all sample results are more than two standard errors

Table 12.2   Equivalent Probabilities, Fractions, and Percents

Probabilities	Fractions	Percents
.80	The event will occur 4/5th of the time or 4 times out of every 5 attempts.	The event will occur 80% of the time or 80 times out of every 100 attempts.
.50	The event will occur 1/2 the time or 1 time out of every 2 attempts.	The event will occur 50% of the time or 50 times out of every 100 attempts.
.10	The event will occur 1/10th of the time or 1 time out of every 10 attempts.	The event will occur 10% of the time or 10 times out of every 100 attempts.
.05	The event will occur 1/20th of the time or 1 time out of every 20 attempts.	The event will occur 5% of the time or 5 times out of every 100 attempts.
.01	The event will occur 1/100th of the time or 1 time out of every 100 attempts.	The event will occur 1% of the time or 1 time out of every 100 attempts.
.003	The event will occur 3/1,000th of the time or 3 times out of every 1,000 attempts.	The event will occur 0.3% of the time or 3 times out of every 1,000 attempts.
.0001	The event will occur 1/10,000th of the time or 1 time out of every 10,000 attempts.	The event will occur 0.01% of the time or 1 time out of every 10,000 attempts.

from the center of the sampling distribution, you can say that the probability of a sample result being more than two standard errors from the center of the distribution is .05.

So, for Step 3 in hypothesis testing, you will be looking for a probability in your SPSS output. This will be a number somewhere between zero and 1.

Another name for the "probability of getting the observed sample results if the null hypothesis is true" is **significance level.** When people talk about the significance level of their results, they are talking about Step 3 in hypothesis testing. They are talking about the probability of getting the sample results they got if the null hypothesis is in fact true.

SPSS TIP

What If SPSS Says the Probability Is .000?

You will sometimes see a probability or significance level of exactly zero in your SPSS output, for example, .000 or .0000. Because sampling distributions in theory extend infinitely far to the left and to the right as their tails get thinner and thinner, it is unlikely that there is truly no chance of the sample result occurring. What you are being told when you see a probability or significance level of all zeros is that the probability is so small that, when rounded to just three or four decimal places, it rounds to all zeros.

A probability in SPSS of .000 actually means the probability is something less than .0005, and a probability in SPSS of .0000 actually means the probability is something less than .00005. Therefore, when you see an SPSS probability of all zeros, you are right to assume the probability is extremely small, but do not assume it is actually zero.

Step 4: Reject or do not reject the null hypothesis.

This is quite a simple step. You have only two choices. You either reject the null hypothesis or you do not.

You may have "not rejected" the null hypothesis based on Step 2 if the sample results were consistent with the null hypothesis. If your sample results were consistent with the research hypothesis, however, you went on to Step 3 and now have a probability—a number between zero and 1.

The question then becomes, "How small must the probability be to justify rejecting the null hypothesis?" Obviously, you would not want to reject the null hypothesis if the probability of getting the sample results you got if the null hypothesis is true is large. Why reject a claim when you got results that are very likely to occur if the claim is correct? So the probability is going to have to be small before you reject the null hypothesis, but how small is small enough?

Since science is cautious and reluctant to eliminate possibilities unless the evidence is overwhelming, the probability is going to have to be quite small. In the social sciences, the most often used rule is that *the probability must be .05 or smaller for you to reject the null hypothesis.* That means you will reject the null hypothesis only if the sample results would have occurred no more than 1/20th of the time, 1 time in 20 attempts, or 5% of the time if the null hypothesis is true.

You will sometimes read studies that use a different probability level. Some studies use a less cautious rule of .10; other studies are extremely cautious—only rejecting the null hypothesis if the probability is no more than .01 or .001. As you can probably guess, you must decide how small a probability must be to reject the null hypothesis *before* looking at the SPSS results. Deciding how small is small enough only after you know the actual probability is unethical. This book will always use the .05 rule. If the probability is .05 or less, reject the null; if it is greater than .05, do not reject the null.

RESEARCH TIP

Do You Reject the Null if the Probability Is .051?

Eventually you will see a probability just slightly above .05, perhaps .051 or .0501. Whether a number like that is greater than .05 or not depends on whether you round it to two decimal places. Analysts differ on what to do in such a case. Ask your instructor how she or he wants you to proceed.

For the examples in this book, a cautious approach has been adopted. If there is any evidence that the probability is greater than .05, then the null hypothesis is not rejected. In the case of .051 or .0501, the null hypothesis would not be rejected.

If you reject the null hypothesis, then you can describe your sample results as statistically significant. The phrase **statistical significance** is properly used only in the context of inferential hypothesis testing, and it is a shorthand way of saying that the researcher was able to reject the null hypothesis. (Do not confuse statistical significance and substantive importance. They are different things. More will be said about the difference in a later chapter.)

When you reject the null hypothesis, are you certain that it is false and should be rejected? The answer is no! The probability that the null hypothesis is true is sufficiently small that you will reject the null hypothesis, but there remains some possibility that your sample was one of those rare samples in the far ends of the sampling distribution that give a result very different from the population parameter. By rejecting the null hypothesis, you might be making an error, but the probability of that error is sufficiently small that you are willing to accept that risk. (Rejecting a null hypothesis that is actually true is called a Type I error. More will be said about types of errors in a later chapter.)

"Rejecting the null hypothesis" means you accept the research hypothesis because it is the only alternative to the null hypothesis, but "not rejecting the null hypothesis" does not mean you accept the null hypothesis or reject the research hypothesis. By not rejecting the null hypothesis, you are leaving your options open. You are saying the null hypothesis may be right or it may be wrong. You will continue to consider it as a possibility until some future time when the evidence is clearer.

RESEARCH TIP

Backwards, Cautious Science

You can begin to see why science (at least the part of science based on inferential hypothesis testing) is sometimes described as moving in a backward fashion. It never proves things to be true. Instead, it eliminates possibilities as false. Furthermore, science is very cautious in eliminating possibilities. The evidence must be overwhelming before a null hypothesis is rejected. If the evidence is against the null hypothesis but not overwhelming, science basically says it will postpone judgment. From a scientific point of view, it is better to proceed slowly in the right direction than to risk moving in the wrong direction.

Hypothesis Testing and the American Justice System

Hypothesis testing may sound pretty strange. But it is actually quite similar to the procedure used in the American justice system for jury trials.

Step 1: A district attorney believes an individual is guilty of a crime. Consider that the research hypothesis. As the trial begins, the judge tells the jury that they should assume that the defendant is innocent. There is your null hypothesis.

Step 2: The prosecution presents its case first, calling witnesses and presenting evidence to support the claim that the defendant is guilty. Once the prosecution has presented its case and before the defense begins its case, the defense attorney can ask the judge for a directed acquittal. The defense lawyer is asking the judge to dismiss the case because the prosecution has failed to present even a minimally adequate case. Just like in Step 2 of hypothesis testing, the judge is being asked to look at the evidence presented thus far and decide which way to proceed. If the evidence supports the research hypothesis that the defendant is guilty, the trial continues, but if the evidence supports the null hypothesis that the defendant is innocent, the judge ends the trial by not rejecting the null hypothesis—in other words, by stating that the defendant is innocent.

Step 3: Assuming the prosecution has presented at least a strong enough case for the trial to continue, the defense now presents its case. Remember that the jury was first told to assume the defendant was innocent. Although most jurors do not think in such quantitative terms, at the beginning of the trial, each juror considers the probability that the null hypothesis of innocence is true to be 1.00. But when one of the witnesses reported that the defendant threatened the victim, perhaps the probability of innocence slipped to .80. Then another witness reported seeing the defendant fleeing from the scene of the homicide. The probability of innocence slips to .45. The murder weapon was a gun owned by the defendant. The probability of innocence drops to .10. Tests show that the defendant fired a gun on the day of the murder. The probability of innocence drops to .01. Of course, it is the defense attorney's job to then raise the probability of innocence in the jurors' minds. When the presentation of evidence and the summary statements by each of the lawyers are concluded, each juror is left with a particular probability that the defendant is innocent.

Step 4: The judge gives the final instructions to the jury. He or she does not tell the jury to reject the claim of innocence only if they are certain. No, the judge tells them to reject the assumption of innocence and render a guilty verdict only if they are sure "beyond a reasonable doubt" that the defendant is not innocent. Of course, each juror is free to determine in his or her own mind what "beyond a reasonable doubt" means. Science is just more upfront about it. For the social sciences, beyond a reasonable doubt means there is only a .05 probability or less that the null hypothesis is true.

If the jury votes guilty, they are rejecting the null hypothesis of innocence. If they vote not guilty, they are not rejecting the null hypothesis of innocence. The entire process bears remarkable similarity to inferential hypothesis testing. One obvious difference, though, is that inferential hypothesis testing is much clearer about how it decides whether to reject or not reject the null hypothesis.

CONCEPT CHECK

Without looking back, can you answer the following questions:

- How can you tell which hypothesis is the null hypothesis and which the research hypothesis?
- What are the four steps in hypothesis testing?
- If at Step 2 in hypothesis testing, the sample results are consistent with the research hypothesis, what do you do? If consistent with the null, what do you do?
- What must the probability level be to reject the null hypothesis?
- When can results be described as "statistically significant"?

If not, go back and review before reading on.

One-Sample *t* Tests

Take another look at the questions at the beginning of this chapter about the GSS young adults in 1980. To answer those questions, we must test a hypothesis about the mean of one variable (e.g., household size) for one population (1980 young adults). Hypothesis tests about the mean of one variable for one population use what is known as a one-sample *t* test.

The one-sample part of the name refers to the fact that we are working with a sample from a single population (1980 young adults). The *t* test part of the name refers to a very commonly used inferential statistic known as *t*. More will be said about *t* later in the chapter.

A First Example

"Did the average household size of 1980 GSS young adults differ significantly from three?"

Step 1: State the research hypothesis and the null hypothesis. The question asked at the start of the chapter directly leads to two competing claims or hypotheses about 1980 young adults: "in the population of 1980 young adults, the average household size was three" and its companion hypothesis, "in the population of 1980 young adults, the average household size was not three." Mathematically, the two hypotheses could be expressed as

$$\overline{\text{HOUSEPOP}} = 3 \text{ and } \overline{\text{HOUSEPOP}} \neq 3$$

The first hypothesis is the null hypothesis because it includes a specific value in its prediction. The mathematical expression of the first hypothesis includes an equal sign, which is an easy way of spotting the null hypothesis. The second hypothesis is the research hypothesis.

Step 2: Check the sample results. Are they consistent with the null hypothesis or the research hypothesis? While many SPSS procedures can produce the sample mean, the *One-Sample T Test* procedure provides both the sample mean needed for Step 2 and the probability needed for Step 3. To access this procedure, pull down the *Analyze* menu, move the cursor over *Compare Means,* and click on *One-Sample T Test.*

Analyze | Compare Means | One-Sample T Test

A dialog similar to Figure 12.2 will appear.

Move the variable about whose mean the claim has been made to the "Test Variable(s)" list. Always pay attention to level of measurement. Since the mean of the test variable will be calculated, the test variable must be interval/ratio.

Then delete the zero in the "Test Value" field and enter the specific value named in the null hypothesis. Finally, click OK. Figure 12.3 shows the output for the test variable HOUSEPOP and a test value of 3.

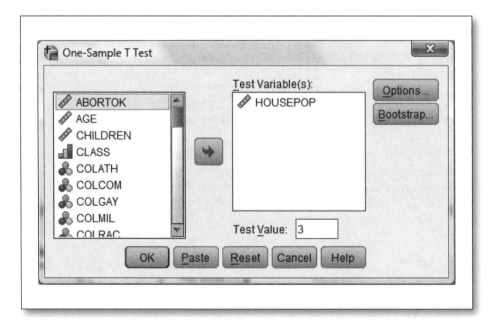

Figure 12.2   Dialog to Produce a One-Sample *t* Test

One-Sample Statistics

	N	Mean	Std. Deviation	Std. Error Mean
HOUSEPOP	327	2.96	1.467	.081

One-Sample Test

	Test Value = 3					
					95% Confidence Interval of the Difference	
	t	df	Sig. (2-tailed)	Mean Difference	Lower	Upper
HOUSEPOP	-.528	326	.598	-.043	-.20	.12

Figure 12.3   *One-Sample t Test* Output for HOUSEPOP = 3 for 1980 GSS Young Adults

The sample mean appears in the "One-Sample Statistics" box. 1980 GSS young adults were living in households that had an average of 2.96 persons.

Step 2 asks if the sample results are consistent with the null hypothesis or the research hypothesis. The null hypothesis said the mean would be exactly 3. The research hypothesis said the mean would not be exactly 3. The sample result is 2.96. While that's close to 3, close isn't enough. The sample result is consistent with the research hypothesis. Therefore, the process moves to Step 3.

Step 3: What is the probability of getting the observed sample results if the null hypothesis is true? The sample result is consistent with the research hypothesis, but that alone is not a sufficient reason to reject the null hypothesis. Perhaps the population mean really is exactly 3, and it was just sampling error that led to a sample mean of 2.96. What we need to know is just how likely it is that a sample result would miss the true mean by as much as .04. If it is very likely, then we should not reject the null hypothesis claim that the true mean is 3; however, if it is very unlikely, then we will reject the claim made by the null hypothesis that the true mean is 3.

The probability of getting the sample result if the null hypothesis is true appears in Figure 12.3 in the "One-Sample Test" box under the heading "Sig. (2-tailed)." The abbreviation "Sig" stands for significance level, which is the same as the probability of getting the observed sample results if the null hypothesis is true. The meaning of "2-tailed" will be discussed later.

The probability is .598. That is the number Step 3 is looking for. A probability of .598 means that if the true value is exactly 3, as stated in the null hypothesis, a sample result based on a sample the size of this one will miss the population parameter by .04 or more 59.8% of the time or almost six times out of every 10 attempts.

Step 4: Reject or do not reject the null hypothesis. Step 3 found that the significance level was .598. Therefore, we do not reject the null hypothesis. We must continue to entertain the possibility that the true mean is 3. If we rejected the null hypothesis, we would be running a 59.8% chance that we are rejecting a null hypothesis that is actually true. As stated in the previous chapter, we will not take on more than a 5% chance of making such an error. The probability must be .05 or less for us to reject the null hypothesis.

Although the sample mean was not 3, the sample evidence was not strong enough to reject the claim that in the population the mean is actually 3. We are not accepting the null hypothesis or saying the null hypothesis is true; we are just not rejecting it. (It is like a juror who suspects the defendant is guilty but reluctantly votes not guilty because the evidence presented at the trial is not strong enough to reject the claim of not guilty.) The results of the hypothesis test would be described as not statistically significant. Only when the null hypothesis is rejected are the results described as statistically significant. The answer to the question, "Did the average household size of 1980 GSS young adults differ significantly from three?" is no.

Congratulations! You just completed your first inferential hypothesis test. It is that simple. Before doing another one, though, it is time to take a closer look at the SPSS output produced by this procedure.

The Confidence Interval

The previous chapter talked about creating a confidence interval, a range of values within which you have a certain level of confidence that the population parameter lies. At the right-hand side of the "One-Sample Test" box in the *One-Sample T Test* output, a 95% confidence interval is reported. However, this is not the confidence interval for the mean. It is actually the confidence interval for the difference between the value of the sample mean and the value of the mean predicted by the null hypothesis. But by simply adding to each of the reported values for the confidence interval the "test value" that you entered to set up the problem and that also appears near the top of the "One-Sample Test" output box, you get the confidence interval for the mean. For this example, −.20 plus 3 equals 2.80, and .12 plus 3 equals 3.12. You can be 95% sure that the true average household size of 1980 young adults was between 2.80 and 3.12.

SPSS TIP

Two Ways of Getting the Confidence Interval

One way of getting the 95% confidence interval for the mean is by adding the test value to both end points of the 95% confidence interval of the difference. There is a second way. The "One-Sample Statistics" output box in Figure 12.3 reports the sample mean and an estimate of the standard error based on the sample data. As described in the previous chapter, you could have doubled the standard error and moved that distance below the sample mean and that distance above the sample mean to obtain the 95% confidence interval for the mean.

These two ways of getting the confidence interval will usually produce the same results. Sometimes there may be a small difference in the results because the guidelines in the previous chapter were only "approximately" correct. They are easy to remember and grossly accurate. SPSS, however, uses more precise rules for calculating margins of error and confidence intervals. Also, SPSS is no longer basing the calculations on the properties of a normal distribution. It has switched to a family of mathematical distributions known as *t* distributions, which are described in this chapter.

So, when they are available, use the SPSS values for the confidence interval rather than calculating the values yourself.

The *t* Distribution

Sampling distributions are normal distributions. We know that from the central limit theorem. But to apply the properties of sampling distributions to interval estimation and hypothesis testing, we need to know the value of the standard error. To get the value of the standard error, we divide the standard deviation in the population by the square root of the sample size. The problem with that was already noted in the last chapter: We do not know the exact value of the standard deviation in the population. To get that would require a census, but all we have is a sample. While it is true that the sample standard deviation provides a reasonable estimate of the population standard deviation, it is only a reasonably good estimate. We basically have a sampling error problem again. It is unlikely that our sample standard deviation perfectly matches the population standard deviation. Our sample standard deviation includes some sampling error.

Statisticians can adjust the sampling distribution to take into account the fact that they only have an estimate of the population sampling distribution. This adjusted distribution is known as a ***t* distribution.** Since the likely amount of sampling error in the estimate of the population standard deviation declines as the size of the sample increases, the *t* distribution is actually a family of distributions. The larger the size of the sample used by the researcher, the smaller the probable amount of sampling error in the estimate of the population standard deviation and the closer the *t* distribution comes to the shape of a normal distribution. Once the sample size reaches 50 or more, the differences between the *t* distribution and the normal distribution are negligible. Since social scientists almost always deal with samples greater than 50, the *t* distributions social scientists deal with are almost exactly like normal distributions. Nevertheless, it is useful to know that the probabilities for this and many other types of hypothesis tests are based on *t* distributions.

Degrees of Freedom

Today, researchers almost always depend on computer software such as SPSS to tell them the probability of getting the sample results they got if the null hypothesis is true. Not that many years ago, however, researchers had to refer to published tables to find those probabilities. Since the *t* distribution is actually a family of distributions, yesterday's statistician or today's software programmer needs to know to which *t* distribution she should go to determine the correct probabilities.

The various *t* distributions can be distinguished by something called **degrees of freedom.** *Degrees of freedom* is often abbreviated as *df*. Calculating the degrees of freedom for a particular hypothesis test is usually easy. As previously noted, the differences between the *t* distributions are a function of sample size.

$$\text{one-sample } t \text{ test: } df = N - 1$$

The degrees of freedom for a one-sample *t* test are simply one less than the sample size. A sample of 100 has 99 degrees of freedom for a one-sample *t* test, and a sample of 1,500 has 1,499 degrees of freedom.

What use is this to you as long as SPSS knows what *t* distribution to use? Since degrees of freedom are routinely included in written reports when researchers state significance levels, you should know what that *df* refers to. Also, when you see the results of a one-sample *t* test with its degrees of freedom, you can easily figure out how large a sample the researcher had. Since the degrees of freedom is *N* minus 1, then

$$\text{one-sample t test: } N = df + 1$$

SPSS reports the degrees of freedom in the "One-Sample Test" box under the heading "df." Figure 12.3 shows 326 degrees of freedom, which corresponds exactly to the number of valid cases in the sample, 327, minus 1.

t Statistic

The SPSS output also reports the value of the **t statistic**. This is like a *z*-score except that it is based on a *t* distribution. It indicates how many standard errors from the center of the distribution the sample result was. Remember that the center of the distribution is based on the null hypothesis' claim about the population parameter. The *t* statistic will be negative if the sample result is below the predicted mean and positive if it is above the predicted mean. The larger the absolute value of the *t* statistic, the further from the predicted mean is the sample result.

Like degrees of freedom, the value of the *t* statistic is usually included when writing up the results of a hypothesis test. For example, a researcher might summarize this first example by stating that "the average household size of 1980 GSS young adults does not differ significantly from three ($t = -.528$, $df = 326$, $p = .598$)." That way, a reader can see the value of the *t* statistic, the degrees of freedom, and the probability. The *p* stands for probability. Sometimes *sig* is used as an abbreviation for significance level instead of *p*.

Don't lose sight of the fact that the answer to Step 3 in hypothesis testing is the probability or significance level. It is important to understand what the *t* statistic and degrees of freedom are, but the decision to reject or not reject the null hypothesis is based on the probability level and only on the probability level—not on the value of the *t* statistic or on the degrees of freedom.

One-Tailed and Two-Tailed Hypothesis Tests

Consider the following null hypotheses:

- The average number of hours of TV watched per day is 3.00. ($\overline{\text{TVHOURS}} = 3.00$)
- The average income of sociology professors is $63,000. ($\overline{\text{INCOME}} = \$63,000$)
- The average GPA of social work majors is 2.75 or higher. ($\overline{\text{GPA}} \geq 2.75$)
- The average number of children Jewish women give birth to is 2.00 or lower. ($\overline{\text{CHILDREN}} \leq 2.00$)

The first two null hypotheses predict a specific value for the mean. The mathematical equivalents of these null hypotheses use a simple equal sign. Think about the sampling distribution for either of these first two null hypotheses. These null hypotheses would be rejected if the sample results fall far from the center of the distribution in either direction. Extreme results *in either tail* of the sampling distribution would be grounds for rejecting the null hypothesis. A hypothesis test with a null hypothesis like either of these is called a **two-tailed hypothesis** test because the rejection area in the sampling distribution is divided between the two tails.

The situation is very different for the third and fourth null hypotheses. These null hypotheses predict a specific value or a value on one side of the specific value. The third null hypothesis predicts a value of 2.75 or any value greater than 2.75; the fourth null hypothesis predicts a value of 2.00 or any value less than 2.00. The mathematical equivalents for these hypotheses use either a "greater than or equal to" sign (≥) or a "less than or equal to" sign (≤). Think about the sampling distributions for these hypotheses. This time, only extreme results *in one particular tail* of the sampling distribution would be grounds for rejecting the null hypothesis. A hypothesis test with a null hypothesis like these is called a **one-tailed hypothesis** test because the rejection area in the sampling distribution resides entirely in just one tail.

For example, consider the third null hypothesis. If the sample result is well below 2.75, the null hypothesis is rejected because a sample result well below 2.75 is very unlikely if the true mean in the population is 2.75 or higher. However, if the sample result is well above 2.75 or even just slightly above 2.75, the null hypothesis is not rejected. A sample result above 2.75, even far above 2.75, is absolutely consistent with the null hypothesis. In fact, upon seeing at Step 2 in hypothesis testing that the sample result is consistent with the null hypothesis, we would go directly to Step 4 and not reject the null hypothesis. A hypothesis test with a null hypothesis like this is known as a one-tailed hypothesis test because the rejection area in the sampling distribution is located in just one tail.

The probability associated with a particular sample result differs depending on whether it is a one-tailed or two-tailed hypothesis test. For the two-tailed hypothesis test, the 5% rejection area is split between the two tails of the sampling distribution, but for the one-tailed test, the 5% rejection area is all located in just one tail of the sampling distribution. Some SPSS procedures will give you an opportunity to specify if you are doing one-tailed or two-tailed hypothesis testing, but most will not. Most will assume you are doing a two-tailed test, and they will report in the output the two-tailed probability. Fortunately, it is very easy to convert two-tailed probabilities to one-tailed probabilities or, for that matter, to convert one-tailed probabilities into two-tailed probabilities. If SPSS reports a two-tailed probability but a one-tailed probability is needed, just divide the two-tailed probability in half.

$$\text{one-tailed probability} = \frac{\text{two-tailed probability}}{2}$$

If SPSS reports a one-tailed probability but a two-tailed probability is required, just multiply the one-tailed probability by 2.

two-tailed probability = one-tailed probability × 2

Of course, this means you need to know whether you are doing a one- or two-tailed hypothesis test. The first example in this chapter had a null hypothesis, "In the population of 1980 young adults, the average household size was three." This calls for a two-tailed hypothesis test. The SPSS output in Figure 12.3 reported a value for "Sig (2-tailed)." We wanted a two-tailed probability; SPSS reported a two-tailed probability. No problem! We used the probability as reported. Had we wanted a one-tailed probability, we would have had to divide the reported probability in half.

Remember to use the correct probability for the type of hypothesis test you are doing. Failing to divide a two-tailed probability in half when a one-tailed probability is needed may result in a wrong conclusion about rejecting or not rejecting the null hypothesis. When SPSS reports one-tailed probabilities for *t* tests, it always identifies them as one-tailed. Two-tailed probabilities for *t* tests are usually identified as two-tailed but not always. If SPSS does not label a *t* test probability, it is a two-tailed probability.

CONCEPT CHECK

Without looking back, can you answer the following questions:

- When is a one-sample *t* test used?
- What is the difference between a two-tailed hypothesis test and a one-tailed hypothesis test?

If not, go back and review before reading on.

A Second Example

"Defining siblings to include full-siblings, half-siblings, and adopted siblings, did 1980 GSS young adults average significantly more than four siblings?"

Step 1: State the research hypothesis and the null hypothesis. The question about the siblings of 1980 GSS young adults translates into two competing hypotheses about 1980 young adults: "in the population of 1980 young adults, the mean number of siblings was more than four" and "in the population of 1980 young adults, the mean number of siblings was four or less." These can be expressed as

$$\overline{\text{SIBLINGS}} > 4 \text{ and } \overline{\text{SIBLINGS}} \leq 4$$

The second hypothesis is the null hypothesis because it includes a specific number. The equal sign (as part of the "less than or equal to" operator) in the mathematical expression of the second hypothesis also identifies it as the null.

This is a one-tailed hypothesis test. To reject the null hypothesis, the sample result must deviate from 4 in one particular direction. To reject the null hypothesis, you must get a result that is a sufficient distance above 4. A sample result below 4, even if it is far below 4, would not be reason to reject the null hypothesis.

One-Sample Statistics

	N	Mean	Std. Deviation	Std. Error Mean
SIBLINGS	327	3.96	2.756	.152

One-Sample Test

	Test Value = 4					
					95% Confidence Interval of the Difference	
	t	df	Sig. (2-tailed)	Mean Difference	Lower	Upper
SIBLINGS	-.281	326	.779	-.043	-.34	.26

Figure 12.4 *One-Sample T Test* Output for $\overline{\text{SIBLINGS}}$ ≤ 4 for 1980 GSS Young Adults

Step 2: Check the sample results. Are they consistent with the null hypothesis or the research hypothesis? The SPSS output from the *One-Sample T Test* procedure appears in Figure 12.4.

The research hypothesis was that 1980 young adults averaged more than four siblings; the null hypothesis was that they averaged four or fewer siblings. In our sample, the average was 3.96. Since the sample result is consistent with the null hypothesis, we go directly to Step 4.

Step 3: What is the probability of getting the observed sample results if the null hypothesis is true? This step is skipped because the sample result is consistent with the null hypothesis. The significance level printed in the output is irrelevant. It has no bearing on your conclusion. It should not even be looked at.

Step 4: Reject or do not reject the null hypothesis. Because the sample result is consistent with the null hypothesis, we do not reject the null hypothesis. This does not prove the null hypothesis is correct. After all, we have sample data, and what we are seeing may simply be sampling error. By not rejecting the null hypothesis, we are only asserting that there is no compelling reason to reject it. Our results can be described as not statistically significant.

A Third Example

"Did the parents of 1980 GSS young adults average significantly less than 12 years of schooling?"

Step 1: State the research hypothesis and the null hypothesis. The pair of hypotheses that follow from this question are "for the population of 1980 young adults, their parents averaged less than 12 years of schooling" and "for the population of 1980 young adults, their parents averaged 12 or more years of schooling." Mathematically, these hypotheses can be represented as

$$\overline{\text{MAPAEDUC}} < 12 \text{ and } \overline{\text{MAPAEDUC}} \geq 12$$

The second hypothesis is the null hypothesis, and this is a one-tailed hypothesis test.

One-Sample Statistics

	N	Mean	Std. Deviation	Std. Error Mean
MAPAEDUC	311	11.465	2.9847	.1692

One-Sample Test

	Test Value = 12					
					95% Confidence Interval of the Difference	
	t	df	Sig. (2-tailed)	Mean Difference	Lower	Upper
MAPAEDUC	-3.163	310	.002	-.5354	-.868	-.202

Figure 12.5   *One-Sample T Test* Output for MAPAEDUC ≥ 12 for 1980 GSS Young Adults

Step 2: Check the sample results. Are they consistent with the null hypothesis or the research hypothesis? The SPSS output appears in Figure 12.5. The research hypothesis predicts the average parental education will be less than 12 years; the null hypothesis predicts that the average will be 12 years or higher. In the sample, the mean is 11.465. The sample result is consistent with the research hypothesis, so we proceed to Step 3.

Step 3: What is the probability of getting the observed sample results if the null hypothesis is true? Figure 12.5 shows a two-tailed significance level of .002. Since this is a one-tailed hypothesis, the one-tailed significance level is .002/2, which is .001.

Step 4: Reject or do not reject the null hypothesis. Because the significance level of .001 is ".05 or less," we reject the null hypothesis. The results support the research hypothesis. They are statistically significant.

1980 GSS Young Adults

The chapter began with some questions about 1980 GSS young adults. On the basis of our analyses, what do we now know?

- The average household size of 1980 GSS young adults did not significantly differ from three ($t = -.528$, $df = 326$, $p = .598$). The average household size of 1980 GSS young adults was 2.96 persons. We can be 95% sure that actual average household size for all 1980 young adults was somewhere between 2.80 and 3.12 persons.
- 1980 GSS young adults did not average significantly more than four siblings. In fact, they averaged less than four siblings—just 3.96 siblings. We can be 95% sure that actual average number of siblings for all 1980 young adults was somewhere between 3.66 and 4.26.

- The parents of 1980 GSS young adults did average significantly less than 12 years of schooling ($t = -3.163$, $df = 310$, $p = .001$). The parents of 1980 GSS twentysomethings averaged just 11.465 years of formal education. We can be 95% sure that the parents of all 1980 young adults actually averaged somewhere between 11.132 and 11.798 years of schooling.

Important Concepts in the Chapter

confidence interval	one-tailed hypothesis
degrees of freedom	research hypothesis
hypothesis	significance level
hypothesis testing	statistical significance
interval estimation	*t* distribution
null hypothesis	*t* statistic
One-Sample T Test procedure	two-tailed hypothesis

Practice Problems

1. What is the difference between "interval estimation" and "hypothesis testing"?

2. Which of the following is different from the others: alternative hypothesis, null hypothesis, research hypothesis, scientific hypothesis?

3. For each of the following, (1) write the companion hypothesis, (2) identify which is the null hypothesis and which the research hypothesis, (3) write the mathematical equivalent of each hypothesis, and (4) state if the hypothesis test would be two-tailed or one-tailed.
   a. For the population of persons in their 20s in 1980, the mean number of hours worked per week was 40. *[handwritten: — Null, 2 tad]*
   b. For the population of persons in their 50s in 1980, the mean number of children was more than four. *[handwritten: — 1 tail]*
   c. For the population of persons in their 50s in 2010, the mean number of children was less than three. *[handwritten: —]*
   d. For the population of persons in their 20s in 2010, the mean number of siblings was three or less. *[handwritten: —]*

4. What are the four steps in hypothesis testing?

5. What should you do after Step 2 in hypothesis testing *[handwritten: one-tail —1 direction]*
   a. if the sample results are consistent with the null hypothesis?
   b. if the sample results are consistent with the research hypothesis?

6. Express each of the following probabilities (1) as a fraction and (2) as a percentage.
   a. .15
   b. .001
   c. .855
   d. .05

7. What is another name for "the probability of getting the observed sample results if the null hypothesis is true"?

8. What are the only two possible conclusions you can reach with hypothesis testing?

9. How small must the significance level be for you to reject the null hypothesis?

10. Why do we switch from the properties of normal distributions to the properties of t distributions to test hypotheses?

11. If there are 701 valid cases, how many degrees of freedom will a one-sample t test have?

12. An author reports the following results of a one-sample t test: $t = 4.12$, $df = 136$, $p = .005$.
    a. How many standard errors from the middle of the hypothesized sampling distribution was the sample result?
    b. Was the sample result higher or lower than the middle of the hypothesized center of the sampling distribution?
    c. How many valid cases did the researcher have?
    d. Did the author reject or not reject the null hypothesis?
    e. Were the results statistically significant?

13. An author reports the following results of a one-sample t test: $t = -1.33$, $df = 13$, $p = .32$.
    a. How many standard errors from the middle of the hypothesized sampling distribution was the sample result?
    b. Was the sample result higher or lower than the middle of the hypothesized center of the sampling distribution?
    c. How many valid cases did the researcher have?
    d. Did the author reject or not reject the null hypothesis?
    e. Were the results statistically significant?

14. SPSS reports the two-tail significance level to be .1000. What is the one-tail significance level?

Problems Requiring SPSS and the *fourGroups.sav* Data Set

For each of the remaining problems, answer the following set of questions:

   a. *State and label the research and the null hypothesis. Is this a one-tailed or two-tailed hypothesis test?*
   b. *What are the sample results? Are they consistent with the null hypothesis or with the research hypothesis?*
   c. *What is the probability of getting the observed sample results if the null hypothesis is true? (If this step is skipped, state that.)*
   d. *Do you reject or not reject the null hypothesis? Are your results statistically significant?*
   e. *What is the 95% confidence interval for the mean?*
   f. *Summarize in a few well-written sentences totaling 100 words or less what you found out.*

15. *(2010 middle-age adults)* Test the hypothesis that 2010 fiftysomethings had an average household size of two persons. (Variables: HOUSEPOP; Select Cases: GROUP = 4)

16. (*2010 young adults*) Test the hypothesis that 2010 twentysomethings had an average of three siblings. (Variables: SIBLINGS; Select Cases: GROUP = 3)

17. (*1980 middle-age adults*) Test the hypothesis that the parents of 1980 fiftysomethings averaged 8 or fewer years of schooling. (Variables: MAPAEDUC; Select Cases: GROUP = 2)

18. (*2010 GSS young adults*) Did the parents of 2010 GSS twentysomethings average significantly more than 12 years of schooling? (Variables: MAPAEDUC; Select Cases: GROUP = 3)

19. (*1980 GSS middle-age adults*) Did 1980 GSS fiftysomethings average significantly more than three children? (Variables: CHILDREN; Select Cases: GROUP = 2)

20. (*2010 GSS middle-age adults*) Did 2010 GSS fiftysomethings average significantly less than three children? (Variables: CHILDREN; Select Cases: GROUP = 4)

21. (*2010 GSS young adults*) Did 2010 GSS twentysomethings average significantly higher than 4 on willingness to allow legal abortion as measured by ABORTOK, an index that ranges from 0 to 6? (Variables: ABORTOK; Select Cases: GROUP = 3)

22. (*2010 GSS middle-age adults*) Did 2010 GSS fiftysomethings average significantly higher than 4 on willingness to allow legal abortion as measured by ABORTOK, an index that ranges from 0 to 6? (Variables: ABORTOK; Select Cases: GROUP = 4)

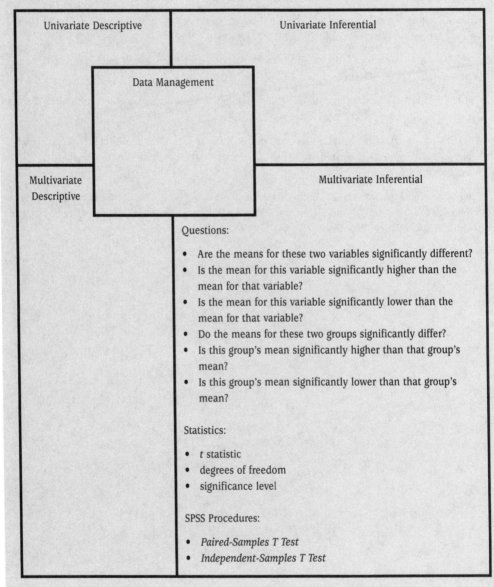

Questions and Tools for Answering Them
(Chapter 13)

Univariate Descriptive

Univariate Inferential

Data Management

Multivariate
Descriptive

Multivariate Inferential

Questions:

- Are the means for these two variables significantly different?
- Is the mean for this variable significantly higher than the mean for that variable?
- Is the mean for this variable significantly lower than the mean for that variable?
- Do the means for these two groups significantly differ?
- Is this group's mean significantly higher than that group's mean?
- Is this group's mean significantly lower than that group's mean?

Statistics:

- t statistic
- degrees of freedom
- significance level

SPSS Procedures:

- *Paired-Samples T Test*
- *Independent-Samples T Test*

Paired- and Independent-Samples *t* Tests

13

In this chapter, you can learn

- how to tell the difference between a paired-samples and an independent-samples t test,
- whether or not to reject a claim that the population means for two variables are identical,
- whether or not to reject a claim that the population mean for one variable is higher than (or lower than) the population mean of another variable,
- whether or not to reject a claim that two populations have identical means on a variable,
- whether or not to reject a claim that one population's mean is higher than (or lower than) another population's mean on the same variable,
- the two kinds of errors you risk when hypothesis testing,
- the difference between statistical significance and substantive importance, and
- why dispersion must not be ignored when comparing group means.

Controversial Persons, Parental Schooling, and Hours Worked

This chapter will answer the following questions about 1980 GSS young adults:

- Were 1980 GSS young adults significantly more willing to let controversial persons give public speeches than to let them teach in college?
- Were the fathers of 1980 GSS young adults significantly better educated than the mothers of 1980 GSS young adults?

- Was the number of hours worked per week by employed 1980 GSS young adults significantly higher for males than for females?
- Was there a significant difference between the employed 1980 GSS young adults and the employed 1980 GSS middle-age adults in the number of hours worked per week?

SPSS TIP

To Duplicate the Examples in This Chapter

To duplicate the examples in this chapter, use the *fourGroups.sav* data set. Before doing the first three examples, set the select cases condition to GROUP = 1. For the final example, set the select cases condition to "all cases."

Overview

Two types of hypothesis tests are introduced in this chapter. Both check to see if a difference between two means is significant. Paired-samples *t* tests compare scores on two different variables but for the same group of cases; independent-samples *t* tests compare scores on the same variable but for two different groups of cases.

The chapter also discusses three hypothesis-testing related topics: types of errors, substantive importance, and significantly different but overlapping distributions.

Paired-Samples *t* Tests

Here are some research hypotheses that can be tested using paired-samples *t* tests:

- The average score of subjects on the posttest is different than the average of those same subjects on the pretest. ($\overline{\text{POSTTEST}} \neq \overline{\text{PRETEST}}$)
- People will listen longer to a female telephone marketer than the very same people will listen to a male telephone marketer. ($\overline{\text{FORAHER}} > \overline{\text{FORAHIM}}$)
- Graduates had higher average salaries 10 years after graduation than they had 5 years after graduation. ($\overline{\text{SALARY10}} > \overline{\text{SALARY5}}$)
- On average, soldiers weighed less after they completed basic training than they weighed before they started. ($\overline{\text{AFTER}} < \overline{\text{BEFORE}}$)
- In a comparison of universities, sociology departments averaged fewer faculty members than did history departments. ($\overline{\text{SOCDEPT}} < \overline{\text{HISTDEPT}}$)
- First-born identical twins live longer, on average, than their second-born birth mates. ($\overline{\text{LIFE1ST}} > \overline{\text{LIFE2ND}}$)
- Husbands average more hours of sleep per night than their wives. ($\overline{\text{HESLEEP}} > \overline{\text{SHESLEEP}}$)

What distinguishes these hypotheses from the one-sample *t* test hypotheses in the last chapter is that each of these hypotheses is making a claim about two means. As always with hypothesis testing, the claim is about the population, but it will be tested using sample data.

It might help to think of it this way: There are two groups of scores. The first is a group of scores on the first variable. The second is a group of scores on the second variable. The mean for each group of scores will be calculated, but first look more closely at the data groups themselves.

Each group is just a sample of the scores that would have been collected if every member of the population had been questioned. But these two groups of sample data are not independent of one another. In most cases, the sample data in the two groups came from the same people. In every case, there is some kind of link between the individual cases that provided the data in the first group and the cases that provided the data in the second group. This link is why the name of the procedure refers to **paired samples.**

Look at the first four hypotheses listed above: subjects who took a pretest and a posttest, persons listening to a female telemarketer and also a male telemarketer, graduates 5 years and then 10 years after graduation, and soldiers weighed before and after basic training. The obvious link between the two groups of scores is that they are both scores for the same group of people.

For the last three hypotheses, however, the two groups of scores are not for the same individuals. Nevertheless, the scores are still linked. The fifth hypothesis compares sociology and history departments within the same universities. The sixth hypothesis compares first-born and second-born children who are twins to one another. The seventh hypothesis compares husbands and wives who are married to one another. For these hypotheses, the units of analysis (what each row in the data set represents) are all things bigger than individual persons. They are universities, sets of twins, and married couples. You can pair up history and sociology departments based on their university, first-born children and second-born children based on what set of twins they represent, and husbands and wives based on the married couples they form.

For each of these research hypotheses, you should be able to form the null hypothesis. For example, the null hypothesis for the first research hypothesis is that the average score of subjects on the posttest is the same as the average of those same subjects on the pretest ($\overline{\text{POSTTEST}} = \overline{\text{PRETEST}}$), and the null hypothesis for the second is that the very same people will listen for the same or shorter time to a female telephone marketer than they will listen to a male telephone marketer ($\overline{\text{FORAHER}} \leq \overline{\text{FORAHIM}}$).

As the seven hypotheses demonstrate, paired-samples *t* testing can be one- or two-tailed. Paired-sample *t* testing proceeds through the same four steps as one-sample *t* tests.

A First Example

"Were 1980 GSS young adults significantly more willing to let controversial persons give public speeches than to let them teach in college?"

Step 1: To answer this question, we form two hypotheses about the population. The research hypothesis is "the average willingness of 1980 young adults to let controversial persons give public speeches was greater than their willingness to let them teach college" ($\overline{\text{OKSPEECH}} > \overline{\text{OKTEACH}}$).

The corresponding null hypothesis is "the average willingness of 1980 young adults to let controversial persons give public speeches was the same or less than their willingness to let them teach college" ($\overline{OKSPEECH} \leq \overline{OKTEACH}$).

These hypotheses are claims about the means on two variables (OKSPEECH and OKTEACH) for one population (1980 young adults). The sample of OKSPEECH scores and the sample of OKTEACH scores are paired samples because the two samples consist of the same persons.

This is a one-tailed hypothesis test since the difference between the means must be sufficiently large and in a particular direction (greater tolerance for speeches than for college teaching) to reject the null hypothesis.

Step 2: The SPSS *Paired-Samples T Test* procedure provides both the sample means and, should it be needed, the significance level. Pull down the *Analyze* menu, move the cursor over *Compare Means,* and click on *Paired-Samples T Test*.

Analyze | Compare Means | Paired-Samples T Test

A dialog similar to Figure 13.1 appears.

Select the two variables whose means will be compared and move them into the "Paired Variables" list. When you select your first variable, it becomes variable1 for pair 1. When you select your second variable, it becomes variable2 for pair 1. Fields open up to specify a second pair, but we will test just one pair at a time.

Pay attention to level of measurement! Since the mean for each variable will be calculated, both variables must be interval/ratio. Once you have moved the pair of variables into the "Paired Variables" list, click OK. Figure 13.2 shows the resulting output.

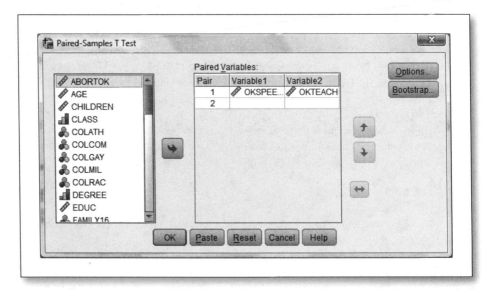

Figure 13.1   Dialog to Produce a Paired-Samples *t* Test

Paired Samples Statistics

		Mean	N	Std. Deviation	Std. Error Mean
Pair 1	OKSPEECH	3.58	293	1.685	.098
	OKTEACH	2.97	293	1.809	.106

Paired Samples Correlations

		N	Correlation	Sig.
Pair 1	OKSPEECH & OKTEACH	293	.619	.000

Paired Samples Test

		Paired Differences				
					95% Confidence Interval of the Difference	
		Mean	Std. Deviation	Std. Error Mean	Lower	Upper
Pair 1	OKSPEECH - OKTEACH	.618	1.530	.089	.442	.794

	t	df	Sig. (2-tailed)
	6.913	292	.000

Figure 13.2   *Paired-Samples T Test* Output for OKSPEECH and OKTEACH for 1980 GSS Young Adults

The "Paired Samples Statistics" shows the mean for each variable. These means are based on the 293 persons in the data set with valid scores on both variables. Cases without valid scores on one or both variables are dropped from the analysis.

In the sample, the average tolerance for giving a public speech is greater than for teaching college. This is consistent with the research hypothesis. So, we proceed to Step 3.

Step 3: Skip over the second box of output, the "Paired Samples Correlations" box. The information in that box is not relevant for a hypothesis about means. The "Paired Samples Correlations" box is testing a hypothesis about the correlation between the two variables. The significance level you see in this second box is *not* the one we want.

The significance level we are looking for is in the "Paired Samples Test" box. This is a single long box as it appears on a computer screen but has been divided into two parts for Figure 13.2. The significance level appears at the extreme right of the box. It is a two-tailed significance. Since we are testing a one-tailed hypothesis, the two-tailed significance must be divided in half, but, of course, .000/2 still is .000.

Before going on to Step 4, however, a few words should be said about the other information in the "Paired Samples Test" box. The degrees of freedom for the hypothesis test are to the left of the significance level. Degrees of freedom for paired-sample t tests are calculated just like for one-sample t tests:

$$\text{paired-samples } t \text{ test: } df = N - 1$$
$$\text{paired-samples } t \text{ test: } N = df + 1$$

The t statistic appears to the left of the degrees of freedom. The value of 6.913 for the t statistic in Figure 13.2 indicates the sample difference in means is almost 7 standard errors to the right of where the null hypothesis says the center of the sampling distribution is. How likely is a sample result this far from the center of the sampling distribution? It is so unlikely that when rounded to just three decimal places, the probability is .000.

Although it is not added to the data set, SPSS actually computes a new variable when it does a paired-samples t test. This new variable is the value of the case's score on the first variable minus the value of the case's score on the second variable. In this example, that would be OKSPEECH minus OKTEACH. The null hypothesis is claiming the mean on this new variable should be 0 or a negative number. The information in the "Paired Samples Test" under the "Paired Differences" heading shows the mean, standard deviation, standard error, and confidence interval for this new variable.

Step 4: The null hypothesis is rejected since the probability of getting the observed sample results if the null hypothesis is true is .000. The results are statistically significant. By rejecting the null hypothesis, support is given to the research hypothesis that 1980 young adults did have more tolerance for controversial persons giving public speeches than for teaching college.

A Second Example

"Were the fathers of 1980 GSS young adults significantly better educated than the mothers of 1980 GSS young adults?"

This question leads directly to two competing hypotheses: "The average years of schooling of the fathers of 1980 young adults was greater than the average years of schooling of the mothers of 1980 young adults" ($\overline{PAEDUC} > \overline{MAEDUC}$) is the research hypothesis; the null hypothesis is "the average years of schooling of the fathers of 1980 young adults was the same or less than the average years of schooling of the mothers of 1980 young adults" ($\overline{PAEDUC} \leq \overline{MAEDUC}$).

The sample of fathers' education scores and the sample of mothers' education scores are paired samples since any particular father's education score can be matched to a particular mother's education score because they are the education scores for the parents of a person who took part in the GSS. The hypothesis test is one-tailed since the difference between the two means must be sufficiently large and in a particular direction to reject the null hypothesis.

The *Paired-Samples T Test* output appears in Figure 13.3.

The fathers averaged 11.54 years of schooling; the mothers averaged 11.52 years. That makes the sample results consistent with the research hypothesis. The means do not differ by much, but they differ—and they differ in the direction predicted by the research hypothesis.

Paired Samples Statistics

		Mean	N	Std. Deviation	Std. Error Mean
Pair 1	PAEDUC	11.54	246	3.643	.232
	MAEDUC	11.52	246	2.709	.173

Paired Samples Correlations

		N	Correlation	Sig.
Pair 1	PAEDUC & MAEDUC	246	.539	.000

Paired Samples Test

		Paired Differences				
					95% Confidence Interval of the Difference	
		Mean	Std. Deviation	Std. Error Mean	Lower	Upper
Pair 1	PAEDUC - MAEDUC	.028	3.158	.201	-.368	.425

t	df	Sig. (2-tailed)
.141	245	.888

Figure 13.3   *Paired-Samples T Test* Output for PAEDUC and MAEDUC for 1980 GSS Young Adults

SPSS TIP

These Are Not the Means We Saw Before!

Back in Chapter 4, the mean for MAEDUC was reported to be 11.41 years, and the mean for PAEDUC was 11.59 years. These are not the means appearing in Figure 13.3. What is going on?

The difference results from how cases with missing data are handled. The *Descriptives* procedure back in Chapter 4 by default used every valid case to calculate the statistics for each variable. All 301 cases with valid data on MAEDUC were used to calculate its mean, and all 256 cases with valid data on PAEDUC were used to calculate its mean.

The *Paired-Samples T Test* procedure, however, can only use cases that have valid values on both of the variables being compared. Only 246 cases in the data set had valid information on both MAEDUC and PAEDUC, and those are the cases being used for this procedure. Dropping the cases with valid data on just one of the two variables accounts for the shift in means.

The two-tailed significance level is .888. Since this is a one-tailed hypothesis, the one-tailed significance level is .888/2, which is .444.

The null hypothesis, which claimed that, on average, the fathers of 1980 young adults had the same or fewer years of schooling as the mothers of 1980 young adults, cannot be rejected. The results are not statistically significant. Whether the fathers had more schooling than the mothers or had equal or less schooling remains an open question.

RESEARCH TIP

One-Sample and Paired-Samples t Tests

With a little bit of extra work, every paired-samples *t* test can be reduced to a one-sample *t* test. It was pointed out that SPSS actually computes a new variable, a difference score, whenever it does a paired-samples *t* test. It then tests the null hypothesis using this new variable.

Well, we could do the same thing. Our first example of paired-samples *t* testing had as a research hypothesis that the average willingness of 1980 young adults to let controversial persons give public speeches was greater than their willingness to let them teach college. We could have calculated a new variable using the *Compute* procedure. It might be named DIFF and calculated as OKSPEECH minus OKTEACH. In terms of this new variable, our research hypothesis would be $\overline{\text{DIFF}} > 0$ and our null hypothesis would be $\overline{\text{DIFF}} \leq 0$. Testing this with a one-sample *t* test would produce values for the *t* statistic, degrees of freedom, and significance level that are identical to the values produced with the paired-samples *t* test procedure. Using the paired-samples *t* test procedure simply saves the effort of computing a new variable!

CONCEPT CHECK

Without looking back, can you answer the following questions:

- Why are paired samples called that?
- Paired-samples *t* tests compare means for how many variables for how many groups of cases?

If not, go back and review before reading on.

Independent-Samples t Tests

Like paired-samples *t* tests, independent-samples *t* tests also test hypotheses about differences between two means; however, the means are for the same variable but for two different populations. The following research hypotheses would use independent-samples *t* tests. (In the mathematical expressions of the hypotheses, the subscript following each variable name indicates the group for which the mean would be calculated.)

- Catholic women average more children than Protestant women. ($\overline{\text{CHILDREN}_{\text{Cath women}}} > \overline{\text{CHILDREN}_{\text{Prot women}}}$)
- Biology graduates have a different average annual income than chemistry graduates. ($\overline{\text{INCOME}_{\text{bio grads}}} \neq \overline{\text{INCOME}_{\text{chem grads}}}$)
- Homicide rates, on average, are higher in Western counties than in Southern counties of the United States. ($\overline{\text{HOMICIDE}_{\text{West counties}}} > \overline{\text{HOMICIDE}_{\text{South counties}}}$)
- Length of life, on average, is shorter for never-married persons than for ever-married persons. ($\overline{\text{LIFE}_{\text{never married}}} < \overline{\text{LIFE}_{\text{ever married}}}$)
- The mean years of schooling of Republicans are different than the mean years of schooling of Democrats. ($\overline{\text{EDUC}_{\text{Republicans}}} \neq \overline{\text{EDUC}_{\text{Democrats}}}$)
- Husbands average more hours of sleep per night than wives. ($\overline{\text{SLEEP}_{\text{husbands}}} > \overline{\text{SLEEP}_{\text{wives}}}$)

As with paired-samples *t* tests, there are again two groups of scores. However, this time, the scores in both groups are scores on the same variable. What distinguishes the groups is that they represent different populations: for example, Catholic women and Protestant women, biology graduates and chemistry graduates, and counties in the West and counties in the South.

Even though all the cases may have been selected in a single sample, it is as if the first group was the result of a sample from the first population (e.g., a sample from the population of Republicans) and the second group was the result of a separate sample from the second population (e.g., a sample from the population of Democrats). There is no reason for pairing up individual cases in one group with individual cases in the other group. In fact, the number of cases in each of the two groups will typically not be the same. The groups (or samples) are independent of one another, thus the name **independent samples.**

The *Independent-Samples T Test* procedure is used to compare just two groups in the population. It would not be used to test a hypothesis about differences in average number of children for Catholic, Protestant, and Jewish women. Comparisons of three or more groups require a different procedure, one presented in the next chapter.

Hypothesis tests using independent-samples *t* tests can be one-tailed or two-tailed. Independent-samples *t* tests use the same four steps in hypothesis testing; however, Step 3 involves an additional decision.

One more thing before starting the first example: At the start of the chapter, the research hypothesis "husbands average more hours of sleep per night than their wives ($\overline{\text{HESLEEP}} > \overline{\text{SHESLEEP}}$)" was said to require a paired-samples *t* test. Now, we have the research hypothesis "husbands average more hours of sleep per night than wives ($\overline{\text{SLEEP}_{\text{husbands}}} > \overline{\text{SLEEP}_{\text{wives}}}$)," and it is said to require an independent-samples *t* test. Why the difference in hypothesis testing techniques?

Although the hypotheses are similar, they are not identical. The first hypothesis talks about husbands and *their* wives. That indicates the cases in the data set represent couples. One of the variables in the data set records how much sleep the husband in the couple gets. A separate variable in the data set records how much sleep the wife in the couple gets. Any HESLEEP score can be paired up with a specific SHESLEEP score, and the basis for the pairing would be that the two scores come from persons who are married to one another. The situation calls for paired-samples *t* testing.

The research hypothesis "husbands average more hours of sleep per night than wives," however, provides no evidence that the husbands and wives are necessarily married to one another. Someone took a sample from the adult population. Everyone in the sample was asked how many hours per day they typically sleep. Some of the persons in the sample were married men; some were married women. The married men in the sample can be viewed as a random sample of all married men in the population. The married women in the sample can be viewed as a random sample of all married women in the population. There is no basis for linking up scores on SLEEP reported by individual husbands with scores on SLEEP reported by individual wives. The situation calls for independent-samples t testing. Unless there is clear evidence that there is a basis for pairing up individual scores, assume you have independent samples.

By the way, there may have been others in the sample besides married men and married women, for example, persons who have never married or persons who are divorced or widowed. Since independent-samples t tests only permit comparisons of two groups, these other cases would be excluded from the analysis.

A First Example

"Was the number of hours worked per week by employed 1980 GSS young adults significantly higher for males than for females?"

Step 1: The research hypothesis for this question is "the average number of hours worked per week by employed 1980 young adults was higher for males than for females" ($\overline{\text{HOURS}_{\text{males}}} > \overline{\text{HOURS}_{\text{females}}}$). The null hypothesis is "the average number of hours worked per week by employed 1980 young adults was the same or lower for males than for females" ($\overline{\text{HOURS}_{\text{males}}} \leq \overline{\text{HOURS}_{\text{females}}}$).

These hypotheses require an independent-samples t test. They are claims about the mean on one variable (HOURS) for two populations (male 1980 young adults and female 1980 young adults). No particular reason exists for pairing up particular male answers with particular female answers.

This is a one-tail hypothesis test since only sample results in which the male average is higher than the female average could lead to the rejection of the null hypothesis.

Step 2: To do an *Independent-Samples T Test* procedure, pull down the *Analyze* menu, move the cursor over *Compare Means,* and click on *Independent-Samples T Test*.

Analyze | Compare Means | Independent-Samples T Test

Figure 13.4 shows the dialog that appears.

Move the variable on whose mean the groups will be compared into the "Test Variable" list. Since means will be calculated for this variable, it must be interval/ratio. Next, the two groups to be compared must be identified. Select the variable whose attributes will define the two groups and move that variable into the "Grouping Variable" field. The grouping variable can be any level of measurement. As soon as a variable is moved into that field, a set of parentheses containing two question marks appears after the name of the variable. SPSS wants to know which codes on this variable

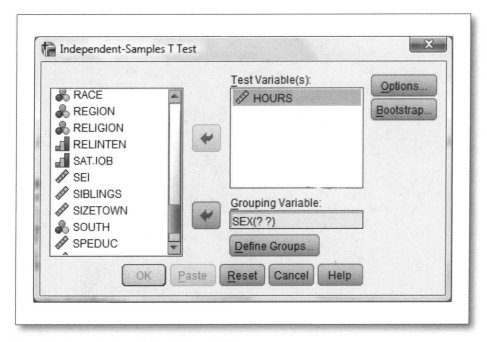

Figure 13.4   Dialog to Produce an Independent-Samples *t* Test

identify the two groups to be compared. Even if the variable is a dichotomy and has just two codes, those codes must be specified. Click on "Define Groups." (The button only becomes active once a grouping variable has been specified.) The dialog in Figure 13.5 appears.

The two groups can be defined specifying exact values or by designating a cut point. When specifying exact values, enter in the "Group 1" field the value that cases must have to be in the first group, and enter in the "Group 2" field the value that cases must have to be in the second group. For this example, 0 was entered for Group 1 since on the variable SEX, males are coded 0, and 1 was entered for Group 2 since females are coded 1.

Designating a cut point will also define two groups to be compared. If the grouping variable was years of schooling, for example, and 13 was entered as the cut point, the first group would include all valid cases with less than 13 years of schooling, and the second group would include all valid cases with 13 or more years of schooling.

After defining the groups, click "Continue" to return to the initial independent-samples *t* test dialog. The question marks behind the grouping variable are now replaced by the codes that define the groups. Click OK to produce output similar to Figure 13.6.

The first box of output, the "Group Statistics" box, shows the sample means. The mean number of hours worked reported by employed males was 43.66, and the mean reported by employed females was 39.76. The sample results are consistent with the research hypothesis that predicted the mean for males would be higher than the mean for females. We proceed to Step 3.

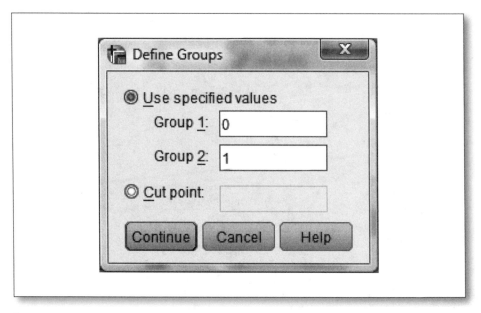

Figure 13.5   Dialog to Identify Two Groups Being Compared

Group Statistics

	SEX	N	Mean	Std. Deviation	Std. Error Mean
HOURS	0 male	106	43.66	13.757	1.336
	1 female	120	39.76	14.638	1.336

Independent Samples Test

		Levene's Test for Equality of Variances				
		F	Sig.	t	df	Sig. (2-tailed)
HOURS	Equal variances assumed	.184	.668	2.057	224	.041
	Equal variances not assumed			2.065	223.126	.040

t-test for Equality of Means			
		95% Confidence Interval of the Difference	
Mean Difference	Std. Error Difference	Lower	Upper
3.902	1.897	.164	7.640
3.902	1.890	.178	7.626

Figure 13.6   *Independent-Samples T Test* Output for HOURS by SEX (0, 1) for 1980 GSS Young Adults

Step 3: This step uses the "Independent Samples Test" output box, which appears on a computer screen as a single long box but has been broken in two parts to better fit in Figure 13.6. But this box contains two lines of results for the independent-samples *t* test. There are two values for the *t* statistic, for degrees of freedom, and for the significance level. Step 3 for the independent-samples *t* tests includes an additional decision because you must decide which result line is the correct one to use.

The reason for two sets of results is that there are two ways of estimating the standard error of the sampling distribution for independent-samples *t* tests. One method assumes that the variance in the male population on number of hours worked is exactly equal to the variance in the female population on number of hours worked. The other method does not assume the population variances are equal. Whether the variances in the two populations are the same or different affects the calculation of the standard error, the value of the *t* statistic, the degrees of freedom, and the probability or significance level.

To reach a conclusion about whether the variances are or are not equal, an entirely separate hypothesis test is done with the null hypothesis that the variances are equal. What appears in the output under the heading "Levene's Test for Equality of Variances" are the results of that separate hypothesis test. If the significance level ("Sig.") of Levene's test is .05 or less, use the second line of *t* test results, the "Equal variances not assumed" line. If the significance level of Levene's test is greater than .05, use the first line of *t* test results, the "Equal variances assumed" line.

Sometimes the two methods of estimating the standard error give you almost identical results (as they do in Figure 13.6), and sometimes they do not. Always check the significance of Levene's test and then use the correct line of *t* test results.

In Figure 13.6, the significance level of Levene's test is .668. Since this is greater than .05, the first line of results is used. The two-tailed significance level for the *t* test for equality of means is .041. Since this is a one-tailed hypothesis, we want the one-tailed significance level, which is .041/2 or .0205. (Make sure you leave Step 3 with the significance level for the *t* test for equality of means. Do *not* leave Step 3 with the significance for Levene's test. Once the significance of Levene's test tells you which row of output to use, you are done with it.)

How degrees of freedom are calculated for independent-samples *t* tests depends on whether equal variances are or are not assumed. When equal variances are assumed, degrees of freedom are simply *N* minus 2. A more complex formula is used when equal variances are not assumed.

The "Independent Samples Test" box also shows you the mean difference, the standard error of the difference, and the 95% confidence interval of the difference. The mean difference is always calculated by subtracting the sample mean for Group 2 from the sample mean for Group 1. If Group 1 has the higher mean, the mean difference will be positive; if Group 2 has the higher mean, the mean difference will be negative. In the sample data, employed males report an average of 3.902 more hours of work per week than employed females.

Step 4: Since the probability is .0205, we reject the null hypothesis. Among the 1980 GSS young adults, employed males did work significantly more hours per week than employed females.

A Second Example

"Was there a significant difference between the employed 1980 GSS young adults and the employed 1980 GSS middle-age adults in the number of hours worked per week?"

The null hypothesis is "the average number of hours worked per week by employed 1980 young adults and by employed 1980 middle-age adults is the same" ($\overline{\text{HOURS}}_{1980\ young\ adults} = \overline{\text{HOURS}}_{1980\ middle\text{-}age\ adults}$). The research hypothesis is "the average number of hours worked per week by employed 1980 young adults and by employed 1980 middle-age adults is different" ($\overline{\text{HOURS}}_{1980\ young\ adults} \neq \overline{\text{HOURS}}_{1980\ middle\text{-}age\ adults}$).

Hypotheses about a difference in means for one variable (HOURS) in two populations (1980 young adults and 1980 middle-age adults) call for an independent-samples t test. This is a two-tailed hypothesis test because a sample difference in either direction could lead to rejecting the null hypothesis.

For setting up the independent-samples t test, the test variable is HOURS and the grouping variable is GROUP. Codes 1 (1980 GSS young adults) and 2 (1980 GSS middle-age adults) define the comparison groups. Cases with codes other than 1 or 2 on GROUP are excluded from the analysis. (Since GROUP is the variable used to identify the comparison groups, *Select Cases* was set to "All cases.") The output appears in Figure 13.7.

Group Statistics

	GROUP	N	Mean	Std. Deviation	Std. Error Mean
HOURS	1 1980 GSS young adults	226	41.59	14.334	.953
	2 1980 GSS middle-age adults	143	39.79	13.020	1.089

Independent Samples Test

		Levene's Test for Equality of Variances				
		F	Sig.	t	df	Sig. (2-tailed)
HOURS	Equal variances assumed	.564	.453	1.216	367	.225
	Equal variances not assumed			1.243	323.296	.215

t-test for Equality of Means		95% Confidence Interval of the Difference	
Mean Difference	Std. Error Difference	Lower	Upper
1.798	1.479	-1.110	4.706
1.798	1.447	-1.049	4.646

Figure 13.7 *Independent-Samples T Test* Output for HOURS by GROUP (1, 2)

In the sample, the mean number of hours worked reported by employed 1980 GSS young adults was 41.59, while the mean reported by 1980 GSS middle-age adults was 39.79. The research hypothesis says the two groups will have different means, and in the sample they do. Therefore, we proceed to Step 3.

The significance level of Levene's test is .453. Since that is greater than .05, we again use the equal variances assumed line of results. The two-tailed significance level of the *t* test for equality of means is .225.

Because the probability of getting the observed sample results if the null hypothesis is true is .225, the null hypothesis is not rejected. The results are not statistically significant. Although young adults and middle-age adults had different average hours of work in our sample, the evidence is not sufficiently strong to reject the possibility that the populations of 1980 young adults and 1980 middle-age adults had the same average number of hours worked. If the null hypothesis was rejected, we would be taking a 22.5% risk that we rejected a null hypothesis that was actually true. We will accept no more than a 5% risk of making such an error!

CONCEPT CHECK

Without looking back, can you answer the following questions:

- Why are independent samples called that?
- Independent-samples *t* tests compare means for how many variables for how many groups of cases?
- If the significance of Levene's test is greater than .05, are "equal variances assumed" or "equal variances not assumed" for the independent-samples *t* test?

If not, go back and review before reading on.

More About Hypothesis Testing

Type I and Type II Errors

Figure 13.8 describes the consequences of rejecting or not rejecting the null hypothesis when the null hypothesis is actually true for the population and when the null hypothesis is actually false for the population.

When a researcher rejects a null hypothesis that is actually false, that is a good outcome. Similarly, when a researcher does not reject a null hypothesis that is actually true, that is also a good outcome. The errors occur when the researcher rejects a null hypothesis that is actually true (Type I error) or does not reject a null hypothesis that is actually false (Type II error).

Of course, researchers do not intentionally commit either of these types of errors. Nor do they know for certain if they have or have not committed an error. In Figure 13.8, you would have to

Based on hypothesis testing using sample results, the researcher	If the researcher did a census, he or she would find	
	The null hypothesis is true	The null hypothesis is false
Rejected the null hypothesis	Type I error	Correct decision
Did not reject the null hypothesis	Correct decision	Type II error

Figure 13.8   Hypothesis-Testing Conclusions by Actual Population Conditions

know what row and what column you are in before you could determine if you made an error or not. But in reality, a researcher never knows what column she is in. To know if the research hypothesis is actually true or actually false, you would have to do a census, which the researcher has not done. She is working with a sample and, based on that sample, rejects or does not reject the null hypothesis. In other words, she knows which row in Figure 13.8 she is in but not which column. When she rejects the null hypothesis, she knows she is either making a correct decision or committing a Type I error. When she does not reject a null hypothesis, she knows she is either making a correct decision or committing a Type II error.

While it is true that when you reject the null hypothesis, you do not know if you are making a correct decision or committing a Type I error, you do know the risk you are taking of making a Type I error. The probability of making a Type I error when rejecting the null hypothesis is equal to the significance level that comes from Step 3 of hypothesis testing. The smaller the significance level is, the less likely that you are rejecting a null hypothesis that is actually true, which also means the less likely that you are committing a Type I error and the greater the likelihood you are making a correct decision.

As noted earlier, science is particularly concerned about rejecting null hypotheses that are actually true. In other words, it is very reluctant to commit Type I errors. That is why the greatest risk we will take of committing a Type I error is .05. But here comes the dilemma! The greater the evidence we require before rejecting a null hypothesis, the greater the risk we run of committing a Type II error.

Both are errors, and both are to be avoided, but rejecting a true null hypothesis (Type I error) is considered a graver problem than not rejecting a false null hypothesis (Type II error). Better to proceed slowly but correctly than rapidly but uncertainly. Null hypotheses not rejected now can always be rejected later if the evidence becomes stronger, but null hypotheses rejected now rarely get further examined.

Whatever decision you make at Step 4, you may be making a correct decision or an error. The significance level indicates the risk of making a Type I error if the null hypothesis is rejected. Usually, social scientists refuse to accept more than a 5% chance of making a Type I error.

RESEARCH TIP

More Parallels Between Science and the American Court System

Rules for the admissibility of evidence in American courts are stringent. Furthermore, jurors are instructed to render a guilty verdict only if they are confident "beyond a reasonable doubt." The system is designed to safeguard against convicting innocent persons. That is the good news. But those same stringent rules of evidence and the requirement that the evidence against a defendant be overwhelming also mean that more guilty persons will get off. That is the bad news. Just like in the system of justice, so also in inferential hypothesis testing, the greater the effort you make to avoid one type of error, the greater the probability of making the other type of error.

In the American justice system, it is considered a more serious error to convict an innocent person than to not convict a guilty one. That is why the rules for evidence are so strict and the requirements for rejecting the assumption of innocence so high. Just like in the justice system, the two types of error are not considered equally bad in inferential hypothesis testing. The graver error is to reject a null hypothesis that is actually true, and to avoid that error, analysts are willing to take on an increased risk of not rejecting a null hypothesis that is actually false.

Significant Versus Important

When testing a hypothesis, data analysts can tell you if the results are statistically significant. When an analyst says those results are statistically significant, he is saying that he rejects the null hypothesis; he is saying the results support the research hypothesis. He is *not* saying the results are substantively important.

In the first example of independent-samples *t* testing, we found that the average number of hours worked per week by employed 1980 GSS young adult males (43.66 hours) was significantly higher than the average hours worked per week by employed 1980 GSS young adult females (39.76 hours)—a difference of 3.90 hours. The difference is statistically significant, but is the difference important? Will a difference that size affect how important work is in a person's definition of self? Will a difference that size impact the allocation of responsibilities within the family? Does a difference that size represent prima facie evidence of workplace discrimination?

If all the analyst knows is that the difference is statistically significant, then the proper answer to these questions is "I do not know." When you ask about *importance,* you are asking a *substantive question,* not a statistical question. The data analyst can tell you with a specified degree of confidence what the difference is between men and women on hours worked per week, but the analyst cannot tell you whether that difference matters.

So, is the data analyst unimportant? Hardly! Unless statistical significance is established, it remains unclear whether the observed sample differences actually exist in the population. Before someone starts talking about the consequences of gender differences in hours worked, he wants to be very confident that those differences aren't just sampling error. To find that out, he needs inferential statistics. But if the results are found to be statistically significant, judgments about the importance of the results are best made by the substantive expert.

Central Tendency Versus Dispersion

This is a good time to briefly restate something discussed several chapters back: In describing the distribution of cases on some variable, central tendency is a useful summary technique, but so is dispersion. Not every case falls right at the mean! Similarly, when comparing scores on two variables within a population or comparing two populations on some variable, differences in means are interesting and sometimes important, but so also are differences or similarities in dispersion.

It is particularly important to remember this when you are testing for significant differences between group means. People sometimes talk about significant differences in means as if every member of the group with the higher mean has a higher score than every member of the group with the lower mean. Such is rarely the case. Graphing the distribution of each group on the variable in question often reveals substantial overlap.

The gender difference in hours worked per week by employed 1980 GSS young adults was statistically significant, with males having a higher average. Because the difference was statistically significant, it is unlikely to have occurred simply by chance. We can be quite sure that the means for the male population and the female population from which these samples came truly did differ. But how did this difference come about? Did almost all employed 1980 young adult males work more hours than almost all employed young adult females? That is hardly the case, as Figure 13.9 shows.

There is considerable overlap in the hours worked by the two groups. For both, 40 was by far the most commonly reported number of hours worked. Many women worked as many or more hours as many men, and many men worked less than many women. Even so, women were a little more likely to work shorter hours and men were a little more likely to work longer hours, and those differences were enough to make the mean difference statistically significant. And that difference in means may, in fact, be important.

The point of this section is not to dismiss differences in means but to also encourage you to examine patterns of dispersion. Be careful (or better, be curious) when you hear about significant gender, race, region, age, or whatever differences. You are probably being told about differences in means. That is valuable information but, to get a fuller picture, also inquire about dispersion.

CONCEPT CHECK

Without looking back, can you answer the following questions:

- When does a researcher risk making a Type I error?
- Does statistical significance indicate substantive importance?
- Can two frequency distributions substantially overlap if their means are significantly different?

If not, go back and review before reading on.

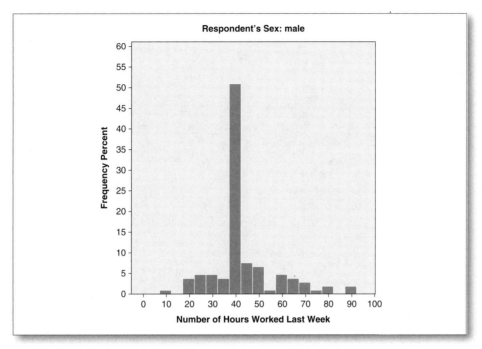

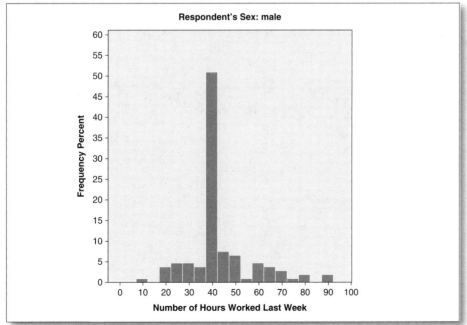

Figure 13.9   Separate Male and Female Histograms for HOURS Worked by 1980 GSS Young Adults

1980 GSS Young Adults

The chapter began with some questions about 1980 GSS young adults. On the basis of our analyses, what do we now know?

- 1980 GSS young adults were significantly more willing to let controversial persons give public speeches than to let them teach in college ($t = 6.913$, $df = 292$, $p = .000$). Their average tolerance for controversial persons giving public speeches was 3.58 on an index that could range from 0 to 5, while their average tolerance for controversial persons teaching college was just 2.97 on an index that also ranged from 0 to 5.
- The fathers of 1980 GSS young adults were not significantly better educated than the mothers of 1980 GSS young adults ($t = 0.141$, $df = 245$, $p = .444$). In our samples, fathers averaged 11.54 years of schooling, and mothers averaged 11.52 years; this difference was too small to reject the possibility that in the full population of 1980 young adults, their fathers averaged the same or even less schooling than their mothers.
- Among employed 1980 GSS young adults, males worked significantly more hours per week than females ($t = 2.057$, $df = 224$, $p = .0205$). In our samples, men worked an average of 43.66 hours per week, and women worked an average of 39.76 hours.
- The difference in hours worked per week between employed 1980 GSS young adults and employed 1980 GSS middle-age adults was not statistically significant ($t = 1.216$, $df = 367$, $p = .225$). Although employed 1980 GSS young adults averaged 41.59 hours of work compared to 39.79 hours for employed 1980 GSS middle-age adults, this difference was too small to reject the possibility that these two populations have the same average weekly hours worked.

Important Concepts in the Chapter

central tendency	statistical significance
dispersion	substantive importance
independent samples	Type I error
Independent Samples T Test procedure	Type II error
paired samples	
Paired-Samples T Test procedure	

Practice Problems

1. Which type of hypothesis test (one-sample *t* test, paired-samples *t* test, or independent-samples *t* test) should be used for each of the following hypotheses?
   a. On average, wives have more education than their husbands.
   b. The average education of wives is 13.4 years.
   c. The average age at first marriage for women is less than 25 years.
   d. The average age at first marriage for women is less than the average age at first marriage for men.
   e. On average, grooms are older than their brides.
   f. The average age at first marriage of persons marrying for the first time in the 1970s was younger than the average age at first marriage of persons marrying for the first time in the 2000s.

2. If you have 1,500 cases, how many degrees of freedom will your paired-samples *t* test have?

3. An author reports the following results of a paired-samples *t* test: $t = 2.12$, $df = 76$, $p = .041$.
   a. How many standard errors from the middle of the hypothesized sampling distribution was the sample result?
   b. How many valid cases did the researcher have?
   c. Did the author reject or not reject the null hypothesis?
   d. Were the results statistically significant?

4. An author reports the following results of an independent-samples *t* test: $t = -0.83$, $df = 215$, $p = .444$.
   a. How many standard errors from the middle of the hypothesized sampling distribution was the sample result?
   b. Did the author reject or not reject the null hypothesis?
   c. Were the results statistically significant?

5. You are doing an independent-samples *t* test. Do you use the "equal variances assumed" or the "equal variances not assumed" set of results for the independent samples *t* test if Levene's test for equality of variances
   a. has a significance level of .05 or less?
   b. has a significance level greater than .05?

6. Define each of the following:
   a. Type I error
   b. Type II error

7. "Significance level" is the same as the risk of making which type of error if you reject the null hypothesis?

8. What is the largest risk social scientists will usually take of making a Type I error?

9. Answer each of the following with an explanation:
   a. If results are statistically significant, does that mean they are substantively important?
   b. If results are *not* statistically significant, does that mean they are *not* substantively important?

10. If the mean for men on aggressiveness is significantly higher than the mean for women on aggressiveness, can we assume that most men are more aggressive than most women? Explain your answer.

Problems Requiring SPSS and the *fourGroups.sav* Data Set

For each of the remaining problems, answer the following set of questions:

   a. *State and label the research and the null hypothesis. Is this a one-tailed or two-tailed hypothesis test?*
   b. *What are the sample results? Are they consistent with the null hypothesis or with the research hypothesis?*
   c. *What is the probability of getting the observed sample results if the null hypothesis is true? (If this step is skipped, state that.)*
   d. *Do you reject or not reject the null hypothesis? Are your results statistically significant?*
   e. *Summarize in a few well-written sentences totaling 100 words or less what you found out.*

11. (*2010 GSS young adults*) Were 2010 GSS twentysomethings significantly more willing to let controversial persons give public speeches than to let them teach in college? (Variables: OKSPEECH, OKTEACH; Select Cases: GROUP = 3)

12. (*2010 GSS middle-age adults*) Was there a significant difference in the willingness of 2010 GSS fiftysomethings to let controversial persons give public speeches and in their willingness to leave the books of controversial persons in libraries? (Variables: OKBOOK, OKSPEECH; Select Cases: GROUP = 4)

13. (*1980 middle-age adults*) Test the hypothesis that the average years of schooling of the fathers and mothers of the 1980 fiftysomethings were the same. (Variables: PAEDUC, MAEDUC; Select Cases: GROUP = 2)

14. (*2010 young adults*) Test the hypothesis that the average years of schooling of the fathers and mothers of 2010 twentysomethings were the same. (Variables: PAEDUC, MAEDUC; Select Cases: GROUP = 3)

15. (*2010 GSS young adults*) Was there a significant difference in the prestige of the occupations held by 2010 GSS young men and women? (Variables: SEI, SEX; Select Cases: GROUP = 3)

16. (*2010 GSS middle-age adults*) Was there a significant difference in the prestige of the occupations held by 2010 GSS middle-age men and women? (Variables: SEI, SEX; Select Cases: GROUP = 4)

17. (*2010 GSS young adults* and *2010 GSS middle-age adults*) Was there a significant difference in the prestige of the occupations held by 2010 GSS twentysomethings and fiftysomethings? (Variables: SEI, GROUP; Select Cases: all cases)

18. (*1980 GSS middle-age adults* and 2010 *GSS middle-age adults*) Did 2010 GSS fiftysomethings have significantly fewer children than 1980 GSS fiftysomethings? (Variables: CHILDREN, GROUP; Select Cases: all cases)

19. (*2010 young adults*) Test the hypothesis that the average years of schooling of the 2010 twentysomethings and the average years of schooling of their spouses were identical. (Variables: EDUC, SPEDUC; Select Cases: GROUP = 3)

20. (*2010 middle-age adults*) Test the hypothesis that there was a difference in the average years of schooling of 2010 fiftysomethings who were liberal and those who were conservative. (Variables: EDUC, POLVIEWS; Select Cases: GROUP = 4)

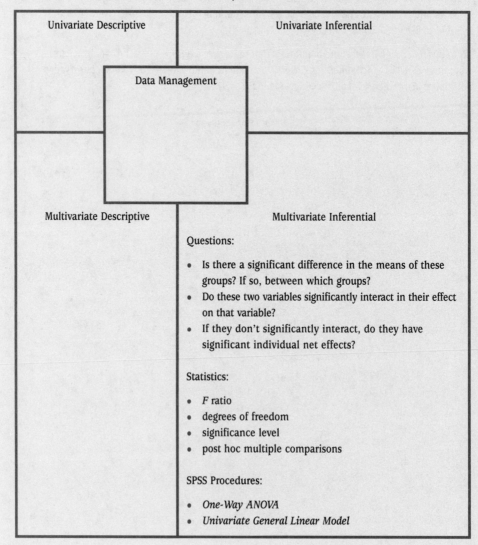

Questions and Tools for Answering Them
(Chapter 14)

Univariate Descriptive	Univariate Inferential

Data Management

Multivariate Descriptive

Multivariate Inferential

Questions:

- Is there a significant difference in the means of these groups? If so, between which groups?
- Do these two variables significantly interact in their effect on that variable?
- If they don't significantly interact, do they have significant individual net effects?

Statistics:

- *F* ratio
- degrees of freedom
- significance level
- post hoc multiple comparisons

SPSS Procedures:

- *One-Way ANOVA*
- *Univariate General Linear Model*

Analysis of Variance

In this chapter, you can learn

- how to tell if there are any significant differences among three or more groups on the mean of a variable,
- how to identify which pairs of groups are significantly different,
- how to examine the effect of two or more discrete independent variables on an interval/ratio dependent variable,
- how to tell if the effect on the dependent variable of one independent variable significantly varies depending on the value of a second independent variable, and
- how to tell if the effect on the dependent variable of an independent variable is significant after controlling for a second independent variable.

Abortion, Hours Worked, and Children

This chapter will answer the following questions about 1980 GSS young adults:

- Were there significant regional differences in average willingness to allow legal abortion among 1980 GSS young adults?
- Were there significant religious affiliation differences in average willingness to allow legal abortion among 1980 GSS young adults?
- Was there a significant interaction effect of marital status and gender on hours worked among 1980 GSS young adults? If the interaction wasn't significant, did marital status and gender have significant individual net effects?

- Was there a significant interaction effect of marital status and gender on number of children among 1980 GSS young adults? If the interaction wasn't significant, did marital status and gender have significant individual net effects?

SPSS TIP

To Duplicate the Examples in This Chapter

To duplicate the examples in this chapter, use the *fourGroups.sav* data set. Before doing any of the statistical procedures, set the select cases condition to GROUP = 1.

Overview

Analysis of variance (ANOVA) and regression are the two most common forms of multivariate analysis in the social sciences. Both use interval/ratio variables as the dependent variable. But while regression is designed for continuous (typically interval/ratio) independent variables, ANOVA is designed for categorical (typically nominal or ordinal) independent variables. (Independent variables are often referred to as factor variables or simply *factors* in analysis of variance.)

Both regression and ANOVA have proven over the years to be quite adaptable procedures. Regression can use ordinal independent variables and even nominal ones if they are converted into dummy variables. ANOVA can make use of continuous independent variables if they are collapsed into discrete categories. In fact, regression and ANOVA share many similarities and are both products of a common statistical approach known as the general linear model.

There is a close connection between ANOVA and the *Means* procedure described in Chapter 6. Both procedures compare group and subgroup means. Both procedures use interval/ratio dependent variables and discrete independent variables. Both procedures reveal main effects and interaction effects. The principal difference is that the *Means* procedure only provides descriptive statistics while ANOVA provides both descriptive and inferential statistics.

We begin with one-way ANOVA. It resembles a *Means* procedure with just a single layer. We then proceed to two-way ANOVA, which resembles a *Means* procedure with a second layer. The chapter concludes by showing how the logic of two-way ANOVA can be applied to ANOVA problems with any number of factors or layers.

One-Way ANOVA

You saw in the last chapter that independent-samples *t* tests reach conclusions about differences in means between two populations. One-way ANOVA reaches conclusions about differences in means among three or more populations. Research hypotheses like the following can be tested using one-way ANOVA:

- There are differences in the average income of sociology, social work, and criminal justice graduates.
- There are differences in average length of life among persons born in the Midwest, the Northeast, the South, and the West.
- There are differences in recidivism rate of persons convicted of burglary, larceny, forgery, and robbery.
- There are differences in average body temperature among persons born under the 12 different astrological signs.
- There are differences in average Apgar score of infants delivered through modern childbirth, natural childbirth, and caesarian childbirth.
- There are differences in average vehicle speed when a police car is visible, when a sign flashing vehicle speed is visible, and when neither is visible.

It is important to understand what these research hypotheses are and are not claiming. They claim that there is some difference in the means for these populations. They are not claiming that every population's mean is different from every other population's mean. The research hypotheses are simply saying they are not all the same. Using the first hypothesis as an example, if sociology and social work graduates had the same average income but the average for criminal justice graduates was different, that would be consistent with the research hypothesis.

The null hypotheses claim that all the populations have the same mean. For example, there is no difference in the average income of sociology, social work, and criminal justice graduates ($\overline{INCOME}_{sociology} = \overline{INCOME}_{social\ work} = \overline{INCOME}_{criminal\ justice}$). While it is easy to mathematically represent the null hypothesis that all group means are identical, there is no way using common mathematical symbols to express the research hypotheses. Replacing the equal signs with not equal signs will not work because only one mean has to be different from the others to satisfy the research hypothesis. Therefore, one-way ANOVA research hypotheses will only be expressed in verbal form.

The F Ratio

The t statistic is not appropriate for testing null hypotheses about three or more groups having identical means. To test these hypotheses, ANOVA makes use of an F ratio. You have seen the F ratio before, but just briefly. Levene's test for equality of variances used an F ratio. At first glance, the F ratio seems an unlikely candidate for testing a hypothesis about group means because the F ratio is a ratio of variances. The top number or numerator of the F ratio is an estimate of the variance in the population on the dependent variable using what is known as the "between-groups" method of estimation. The bottom number or denominator of the F ratio is an alternative estimate of the variance in the population on the dependent variable using the "within-groups" method of estimation.

How this ties back to means is that when the populations being compared have the same means, the two methods of estimating variance yield the same estimate, and the value of the F ratio is 1. When the populations being compared have different means, however, the between-groups method of estimating the population variance yields a larger estimate of the population variance, and the value of the F ratio is greater than 1.

Even if the population groups have identical means, however, sampling error usually produces groups with at least slightly different means and an F ratio with a value different from 1. What a researcher needs to know is the probability of getting a particular value for the F ratio if, in fact, the null hypothesis of equal means is true. In other words, we need to know about the sampling distribution of the F ratio. Although different from the normal distribution and the t distribution, statisticians know quite a bit about the F distribution and the probability of getting particular sample values for the F ratio.

Degrees of Freedom

Like the t distribution, the F distribution is actually a family of distributions. Which particular distribution should be used depends on the degrees of freedom for the hypothesis test. Unlike the t statistic, which had one number to indicate its degrees of freedom, the F ratio has two degrees of freedom numbers. The two numbers are based on the two methods of estimating the population variance.

$$\text{one-way ANOVA: } df = (K - 1 \text{ and } N - K)$$

The first degrees of freedom number is $K - 1$, where K is the number of groups being compared. The second degrees of freedom number is $N - K$, where N is the number of cases and K is still the number of groups.

In the old days, researchers needed both these numbers to locate the correct F distribution with its probabilities of getting particular values for the F ratio. Statistical software has eliminated the need to look up F ratio probabilities. Nevertheless, the two degrees of freedom numbers are still routinely reported along with the value of the F ratio and its probability. You can use the two degrees of freedom numbers to determine how many groups a researcher was comparing and how large the sample was.

$$\text{one-way ANOVA: } K = df_1 + 1$$

$$\text{one-way ANOVA: } N = df_2 + K$$

K, the number of groups being compared, is the first degrees of freedom number plus 1. N, the number of valid cases, is the second degrees of freedom number plus K, the number of groups being compared. For example, you are reading a report and come across the following information: $F = 8.45$, $df = 4$ and 1,230, $p = .04$. You are being told that the value of the F ratio is 8.45, and the probability of getting a value that high or higher in a sampling distribution with 4 and 1,230 degrees of freedom is .04. (So you will reject the null hypothesis of identical means!) From the degrees of freedom numbers, you can also determine that five groups were being compared (4 + 1 = 5), and the sample had 1,235 cases (1,230 + 5 = 1,235).

Nondirectional Hypotheses

If the bad news about F ratio hypotheses is that there are not one but two degrees of freedom numbers, the good news is that all F ratio hypotheses are nondirectional. They make claims about parameters being equal to or not equal to each other, but they do not claim certain parameters are greater than or less than other parameters or values. Therefore, hypothesis tests using F ratios are not separated into one-tailed or two-tailed hypotheses.

Post Hoc Multiple Comparisons

Is one-way ANOVA really necessary since we already know how to do independent-samples t tests? Could any comparison of three or more groups simply be reduced to a series of two-group comparisons? Could the hypothesis "there are differences in the average income of sociology, social work, and criminal justice graduates" be reduced to three separate independent-samples t tests using the following research hypotheses?

- There is a difference in the average income of sociology and social work graduates.
- There is a difference in the average income of sociology and criminal justice graduates.
- There is a difference in the average income of social work and criminal justice graduates.

Using the same logic, could a one-way ANOVA comparison of four groups be reduced to 6 separate two-group comparisons, a comparison of five groups to 10 separate two-group comparisons, and so on?

The problem with doing that is not simply that it would involve more work. The problem has to do with the risk of making a Type I error. When a researcher does one hypothesis test and only rejects the null hypothesis if the probability is .05 or less, he runs a .05 risk of making a Type I error. However, when he does 3 hypothesis tests, each requiring a .05 probability to reject the null, his chance of making at least one Type I error rises to .14; when he does 6 hypothesis tests, his chance of making at least one Type I error rises to .26; and when he does 10 hypothesis tests, his chance of making at least one Type I error rises to .40. The more t tests the researcher does, the greater the risk of committing a Type I error somewhere in the t testing—even though every individual t test took no more than a .05 risk.

To avoid this problem, we should initially do a single hypothesis test using an F ratio. The null hypothesis for this test will be that all of the groups have the same mean; the research hypothesis will be that all of the groups do not have the same mean. Only if we are able to reject this initial null hypothesis will we then investigate pairs of groups using t tests to see which groups differ from which other groups. If and when we proceed to comparing pairs of groups, we will adjust the requirements for statistical significance so that we continue to take on only a 5% risk overall of making a Type I error. These comparisons of pairs of groups are known as post hoc multiple comparisons.

Each of these comparisons of pairs of groups is a separate hypothesis test and could be broken down into the standard four steps. However, the whole set of comparisons will be treated as a fifth step in hypothesis testing. We will take this fifth step only with one-way analysis of variance, and it is a step that is not always needed. We proceed to this fifth step of identifying significantly different pairs only if we are able to reject the original null hypothesis that all the groups have the same population mean.

A First Example

"Were there significant regional differences in average willingness to allow legal abortion among 1980 GSS young adults?" (regional categories: Midwest, Northeast, South, and West)

Step 1: The research hypothesis is "there were differences in average willingness to allow legal abortion between some of the following groups of 1980 young adults: Midwesterners, Northeasterners, Southerners, and Westerners." The null hypothesis is "there were no differences in average willingness to allow legal abortion between any of the following groups of 1980 young adults: Midwesterners, Northeasterners, Southerners, and Westerners." Expressed mathematically, the null hypothesis is

$$\overline{\text{ABORTOK}_{\text{Midwest}}} = \overline{\text{ABORTOK}_{\text{Northeast}}} = \overline{\text{ABORTOK}_{\text{South}}} = \overline{\text{ABORTOK}_{\text{West}}}$$

Step 2: To get the sample group means, pull down the *Analyze* menu, move the cursor over *Compare Means,* and click on *One-Way ANOVA.*

Analyze | Compare Means | One-Way ANOVA

A dialog similar to Figure 14.1 appears.

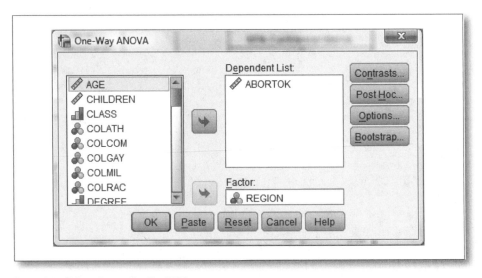

Figure 14.1   Dialog to Create a One-Way ANOVA

Move the variable whose means will be calculated to the "Dependent List." This variable must be interval/ratio. Move the variable whose attributes will define the groups to be compared to the "Factor" field. This variable can be any level of measurement. Discrete variables with no more than six or seven categories are usually used.

Click on "Options," and a dialog similar to Figure 14.2 will appear. Check "Descriptive." This will give you the sample group means that you need for this second step in hypothesis testing. Click "Continue" to return to the main dialog.

Now click "Post Hoc." A dialog similar to Figure 14.3 will appear. There are many alternative methods of doing post hoc multiple comparisons. The techniques generally reach the same conclusions but use different statistical procedures along the way. This book uses the "Tukey" method, but check with your instructor about which method she or he prefers. The multiple-comparison output being requested here will be of use in Step 5 *if* we proceed to Step 5. Click "Continue" to return to the initial dialog.

Finally, click OK. Figure 14.4 shows most of the output produced by these dialogs. The "Descriptives" output box is used for Step 2 in hypothesis testing, the "ANOVA" output box assists with Step 3, and the "Multiple Comparisons" output box is for Step 5. Requesting Tukey multiple comparisons also produces a "Homogeneous Subjects" output box, but we will not use that.

The sample group means appear in the Descriptives output box. As long as at least two groups have different sample means, the sample results are consistent with the research hypothesis since the null hypothesis says all means will be identical. In the sample, 1980 GSS young adults living in the Northeast would

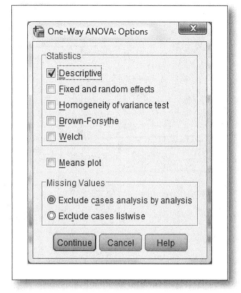

Figure 14.2   Dialog to Request Sample Means

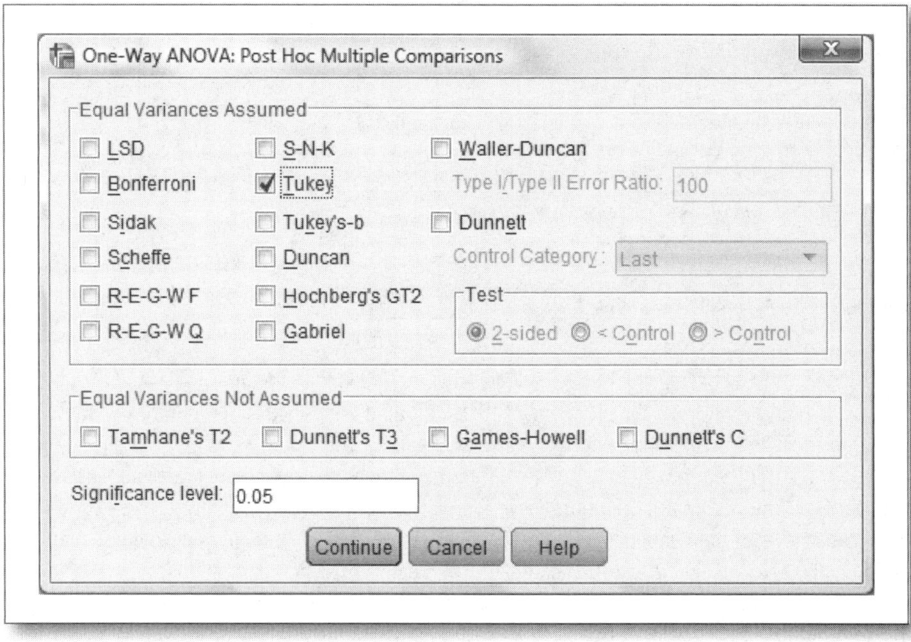

Figure 14.3   Dialog to Request Tukey Multiple Comparisons

Descriptives

ABORTOK

	N	Mean	Std. Deviation	Std. Error	95% Confidence Interval for Mean		Minimum	Maximum
					Lower Bound	Upper Bound		
1 Northeast	58	4.95	1.791	.235	4.48	5.42	0	6
2 Midwest	80	3.54	1.993	.223	3.09	3.98	0	6
3 South	104	4.00	1.961	.192	3.62	4.38	0	6
4 West	54	4.94	1.522	.207	4.53	5.36	1	6
Total	296	4.23	1.946	.113	4.01	4.46	0	6

ANOVA

ABORTOK

	Sum of Squares	df	Mean Square	F	Sig.
Between Groups	101.350	3	33.783	9.714	.000
Within Groups	1015.566	292	3.478		
Total	1116.916	295			

Multiple Comparisons

ABORTOK
Tukey HSD

(I) REGION	(J) REGION	Mean Difference (I-J)	Std. Error	Sig.	95% Confidence Interval	
					Lower Bound	Upper Bound
1 Northeast	2 Midwest	1.411*	.322	.000	.58	2.24
	3 South	.948*	.306	.011	.16	1.74
	4 West	.004	.353	1.000	-.91	.92
2 Midwest	1 Northeast	-1.411*	.322	.000	-2.24	-.58
	3 South	-.462	.277	.343	-1.18	.25
	4 West	-1.407*	.328	.000	-2.26	-.56
3 South	1 Northeast	-.948*	.306	.011	-1.74	-.16
	2 Midwest	.462	.277	.343	-.25	1.18
	4 West	-.944*	.313	.015	-1.75	-.14
4 West	1 Northeast	-.004	.353	1.000	-.92	.91
	2 Midwest	1.407*	.328	.000	.56	2.26
	3 South	.944*	.313	.015	.14	1.75

*. The mean difference is significant at the 0.05 level.

Figure 14.4   *One-Way ANOVA* Output for ABORTOK by REGION for 1980 GSS Young Adults

allow abortions in an average of 4.95 situations, while those living in the Midwest would allow abortions only in an average of 3.54 situations. We have found a difference in sample means; therefore, the sample results are consistent with the research hypothesis. The process moves to Step 3.

Step 3: What is the probability of getting differences among the sample means as large as we did if, in fact, all four regional populations have identical means? The ANOVA output box shows the significance level of the F ratio to be .000. We would get differences as large as we did less than five times in 10,000 samples if the groups had identical means in the population!

Before going on, note from the ANOVA output box that the F ratio has 3 and 292 degrees of freedom. Adding 1 to the first degrees of freedom number tells us there were four groups being compared, which is true; adding the number of groups being compared, which we just established to be four, to the second degrees of freedom number tells us there were 296 valid cases included in the analysis, which is also true as we can see in the Descriptives output box.

Step 4: We reject the null hypothesis. The results are statistically significant. The results support the claim that there are differences in the regional populations. Therefore, we proceed to Step 5 to identify which pairs of populations probably differ.

Step 5: The Tukey results appear in the Multiple Comparisons output box. At the left of the box, each of the regional groups is matched against every other regional group. That means that each pair actually appears twice, once with the first group listed first and once with the second group listed first. For our purposes, it does not matter which group is listed first; the statistical significance information we want about each pair of groups is identical either way! For each pair, the Multiple Comparisons output box shows the difference in means, the estimated standard error of the sampling distribution for the difference in means, the two-tailed significance level, and the 95% confidence interval for the difference between the group means.

Post hoc multiple-comparison tests use the t statistic, which means they can be one- or two-tailed. The SPSS output assumes each comparison of two group means is a two-tailed hypothesis test in which the research hypothesis is simply predicting the means differ and the null hypothesis is predicting they do not. The significance levels that are printed in the multiple-comparisons output are two-tailed, even though they are not labeled as such. As long as you are doing two-tailed comparisons, spotting the statistically significant comparisons is easy. You can just scan down the significance level column looking for values of .05 or less. The significant comparisons are also marked with a small asterisk in the mean difference column. Don't be confused by the fact that every pair of groups is listed twice in the Multiple Comparisons output box. If *four* mean differences are marked with asterisks, there are *two* pairs with significant differences! The number of pairs that are significantly different is always half the number of asterisks appearing in the mean difference column.

If your research hypotheses for the multiple comparisons are predicting differences in particular directions, then you are doing one-tail hypothesis testing. For comparisons to be statistically significant, the sample means must differ in the direction predicted by the research hypothesis, and the one-tail significance level must be .05 or less. To get the one-tail significance levels, divide the significance levels appearing in the multiple-comparisons output, which are two-tail levels, in half. Do not depend on the asterisks to identify significant differences when you are testing one-tailed post hoc comparisons.

Our research hypothesis simply predicted there were differences among the groups in mean tolerance of abortion; no specific directions were predicted for the differences. Therefore, we are looking for two-tailed significance levels of .05 or less in our multiple comparisons. Scanning down the Multiple Comparisons table, the first significant difference is between the Northeast and the Midwest. The next significant difference is between the Northeast and the South. The next significant difference is between the Midwest and the Northeast, but that is simply a duplication of the previous Northeast–Midwest pair. Continuing down the multiple comparisons results, looking for new pairs and ignoring duplications, we end up with four significantly different pairs: Northeast–Midwest, Northeast–South, Midwest–West, and South–West. The pairs that do not significantly differ are Northeast–West and Midwest–South.

RESEARCH TIP

Pairs With Larger Differences Aren't Always Significant

Although it did not occur in Figure 14.4, you will sometimes be reviewing multiple-comparison results and find pairs of groups with large differences that aren't significant while pairs with smaller differences are. How can that be? It can be because the significance test considers not only the size of the difference between means but also the sample size of the groups and the variability within the groups. A large mean difference may not be significant if one or both groups are represented by a small number of cases in the sample or have a lot of variability on the dependent variable.

A Second Example

"Were there significant religious affiliation differences in average willingness to allow legal abortion among 1980 GSS young adults?" (religious affiliation categories: Protestants, Catholics, Jews, members of other religions, and members of no religion)

Step 1: The research hypothesis is "there are differences in average willingness to allow legal abortion between some of the following groups of 1980 young adults: Protestants, Catholics, Jews, members of other religions, and members of no religion." The null hypothesis is "there are no differences in average willingness to allow legal abortion between any of the following groups of 1980 young adults: Protestants, Catholics, Jews, members of other religions, and members of no religion." Mathematically, the null hypothesis can be expressed as follows:

$$\overline{ABORTOK_{Prot}} = \overline{ABORTOK_{Cath}} = \overline{ABORTOK_{Jew}} = \overline{ABORTOK_{other}} = \overline{ABORTOK_{none}}$$

Step 2: Figure 14.5 shows the output from the one-way ANOVA procedure.

The sample means in the Descriptives output box show religious differences in tolerance of abortion, which means the sample results are consistent with the research hypothesis. We proceed to Step 3.

Step 3: The ANOVA output box shows a significance level for the *F* ratio of .087.

Step 4: Because the probability of the sample results is greater than .05, we do not reject the null hypothesis. While the abortion tolerance of 1980 young adults may have differed by region, the sample evidence is not strong enough to reject the possibility that the average tolerance was the same between Protestants, Catholics, Jews, other religionists, and no religionists. Our results are not statistically significant.

Step 5: Because the ANOVA results were not statistically significant, we skip Step 5. There would be no point in looking for pairs that significantly differ in the population when we cannot eliminate the possibility that in the population, all groups have the identical mean.

Descriptives

ABORTOK

	N	Mean	Std. Deviation	Std. Error	95% Confidence Interval for Mean		Minimum	Maximum
					Lower Bound	Upper Bound		
1 Protestant	167	4.03	1.906	.147	3.74	4.32	0	6
2 Catholic	88	4.27	2.016	.215	3.85	4.70	0	6
3 Jewish	6	4.83	2.401	.980	2.31	7.35	0	6
4 Other	5	4.60	1.949	.872	2.18	7.02	2	6
5 none	30	5.07	1.721	.314	4.42	5.71	0	6
Total	296	4.23	1.946	.113	4.01	4.46	0	6

ANOVA

ABORTOK

	Sum of Squares	df	Mean Square	F	Sig.
Between Groups	30.711	4	7.678	2.057	.087
Within Groups	1086.205	291	3.733		
Total	1116.916	295			

Multiple Comparisons

ABORTOK
Tukey HSD

(I) RELIGION	(J) RELIGION	Mean Difference (I-J)	Std. Error	Sig.	95% Confidence Interval	
					Lower Bound	Upper Bound
1 Protestant	2 Catholic	-.243	.254	.875	-.94	.46
	3 Jewish	-.803	.803	.855	-3.01	1.40
	4 Other	-.570	.877	.967	-2.98	1.84
	5 none	-1.037	.383	.055	-2.09	.01
2 Catholic	1 Protestant	.243	.254	.875	-.46	.94
	3 Jewish	-.561	.815	.959	-2.80	1.68
	4 Other	-.327	.888	.996	-2.77	2.11
	5 none	-.794	.408	.297	-1.92	.33
3 Jewish	1 Protestant	.803	.803	.855	-1.40	3.01
	2 Catholic	.561	.815	.959	-1.68	2.80
	4 Other	.233	1.170	1.000	-2.98	3.44
	5 none	-.233	.864	.999	-2.61	2.14
4 Other	1 Protestant	.570	.877	.967	-1.84	2.98
	2 Catholic	.327	.888	.996	-2.11	2.77
	3 Jewish	-.233	1.170	1.000	-3.44	2.98
	5 none	-.467	.933	.987	-3.03	2.10
5 none	1 Protestant	1.037	.383	.055	-.01	2.09
	2 Catholic	.794	.408	.297	-.33	1.92
	3 Jewish	.233	.864	.999	-2.14	2.61
	4 Other	.467	.933	.987	-2.10	3.03

Figure 14.5 *One-Way ANOVA* Output for ABORTOK by RELIGION for 1980 GSS Young Adults

CONCEPT CHECK

Without looking back, can you answer the following questions:

- When is an independent-samples *t* test used to compare group means and when is a one-way ANOVA used?
- Does the one-way ANOVA research hypothesis claim that in the population, every group's mean differs from every other group's mean?
- When are post hoc multiple-comparison results examined and when are they not examined?

If not, go back and review before reading on.

Two-Way ANOVA

One-way ANOVA is limited to examining the effect of a single independent variable on a dependent variable. Two-way ANOVA introduces a second independent variable and, in so doing, provides information about each factor's net effect.

Main Effects and Interaction Effects

The discussion of the *Means* procedure in Chapter 6 introduced the terms *main effect* and *interaction effect*. A main effect is the difference in means that you see when you create groups based on the attributes of just one variable. An interaction effect is the difference that you see in the size and/or direction of the effect of one of the independent variables on the dependent variable depending on the value of the other independent variable. Chapter 6 examined the main effect of gender on education (the difference in mean education between men and women) and the main effect of race on education (the differences in mean education between whites and blacks). It also examined the interaction effect of race and gender on education (how the size of the gender gap in education varied between the racial groups).

When doing descriptive statistics as we were in Chapter 6, main effects and interaction effects can be identified simply by examining means for the various subgroups. The situation becomes more complex when doing inferential statistics. Even if there are differences in the sample subgroup means, they could be due simply to sampling error. Are those sample differences large enough to conclude that the interaction effect or the main effects probably also exist in the population? Two-way ANOVA answers those questions.

A Series of Hypothesis Tests

Two-way ANOVA can be understood as a series of hypothesis tests. The result of each hypothesis test determines whether additional hypothesis tests are performed. The process is illustrated in Figure 14.6.

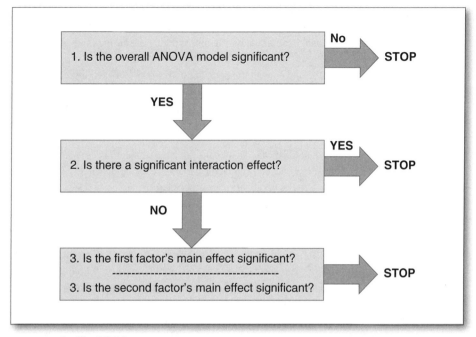

Figure 14.6   Two-Way ANOVA Sequence

RESEARCH TIP

What About the Four Steps of Hypothesis Testing?

Each round of questions for a two-way ANOVA problem could be broken down into the familiar four steps of hypothesis testing. We are switching to a more abbreviated procedure to speed up the process a bit, but if you read the description in the text of each round, you will see the research and null hypotheses mentioned (Step 1), reference to the significance level (Step 3), and a conclusion about whether the results are significant or not (Step 4). Only Step 2, where the sample results are checked, is actually being skipped here. We are assuming the sample results to be consistent with the research hypothesis. As we saw in Chapter 6 with the *Means* procedure, this is a very safe assumption. There are almost always differences in the *sample* group and subgroup means.

Round 1: Is the Overall ANOVA Model Significant?

This first round asks a very broad question: Is the evidence from the sample at least strong enough to conclude that in the population, some kind of relationship exists between the factor variables and the dependent variable? Only if the evidence is strong enough do we proceed to other hypothesis tests to learn the specifics of the relationship.

In this first round, the research hypothesis is that in the population, there are some differences in the subgroup means on the dependent variable. The null hypothesis is that in the population, all the subgroups have the same mean. In other words, the null hypothesis is saying there are no mean differences to explain!

If the sample evidence is not strong enough to reject that null hypothesis, then there is no point in trying to pin down the nature of the relationship between the factor variables and the dependent variable because we cannot be sure there is a relationship to pin down. Our investigation would stop right here. We describe the overall model as not significant and do not do any of the hypothesis tests described in the following rounds.

However, if the overall model is statistically significant, we have reason to believe some kind of relationship exists in the population between the factor variables and the dependent variable. To find out what exactly is occurring in the population, we proceed to the next round.

Round 2: Is There a Significant Interaction Effect?

If the overall model is significant, the next test is for a significant interaction effect. We test for an interaction effect before testing for main effects. The rationale for this, as noted in Chapter 6, is that interaction effects trump or supersede main effects. If an interaction effect is present, that means discussions of main effects are not relevant or, at least, are much less relevant. An interaction effect means that the size and possibly even the direction of one factor's effect on the dependent variable depend on the value of the second factor. When an interaction effect is present, it makes less sense to talk about the *single* effect of a factor since what that effect is varies depending on the value of the second factor.

Interaction effects could be described as symmetrical. If an interaction effect is present, not only will the effect of the first factor depend on the second, but also the effect of the second factor will depend on the first. For example, if the effect of gender on education varies by race, then the effect of race on education will vary by gender.

The research hypothesis for this second round is that in the population, the two factors interact in their effect on the dependent variable. The null hypothesis is that they do not.

If the interaction effect is statistically significant, we have reason to believe that in the population, the effect of one factor on the dependent variable varies depending on the value of the second factor. When the interaction is significant, we stop hypothesis testing. We do *not* then test for main effects. The reason for stopping is that discussing main effects would now be simplistic. We have evidence that the world works in a more complicated fashion. Describing the effects of individual variables would be misleading since the significant interaction effect tells us the factor variables work in concert.

If the interaction effect is not significant, we proceed to test for significant main effects. The factor variables may or may not individually affect the dependent variable, but we know they do not work in concert—more accurately, we have looked and not found compelling evidence that they work in concert.

Round 3: Are the Main Effects Significant?

If we have reason to believe some kind of relationship exists between the factor variables and the dependent variable (because the overall model was found to be significant) but the interaction effect was not significant, we then check for significant main effects. Each factor variable is tested for a significant main effect. We may find both main effects are significant. We may find just one is significant. We may even find neither main effect to be significant, but this occurs rarely.

Hypothesis testing for main effects resembles one-way analysis of variance except that what are being examining are net effects. The main effect of one of the factor variables is being examined while controlling for the effect of the other. For each factor variable, the research hypothesis is that in the population, after controlling for the other factor, there is some difference in subgroup means; the null hypothesis is that in the population, after controlling for the other factor, the subgroups means are identical.

Regardless of the result of the hypothesis test for the first main effect, the procedure is repeated for the second factor variable. Once both main effects have been tested for significance, the rounds of hypothesis testing for two-way ANOVA are completed.

RESEARCH TIP

Post Hoc Multiple Comparisons With Two-Way ANOVA

When main effects are found to be statistically significant, post hoc multiple comparisons can be done to determine which pairs of groups are significantly different. The process of interpreting those tests is identical to the process for one-way ANOVA. To request post hoc multiple comparisons for a two-way ANOVA, click "Post Hoc" on the initial two-way ANOVA dialog and choose which version of the tests you want.

To review, the sequence of hypothesis tests has several possible stopping points. If the overall model *is not found* to be statistically significant, you stop. If the interaction effect *is found* to be statistically significant, you stop. Following the hypothesis tests for the two main effects, regardless of their outcomes, you have reached the end of the sequence and therefore stop. One place that is never a stopping point is after the first test for a main effect, if you reach the third round of hypothesis testing, you are committed to testing both main effects. Whether the first main effect is or is not significant, you test the second.

A First Example

"Was there a significant interaction effect of marital status and gender on hours worked among 1980 GSS young adults? If the interaction wasn't significant, did marital status and gender have significant individual net effects?"

We first answer a question about the overall model (Round 1), and should the interaction effect not be significant (Round 2), we will answer two questions about main effects (Round 3).

The *Univariate General Linear Model* procedure provides the necessary SPSS output. Pull down the *Analyze* menu, move the cursor over *General Linear Model,* and click on *Univariate.*

Analyze | General Linear Model | Univariate

A dialog similar to Figure 14.7 appears.

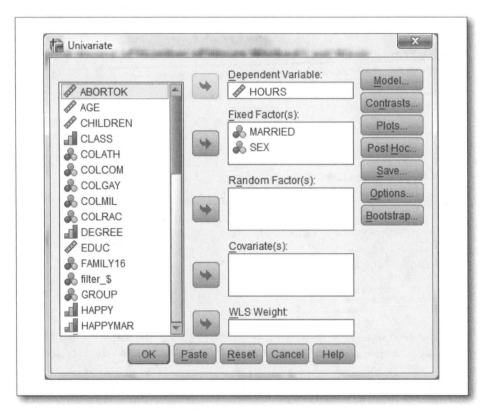

Figure 14.7   Dialog to Produce a Two-Way ANOVA

Begin by moving the dependent variable into the "Dependent Variable" list. This variable should be interval/ratio since its mean will be calculated for each of the subgroups. Next move the independent variables into the "Fixed Factor(s)" list. These variables can be any level of measurement but should be discrete variables with a limited number of categories. Usually, they will be nominal or ordinal.

Next, click "Options." A dialog similar to Figure 14.8 will appear. Check "Descriptive statistics" so that subgroup means are included in the output. Click "Continue" to return to the initial dialog.

Next, click "Plots." A dialog similar to Figure 14.9 will appear. In the field labeled "Factors" are the names of the variables listed as fixed factors in the initial dialog. Move the factor with more attributes into the "Horizontal Axis" field and the factor with the less attributes into the "Separate Lines" field.

Figure 14.8   Dialog to Request Subgroup Means

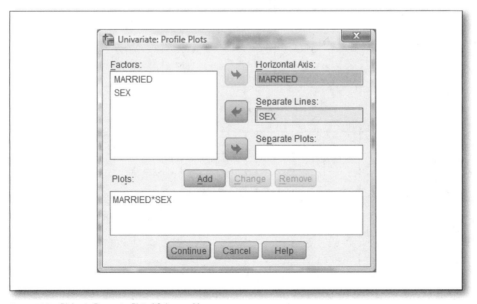

Figure 14.9   Dialog to Request a Plot of Subgroup Means

Then click "Add." The chart that will appear in the output because of this dialog will enable you to more easily see if there is an interaction effect in the sample data and, if there is, its nature. Click "Continue."

Finally, click OK to have SPSS carry out the two-way ANOVA problem.

Figure 14.10 shows some of the output that was produced. Number of hours of paid employment (HOURS) is the dependent variable; gender (SEX) and a three-attribute version of marital status (MARRIED) are the factor variables. Descriptive statistics and a profile plot are displayed. For the profile plot, marital status defines the horizontal axis, and there are separate lines to represent each gender.

Round 1: Is the overall ANOVA model significant? Looking at the "Corrected Model" line in the "Tests of Between-Subjects Effects" box, we see a significance level of .013. The overall model is statistically significant. We have reason to believe there is some relationship in the population between hours worked and the two factor variables, marital status and gender. We proceed to the next round.

Round 2: Is there a significant interaction effect? The "MARRIED*SEX" line in the "Tests of Between-Subjects Effects" box shows a significance level of .008. The interaction effect is significant. We have reason to believe that among 1980 young adults, marital status made a difference

Descriptive Statistics

Dependent Variable:HOURS

MARRIED	SEX	Mean	Std. Deviation	N
1 never married	0 male	40.42	10.406	50
	1 female	43.33	11.934	42
	Total	41.75	11.163	92
2 currently married	0 male	47.26	16.146	50
	1 female	37.72	16.274	65
	Total	41.87	16.831	115
3 divorced, separated, widowed	0 male	40.67	10.633	6
	1 female	38.38	12.514	13
	Total	39.11	11.704	19
Total	0 male	43.66	13.757	106
	1 female	39.76	14.638	120
	Total	41.59	14.334	226

Tests of Between-Subjects Effects

Dependent Variable:HOURS

Source	Type III Sum of Squares	df	Mean Square	F	Sig.
Corrected Model	2914.171[a]	5	582.834	2.960	.013
Intercept	190216.252	1	190216.252	966.176	.000
MARRIED	129.177	2	64.589	.328	.721
SEX	245.708	1	245.708	1.248	.265
MARRIED * SEX	1968.206	2	984.103	4.999	.008
Error	43312.559	220	196.875		
Total	437117.000	226			
Corrected Total	46226.730	225			

a. R Squared = .063 (Adjusted R Squared = .042)

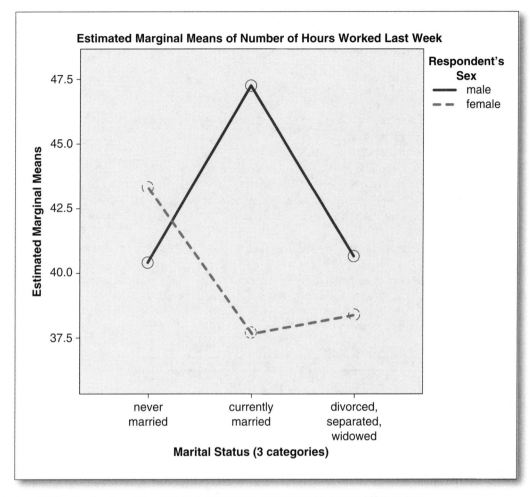

Figure 14.10 *Univariate General Linear Model* Output for HOURS by MARRIED and SEX for 1980 GSS Young Adults

in hours worked, but how marital status affected hours worked differed for women and men. Since interactions work both ways, we could also conclude that among 1980 young adults, gender made a difference in hours worked, but how gender affected hours worked differed for never-married, currently married, and previously married persons.

Examination of the plot in Figure 14.10 shows what the interaction looked like in the sample. The gender gap in hours worked was clearly larger among the currently married than among the never married or the previously married. We can also see that while men worked more hours than women among the currently married and the previously married, it was women who averaged more hours among the never married. While we could reach the same conclusion from the Descriptive Statistics in Figure 14.10, the plot makes the nature of the interaction quickly apparent.

Round 3: Are the main effects significant? Because the interaction in this example was significant, this round is skipped—we know that both marital status and gender affect hours worked for 1980 young adults, but they work in combination rather than independently.

A Second Example

"Was there a significant interaction effect of marital status and gender on number of children among 1980 GSS young adults? If the interaction wasn't significant, did marital status and gender have significant individual net effects?"

In setting up the SPSS procedure, number of children (CHILDREN) is the dependent variable; the collapsed version of marital status (MARRIED) and gender (SEX) are the factor variables. Descriptive statistics and a profile plot are requested. For the profile plot, marital status defines the horizontal axis, and there will be separate lines to represent each gender. Figure 14.11 shows the output that was produced.

Round 1: Looking at the corrected model line in the "Tests of Between-Subjects Effects" box, we see a significance level of .000. The overall model is statistically significant. We have reason to believe there is some relationship in the population between number of children and the two factor variables, marital status and gender. We proceed to the next round.

Descriptive Statistics

Dependent Variable:CHILDREN

MARRIED	SEX	Mean	Std. Deviation	N
1 never married	0 male	.04	.208	67
	1 female	.21	.669	58
	Total	.12	.485	125
2 currently married	0 male	1.00	.851	59
	1 female	1.12	1.078	113
	Total	1.08	1.005	172
3 divorced, separated, widowed	0 male	1.00	1.155	7
	1 female	2.00	1.348	23
	Total	1.77	1.357	30
Total	0 male	.52	.794	133
	1 female	.95	1.153	194
	Total	.78	1.043	327

Tests of Between-Subjects Effects

Dependent Variable:CHILDREN

Source	Type III Sum of Squares	df	Mean Square	F	Sig.
Corrected Model	106.055[a]	5	21.211	27.383	.000
Intercept	118.283	1	118.283	152.701	.000
MARRIED	75.033	2	37.517	48.433	.000
SEX	6.770	1	6.770	8.739	.003
MARRIED * SEX	3.703	2	1.852	2.391	.093
Error	248.648	321	.775		
Total	552.000	327			
Corrected Total	354.703	326			

a. R Squared = .299 (Adjusted R Squared = .288)

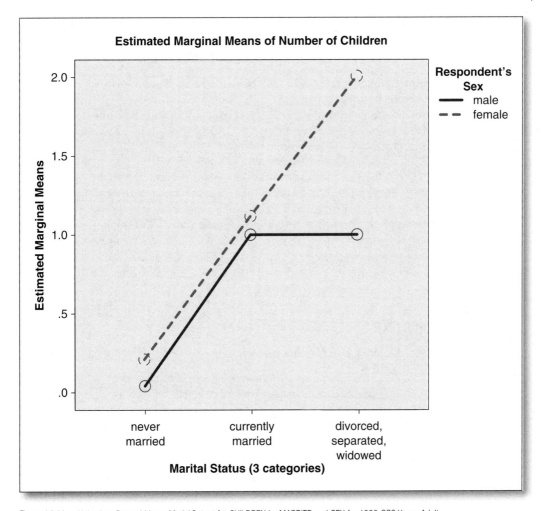

Figure 14.11   *Univariate General Linear Model* Output for CHILDREN by MARRIED and SEX for 1980 GSS Young Adults

Round 2: The MARRIED*SEX line in the "Tests of Between-Subjects Effects" box shows a significance level of .093. The interaction effect is not significant. Even though the descriptive statistics and plot in Figure 14.11 show an interaction effect in the sample data, the evidence is not strong enough to conclude there is an interaction effect in the population.

As the plot in Figure 14.11 shows, the small gender gap in number of children is very similar for never married and for currently married. The gap is much wider, though, for those in the previously married category. When the size of the gap shifts dramatically like that, it indicates an interaction effect. But the previously married category is a very small category in the data set. The descriptive statistics show it includes only 30 persons: 7 men and 23 women. Because the evidence for this much-wider gender gap is based on so few cases, the possibility that there is no interaction effect in the population cannot be rejected. What we see in the sample may just be sampling error.

At this point, we know the answer to our original question. There is not a significant interaction effect of marital status and gender on number of children among 1980 GSS young adults. Getting a negative answer to our original query, we then raise two additional questions:

- Net of the effect of gender, did marital status have a significant main effect on number of children among 1980 young adults?
- Net of the effect of marital status, did gender have a significant main effect on number of children among 1980 young adults?

Round 3: The significance level for the main effect of MARRIED is .000. That is statistically significant. The descriptive statistics in Figure 14.11 show that among 1980 GSS young adults, never-married persons reported an average of 0.12 children, currently married an average of 1.08, and previously married an average of 1.77. These sample differences are large enough to conclude, based on the significance level, that they are unlikely to be just sampling error.

The significance level for the main effect of SEX is .003—also statistically significant. Female 1980 GSS young adults reported an average of 0.95 children while male 1980 GSS young adults reported an average of just 0.52. Regardless of marital status, women reported more children.

RESEARCH TIP

A Gender Difference in Number of Children?

That marital status has a significant main effect on number of children probably comes as no surprise. That gender also has a significant main effect is more unexpected. Several possible explanations come to mind for why men might report fewer children: Men may father children at later ages than women mother children, some men may not know about the children they have fathered, and some men may underreport their number of children, perhaps not counting children from past marriages. Whatever the reason, the results of the hypothesis testing suggest that this is a real difference and not just sampling error.

CONCEPT CHECK

Without looking back, can you answer the following questions:

- What is a main effect?
- What is an interaction effect?
- What are the three rounds for analyzing a two-way ANOVA?
- If the first factor's main effect is not significant, do you check the second factor's significance level?

If not, go back and review before reading on.

Extending the ANOVA Model for More Factor Variables

We have now seen examples of analysis of variance with one and two factor variables. ANOVA can handle even more complex models with three, four, or more factor variables. Although the ANOVA output and interpretation become much more complex, the logic of the analysis remains similar.

You always begin by checking to see if the overall model is significant. If it is, you proceed on. If it is not, you are done. If the overall model is statistically significant, you then begin checking for specific effects, beginning with the most complex interactions and moving eventually to main effects. The process stops either when the only remaining effects to check are simply subsets of more complex interactions already found to be significant or when there are no more effects to check.

Consider the three-way ANOVA problem shown in Table 14.1. The three factor variables are represented by the letters A, B, and C.

Table 14.1   Sample Three-Way ANOVA Problem

Round 1: overall model	overall model (sig. = .000)		
Round 2: three-way interaction	$A \times B \times C$ (sig. = .463)		
Round 3: two-way interactions	$A \times B$ (sig. = .031)	$A \times C$ (sig. = .168)	$B \times C$ (sig. = .255)
Round 4: main effects	A	B	C (sig. = .336)

The overall model is statistically significant. We have reason to believe some relationship exists in the population between the dependent variable and at least some of the factor variables. If the overall model were not significant, that would be a stopping point.

Next check the most complex possibility. That would be an interaction effect involving all of the factor variables ($A \times B \times C$). If it is significant, then we know that in the population, each of the factors probably affects the dependent variable, but the magnitude and, possibly, even the direction of each variable's effect depend on the level of each of the other factors. If the three-way interaction were significant, that would be a stopping point because each of the lower order effects (the two-way interactions and the main effects) that could be tested are simply subsets of significant higher order effects (the three-way interaction). In Table 14.1, the three-way interaction is not significant, so we continue on.

With three factor variables, there are three different two-way interactions possible: $A \times B$, $A \times C$, and $B \times C$. Since the three-way interaction was not significant, each of the two-way interactions must be checked. All, some, or none may be significant. In Table 14.1, only the two-way interaction $A \times B$ is significant.

We continue on because not all of the lower order effects (the main effects) are subsets of higher order effects already found to be significant. Specifically, we need to test for a significant main effect of C since this factor has not been involved in any significant higher order effects. We would not check for significant main effects for A or B since both of these effects are simply subsets of a higher order effect (the two-way interaction A × B) already found to be significant. In Table 14.1, the main effect of C is not significant.

There being no more effects to check, the three-way ANOVA is complete. We would conclude that Factors A and B both significantly affect the dependent variable but that they do so in interaction. How one factor affects the dependent variable depends on the value of the other. We would also conclude that Factor C does not have a significant effect on the dependent variable.

No matter the number of factors involved, ANOVA problems all employ the same logic. First test the overall model. If it is significant, begin with the most complicated interaction and sequentially move to simpler interactions and finally main effects. Lower order effects that are subsets of higher order effects already found to be significant need not be tested.

1980 GSS Young Adults

The chapter began with some questions about 1980 GSS young adults. On the basis of our analyses, what do we now know?

- There were significant regional differences in average willingness to allow legal abortion ($F = 9.714$, $df = 3$ and 292, $p = .000$). On an abortion tolerance index that ranged from 0 to 6, 1980 GSS young adults living in the Northeast (mean = 4.95) and in the West (mean = 4.94) significantly differed from those living in the South (mean = 4.00) and in the Midwest (mean = 3.54).
- Although there were religious affiliation differences in willingness to allow legal abortion in our sample of 1980 GSS young adults, these differences were not significant ($F = 2.057$, $df = 4$ and 291, $p = .087$). On the basis of our evidence, we cannot reject the possibility that in the population of 1980 young adults, Protestants, Catholics, Jews, other religionists, and no religionists all averaged the same willingness to allow legal abortion.
- There was a significant interaction effect of marital status and gender on hours worked among 1980 GSS young adults ($F = 4.999$, $df = 2$ and 220, $p = .008$). Among the never married, employed women worked more hours than men (women's mean = 43.33, men's mean = 40.42), but among the currently married and previously married, employed men worked more (currently married men's mean = 47.26, currently married women's mean = 37.72, previously married men's mean = 40.67, previously married women's mean = 38.38). The size of the gender gap in hours worked was largest for employed persons currently married.
- There was not a significant interaction effect of marital status and gender on number of children among 1980 GSS young adults ($F = 2.391$, $df = 2$ and 321, $p = .093$). However, the main effects of both marital status ($F = 48.433$, $df = 2$ and 321, $p = .000$) and gender ($F = 8.739$, $df = 1$ and 321, $p = .003$) were significant. Among the 1980 GSS young adults, never-married persons averaged just 0.12 children compared to 1.08 children for those currently married and 1.77 for those previously married. Women reported an average of 0.95 children compared to just 0.52 for men.

Important Concepts in the Chapter

analysis of variance (ANOVA)	main effect
F ratio	*One-Way ANOVA* procedure
factor variable	post hoc multiple comparisons
interaction effect	*Univariate General Linear Model* procedure

Practice Problems

1. Which type of hypothesis test (one-sample *t* test, paired-samples *t* test, independent-samples *t* test, one-way ANOVA, or two-way ANOVA) should be used for each of the following hypotheses?
    a. Differences by ethnicity of the defendant in average sentence for armed robbery first conviction vary by state.
    b. The average sentence for an armed robbery first conviction is less than 10 years.
    c. The average sentence for an armed robbery second conviction is 15.3 years.
    d. The average sentence for persons convicted of armed robbery a second time is longer than the average sentence of those same persons on their first armed robbery conviction.
    e. The average sentence for armed robbery first conviction for Hispanics is more than 12 years.
    f. The average sentence for armed robbery first conviction for Hispanics is longer than for African Americans.
    g. There are differences in the average sentence for armed robbery first conviction in Texas, Wisconsin, Iowa, and Illinois.
    h. The effect of ethnicity on average sentence for armed robbery varies depending on whether it is a first or second conviction.

2. When comparing the means for three or more groups, why don't we just do repeated independent-samples *t* tests?

3. If seven groups are being compared using a data set of 1,200 cases, how many degrees of freedom will the *F* ratio have?

4. An author reports the following results of a one-way ANOVA: $F = 1.78$; $df = 11$ and $2,000$; $p = .13$.
    a. How many groups were being compared?
    b. How big was the sample?
    c. Did the author reject or not reject the null hypothesis?
    d. Were the results statistically significant?
    e. Were the post hoc multiple-comparison results used?

5. An author reports the following results of a one-way ANOVA: $F = 3.92$; $df = 4$ and 298; $p = .004$.
    a. How many groups were being compared?
    b. How big was the sample?

   c. Did the author reject or not reject the null hypothesis?

   d. Were the results statistically significant?

   e. Were the post hoc multiple-comparison results used?

6. For both one-way and two-way ANOVA, what is the lowest level of measurement permissible for

   a. the dependent variable?

   b. factor variables?

7. For one-way ANOVA, when do you go on to examine post hoc multiple-comparison results?

8. When doing a two-way analysis of variance, do you stop or go on if

   a. the overall model is not significant?

   b. the interaction effect is not significant?

   c. the first main effect is not significant?

9. You are looking at the effect of highest degree and religion on income.

   a. The interaction effect is significant. What does that tell you about how highest degree and religion affect income?

   b. The interaction effect is not significant but both main effects are significant. What does that tell you about how highest degree and religion affect income?

   c. The interaction effect is not significant; the main effect of highest degree is significant, but the main effect of religion is not significant. What does that tell you about how highest degree and religion affect income?

Problems Requiring SPSS and the *fourGroups.sav* Data Set

For problems 10 through 14, do the following:

   a. *State and label the research and the null hypothesis.*

   b. *What are the sample results? Are they consistent with the null hypothesis or with the research hypothesis?*

   c. *What is the probability of getting the observed sample results if the null hypothesis is true? (If this step is skipped, state that.)*

   d. *Do you reject or not reject the null hypothesis? Are your results statistically significant?*

   e. *Report which pairs of groups significantly differ from each other. (If this step was skipped because of earlier conclusions, state that this step was "skipped.")*

   f. *Summarize in a few well-written sentences totaling 100 words or less what you found out.*

10. *(2010 young adults)* Test the hypothesis that among 2010 young adults, there were differences in abortion attitudes between religious affiliations. (Variables: ABORTOK, RELIGION; Select Cases: GROUP = 3)

11. *(2010 GSS middle-age adults)* Were there significant differences between regions in tolerance of abortion for 2010 GSS middle-age adults? (Variables: ABORTOK, REGION; Select Cases: GROUP = 4)

12. *(2010 GSS young adults)* Were there significant differences between regions in years of schooling for 2010 GSS young adults ages 25 and older? (Variables: EDUC, REGION; Select Cases: GROUP = 3 and AGE >= 25)

13. (*2010 GSS middle-age adults*) Did the number of children reported by 2010 GSS middle-age adults significantly differ by religious affiliation? (Variables: CHILDREN, RELIGION; Select Cases: GROUP = 4)

14. (*2010 GSS middle-age adults*) Were there significant differences in income by highest educational degree for those 2010 GSS fiftysomethings who were working full-time? (Variables: INCOME86, DEGREE; Select Cases: GROUP = 4 and WORKSTAT = 1)

    For each of the remaining problems, answer this set of questions:

    a. *Is the overall model statistically significant?*
    b. *Is the interaction effect statistically significant? (If this step was skipped, state that.)*
    c. *Is the first factor's main effect statistically significant? Be sure to identify which variable you are referring to. (If this step was skipped, state that.)*
    d. *Is the second factor's main effect statistically significant? Be sure to identify which variable you are referring to. (If this step was skipped, state that.)*
    e. *Summarize in a few well-written sentences totaling 100 words or less what you found out.*

15. (*2010 GSS young adults*) Was there a significant interaction effect of marital status and gender on number of hours worked among 2010 GSS young adults? Be sure to use MARRIED, which is the shortened version of marital status. (Variables: HOURS, MARRIED, SEX; Select Cases: GROUP = 3)

16. (*2010 GSS middle-age adults*) Was there a significant interaction effect of marital status and gender on number of hours worked among 2010 GSS middle-age adults? Be sure to use MARRIED, which is the shortened version of marital status. (Variables: HOURS, MARRIED, SEX; Select Cases: GROUP = 4)

17. (*2010 GSS middle-age adults*) Was there a significant interaction effect of highest educational degree and gender on number of children among 2010 GSS middle-age adults? (Variables: CHILDREN, DEGREE, SEX; Select Cases: GROUP = 4)

18. (*2010 GSS young adults*) Was there a significant interaction effect of race and gender on years of schooling among 2010 GSS young adults ages 25 and older? (Variables: EDUC, RACE, SEX; Select Cases: GROUP = 3 and AGE >= 25)

19. (*all four groups*) Was there a significant interaction effect of GSS group and gender on tolerance for abortion? (Variables: ABORTOK, GROUP, SEX; Select Cases: all cases)

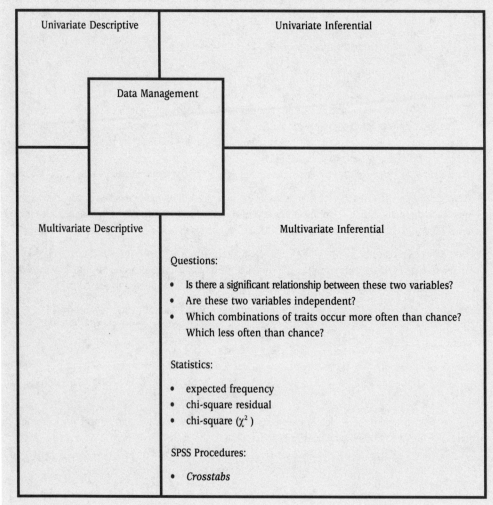

Questions and Tools for Answering Them
(Chapter 15)

Univariate Descriptive

Univariate Inferential

Data Management

Multivariate Descriptive

Multivariate Inferential

Questions:

- Is there a significant relationship between these two variables?
- Are these two variables independent?
- Which combinations of traits occur more often than chance? Which less often than chance?

Statistics:

- expected frequency
- chi-square residual
- chi-square (χ^2)

SPSS Procedures:

- *Crosstabs*

Chi-Square 15

In this chapter, you can learn

- how to tell if two discrete variables are significantly related and
- how to find out which combinations of attributes occurred more often and less often than expected by chance in the sample.

Rural or Urban Backgrounds

This chapter will answer the following questions about 1980 GSS young adults:

- Was there a significant relationship between the region of the country in which a GSS young adult lived in 1980 and the type of place in which he or she grew up?
- Was there a significant relationship between the political orientation of 1980 GSS young adults and the type of place in which they grew up?
- Was there a significant relationship between the marital status of 1980 GSS young adults and the type of place in which they grew up?

SPSS TIP

To Duplicate the Examples in This Chapter

To duplicate the examples in this chapter, use the *fourGroups.sav* data set. Before doing any of the statistical procedures, set the select cases condition to GROUP = 1.

Overview

Thus far, every inferential test we have done has involved at least one interval/ratio variable. This chapter introduces a widely used inferential statistic that can be used to test the significance of relationships involving discrete variables with any level of measurement. That statistic is **chi-square.** It is often represented as χ^2. Although chi-square itself is not a measure of association, several nominal measures of association described in Chapter 8 are chi-square based. Like those measures of association, chi-square is based on data arranged in a crosstab table.

Step 1: Hypotheses About Independence

Chi-square is used to test a very broad type of research hypothesis and null hypothesis. The research hypothesis is simply a claim that two variables are related. For example, belief in miracles and belief in God are related or social class and liking of opera are related. The corresponding null hypothesis is always a claim that the two variables are not related. For example, belief in miracles and belief in God are not related or social class and liking of opera are not related. Another way of saying not related is that the variables are independent: Belief in miracles and belief in God are independent or social class and liking of opera are independent.

The two variables mentioned in a chi-square hypothesis must both be discrete (categorical) variables. They will usually be nominal or ordinal but could even be discrete interval/ratio variables. Discrete variables with a large number of attributes usually do not work well because they tend to spread cases quite thinly across a large crosstab table. That not only makes visual comprehension of a relationship difficult but also creates some statistical problems for chi-square. More will be said about those statistical problems later. Chi-square does not require the variables in the hypothesis to be identified as independent and dependent.

The absence of a relationship is called **independence** because the percentage distribution of cases on one variable is independent (not affected by) the value of the other variable. For example, if social class and liking opera are independent and if 65% of persons in the lower social class like opera and 35% do not, we would find that same 65/35 split in the middle class and in the upper class. This independence works the same if we look at the distribution of the other variable. If 30% of those who like opera are lower class, 60% are middle class, and 10% are upper class, then we would find this same 30/60/10 split for those who do not like opera.

The research hypothesis with its claim of a relationship between the variables is simply asserting that this complete state of independence does not exist. The research hypothesis argues that, in the population from which the sample came, the percentage distribution of cases on one variable differs, at least slightly, depending on the value of the other variable.

CONCEPT CHECK

Without looking back, can you answer the following questions:

- Variables included in a chi-square hypothesis test can have which levels of measurement?
- What does it mean if two variables are independent? If two variables are related?

If not, go back and review before reading on.

Step 2: Sample Results and Residuals

If in the sample the two variables mentioned in the hypothesis are independent, that would be consistent with the null hypothesis, and we would proceed directly to Step 4 and not reject the null. If in the sample there is evidence of a relationship, however, that would be consistent with the research hypothesis, and we would proceed to Step 3. So how can we tell if the sample data show independence or not?

There are several different ways of finding out. All of them begin by displaying the data in a crosstab table. Figure 15.1 displays two crosstab tables. Both tables use made-up data. The first shows the relationship between manual preference (being left- or right-handed) and job satisfaction; the second shows the relationship between sex and job satisfaction.

A simple way to check for independence is to have SPSS calculate column percentages. If the two variables in the crosstab are independent, the column percentages in each column will be absolutely identical. Figure 15.2 shows the column percentages for the two tables.

The percentages in the columns of the first table perfectly match. Manual preference and job satisfaction are independent. There is no relationship between the two. The percentages in the columns of the second table, however, do not match one another. Sex and job satisfaction are not independent. Rather, they are related. (We could have reached the same conclusions had we calculated row percentages instead of column percentages. The percentages in any row of the first table would have perfectly matched the percentages in any other row. That would not have been true in the second table.)

While examining column percentages (or row percentages) is an easy way to tell if two variables are independent or not, it does not provide some information that will be needed in a later hypothesis-testing step. Therefore, we will use a different method for determining if the variables in a crosstab are independent. We will calculate for each cell in the table the number of cases that we

JOBSAT * MANUAL Crosstabulation

Count

		MANUAL		Total
		1 left	2 right	
JOBSAT	1 dislike very much	10	30	40
	2 dislike somewhat	20	60	80
	3 like fairly well	30	90	120
	4 like very much	40	120	160
Total		100	300	400

JOBSAT * SEX Crosstabulation

Count

		SEX		Total
		0 male	1 female	
JOBSAT	1 dislike very much	12	28	40
	2 dislike somewhat	32	48	80
	3 like fairly well	60	60	120
	4 like very much	96	64	160
Total		200	200	400

Figure 15.1   Two Crosstab Tables With Cell Counts

would expect in that cell *if the variables were independent*. This number is referred to as the **expected count**. We will then calculate the difference between the actual number of cases in the cell (known as the **observed count**) and the expected count. That difference is known as the **cell residual**. If the two variables in the table are independent, all of the cell residuals will be zero. If any of the cell residuals is not zero, then the variables are related.

To calculate an expected count for a cell, multiply the total number of cases in the row in which the cell is located by the total number of cases in the column in which the cell is located. Then take that product and divide by the total number of cases in the entire table.

$$\text{expected count} = \frac{\text{row total} \times \text{column total}}{\text{table total}}$$

If we were calculating the expected frequency for the upper left cell in the JOBSAT by SEX crosstab, we would multiply 40 (the row total) by 200 (the column total) and divide that product by 400 (the table total). That would give us an expected count of 20.

JOBSAT * MANUAL Crosstabulation

			MANUAL		Total
			1 left	2 right	
JOBSAT	1 dislike very much	Count	10	30	40
		% within MANUAL	10.0%	10.0%	10.0%
	2 dislike somewhat	Count	20	60	80
		% within MANUAL	20.0%	20.0%	20.0%
	3 like fairly well	Count	30	90	120
		% within MANUAL	30.0%	30.0%	30.0%
	4 like very much	Count	40	120	160
		% within MANUAL	40.0%	40.0%	40.0%
Total		Count	100	300	400
		% within MANUAL	100.0%	100.0%	100.0%

JOBSAT * SEX Crosstabulation

			SEX		Total
			0 male	1 female	
JOBSAT	1 dislike very much	Count	12	28	40
		% within SEX	6.0%	14.0%	10.0%
	2 dislike somewhat	Count	32	48	80
		% within SEX	16.0%	24.0%	20.0%
	3 like fairly well	Count	60	60	120
		% within SEX	30.0%	30.0%	30.0%
	4 like very much	Count	96	64	160
		% within SEX	48.0%	32.0%	40.0%
Total		Count	200	200	400
		% within SEX	100.0%	100.0%	100.0%

Figure 15.2   Two Crosstab Tables With Column Percents

To calculate a cell's residual, begin with the observed count and subtract the expected count.

$$\text{cell residual} = \text{observed count} - \text{expected count}$$

If the residual is positive, there are more cases in that cell than expected if the variables were independent. If the residual is negative, there are fewer cases in the cell than expected if the variables were independent. And if the residual is zero, there are exactly as many cases as expected if the variables were independent. Be sure to start the subtraction with the observed count—otherwise, you will misinterpret nonzero residuals.

To calculate the residual for the upper left cell in the JOBSAT by SEX crosstab, we would begin with 12 (the observed count) and subtract 20 (the expected count). That would give us a residual of

–8. There are 8 fewer males who say they dislike their job very much than we would have expected if sex and job satisfaction were independent.

Figure 15.3 shows the two tables with the observed counts, the expected counts, and the residuals. For the sample data to be independent, every residual must be zero. If any residuals are anything other than zero, the sample data are not independent.

JOBSAT * MANUAL Crosstabulation

			MANUAL		Total
			1 left	2 right	
JOBSAT	1 dislike very much	Count	10	30	40
		Expected Count	10.0	30.0	40.0
		Residual	.0	.0	
	2 dislike somewhat	Count	20	60	80
		Expected Count	20.0	60.0	80.0
		Residual	.0	.0	
	3 like fairly well	Count	30	90	120
		Expected Count	30.0	90.0	120.0
		Residual	.0	.0	
	4 like very much	Count	40	120	160
		Expected Count	40.0	120.0	160.0
		Residual	.0	.0	
Total		Count	100	300	400
		Expected Count	100.0	300.0	400.0

JOBSAT * SEX Crosstabulation

			SEX		Total
			0 male	1 female	
JOBSAT	1 dislike very much	Count	12	28	40
		Expected Count	20.0	20.0	40.0
		Residual	-8.0	8.0	
	2 dislike somewhat	Count	32	48	80
		Expected Count	40.0	40.0	80.0
		Residual	-8.0	8.0	
	3 like fairly well	Count	60	60	120
		Expected Count	60.0	60.0	120.0
		Residual	.0	.0	
	4 like very much	Count	96	64	160
		Expected Count	80.0	80.0	160.0
		Residual	16.0	-16.0	
Total		Count	200	200	400
		Expected Count	200.0	200.0	400.0

Figure 15.3   Two Crosstab Tables With Observed Counts, Expected Counts, and Cell Residuals

Figure 15.3 confirms what we already know. Manual preference and job satisfaction are independent in the sample data. This is consistent with the null hypothesis of independence. We would proceed directly to Step 4 and not reject the null hypothesis. Sex and job satisfaction, however, are not independent in the sample. The sample data are consistent with the research hypothesis of a relationship between the variables. We would go to Step 3 for this pair of variables.

Step 3: Probabilities and Chi-Square

The fact that the sample data show a relationship does not prove that a relationship between these variables exists in the population. In the population, the variables may be independent, and our nonzero residuals may simply be the result of sampling error. To determine the probability of getting residuals as large as those observed in the sample data if in the population the variables are independent, we use the chi-square statistic.

The value of the chi-square statistic itself is a function of the observed and expected frequencies in each cell of the crosstab. The formula for chi-square is

$$\text{chi-square} = \sum \frac{\text{cell residual}^2}{\text{expected count}}$$

To determine the value of chi-square, a separate calculation is done for each cell. The cell residual is squared and then divided by the cell's expected frequency. The results from all the cells are then added together to obtain the value of chi-square. Table 15.1 shows the calculation of chi-square for JOBSAT by SEX.

Table 15.1 shows the value of chi-square to be 16.0. But we need to leave Step 3 in hypothesis testing with a probability, and the value of chi-square is not a probability. We need to know the probability of getting the observed sample results if the null hypothesis of independence is true. Thus far in this book, we have obtained probabilities based on the normal distribution, the t distribution, and the F distribution. Now we will use the chi-square distribution to determine the probability of getting a chi-square of 16.0 or greater if the null hypothesis is actually true.

Like the t and F distributions, the chi-square distribution is a family of distributions. Which specific distribution to use is referenced by the degrees of freedom, and that is determined by the size of the crosstab table. Like the t distribution, chi-square has just a single degrees of freedom number, and it is easy to calculate. Degrees of freedom for a chi-square problem are obtained by multiplying the number of rows in the crosstab table minus 1 by the number of columns minus 1.

chi-square: $df = (\text{\# of rows} - 1) \times (\text{\# of columns} - 1)$

There are four rows and two columns in the JOBSAT by SEX crosstab; therefore, chi-square has three (3×1) degrees of freedom.

Table 15.1   Calculation of Chi-Square for JOBSAT by SEX

Cell	Observed	Expected	Residual	Residual^2	Residual^2 / Expected
Dislike very much and male	12	20	−8	64	3.2
Dislike very much and female	28	20	8	64	3.2
Dislike somewhat and male	32	40	−8	64	1.6
Dislike somewhat and female	48	40	8	64	1.6
Like fairly well and male	60	60	0	0	0
Like fairly well and female	60	60	0	0	0
Like very much and male	96	80	16	256	3.2
Like very much and female	64	80	−16	256	3.2
Chi-square =					16.0

To complete Step 3, then, we need the probability of getting a chi-square of 16.0 from a crosstab with 3 degrees of freedom. That could be found by either checking a printed volume of statistical tables or using a statistical software package that includes those probabilities. SPSS reports the probabilities for chi-square in its output.

Like hypotheses tested with F ratios, hypotheses tested with chi-square are nondirectional. They are not described as one-tailed or two-tailed.

Step 4: Conclusions

As always, Step 4 is straightforward. If the probability from the previous step is .05 or less, the null hypothesis of independence is rejected. The result is statistically significant and supports the research hypothesis claim that the variables are related in the population. When chi-square is significant, most researchers then proceed to describe the relationship in the crosstab table using a measure of association and a comparison of column modes, medians, or percentages.

If the probability from Step 3 is greater than .05, the claim of independence made by the null hypothesis cannot be rejected. The result is not statistically significant. We must continue to consider as a possibility that the two variables are not related in the population.

Limitations of Chi-Square

Before looking at how to set up a chi-square procedure with SPSS, two cautions about chi-square should be mentioned. First, chi-square should not be used when the expected counts in the crosstab are very small. Second, the value of the chi-square statistic should not be interpreted as an indicator of the strength of the relationship between the variables.

Cases Spread Too Thinly Across a Table

When crosstab tables have low expected counts in some of the cells, the value of chi-square becomes unstable. Differences in the attributes of just a few cases in the sample can dramatically change the value of chi-square.

A statistical guideline that is widely accepted is *not to use chi-square if even one cell has an expected count of less than 1 or if more than one fifth of the cells have expected counts of less than 5.* In those situations, shifts in the attributes of even a few of the cases could substantially change the size and probability of chi-square and the conclusion about the significance of the results.

You need to check the expected counts in the crosstab before using the chi-square results. If any cells have an expected count of less than 1 or if more than 20% of the cells have expected counts less than 5, chi-square should not be used. What do you do then? Often the solution is to combine similar attributes of one or both variables using the *Recode* procedure. In particular, look to combine attributes that were rarely used. This will reduce the size of the crosstab and increase the expected counts in the cells.

Not a Measure of Association

The second caution arises out of the wide use of chi-square as an inferential test. Researchers often find themselves interested in the relationship between two discrete variables and, as a result, often make use of chi-square. Because chi-square looks for any deviations from independence in a table, it is tempting to interpret the size of the chi-square statistic as an indication of the strength of the relationship between the two variables: The closer the value of chi-square to zero, the weaker the relationship; the further from zero, the stronger the relationship. Although it may be tempting to interpret chi-square in that way, it is incorrect.

While the probability of getting a particular value of chi-square is a good indication of whether the variables are independent or not in the population, the size of the chi-square statistic itself does not indicate the strength of the relationship. Chi-square fails as a measure of association on at least two counts. First, the size of chi-square is affected by the size of the sample. For example, doubling the number of observed cases in each cell of a crosstab does not change the nature of the relationship between the two variables, but it does increase the size of the chi-square statistic. While a relationship based on a larger number of cases is more likely to be statistically significant, a relationship based on a larger number of cases is not automatically a stronger relationship. Second, the chi-square statistic has no maximum upper limit. It cannot go below zero, but it can go infinitely high. That would make it impossible to determine what constitutes a weak, moderate, or strong relationship.

RESEARCH TIP

Chi-Square-Based Measures of Association

If chi-square is not a measure of association, how can some nominal measures of association be chi-square based? Although the coefficient of contingency, Cramer's V, and phi all include chi-square in their formulas, each in its own way modifies the chi-square value to eliminate its sensitivity to sample size and impose an upper limit at or near the value of 1. With these adjustments to chi-square, they function well as nominal measures of association.

CONCEPT CHECK

Without looking back, can you answer the following questions:

- What does a positive cell residual tell you? A negative cell residual? A zero cell residual?
- What can you do if the expected cell frequencies are too small for a chi-square hypothesis test?

If not, go back and review before reading on.

A First Example

The remainder of this chapter looks at three hypothesis tests that employ chi-square. All three use as one of the variables the type of place where the 1980 GSS young adult was living when she or he was age 16 (PLACE16). This nominal variable consists of five attributes: farm/countryside, small city, medium city, suburb of large city, and large city.

"Was there a significant relationship between the region of the country in which a GSS young adult lived in 1980 and the type of place in which he or she grew up?"

Step 1: The research hypothesis is "the type of place in which 1980 young adults grew up and their political orientation are related." The null hypothesis is "they are independent."

Step 2: Chi-square hypotheses are tested using output produced by the *Crosstabs* procedure. For this first example, REGION will be the column variable and PLACE16 the row variable.

From the initial *Crosstabs* dialog, click "Cells." A dialog similar to Figure 15.4 appears.

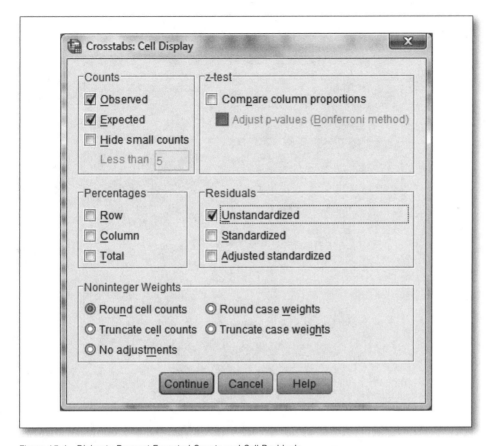

Figure 15.4   Dialog to Request Expected Counts and Cell Residuals

This is the dialog we used to request cell percents. It is also the dialog used to request observed counts, expected counts, and cell residuals. By default, SPSS provides observed counts. That box is already checked. Indicate by a checkmark that you also want the expected counts and the unstandardized residuals. The formula for residuals that was presented earlier is the formula for unstandardized residuals. Click "Continue" to return to the initial *Crosstabs* dialog.

From that initial *Crosstabs* dialog, click "Statistics" to open the dialog that appears in Figure 15.5.

This is the dialog used to request measures of association, and it is also the dialog for requesting chi-square. Check "Chi-square" and then click "Continue" to return to the initial dialog. From there, click OK to give the problem to SPSS.

Figure 15.6 shows the result. A glance at the crosstab table reveals nonzero residuals. That means the sample data are consistent with the research hypothesis of a relationship between the variables.

Step 3: Before checking the probability of the chi-square statistic, we need to confirm that there are no cells with an expected frequency of less than 1 and that there are no more than one fifth of

Figure 15.5   Dialog to Request Chi-Square

the cells with expected counts of less than 5. SPSS saves us the effort of a visual inspection of the table. Printed below the "Chi-Square Tests" box in the output is a message stating that no cells have expected counts of less than 5.

When chi-square is requested, SPSS provides several related statistics. For our hypothesis test, we use "Pearson Chi-Square." The value of chi-square is 52.149, and there are 12 degrees of freedom. The significance level (or probability of getting a chi-square of 52.149 or higher in a crosstab with 12 degrees of freedom if the null hypothesis is true) is .000.

Step 4: With a probability of .000, we reject the null hypothesis of independence. We conclude that region and type of place in which raised are probably related. The result is statistically significant.

Now that we have reason to believe region and type of place in which raised were related for the 1980 young adults, we go on to discuss the nature of the relationship as it appears in the sample data by talking about a measure of association and comparing column modes, medians, or percentages. We could have requested a measure of association and column percents when setting up the original SPSS

PLACE16 * REGION Crosstabulation

			REGION				
			1 Northeast	2 Midwest	3 South	4 West	Total
PLACE16	1 country, farm	Count	10	32	28	4	74
		Expected Count	14.5	20.1	26.5	12.9	74.0
		Residual	-4.5	11.9	1.5	-8.9	
	2 small city	Count	19	22	51	8	100
		Expected Count	19.6	27.2	35.8	17.4	100.0
		Residual	-.6	-5.2	15.2	-9.4	
	3 medium city	Count	8	13	17	13	51
		Expected Count	10.0	13.9	18.2	8.9	51.0
		Residual	-2.0	-.9	-1.2	4.1	
	4 suburb of large city	Count	13	10	7	14	44
		Expected Count	8.6	12.0	15.7	7.7	44.0
		Residual	4.4	-2.0	-8.7	6.3	
	5 large city	Count	14	12	14	18	58
		Expected Count	11.4	15.8	20.8	10.1	58.0
		Residual	2.6	-3.8	-6.8	7.9	
Total		Count	64	89	117	57	327
		Expected Count	64.0	89.0	117.0	57.0	327.0

Chi-Square Tests

	Value	df	Asymp. Sig. (2-sided)
Pearson Chi-Square	52.149[a]	12	.000
Likelihood Ratio	53.058	12	.000
Linear-by-Linear Association	2.356	1	.125
N of Valid Cases	327		

a. 0 cells (.0%) have expected count less than 5. The minimum
expected count is 7.67.

Figure 15.6   *Crosstabs* Output With Chi-Square for PLACE16 by REGION for 1980 GSS Young Adults

chi-square problem and simply held the discussion of them in reserve until we saw if our chi-square results were significant. Doing so, however, results in a more crowded crosstab table, which can easily become confusing. Figure 15.7 shows a crosstab with column percentages and the value of Cramer's *V*.

Cramer's *V* indicates a moderate relationship between region and type of place in which raised. The value of Cramer's *V* is .231. For 1980 GSS young adults, the modal type of place in which raised was in the country or on a farm for those living in the Midwest, in a small city for those in the Northeast and in the South, but in a large city for young adults living in the West. A glance at the column percents shows that of the four regions, persons in the West were least likely to have been raised in the country, on a farm, or in a small city and were most likely to have been raised in a large city or one of its suburbs. (If this comes as a surprise, you are possibly confusing population density with percent urban. While the West has hundreds of thousands of square miles of sparsely

PLACE16 * REGION Crosstabulation

			REGION				
			1 Northeast	2 Midwest	3 South	4 West	Total
PLACE16	1 country, farm	Count	10	32	28	4	74
		% within REGION	15.6%	36.0%	23.9%	7.0%	22.6%
	2 small city	Count	19	22	51	8	100
		% within REGION	29.7%	24.7%	43.6%	14.0%	30.6%
	3 medium city	Count	8	13	17	13	51
		% within REGION	12.5%	14.6%	14.5%	22.8%	15.6%
	4 suburb of large city	Count	13	10	7	14	44
		% within REGION	20.3%	11.2%	6.0%	24.6%	13.5%
	5 large city	Count	14	12	14	18	58
		% within REGION	21.9%	13.5%	12.0%	31.6%	17.7%
Total		Count	64	89	117	57	327
		% within REGION	100.0%	100.0%	100.0%	100.0%	100.0%

Symmetric Measures

		Value	Approx. Sig.
Nominal by Nominal	Phi	.399	.000
	Cramer's V	.231	.000
N of Valid Cases		327	

Figure 15.7   *Crosstabs* Output for PLACE16 by REGION for 1980 GSS Young Adults

populated land, the population of the West is actually more concentrated in large urban areas than any other region of the country.)

A Second Example

"Was there a significant relationship between the political orientation of 1980 GSS young adults and the type of place in which they grew up?"

Step 1: The research hypothesis is "the type of place in which 1980 young adults grew up and their political orientation are related." The null hypothesis is "they are independent."

Step 2: Figure 15.8 shows the *Crosstabs* output. The presence of nonzero residuals indicates that the two variables are related in the sample. This is consistent with the research hypothesis.

Step 3: No cells have expected counts less than 5, so chi-square can be used. Chi-square's actual value is 6.072. There are 8 degrees of freedom in the crosstab table. The probability of getting a chi-square of 6.072 or larger in a table with 8 degrees of freedom when the two variables are independent in the population is .639.

Step 4: On the basis of that probability, we do not reject the null hypothesis of independence. The results are not statistically significant. We must continue to entertain the possibility that for 1980 young adults, the type of place in which raised and their political orientation were unrelated.

POLVIEWS * PLACE16 Crosstabulation

			PLACE16					
			1 country, farm	2 small city	3 medium city	4 suburb of large city	5 large city	Total
POLVIEWS	1 liberal	Count	23	37	20	22	24	126
		Expected Count	28.6	38.3	19.7	17.0	22.4	126.0
		Residual	-5.6	-1.3	.3	5.0	1.6	
	2 moderate	Count	31	32	19	12	21	115
		Expected Count	26.1	34.9	18.0	15.5	20.5	115.0
		Residual	4.9	-2.9	1.0	-3.5	.5	
	3 conservative	Count	20	30	12	10	13	85
		Expected Count	19.3	25.8	13.3	11.5	15.1	85.0
		Residual	.7	4.2	-1.3	-1.5	-2.1	
Total		Count	74	99	51	44	58	326
		Expected Count	74.0	99.0	51.0	44.0	58.0	326.0

Chi-Square Tests

	Value	df	Asymp. Sig. (2-sided)
Pearson Chi-Square	6.072[a]	8	.639
Likelihood Ratio	6.040	8	.643
Linear-by-Linear Association	2.487	1	.115
N of Valid Cases	326		

a. 0 cells (.0%) have expected count less than 5. The minimum expected count is 11.47.

Figure 15.8 *Crosstabs* Output With Chi-Square for POLVIEWS by PLACE16 for 1980 GSS Young Adults

Because the results are not significant, we would not spend time describing the relationship that existed in the sample data. Without evidence that a relationship exists in the population, most persons would not be interested in the relationship that occurred in the sample data since any apparent relationships in the sample data may just be sampling error.

A Third Example

"Was there a significant relationship between the marital status of 1980 GSS young adults and the type of place in which they grew up?"

Step 1: The research hypothesis is "there was a relationship between the type of place in which 1980 young adults grew up and their marital status." The null hypothesis is "for 1980 young adults, type of place in which raised and marital status were independent."

Step 2: Figure 15.9 shows the SPSS output from the *Crosstabs* procedure. For marital status, the variable MARITAL is used, which has five attributes: married, widowed, divorced, separated, and never married. No 1980 GSS young adults were widowed, so that attribute does not appear in the

MARITAL * PLACE16 Crosstabulation

			PLACE16					
			1 country, farm	2 small city	3 medium city	4 suburb of large city	5 large city	Total
MARITAL	1 married	Count	52	52	22	22	24	172
		Expected Count	38.9	52.6	26.8	23.1	30.5	172.0
		Residual	13.1	-.6	-4.8	-1.1	-6.5	
	3 divorced	Count	3	2	5	1	7	18
		Expected Count	4.1	5.5	2.8	2.4	3.2	18.0
		Residual	-1.1	-3.5	2.2	-1.4	3.8	
	4 separated	Count	5	2	1	0	4	12
		Expected Count	2.7	3.7	1.9	1.6	2.1	12.0
		Residual	2.3	-1.7	-.9	-1.6	1.9	
	5 never married	Count	14	44	23	21	23	125
		Expected Count	28.3	38.2	19.5	16.8	22.2	125.0
		Residual	-14.3	5.8	3.5	4.2	.8	
Total		Count	74	100	51	44	58	327
		Expected Count	74.0	100.0	51.0	44.0	58.0	327.0

Chi-Square Tests

	Value	df	Asymp. Sig. (2-sided)
Pearson Chi-Square	32.451[a]	12	.001
Likelihood Ratio	34.338	12	.001
Linear-by-Linear Association	7.878	1	.005
N of Valid Cases	327		

a. 9 cells (45.0%) have expected count less than 5. The minimum expected count is 1.61.

Figure 15.9 *Crosstabs* Output With Chi-Square for MARITAL by PLACE16 for 1980 GSS Young Adults

crosstab. The presence of nonzero residuals in the crosstab shows the sample data to be consistent with the research hypothesis.

Step 3: At this step, we want to know the probability of getting the sample results we got if the null hypothesis of independence is true. However, there is a problem with using chi-square. Although no cells have expected counts less than 1, too many cells (45%) have expected counts less than 5. For chi-square to be interpretable, no more than 20% of the cells may have expected counts below 5.

Look at the crosstab table to see where the cells are with low expected counts. They are in the rows representing persons who were divorced or separated. Combining these categories of marital status should solve our low expected frequencies chi-square problem. Furthermore, combining these categories along with "widowed" makes substantive sense since all three categories represent persons who have been married but, for a variety of reasons, are no longer living with their spouse. The variable MARRIED already in our data set combines marital statuses in just that way. The new crosstab of MARRIED by PLACE16 appears in Figure 15.10.

MARRIED * PLACE16 Crosstabulation

			PLACE16					
			1 country, farm	2 small city	3 medium city	4 suburb of large city	5 large city	Total
MARRIED	1 never married	Count	14	44	23	21	23	125
		Expected Count	28.3	38.2	19.5	16.8	22.2	125.0
		Residual	-14.3	5.8	3.5	4.2	.8	
	2 currently married	Count	52	52	22	22	24	172
		Expected Count	38.9	52.6	26.8	23.1	30.5	172.0
		Residual	13.1	-.6	-4.8	-1.1	-6.5	
	3 divorced, separated, widowed	Count	8	4	6	1	11	30
		Expected Count	6.8	9.2	4.7	4.0	5.3	30.0
		Residual	1.2	-5.2	1.3	-3.0	5.7	
Total		Count	74	100	51	44	58	327
		Expected Count	74.0	100.0	51.0	44.0	58.0	327.0

Chi-Square Tests

	Value	df	Asymp. Sig. (2-sided)
Pearson Chi-Square	28.354[a]	8	.000
Likelihood Ratio	29.915	8	.000
Linear-by-Linear Association	1.218	1	.270
N of Valid Cases	327		

a. 2 cells (13.3%) have expected count less than 5. The minimum expected count is 4.04.

Figure 15.10   *Crosstabs* Output With Chi-Square for MARRIED by PLACE16 for 1980 GSS Young Adults

The research and null hypotheses remain the same. The sample results still support the research hypothesis. This time, there is no expected count problem to prevent the use of chi-square. Only 13.3% of the cells (two cells) have an expected frequency of less than 5, and no cells have expected frequencies below 1. Chi-square has a value of 28.354 with 8 degrees of freedom. Its significance level is .000.

Step 4: On the basis of our sample evidence, we reject the null hypothesis that the variables were independent. We have found that there was a significant relationship between the type of place in which 1980 GSS young adults grew up and their marital status at the time of the survey. Since we have a significant result, we then proceed to describe the relationship as it exists in the sample.

Figure 15.11 shows a moderate relationship between type of place in which raised and marital status (Cramer's $V = .208$). The 1980 GSS young adults raised on farms or in the country were more likely to be currently married and less likely to be never married than those who were raised elsewhere.

MARRIED * PLACE16 Crosstabulation

			PLACE16					
			1 country, farm	2 small city	3 medium city	4 suburb of large city	5 large city	Total
MARRIED	1 never married	Count	14	44	23	21	23	125
		% within PLACE16	18.9%	44.0%	45.1%	47.7%	39.7%	38.2%
	2 currently married	Count	52	52	22	22	24	172
		% within PLACE16	70.3%	52.0%	43.1%	50.0%	41.4%	52.6%
	3 divorced, separated, widowed	Count	8	4	6	1	11	30
		% within PLACE16	10.8%	4.0%	11.8%	2.3%	19.0%	9.2%
Total		Count	74	100	51	44	58	327
		% within PLACE16	100.0%	100.0%	100.0%	100.0%	100.0%	100.0%

Symmetric Measures

		Value	Approx. Sig.
Nominal by Nominal	Phi	.294	.000
	Cramer's V	.208	.000
N of Valid Cases		327	

Figure 15.11 *Crosstabs* Output for MARRIED by PLACE16 for 1980 GSS Young Adults

1980 GSS Young Adults

The chapter began with some questions about 1980 GSS young adults. On the basis of our analyses, what do we now know?

- There was a significant relationship between region of residence and type of place in which raised ($\chi^2 = 52.149$, $df = 12$, $p = .000$). The relationship is of moderate strength (Cramer's $V = .231$). Those 1980 GSS young adults residing in the West were most likely and those residing in the South were least likely to have been raised in a large city or one of its suburbs.
- The type of place in which 1980 GSS young adults grew up and their political orientation were not significantly related ($\chi^2 = 6.072$, $df = 8$, $p = .639$). We must continue to entertain the possibility these two factors are completely independent.
- There was a significant relationship between the type of place in which 1980 GSS young adults grew up and their marital status at the time of the survey ($\chi^2 = 28.354$, $df = 8$, $p = .000$). It is moderate in strength (Cramer's $V = .208$). 1980 GSS young adults raised in the country or on a farm were least likely to report being never married and most likely to report being currently married.

Important Concepts in the Chapter

cell residual

chi-square

Crosstabs procedure

expected count

independence

observed count

Practice Problems

1. Which type of hypothesis test (one-sample *t* test, paired-samples *t* test, independent-samples *t* test, one-way ANOVA, two-way ANOVA, or chi-square) should be used for each of the following hypotheses?
   a. The gate from which a horse starts a race and the horse's finishing position are related.
   b. The effect of sex on income varies by occupation.
   c. There are differences in mean salary between administrators, faculty, clerical staff, and student workers.
   d. There are differences in mean salary between electricians and carpenters.
   e. On average, full professors make the same salary they made when they were assistant professors.
   f. The mean annual salary of assistant professors is less than $45,000.
   g. Religious affiliation and political party affiliation are related.
   h. The effect of being raised by a single parent on the child's educational attainment varies by social class.
   i. The mean batting average of baseball players who use steroids is higher than the mean average for baseball players who don't.
   j. Astrological sign and happiness with life are independent.

2. For a chi-square table with five rows and three columns, how many degrees of freedom would there be?

3. For the following problems, begin with this table:

	Goes to Church		
Owns Pets	No	Yes	
No	20	20	40
Yes	20	40	60
	40	60	100

   a. Calculate the expected frequency for each cell.
   b. Calculate the residual for each cell.

c. For the data in the table, are going to church and owning pets independent?

d. Calculate the value of chi-square. (You'll need a calculator. Round numbers to just two decimal places.)

e. How many degrees of freedom does this table have?

4. Calculate the value of chi-square for the following table. (You'll need a calculator. Round numbers to just two decimal places.)

Goes to Church

Owns Pets	No	Yes	
No	40	40	80
Yes	40	80	120
	80	120	200

5. If either of two situations regarding expected frequencies is true, chi-square should not be used.

a. What are those two conditions?

b. If either of those situations is true, what can be done to remedy the situation and then legitimately use chi-square?

6. Why can't the value of chi-square be used as a nominal measure of association?

Problems Requiring SPSS and the *fourGroups.sav* Data Set

For each of the remaining problems, do the following:

a. *State and label the research and the null hypothesis.*

b. *Are the sample results consistent with the null hypothesis or with the research hypothesis?*

c. *What is the probability of getting the observed sample results if the null hypothesis is true? (If this step is skipped, state that.)*

d. *Do you reject or not reject the null hypothesis? Are your results statistically significant?*

e. *Only if the results are significant*

   i. *report the value of a measure of association and note its strength and, if appropriate, its direction.*

   ii. *illustrate what the measure of association found about the strength and, if appropriate, the direction of the relationship by comparing column modes, medians, or percents in the crosstab.*

f. *Summarize in a few well-written sentences totaling 100 words or less what you found out.*

7. (*2010 GSS young adults*) Was there a significant relationship between region of the country and race of the 2010 GSS twentysomethings? (Variables: REGION, RACE; Select Cases: GROUP = 3)

8. (*2010 GSS young adults*) Was there a significant relationship between the type of place in which 2010 GSS twentysomethings grew up and their political orientation? (Variables: PLACE16, POLVIEWS; Select Cases: GROUP = 3)

9. (*2010 GSS young adults*) Was there a significant relationship between race of the 2010 GSS twentysomethings and their marital status? Be sure to use MARRIED, which is the shortened version of marital status. (Variables: RACE, MARRIED; Select Cases: GROUP = 3)

10. (*2010 GSS middle-age adults*) Was there a significant relationship between race of the 2010 GSS fiftysomethings and their marital status? Be sure to use MARRIED, which is the shortened version of marital status. (Variables: RACE, MARRIED; Select Cases: GROUP = 4)

11. (*2010 GSS young adults*) Was there a significant relationship between race and political orientation among 2010 GSS twentysomethings? (Variables: RACE, POLVIEWS; Select Cases: GROUP = 3)

12. (*2010 GSS middle-age adults*) Was there a significant relationship between race and the strength of religious affiliation among 2010 GSS fiftysomethings? (Variables: RACE, RELINTEN; Select Cases: GROUP = 4)

13. (*2010 GSS middle-age adults*) Was there a significant relationship between belief in an afterlife and current overall happiness among 2010 GSS fiftysomethings? (Variables: POSTLIFE, HAPPY; Select Cases: GROUP = 4)

14. (*2010 GSS young adults*) Were the type of family in which a person was raised and a person's current overall happiness significantly related for 2010 GSS twentysomethings? (Variables: FAMILY16, HAPPY; Select Cases: GROUP = 3)

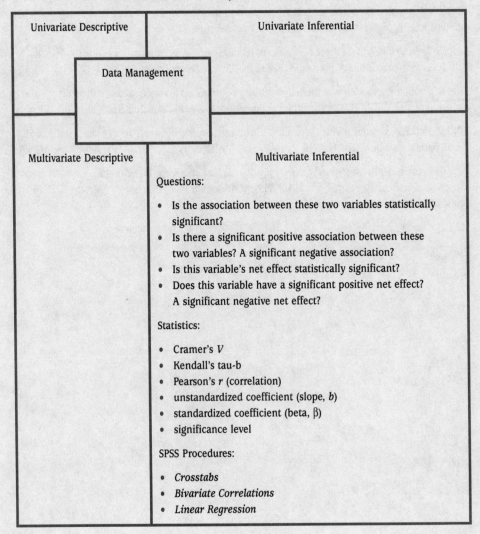

Questions and Tools for Answering Them
(Chapter 16)

Univariate Descriptive	Univariate Inferential

Data Management

Multivariate Descriptive	Multivariate Inferential

Multivariate Inferential

Questions:

- Is the association between these two variables statistically significant?
- Is there a significant positive association between these two variables? A significant negative association?
- Is this variable's net effect statistically significant?
- Does this variable have a significant positive net effect? A significant negative net effect?

Statistics:

- Cramer's V
- Kendall's tau-b
- Pearson's r (correlation)
- unstandardized coefficient (slope, b)
- standardized coefficient (beta, β)
- significance level

SPSS Procedures:

- *Crosstabs*
- *Bivariate Correlations*
- *Linear Regression*

Hypothesis Testing With Measures of Association and Regression

16

In this chapter, you can learn

- how to tell if associations measured by Cramer's *V*, Kendall's tau-b, and Pearson's *r* are statistically significant;
- how to determine if a regression model is statistically significant; and
- how to tell if the net effects of independent variables in regression models are statistically significant.

Old Questions Revisited

In this chapter, we revisit some of the analyses from the descriptive statistics part of this book, but this time we ask questions about 1980 GSS young adults that require inferential statistics to answer:

- Is the association between gender and primary work activity statistically significant?
- Is the weak association we found between highest degree and happiness statistically significant?
- Is there a significant positive correlation between the educational levels of the mothers and fathers of 1980 GSS young adults?
- Are the net effects on income of education, gender, age, and region each statistically significant?

SPSS TIP

To Duplicate the Examples in This Chapter

To duplicate the examples in this chapter, use the *fourGroups.sav* data set. Before doing the hypotheses about measures of association, set the select cases condition to GROUP = 1. Before doing the regression-based hypotheses, set the select cases condition to GROUP = 1 and AGE >= 25 and WORKSTAT = 1 and INCOME86 < 139297.

Overview

This inferential part of the book will conclude by quickly showing how to test some additional hypotheses. We can proceed through these more swiftly not only because by now you are familiar with the steps of hypothesis testing but also because there are no new SPSS procedures to learn here. We are revisiting the measures of association and regression material covered in Part Two of the book. The output you learned to generate in those earlier chapters included information about significance levels (and, therefore, hypothesis testing), but it was passed over at the time. Now, we will use those parts of the output.

Hypotheses About Measures of Association

Here are some examples of research hypotheses about the association between two variables:

- There is an association (as indicated by Cramer's *V*) between religious affiliation and belief in miracles. (Cramer's $V_{\text{religion,miracle}} \neq .00$)
- There is an association (as indicated by tau-b) between marital satisfaction and job satisfaction. (tau-$b_{\text{marital satisfaction,job satisfaction}} \neq .00$)
- There is a negative association (as indicated by tau-b) between highest educational degree and belief in miracles. (tau-$b_{\text{degree,miracles}} < .00$)
- There is an association (as indicated by Pearson's *r*) between income and number of visits to a physician's office. ($r_{\text{income,doctor visits}} \neq .00$)
- Years of schooling and number of children are negatively correlated. ($r_{\text{school years,children}} < .00$)

Sometimes the claim is simply that two variables are associated. The first, second, and fourth examples illustrate this type of claim. A claim that two variables are associated is really a claim about the strength of the association. It is a claim that the value of the measure of association in the population is not zero. The claim does not state how strong the association is, just that there is some association.

Of course, when one or both of the variables are nominal, the hypothesis can only be about the existence of the association. When neither variable is nominal, however, the hypothesis may make a claim about both the existence of an association and its direction. The third and fifth examples illustrate this. Hypothesis tests involving ordinal and interval/ratio measures of association must be identified as one-tailed or two-tailed to perform the test properly.

Before proceeding further, three things about the sample hypotheses should be pointed out. First, hypotheses about any of the measures of association covered in this book could be made. Cramer's *V*, Kendall's tau-b, and Pearson's *r* are used only as examples of hypotheses involving measures of association.

Second, the term *association* in the hypotheses is to distinguish them from chi-square hypotheses for which the term *relationship* is used. Observing this distinction will make it easier for you to distinguish between hypotheses calling for tests based on chi-square and hypotheses based on measures of association. While that will make life simpler for now, as you might expect, this distinction is not always observed outside of this book. Usually, however, you will be able to tell from the context whether a researcher is making a claim about a measure of association or about chi-square.

Third, Chapter 8 noted that a variety of measures of association exist, each designed to detect most types of association but often blind to certain types of association. Any claim that an association exists between two variables is really a claim that a particular measure of association will detect an association between the two variables. For that reason, each of the sample hypotheses mentions a specific measure of association.

The fifth example above of a research hypothesis about an association between variables was "Years of schooling and number of children are negatively correlated." Contrary to the general observations just made about hypotheses involving associations, this hypothesis does not refer to an association or mention a specific statistic. Because Pearson's *r* is such a commonly used correlation coefficient, you can safely assume that any hypothesis that talks about two variables being correlated is referring to an association as indicated by Pearson's *r*.

Cramer's *V*

"Is the association between gender and primary work activity for 1980 GSS young adults statistically significant?"

We begin by testing the research hypothesis "there is an association (as indicated by Cramer's *V*) between gender and work status" (Cramer's $V_{\text{gender,work status}} \neq .00$). The null hypothesis is "there is no association" (Cramer's $V_{\text{gender,work status}} = .00$).

The second step is to see if the sample results are consistent with the research hypothesis or with the null hypothesis. Figure 16.1 shows a value of .386 for Cramer's *V* for gender and primary work activity for 1980 GSS young adults. Thus, the sample results are consistent with the research hypothesis, and we go on to Step 3. (Had the Cramer's *V* for the sample data been precisely .000, we would have gone on to Step 4 and not rejected the null hypothesis.)

Step 3 asks the probability of getting the observed sample results if the null hypothesis is true. As Figure 16.1 indicates, the significance level is .000. (Because Cramer's *V* is a chi-square-based measure, its significance level is identical to the significance level of chi-square.)

In Step 4, we reject the null hypothesis of no association. The results are statistically significant. The results support the claim that gender and work status were associated for 1980 GSS young adults.

Symmetric Measures

		Value	Approx. Sig.
Nominal by Nominal	Phi	.386	.000
	Cramer's V	.386	.000
N of Valid Cases		327	

Figure 16.1   Cramer's V for WORKSTAT by SEX for 1980 GSS Young Adults

RESEARCH TIP

Why the "Approximate" Significance?

The *Crosstabs* output reports "approximate" significance levels. That is because the significance of lambda, Goodman and Kruskal tau, and the uncertainty coefficient are based on an estimated *t* statistic, and the significance of phi, Cramer's *V*, and the contingency coefficient is based on the significance of the chi-square statistic. The significance levels for the ordinal measures of association will also be labeled as approximate. For our purposes, there is no problem in using the approximate significance level.

In fact, however, many researchers, when examining the association between nominal and ordinal variables, first do a chi-square test to see if the relationship is significant. Chi-square has the advantage of not having any blind spots but the disadvantage of not indicating the strength or, in the case of ordinal variables, the strength and direction of the relationship. If chi-square is significant, the researcher then goes on to report the value of a measure of association. Some researchers, however, skip chi-square and do their hypothesis testing using the measure of association.

No matter which path is taken, a researcher should include a discussion of the modes, medians, or percentages within the crosstab when the relationship/association is significant. This information will give a reader or listener an easy to understand view of the relationship between the variables.

Kendall's tau-b

"Is the weak association we found between highest degree and happiness statistically significant?"

Our research hypothesis is "there is an association (as indicated by tau-b) between degree and happiness" (tau-b$_{degree,happiness}$ ≠ .00). The null hypothesis is "there is no association between degree and happiness" (tau-b$_{degree,happiness}$ = .00). For ordinal measures of association, hypotheses can be one- or two-tailed. In this case, we have a two-tailed hypothesis.

As Figure 16.2 shows, tau-b has a value in our sample of .129. That is consistent with the research hypothesis, which predicted a nonzero association, so we proceed to Step 3. (Had the sample tau-b been .000, we would have gone to Step 4 and not rejected the null hypothesis.)

Symmetric Measures

		Value	Asymp. Std. Error[a]	Approx. T[b]	Approx. Sig.
Ordinal by Ordinal	Kendall's tau-b	.129	.050	2.525	.012
N of Valid Cases		327			

a. Not assuming the null hypothesis.
b. Using the asymptotic standard error assuming the null hypothesis.

Figure 16.2   Kendall's Tau-b for HAPPY by DEGREE for 1980 GSS Young Adults

We have a two-tailed hypothesis test, and the two-tailed approximate significance level is .012. (Recall that when significance levels for t statistics are not identified as one- or two-tailed, they are two-tailed.) Therefore, we reject the null hypothesis. The results are statistically significant. We have reason to believe there is an association in the population of 1980 young adults between highest educational degree and level of happiness.

RESEARCH TIP

If an Association Is Weak, Shouldn't It Be Nonsignificant?

There was only a weak association between degree and happiness for the 1980 GSS young adults, and yet it was significant. How could that be?

As this example shows, the fact that a sample association is weak does not prevent it from being statistically significant. Statistical significance does not mean the association is strong or important. It simply means the association exists in the population.

Just as weak associations aren't always nonsignificant, strong and very strong associations aren't always significant. Strong and even very strong associations may be nothing more than sampling error when based on small samples!

Pearson's r

"Is there a significant positive correlation between the educational levels of the mothers and fathers of 1980 GSS young adults?"

The research hypothesis is "mother's and father's years of schooling are positively correlated" ($r_{maeduc,paeduc} > .000$). The null hypothesis is "mother's and father's years of schooling are not correlated or are negatively correlated" ($r_{maeduc,paeduc} \leq .000$).

In Chapter 9, the correlations between mother's schooling, father's schooling, respondent's schooling, and, if married, respondent's spouse's schooling were examined. That correlation matrix is reproduced here as Figure 16.3.

In the sample, mother's and father's years of schooling show a strong, positive correlation (r = .539). This is consistent with the research hypothesis, so we proceed to examine the significance level. (Of course, had the correlation been zero or negative, we would have gone directly to Step 4 and not rejected the null hypothesis.)

The significance level for each correlation in the matrix appears directly below the correlation. The two-tailed significance level for the correlation of MAEDUC and PAEDUC is .000. Since this is a one-tailed hypothesis, we want the one-tailed significance level, which is .000/2 or .000. Based on this significance level, the null hypothesis is rejected. The results are statistically significant. We conclude that the years of schooling of the mothers and fathers of 1980 young adults probably are positively correlated.

We could also test the research hypothesis that the educational level of 1980 GSS young adults who were currently married and the educational level of their spouses were positively correlated. Figure 16.3 shows the sample correlation to be .389. The correlation is in the direction predicted by the research hypothesis, and the one-tailed significance level is .000. Our results our statistically significant and support the claim that the educational levels of 1980 young adults and their spouses

Correlations

		MAEDUC	PAEDUC	EDUC	SPEDUC
MAEDUC	Pearson Correlation	1	.539**	.325**	.248**
	Sig. (2-tailed)		.000	.000	.002
	N	301	246	301	155
PAEDUC	Pearson Correlation	.539**	1	.371**	.344**
	Sig. (2-tailed)	.000		.000	.000
	N	246	256	256	132
EDUC	Pearson Correlation	.325**	.371**	1	.389**
	Sig. (2-tailed)	.000	.000		.000
	N	301	256	327	169
SPEDUC	Pearson Correlation	.248**	.344**	.389**	1
	Sig. (2-tailed)	.002	.000	.000	
	N	155	132	169	169

**. Correlation is significant at the 0.01 level (2-tailed).

Figure 16.3 *Bivariate Correlations* Output for MAEDUC, PAEDUC, EDUC, and SPEDUC for 1980 GSS Young Adults

are positively correlated. The correlation matrix in Figure 16.3 could also be used to test the hypothesis that there is a positive correlation between the years of schooling of 1980 young adults and the years of schooling of their mothers, as well as a positive correlation between the years of schooling of 1980 young adults and the years of schooling of their fathers.

By default, the *Bivariate Correlations* procedure reports two-tailed significance levels. One-tailed significance levels can be requested in the same dialog that identifies the variables to be included in the matrix (see Figure 9.1).

CONCEPT CHECK

Without looking back, can you answer the following questions:

- Hypothesis tests for which measures of association must be identified as one-tailed or two-tailed?
- Are weak associations between variables always nonsignificant? Are strong associations always significant?

If not, go back and review before reading on.

Regression Hypotheses

Information about statistical significance has also been appearing in the bivariate and multiple regression outputs. The research hypotheses for regression usually pertain to the net effects of variables. Here are some examples:

- After controlling for the number of classes attended and the percent of the textbook read, hours spent studying has an effect on test grade. ($beta_{hours} \neq .000$)
- Among full-time workers, being female has a negative effect on earnings even after controlling for education, age, and geographic region of residence. ($beta_{sex(female)} < .000$)

Just like with the measures of association, the research hypotheses are claiming there is a non-zero net effect but are not making a claim about how strong the net effect is. Sometimes the hypothesis predicts a direction for this net effect such as in the second example where being female is claimed to have a negative effect. This is a one-tailed hypothesis. Other times, the hypothesis makes no claim about the direction of the net effect. The first example simply predicts that hours spent studying has an effect but does not predict its direction. This is a two-tailed hypothesis.

Chapter 10 included a multiple regression for 1980 GSS young adults with income as the dependent variable and years of schooling, age, gender, and geographic region as independent variables. SEX was coded 0 for males and 1 for females. The analysis was limited to persons who reported they were currently working full-time, made less than $139,297 the previous year, and were at least 25 years old. Figure 16.4 shows the relevant parts of the *Linear Regression* output.

Before looking at individual net effects, researchers check to see if the overall regression model is statistically significant. To check this, the significance level of the *F* ratio in the output box labeled "ANOVA" is used. In this example, the significance level is .000. The overall model is statistically significant. This tells us that the set of independent variables probably does have some effect on income.

Knowing that the overall model is significant, we proceed to examine the significance of the individual net effects. For this, we move to the Coefficients output box. Hypotheses about individual

Model Summary

Model	R	R Square	Adjusted R Square	Std. Error of the Estimate
1	.608[a]	.369	.322	7424.529

a. Predictors: (Constant), WEST, AGE, EDUC, SEX, NOREAST, SOUTH

ANOVA[b]

Model		Sum of Squares	df	Mean Square	F	Sig.
1	Regression	2.582E9	6	4.303E8	7.807	.000[a]
	Residual	4.410E9	80	55123628.48		
	Total	6.992E9	86			

a. Predictors: (Constant), WEST, AGE, EDUC, SEX, NOREAST, SOUTH
b. Dependent Variable: INCOME86

Coefficients[a]

Model		Unstandardized Coefficients		Standardized Coefficients	t	Sig.
		B	Std. Error	Beta		
1	(Constant)	-8136.639	17004.221		-.479	.634
	EDUC	1459.651	361.261	.368	4.040	.000
	AGE	428.827	603.294	.064	.711	.479
	SEX	-8022.563	1659.835	-.447	-4.833	.000
	NOREAST	-1947.002	2472.013	-.094	-.788	.433
	SOUTH	-3551.716	2272.454	-.192	-1.563	.122
	WEST	2661.086	2652.157	.112	1.003	.319

a. Dependent Variable: INCOME86

Figure 16.4   Output From Regressing INCOME86 on EDUC, AGE, SEX, NOREAST, SOUTH, and WEST for 1980 GSS Young Adults

net effects are tested using t tests. Toward the right of the output box, you see the values of the various t statistics and the significance levels of the t statistics. Although the significance level of the t statistic for the Y intercept (Constant) is reported, researchers are usually more interested in the significance of the independent variables. If the research hypothesis is simply that a variable has a nonzero net effect, then all we have to do is note the printed significance level. If it is .05 or less, the net effect is significant. If the research hypothesis claims that a variable has a net effect in a particular direction, then we have to check to see if the net effect is in the predicted direction (the slope or the beta will tell us this), and if it is in the correct direction, we need to divide the significance level in half since the printed significance levels are two-tailed and we have a one-tailed hypothesis.

Let's assume we had predicted education and age would both have positive net effects on income and being female would have a negative effect. Each of these predictions is a one-tailed research hypothesis about the value of the standardized coefficient (or, for that matter, the unstandardized coefficient) being in a particular direction. The null hypotheses are that in the population, the net effects are zero or in the opposite direction. Let's assume we also predicted there would be regional net differences in income but did not predict specific directions for those differences. That means we are making two-tailed hypotheses about the net effect of each of the regional variables in the equation. Our research hypothesis for each region included in the equation is that in the population, the standardized coefficient is not zero; the null hypothesis is that the standardized coefficient is zero.

Having confirmed that the overall regression model is statistically significant, we check to see if the net effects are consistent with the research or null hypotheses.

All of the standardized coefficients (and unstandardized coefficients) are consistent with the research hypotheses. The net effects of education and age are positive, the net effect of being female is negative, and the net effects of living in the Northeast, the South, or the West (all compared to the effect of living in the Midwest, which is the omitted category) are nonzero.

We now proceed to check the significance levels. The printed significance levels are two-tailed. Since our hypotheses about education, age, and being female are one-tailed, we divide those significance levels in half. The one-tailed significance level for education is .000 (.000/2), which is statistically significant. We reject the null hypothesis and conclude that education did have a positive effect on income for 1980 young adults even after controlling for age, gender, and region.

The one-tailed significance level for age is .2395 (.479/2), which is not statistically significant. We cannot reject the null hypothesis that after controlling for education, gender, and region, age had no effect or a negative effect on income. (Remember that age only ranged from 25 to 29 for the 1980 GSS young adults included in the analysis.)

The one-tailed significance level for being female (having a code of 1 on SEX) is .000 (.000/2), which is statistically significant. We reject the null hypothesis and conclude that for 1980 young adults, being female did have a negative effect on income even after controlling for education, age, and region.

Since no directions were predicted for the net effects of geographic region, we do not divide the printed significance in half. The significance levels for the Northeast, South, and West are .433, .122, and .319. None of these regions significantly differ from the Midwest (the omitted category). We must continue to entertain the possibility that the geographic region in which 1980 young adults lived had no effect on income once education, age, and gender are taken into account.

CONCEPT CHECK

Without looking back, can you answer the following questions:

- Before checking the significance levels of the net effects of the independent variables in a multiple regression, the significance of what should be checked?
- Are the significance levels that appear in the output for the net effects of the independent variables in regression one-tailed or two-tailed significance levels?

If not, go back and review before reading on.

1980 GSS Young Adults

The chapter began with some questions about 1980 GSS young adults. On the basis of our analyses, what do we now know?

- There was a significant association between gender and primary work activity for 1980 GSS young adults (approx. $p = .000$). In our sample, these variables were moderately associated (Cramer's $V = .386$). Men were more likely to be employed full-time. Women were much more likely to be not employed but keeping house.
- The weak positive association between highest educational degree and happiness (tau-b = .129) was statistically significant (approx. $t = 2.525$, approx. $p = .012$). Our results support the claim that in the population of 1980 young adults, degree and happiness are associated.
- The strong positive correlation ($r = .539$) between the educational levels of the mothers and fathers of 1980 GSS young adults was statistically significant ($p = .000$). In choosing one another, the parents of 1980 young adults chose partners with similar years of schooling. We also found that their children showed early signs of maintaining this pattern of educational homogamy. For those 1980 GSS young adults married at the time of the survey, the correlation between their years of schooling and their spouse's was .389, which was statistically significant ($p = .000$).
- Education's positive net effect on income was statistically significant for the 1980 GSS young adults ($t = 4.040$, $p = .000$), as was the negative net effect on income of being female ($t = -4.833$, $p = .000$). In our sample, the net effect of gender was strong (beta$_{income,sex}$ = $-.447$), and the net effect of education was moderate (beta$_{income,education}$=.368). Controlling for other factors, each additional year of schooling resulted in approximately $1,460 of additional income. Controlling for other factors, being female carried an income penalty of about $8,023. Age did not have a significant positive net effect ($t = .711$, $p = .2395$). Net of other factors, regional differences were not significant.

A Final Note

The examples in the chapters of this book gave you answers to many specific questions about 1980 GSS young adults. The practice problems provided you with opportunities to answer an even greater number of specific questions about 2010 GSS young adults and 2010 GSS middle-age adults. But more important than the answers to these specific questions, you hopefully have learned *how* to ask empirical questions and *how* to find answers.

Statistics are simply tools for answering questions. They aren't magical, they aren't mystical, and they aren't beyond the grasp of ordinary persons! Now that you have acquired all these new tools, use them. Use them to answer your own individual questions, job-related questions, and community questions. There are so many questions needing answers. Best wishes in the future.

Important Concepts in the Chapter

Bivariate Correlations procedure

bivariate regression

Crosstabs procedure

Cramer's *V*

Kendall's tau-b

Linear Regression procedure

multiple regression

net effect

one-tailed hypothesis

Pearson's *r*

two-tailed hypothesis

Practice Problems

1. For each of the following inferential statistics, indicate if you must identify hypotheses as one-tailed or two-tailed:
   a. chi-square
   b. *F* ratio
   c. *t* statistic

2. For each of the following inferential statistics, are degrees of freedom indicated by one or two numbers?
   a. chi-square
   b. *F* ratio
   c. *t* statistic

3. For each of the following, indicate whether the hypothesis test is based on the chi-square, the *F* ratio, or the *t* statistic.
   a. hypotheses about Cramer's *V*
   b. hypotheses about Kendall's tau-b

    c. hypotheses about Pearson's r

    d. hypotheses about the overall regression model

    e. hypotheses about beta coefficients

4. (*2010 GSS young adults*) Answer each of the following questions based on this matrix of Kendall's tau-b values for 2010 GSS twentysomethings. (High scores on POLVIEWS represent conservative views; low scores represent liberal views.)

Correlations

			CLASS	DEGREE	HEALTH	POLVIEWS
Kendall's tau_b	CLASS	Correlation Coefficient	1.000	.247**	.190**	-.102*
		Sig. (2-tailed)	.	.000	.003	.039
		N	339	339	210	329
	DEGREE	Correlation Coefficient	.247**	1.000	.188**	-.010
		Sig. (2-tailed)	.000	.	.002	.835
		N	339	341	212	330
	HEALTH	Correlation Coefficient	.190**	.188**	1.000	-.019
		Sig. (2-tailed)	.003	.002	.	.763
		N	210	212	212	206
	POLVIEWS	Correlation Coefficient	-.102*	-.010	-.019	1.000
		Sig. (2-tailed)	.039	.835	.763	.
		N	329	330	206	330

**. Correlation is significant at the 0.01 level (2-tailed).
*. Correlation is significant at the 0.05 level (2-tailed).

    a. Was there a significant positive association between social class and highest degree?

    b. Was there a significant positive association between social class and health?

    c. Was there a significant positive association between social class and conservative political views?

    d. Was there a significant positive association between highest degree and health?

    e. Was there a significant negative association between highest degree and conservative political views?

    f. Was there a significant association between health and political views?

5. (*2010 GSS middle-age adults*) Answer each of these questions based on the following matrix of Pearson's r values for 2010 GSS fiftysomethings.

    a. Was there a significant negative association between years of schooling and number of children?

    b. Was there a significant positive association between years of schooling and willingness to allow legal abortion?

    c. Was there a significant positive association between years of schooling and willingness to let controversial persons teach college?

    d. Was there a significant negative association between number of children and willingness to allow legal abortion?

e. Was there a significant association between number of children and willingness to let controversial persons teach college?

f. Was there a significant positive association between willingness to allow legal abortion and willingness to let controversial persons teach college?

Correlations

		EDUC	CHILDREN	ABORTOK	OKTEACH
EDUC	Pearson Correlation	1	-.286**	.180**	.250**
	Sig. (2-tailed)		.000	.009	.000
	N	377	377	208	211
CHILDREN	Pearson Correlation	-.286**	1	-.132	-.162*
	Sig. (2-tailed)	.000		.058	.018
	N	377	378	208	211
ABORTOK	Pearson Correlation	.180**	-.132	1	.171*
	Sig. (2-tailed)	.009	.058		.018
	N	208	208	208	191
OKTEACH	Pearson Correlation	.250**	-.162*	.171*	1
	Sig. (2-tailed)	.000	.018	.018	
	N	211	211	191	211

**. Correlation is significant at the 0.01 level (2-tailed).
*. Correlation is significant at the 0.05 level (2-tailed).

Problems Requiring SPSS and the *fourGroups.sav* Data Set

6. (*2010 GSS young adults*) This problem asks if education, age, and gender significantly affected income for the 2010 GSS twentysomethings. Regress income on years of schooling, age, and gender. You are predicting positive net effects for years of schooling and age but a negative net effect for being female. (Variables: INCOME86, EDUC, AGE, SEX; Select Cases: GROUP = 3 and AGE >= 25 and WORKSTAT = 1)

a. Is the overall model significant? If it is significant, what proportion of the differences in income in the sample is explained by the model?

b. Was there a significant positive net effect of years of schooling? If it was significant, how strong was the net effect in the sample? (If the step is skipped, state that.)

c. Was there a significant positive net effect of age? If it was significant, how strong was the net effect in the sample? (If the step is skipped, state that.)

d. Was there a significant negative net effect of being female? If it was significant, how strong was the net effect in the sample? (If the step is skipped, state that.)

e. Summarize in a few well-written sentences totaling 100 words or less what you found out.

7. (*2010 GSS young adults*) This problems looks to see if the effects of education, gender, and religion on willingness to allow legal abortion were significant for the 2010 GSS twentysomethings. Regress willingness to allow legal abortion on years of schooling, gender, and strength of religious affiliation. You are predicting a positive net effect for years of schooling and a negative net effect for strength of religious affiliation. You are not predicting a direction for the net effect of gender. (Variables: ABORTOK, EDUC, SEX, RELINTEN; Select Cases: GROUP = 3)
   a. Is the overall model significant? If it is significant, what proportion of the differences in willingness to allow legal abortion in the sample is explained by the model?
   b. Was there a significant positive net effect of years of schooling? If it was significant, how strong was the net effect in the sample? (If the step is skipped, state that.)
   c. Was there a significant net effect of gender? If it was significant, how strong and in what direction was the net effect in the sample? (If the step is skipped, state that.)
   d. Was there a significant negative net effect of strength of religious affiliation? If it was significant, how strong was the net effect in the sample? (If the step is skipped, state that.)
   e. Summarize in a few well-written sentences totaling 100 words or less what you found out.

8. (*2010 GSS middle-age adults*) This problem asks if education, siblings, and religion significantly affected the completed fertility of the 2010 GSS fiftysomethings. Regress number of children on years of schooling, number of siblings, and strength of religious affiliation. You are predicting a negative net effect for years of schooling but positive net effects for number of siblings and strength of religious affiliation. (Variables: CHILDREN, EDUC, SIBLINGS, RELINTEN; Select Cases: GROUP = 4)
   a. Is the overall model significant? If it is significant, what proportion of the differences in number of children in the sample is explained by the model?
   b. Was there a significant negative net effect of years of schooling? If it was significant, how strong was the net effect in the sample? (If the step is skipped, state that.)
   c. Was there a significant positive net effect of number of siblings? If it was significant, how strong was the net effect in the sample? (If the step is skipped, state that.)
   d. Was there a significant positive net effect of strength of religious affiliation? If it was significant, how strong was the net effect in the sample? (If the step is skipped, state that.)
   e. Summarize in a few well-written sentences totaling 100 words or less what you found out.

9. (*1980 GSS middle-age adults*) This problem asks if education, siblings, and religion significantly affected the completed fertility of the 1980 GSS fiftysomethings. Regress number of children on years of schooling, number of siblings, and strength of religious affiliation. You are predicting a negative net effect for years of schooling but positive net effects for number of siblings and strength of religious affiliation. (Variables: CHILDREN, EDUC, SIBLINGS, RELINTEN; Select Cases: GROUP = 2)
   a. Is the overall model significant? If it is significant, what proportion of the differences in number of children in the sample is explained by the model?
   b. Was there a significant negative net effect of years of schooling? If it was significant, how strong was the net effect in the sample? (If the step is skipped, state that.)
   c. Was there a significant positive net effect of number of siblings? If it was significant, how strong was the net effect in the sample? (If the step is skipped, state that.)
   d. Was there a significant positive net effect of strength of religious affiliation? If it was significant, how strong was the net effect in the sample? (If the step is skipped, state that.)
   e. Summarize in a few well-written sentences totaling 100 words or less what you found out.

For each of the following problems, do the following:

  a. *State and label the research and the null hypothesis. If appropriate, indicate if this is a one- or two-tailed hypothesis test.*

  b. *What are the sample results? Are they consistent with the null hypothesis or with the research hypothesis?*

  c. *What is the probability of getting the observed sample results if the null hypothesis is true? (If this step is skipped, state that.)*

  d. *Do you reject or not reject the null hypothesis? Are your results statistically significant?*

  e. *Summarize in a few well-written sentences totaling 100 words or less what you found out.*

10. (*2010 GSS young adults*) Was there a significant association (as indicated by Cramer's *V*) between gender and work status among 2010 GSS twentysomethings? (Variables: SEX, WORKSTAT; Select Cases: GROUP = 3)

11. (*2010 GSS middle-age adults*) Was there a significant association (as indicated by Cramer's *V*) between gender and work status among 2010 GSS fiftysomethings? (Variables: SEX, WORKSTAT; Select Cases: GROUP = 4)

12. (*2010 GSS young adults*) Was there a significant association (as indicated by tau-b) between highest educational degree and happiness among 2010 GSS twentysomethings? (Variables: DEGREE, HAPPY; Select Cases: GROUP = 3)

13. (*2010 GSS middle-age adults*) Was there a significant association (as indicated by tau-b) between highest educational degree and happiness among 2010 GSS fiftysomethings? (Variables: DEGREE, HAPPY; Select Cases: GROUP = 4)

14. (*2010 GSS young adults*) Was there a significant positive correlation between the educational levels of the mothers and fathers of 2010 GSS twentysomethings? (Variables: PAEDUC, MAEDUC; Select Cases: GROUP = 3)

15. (*2010 GSS middle-age adults*) Was there a significant positive correlation between the income and the occupational prestige of full-time employed 2010 GSS fiftysomethings? (Variables: INCOME86, SEI; Select Cases: GROUP = 4 and WORKSTAT = 1)

16. (*2010 GSS young adults*) Both of the following questions can be answered using output from a single *Crosstabs* procedure. Be sure to use MARRIED, which is the shortened version of marital status. (Variables: MARRIED, HAPPY, SEX; Select Cases: GROUP = 3)

  a. Was there a significant association (as indicated by Cramer's *V*) between marital status and happiness among 2010 GSS young men?

  b. Was there a significant association (as indicated by Cramer's *V*) between marital status and happiness among 2010 GSS young women?

17. (*2010 GSS middle-age adults*) Both of the following questions can be answered using output from a single *Crosstabs* procedure. (Variables: HEALTH, HAPPY, SEX; Select Cases: GROUP = 4)

  a. Was there a significant association (as indicated by Kendall's tau-b) between health and happiness among 2010 GSS middle-age men?

  b. Was there a significant association (as indicated by Kendall's tau-b) between health and happiness among 2010 GSS middle-age women?

Glossary

analysis of variance (ANOVA): a statistical procedure that examines the effect of one or more discrete independent variables known as factors on an interval/ratio dependent variable.

asymmetric measure: a measure of association whose value may differ depending on which of the pair of variables is the dependent variable and which is the independent variable.

attribute: a category of a variable; a possible score or value a case may receive on a variable.

bar chart: a univariate chart that uses a series of columns to represent the distribution of cases across the attributes of a variable.

best-fitting straight line: the line that minimizes the sum of the squared vertical distances of the points in a scatterplot from the line.

bimodal: a variable whose frequency distribution has two attributes that exactly or nearly tie for most frequently occurring.

bivariate regression: regression analysis using just one independent variable.

bivariate statistic: a statistic that summarizes or draws conclusions about the relationship between two variables.

cases: the subjects, participants, objects, or observations that make up a data set; cases may be individual persons, groups, social interactions, or artifacts; the cases correspond to the rows in a data matrix.

cell: where a row and column cross in a data matrix, crosstab table, or correlation matrix.

cell residual: the difference between the observed count and the expected count for a cell of a crosstab.

census: when every element in a population is measured.

central limit theorem: the mathematical demonstration that sampling distributions based on samples of size 30 or larger are normal distributions.

central tendency: what is common, typical, or representative of the values of cases on a variable.

chi-square (χ^2): an inferential statistic used to assess the fit between an observed set of values (e.g., observed counts in crosstab cells) and an expected set of values (e.g., expected counts under an assumption of independence).

clustered bar chart: a multivariate chart in which cases are first divided into groups based on their attribute on one variable and then each group's distribution of cases on a second variable is presented as a separate bar chart.

coefficient of alienation: the proportion of the variance in the dependent variable that is not explained (not accounted for) by the independent variables in a regression analysis.

coefficient of determination (R^2): the proportion of the variance in the dependent variable that is explained (accounted for) by the independent variables in a regression analysis.

column percent: the percent of cases in a crosstab column that are in a particular cell.

concordant pair: when the scores on two variables for a pair of cases are being compared and the same case has a higher score on both variables.

confidence interval: a range of values within which a researcher has a certain level of confidence that the parameter lies.

confidence level: how confident a researcher is that the parameter lies within the confidence interval.

constant: a dimension on which the cases in a data set do not differ.

contingency coefficient: a symmetric nominal measure of association whose values range from 0.00 to approximately 1.00.

continuous variable: a variable having a large, theoretically infinite number of attributes.

control variable: a variable whose influence on the dependent variable a researcher wants to eliminate or, at least, isolate to more correctly determine the influence of the independent variable on the dependent variable.

covariation: the existence of a nonzero statistical relationship between two variables; demonstrating covariation is one requirement for proving causality.

Cramer's *V*: a symmetric nominal measure of association whose values range from 0.00 to 1.00.

Cronbach's alpha (coefficient alpha, alpha): a way of assessing the reliability of an index by measuring its internal consistency; used to determine if all the items appear to be reflecting a common underlying dimension.

degrees of freedom: identifies which distribution in a family of distributions is the correct one to use to determine the significance level in hypothesis testing.

dependent variable: in a relationship in which one variable influences another variable, the dependent variable is the one being influenced.

descriptive statistic: a statistic that summarizes the values on one or more variables for the cases in a data set and only the cases in the data set.

dichotomy: a variable having just two attributes.

direction of a relationship: whether higher values on one variable are associated with higher values or lower values on a second variable; the relationship is positive if they are associated with higher values but negative (or inverse) if they are associated with lower values.

discordant pair: when the scores on two variables for a pair of cases are being compared and one case scores higher on the first variable but the other case scores higher on the second variable.

discrete variable: a variable having a finite and usually small number of attributes.

dispersion: the variety or differences in the values of cases on a variable.

dummy variable: one of a series of dichotomous variables created to include in a regression analysis the information contained in a nominal variable with three or more attributes.

ecological fallacy: the incorrect assumption that what is true about groups must inevitably be true of the members of those groups.

element: a member of a population.

expected count: the number of cases that would be in a cell of a crosstab if the column variable and row variable were independent in the data set.

F ratio: an inferential statistic that is the ratio of two estimates of population variance.

factor variable: term for discrete independent variables in analysis of variance.

frequency distribution: how often each attribute of a variable occurs in a data set.

gamma: a symmetric ordinal measure of association whose values range from -1.00 to 1.00.

histogram: a univariate chart that uses a series of columns (bins) corresponding to intervals on a number line to represent the distribution of cases on an interval/ratio variable.

hypothesis: a prediction or claim about a population parameter.

hypothesis testing: a branch of inferential statistics in which sample results are used to reject or not reject claims about population parameters.

independence: the absence of a statistical relationship between variables.

independent samples: two groups of scores on the same variable, each group based on a sample from a different population, for which there exists no logical reason for matching individual scores in one group with individual scores in the other.

independent variable: in a relationship in which one variable influences another variable, the variable that is doing the influencing.

index: a set of items all assumed to be of approximately equal importance in measuring a single underlying concept that are then combined to yield a single overall score on the underlying concept.

inferential statistic: a statistic that draws a conclusion about a population parameter based on data from a probability sample.

interaction effect: when the size and/or direction of one factor's effect on the dependent variable varies depending on the value of one or more other factors.

interval estimation: a branch of inferential statistics in which sample results are used as the basis for probabilistic statements about population parameters.

interval/ratio: highest level of measurement; attributes of a variable cover all possibilities without overlapping, can be put in a natural order from low to high, and form a numeric scale.

interval/ratio measure of association: a measure of association that assumes the attributes that make up each of the variables are different, have rank order, and represent a numeric scale.

Kendall's tau-b: a symmetric ordinal measure of association whose values range from -1.00 to 1.00 for tables with equal numbers of rows and columns and approximately from -1.00 to 1.00 for other tables; pairs of cases tied on just one of the variables are taken as evidence of a weak relationship.

Kendall's tau-c: a symmetric ordinal measure of association whose values range from -1.00 to 1.00 for tables with equal numbers of rows and columns and approximately from -1.00 to 1.00 for other tables; table size is taken into account, but tied pairs of cases are not.

lambda: a nominal measure of association whose values range from 0.00 to 1.00; it comes in both a symmetric and an asymmetric version.

level of measurement: a classification system for variables based on the properties of a variable's attributes; important levels of measurement for data analysis are nominal, ordinal, and interval/ratio.

listwise deletion: when cases missing data on any of the variables involved in a statistical procedure are excluded from all parts of the statistical procedure; ensures that all parts of the procedure are based on the same cases but reduces the number of cases on which the procedure is based.

main effect: the differences in means on the dependent variable of groups of cases formed by the attributes of an independent variable.

margin of error: the distance from the center of the confidence interval (which is the sample result) to either end of the confidence interval.

maximum: an ordinal-level measure of dispersion that identifies the highest attribute on a variable used by at least one case.

mean: an interval/ratio measure of central tendency that identifies the average of the values for the cases on a variable.

measure of association: a statistic that describes the strength and, for ordinal and interval/ratio measures of association, also the direction of the relationship between two variables.

median: an ordinal-level measure of central tendency that identifies the attribute of a variable used by the middle case when the cases have been ordered from low to high based on their attribute on the variable.

minimum: an ordinal-level measure of dispersion that identifies the lowest attribute on a variable used by at least one case.

mode: a nominal-level measure of central tendency that identifies the most frequently occurring attribute of a variable.

multicollinearity: a problem that occurs when two or more independent variables in a regression analysis are very strongly correlated; results in standardized and unstandardized coefficients that are highly sensitive to small changes in data set values.

multimodal: a variable whose frequency distribution has two or more attributes that exactly or nearly tie for most frequently occurring.

multiple correlation coefficient (R): a measure of association between the dependent variable in a regression analysis and the set of independent variables; the correlation between the actual values of the cases on the dependent variable and the predicted values based on the regression equation.

multiple regression: regression analysis using more than one independent variable.

multivariate statistic: a statistic that summarizes or draws conclusions about the relationship between two or more variables.

net effect: the effect of an independent variable on a dependent variable after other independent variables have been controlled.

nominal: lowest level of measurement; attributes of a variable cover all possibilities without overlapping but cannot be put in a natural order from low to high.

nominal measure of association: a measure of association that only assumes the attributes that make up each of the variables are different.

nonprobability sampling techniques: methods of taking samples in which not every element in the population has some chance of being selected or the probability of any particular element being selected cannot be calculated; common nonprobability sampling techniques are convenience (accidental, reliance on available subjects), purposive (judgmental), quota, and snowball.

nonspuriousness: a nonzero net effect of one variable on another even after all other variables have been controlled; demonstrating nonspuriousness is a requirement for proving causality.

normal distribution: a mathematical distribution resembling a bell shape whose properties include that it is symmetrical; its mean, median, and mode are identical; and approximately 68% of the distribution is within one standard deviation of the center, approximately 95% within two standard deviations, and approximately 99.7% within three standard deviations.

null hypothesis: a hypothesis whose prediction about the population parameter includes a specific value; it is the null hypothesis that is tested in hypothesis testing (see *research hypothesis*).

numeric variable: an SPSS variable type that only allows variable values consisting of numbers, decimal points, positive signs, and negative signs.

observed count: the actual number of cases in a cell of a crosstab.

one-tailed hypothesis: a hypothesis test in which the null hypothesis will be rejected only if the sample result falls far from the claimed center of the sampling distribution in one particular direction.

open-ended attribute: an attribute with no fixed lower limit or no fixed upper limit; for example, seven or more children, an IQ score of less than 85.

operational definition: an explanation in concrete, specific terms of how a variable will be measured; should include an indication of the attributes that make up the variable and the process by which the appropriate attribute for each case is determined.

ordinal: intermediate level of measurement; attributes of a variable cover all possibilities without overlapping, can be put in a natural order from low to high, but do not form a numeric scale.

ordinal measure of association: a measure of association that assumes the attributes that make up each of the variables are not only different but also have rank order.

paired samples: two equal-size groups of scores, each based on a sample from the population and each measuring a different variable, for which there exists a logical reason for matching individual scores in one group with individual scores in the other—the most common reason being they are two scores for the same person such as a pretest and a posttest score.

pairwise deletion: when cases missing data on some of the variables involved in a statistical procedure are excluded only from those parts of the statistical procedure that involve the variables for which the data are missing; maximizes the number of cases on which each part of the procedure is based but reduces comparability of different parts of the procedure.

parameter: characteristic of a population (see *statistic*).

Pearson's *r*: a symmetric interval/ratio measure of association whose values range from −1.00 to 1.00.

percent distribution: a nominal-level measure of dispersion that shows the percent of valid cases in each attribute of a variable.

percentile: an ordinal-level measure of dispersion; the value of the nth percentile tells you that the lowest $n\%$ of the cases had that value or a lower value on the variable.

phi: a symmetric nominal measure of association whose values range from −1.00 to 1.00 for tables with just two rows and two columns and from 0.00 to approximately 1.00 in larger tables.

pie chart: a univariate chart that divides a circle into sections to represent the distribution of cases across the attributes of a variable.

population: a group of entities (perhaps persons, families, organizations, or nations) about which a researcher would ultimately like to draw conclusions.

post hoc multiple comparisons: consecutive t tests of differences between pairs of groups in which the significance level is adjusted because the same data are being repeatedly tested so that the risk of making a Type I error across the entire set of t tests remains at a predetermined level, usually .05.

predicted value: the value a case would be expected to have on the dependent variable based on the regression equation and the case's values on the independent variables.

probability sampling techniques: methods of taking samples so that every element in the population has some chance of being selected and the probability of any particular element being selected can be calculated; common probability sampling techniques are simple random, systematic random, stratified, and multistage cluster.

range: an ordinal-level measure of dispersion that indicates the number of attributes (or distance on the number line) from the maximum to the minimum.

regression equation: the equation for the best-fitting straight line.

regression residual: the difference between a case's actual value on the dependent variable and its predicted value.

reliability: consistency of measurement; for example, cases assigned a particular attribute on a variable should be assigned the same or a closely similar attribute if they were remeasured after only a short interval of time; it is important that operational definitions be reliable.

research hypothesis (alternative hypothesis, scientific hypothesis): a hypothesis whose prediction about the population parameter does not include a specific value; the research hypothesis and null hypothesis together form a set such that one hypothesis must be a true description of the population and they cannot both be true (see *null hypothesis*).

response bias: when the distribution of values on a variable differs from what the distribution of values on that same variable would have been had there been no missing cases.

row percent: the percent of cases in a crosstab row that are in a particular cell.

sampling: the process by which a subset of elements from a population is selected.

sampling distribution: how often every possible sample result would occur if every possible sample of a particular size from a particular population were taken.

sampling error: the difference between a sample result (the value of a statistic) and a census result (the value of a parameter); the amount the sample missed the true value in the population by.

scale: (1) the name used by SPSS for interval/ratio level of measurement; (2) a set of items used to yield a single overall score on an underlying concept where the items are believed to have some internal structure such that they could be ranked in terms of how highly they reflect the underlying concept.

scatterplot: an interval/ratio chart that plots cases on a two-dimensional graph using a horizontal axis corresponding to the independent variable and a vertical axis corresponding to the dependent variable.

significance level: the probability of getting the observed sample results if the null hypothesis is true; the risk of making a Type I error if the null hypothesis is rejected.

skewness coefficient: an interval/ratio measure of dispersion that indicates how far the distribution of values on a variable deviates from being balanced around the mean and, if it is not balanced, the direction (positive or negative) that the distribution is being pulled out of balance by extreme values.

Somers' *d*: an ordinal measure of association whose values range from -1.00 to 1.00; it comes in both a symmetric and an asymmetric version.

Spearman's correlation: a symmetric ordinal measure of association whose values range from -1.00 to 1.00.

standard deviation: an interval/ratio measure of dispersion that indicates the approximate average distance of cases from the mean.

standard error: a measure of dispersion in a sampling distribution; the approximate average amount of sampling error in the samples that make up a sampling distribution; the approximate average distance of sample results from the population parameter.

standardized coefficient (beta, β): the slopes for the regression equation when variables are converted to z-scores; indicates the direction and strength of the net effects of the independent variables.

statistic: characteristic of a sample (see *parameter*).

statistical significance: sample results are said to be statistically significant when the null hypothesis can be rejected.

strength of a relationship: the degree to which the probability of a case having a particular attribute on one variable varies depending on the case's attribute on another variable.

string variable: an SPSS variable type that allows variable values consisting of numbers, symbols, spaces, letters, punctuation, or any other characters.

substantive importance: a research finding that, in the opinion of experts in the field, calls for a change in behavior, policy, or program.

symmetric measure: a measure of association whose value does not differ depending on which is the dependent variable and which is the independent variable.

system missing: an SPSS missing data code that results when a cell in a data matrix is left empty; cases with system-missing values on a variable are normally excluded from analyses involving that variable.

***t* distribution:** a family of mathematical distributions whose properties increasingly resemble those of a normal distribution as the degrees of freedom on which the distribution is based increase; sampling distributions in which the standard deviation in the population is unknown and must be estimated from the sample are better described by t distributions than by the normal distribution.

***t* statistic:** indicates how many standard errors the sample result is above or below the hypothesized center of the t distribution.

temporal sequence: the order in time in which variables occur or change values; which variable happens first or changes first, which happens or changes second; establishing temporal sequence is a requirement for proving causality.

theoretical definition (nominal definition): an explanation in abstract terms of what a researcher means by a certain variable name.

tied pair: when the scores on two variables for a pair of cases are being compared and the cases have identical scores on one or both of the variables.

total percent: the percent of cases in a crosstab that are in a particular cell.

two-tailed hypothesis: a hypothesis test in which the null hypothesis will be rejected if the sample result falls far in either direction from the claimed center of the sampling distribution.

Type I error: rejecting a null hypothesis that is actually true.

Type II error: not rejecting a null hypothesis that is actually false.

uncertainty coefficient: a nominal measure of association whose values range from 0.00 to 1.00; it comes in both a symmetric and an asymmetric version.

units of analysis: what the cases in a data set represent; common units of analysis are persons, families, or nations.

univariate chart: a visual display that summarizes the results on a single variable.

univariate statistic: a statistic that summarizes or draws conclusions about the values on one variable.

unstandardized coefficient (slope, *b*): the Y intercept and the slopes for the regression equation when variables are kept in their original metric; indicates the direction of the net effects of the independent variables but not the strength.

user-missing: an SPSS missing data code that must be defined by the user; cases with user-missing values on a variable are normally excluded from analyses involving that variable.

validity: measuring what you intend to measure; operational definitions should be valid—that is, they should be measuring what the variable's theoretical definition says the variable is about.

variable: a dimension on which the cases in a data set differ.

variance: an interval/ratio measure of dispersion that indicates the approximate average squared distance of the cases from the mean.

z-scores: a way of standardizing scores on an interval/ratio variable such that each case's raw score on the variable is expressed in terms of the number of standard deviations the raw score falls above or below the mean.

Index

NOTE: In page references, f indicates figures and t indicates tables.

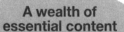